Twentieth-Century
Short Story Explication
New Series

Volume V   1997–1998

With Checklists of Books and Journals Used

Wendell M. Aycock
Professor of English
Texas Tech University

The Shoe String Press, 2002

© 2002 The Shoe String Press, Inc.
All rights reserved.
First published by The Shoe String Press, Inc.,
2 Linsley Street, North Haven, Connecticut 06473.
www.shoestringpress.com

Library of Congress Cataloging-in-Publication Data

Walker, Warren S.
Twentieth-century short story explication : new series; with checklists of books and
journals used/Warren S. Walker.
p.   cm.
Includes bibliographical references and index. Summary: Contains nearly 26,000
entries that provide a bibliography of interpretations that have appeared since 1900 of
short stories published since 1800.
1. Short stories—Indexes.   [1. Short stories—Indexes.]
I. Title
Z5917.S5W35   1993   [PN3373]   92-22790
016.8093′1—dc20   ISBN 0-208-02340-2 (v. 1)

*Twentieth-Century Short Story Explication, with Checklists of Books
and Journals Used*

	Coverage	Published	ISBN
Edited by Warren S. Walker			
Third Edition	1961–1975	1977	0-208-01570-1
Supplement I	1976–1978	1980	0-208-01813-1
Supplement II	1979–1981	1984	0-208-02005-5
Supplement III	1982–1984	1987	0-208-02122-1
Supplement IV	1985–1986	1989	0-208-02188-4
Supplement V	1987–1988	1991	0-208-02299-6
Index	1961–1991	1992	0-208-02320-8

*Twentieth-Century Short Story Explication, New Series, with Checklists of Books
and Journals Used*

	Coverage	Published	ISBN
Edited by Warren S. Walker			
Volume 1	1989–1990	1993	0-208-02340-2
Edited by Wendell M. Aycock			
Volume 2	1991–1992	1995	0-208-02370-4
Volume 3	1993–1994	1997	0-208-02419-0
Volume 4	1995–1996	1999	0-208-02493-X
Volume 5	1997–1998	2002	0-208-02508-1

The paper in this publication meets the minimum requirements of American National
Standard for Information Science—Permanence of Paper for Printed Library
Materials, ANSI Z39.48-1984 ⊗

Printed in the United States of America

To Diane, of course

Contents

Preface

This fifth volume of the New Series carries the coverage of *Twentieth-Century Short Story Explication* forward through December 31, 1998. It includes more than 4,920 entries. Of the 887 authors cited, 268 appear here for the first time, bringing to 3,571 the total number of authors represented in both the original and New Series of *Twentieth-Century Short Story Explication*. As in the previous two or three volumes, interest in multiculturalism accounts for the great diversity of countries and cultures that the new writers represent. The famous short story artists of the past, however, still appear along with the names of writers who are listed here for the first time. Borges, Conrad, Hemingway, James, Melville, Mann, Poe, Welty, and others are certainly not being ignored by scholars nowadays.

No matter what language the short stories were originally composed in, the explications within are limited to those published in the major languages of Western Europe. Although certainly some explications are excluded by these parameters, the vast majority of the studies are written in these languages.

As in the past, this volume of *Twentieth-Century Short Story Explication* is a bibliography of interpretations that have appeared since 1900 of short stories published since 1800. The term *short story* here has the same meaning it carries in the Wilson Company's *Short Story Index*: "A brief narrative of not more than 150 average-sized pages." *Explication* is meant to suggest simply interpretation or explanation of the meaning of the story, including observations on theme, symbol, and sometimes structure. This definition excludes from the bibliography what are essentially studies of source, biographical data, and background materials. Occasionally there are explicatory passages cited in works otherwise devoted to these external considerations. All pages refer strictly to interpretative passages, not to the longer works in which they occur.

Over the years, Professor Warren Walker, who originated this bibliography, developed a very convenient, useful system for handling great numbers of explications. We continue to follow his system in this volume. Each book is cited by author or editor and a short title; the full title and publication data are provided in "A Checklist of Books Used"—and 625 were used in the compilation of this volume. For an article in a journal or an essay in a critical collection, the full publication information is provided in the text the first time the study is cited. In subsequent entries, only the critic's or scholar's name and a short title are used as long as these entries appear under the name of the same short story author. If an article or essay explicates stories of two or more authors, a complete initial entry is made for each author. As in previous volumes, we have included a "Checklist of Journals Used"—and this time 330 were used. This information should be especially helpful to students who may not be familiar with titles of professional journals, much less the abbreviations for such titles.

Although most of the entries in Volume V were published in 1997 and 1998, there are some entries with earlier dates. A few of these are earlier interpretations that were either unavailable or overlooked previously. A few are reprintings of earlier studies and these are preceded by a plus sign (+). Any such entry can be located in the original series by consulting the *Index to the Third Edition and Its Five Supplements, 1961–1991.*

In preparing this book, I have been indebted to a number of people. Warren Walker has been a constant source of information, help, and encouragement. In addition, I must acknowledge the contributions from such journals as *PMLA, Studies in Short Fiction,* and *Journal of Modern Literature.* I depend constantly upon the considerable support and help from the Texas Tech University Library, especially from Jan Kemp, Marina Oliver, Janie Boyd, and Vicky Brown in Acquisitions, and from Carol Roberts and her staff in the Department of Interlibrary Loan of the Texas Tech University Library. I also extend my appreciation for the great help of some very capable students: Natalie Tarenko, Laura Butler, Doris Miller, and Wei Yan. Finally, for her patience, assistance, and encouragement, I want to thank my wife Diane.

Wendell Aycock
Texas Tech University

Short Story Explications

SAIFUR RAHMAN ABBAD

"The Immigrant"
Rahim, Habibeh. "The Mirage of Faith and Justice: Some
Sociopolitical and Cultural Themes in Post-Colonial Urdu Short
Stories," in Hawley, John C., Ed. *The Postcolonial Crescent* . . . ,
238–239.

ABE AKIRA

"Peaches"
Charters, Ann, and William E. Sheidley. *Resources* . . . , 5th ed., 1.

ABE KŌBŌ

"Magic Chalk"
Ford, Joh, and Marjorie Ford. *Instructor's Manual* . . . , 74–75.

CHINUA ACHEBE

"Akueke"
Ezenwa-Ohaeto. *Chinua Achebe: A Biography*, 76.
"Chike's School Days"
Ezenwa-Ohaeto. *Chinua Achebe* . . . , 11, 75–76.
"Civil Peace"
Charters, Ann, and William E. Sheidley. *Resources* . . . , 5th ed., 2–3.
Ezenwa-Ohaeto. *Chinua Achebe* . . . , 165.
"Dead Men's Path"
Ezenwa-Ohaeto. *Chinua Achebe* . . . , 49.
"In a Village Church"
Ezenwa-Ohaeto. *Chinua Achebe* . . . , 41–42.
"The Mad Man"
Ezenwa-Ohaeto. *Chinua Achebe* . . . , 159.
Ford, Joh, and Marjorie Ford. *Instructor's Manual* . . . , 80–81.
"The Old Order in Conflict with the New"
Ezenwa-Ohaeto. *Chinua Achebe* . . . , 47.
"Polar Undergraduate"
Ezenwa-Ohaeto. *Chinua Achebe* . . . , 39.

1

"The Sacrificial Egg"
Ezenwa-Ohaeto. *Chinua Achebe* . . . , 69–70.

"Sugar Baby"
Ezenwa-Ohaeto. *Chinua Achebe* . . . , 169.

"Uncle Ben's Choice"
Ezenwa-Ohaeto. *Chinua Achebe* . . . , 111–112.

"Vengeful Creditor"
Ezenwa-Ohaeto. *Chinua Achebe* . . . , 160.

"The Voter"
Ezenwa-Ohaeto. *Chinua Achebe* . . . , 106.

SOLEDAD ACOSTA DE SAMPER

"El crimen"
Rodríguez-Arenas, Flor María. "La marginación de la narrativa de
escritoras decimonónicas colombianas: 'El crimen' de Soledad
Acosta de Samper," in Bacarisse, Pamela, Ed. *Tradición y
actualidad* . . . , 153–158.

SHMUEL [SHAY] YOSEF AGNON [SHMUEL YOSEF CZACZKES]

"According to the Pain is the Reward"
Fisch, Harold. *New Stories for Old* . . . , 195–198.

"Knots upon Knots"
Fisch, Harold. *New Stories* . . . , 193–194.

JOSÉ AGUSTÍN

"Cuál es la onda"
Vaquera, Santiago. " 'Cuál es la onda': Vagando por la ciudad
posmoderna," in Herrera, Sara P., Ed. *El cuento mexicano* . . . ,
446–457.

AH CHENG [ZHONG ACHENG]

"The King of Chess"
McDougall, Bonnie S., and Kam Louie. *The Literature of China* . . . ,
400–401.

ILSE AICHINGER

"Ajax"
Thums, Barbara. "Name, Mythos und Geschichte in Ilse Aichingers
Erzählung 'Ajax,' " *Zeitschrift für Germanistik*, 7 (1997), 292–302.

"Das Fenster-Theater"
McDonald, Edward R. "Out from the Shadows!—Ilse Aichinger's Poetic Dreams of the Unfettered Life," in Lamb-Faffelberger, Margarete, Ed. *Out from the Shadows . . .* , 24–25.

"Der Gefesselte"
McDonald, Edward R. "Out from . . . ," 28–30.

"Die geöffnete Order"
McDonald, Edward R. "Out from . . . ," 26–27.

"Der Hauslehrer"
McDonald, Edward R. "Out from . . . ," 25–26.

"Der junge Leutnant"
McDonald, Edward R. "Out from . . . ," 22–23.

"Die Maus"
McDonald, Edward R. "Out from . . . ," 23–24.

"Mein grüner Esel"
McDonald, Edward R. "Out from . . . ," 27–28.

"Das Plakat"
McDonald, Edward R. "Out from . . . ," 20.

"Spiegelgeschichte"
Gerlach, U. Henry. "Ilse Aichingers 'Spiegelgeschichte': eine einzigartige Erzählung," *Österreich Geschichte*, 40 (1996), 37–45.

"Wisconsin und Apfelreis"
Reiter, Andrea. "Ilse Aichinger: The Poetics of Silence," in Williams, Arthur, Stuart Parkes, and Julian Preece, Eds. *Contemporary . . .* , 214–220.

"Wo ich wohne"
McDonald, Edward R. "Out from . . . ," 21–22.

AMA ATA AIDOO

"No Sweetness Here"
Baldwin, Dean. *Instructor's Resource . . .* , 178–179.

CONRAD AIKEN

"Silent Snow, Secret Snow"
Baldwin, Dean. *Instructor's Resource . . .* , 118–120.

SALIM ALAFENISCH

"Der Gast mit den blauen Augen"
Berman, Nina. "German and Middle Eastern Literary Traditions in a Novel by Salim Alafenisch: Thoughts on a Germanophone Beduin Author from the Negev," *Germ Q*, 71 (1998), 275.

"Der gelehrte Esel"
Berman, Nina. "German and Middle . . . ," 275, 277.
"Das Kamel mit dem Nasenring"
Berman, Nina. "German and Middle . . . ," 275, 277.
"Die Sieben-Brunnen-Stadt"
Berman, Nina. "German and Middle . . . ," 274–275.

BOZORG ALAVI

"Dance of Death"
Zarrin, Ali. "The Rhetoric of Self and Other in Selected Iranian Short
Stories, 1906–1979," *Int'l Fiction R*, 24, i–ii (1997), 37.

A. ALBERTS

"The Hunt"
Beekman, E. M. *Troubled Pleasures* . . . , 591–592.
"The Thief"
Beekman, E. M. *Troubled Pleasures* . . . , 582.

LOUISA MAY ALCOTT

"Agatha's Confession"
Stern, Madeleine B. *Louisa May Alcott* . . . , 53.

"Behind a Mask"
Dawson, Melanie. "A Woman's Power: Alcott's 'Behind a Mask' and
the Usefulness of Dramatic Literacies in the Home," *ATQ*, 11, N.S.
(1997), 19–40.
Goddu, Teresa A. *Gothic America* . . . , 122–125.

"The Brothers" [same as "My Contraband"]
Klimasmith, Betsy. "Slave, Master, Mistress, Slave: Genre and
Interracial Desire in Louisa May Alcott's Fiction," *ATQ*, 11, N.S.
(1997), 120, 124–126.
Patterson, Mark. "Racial Sacrifice and Citizenship: The Construction
of Masculinity in Louisa May Alcott's 'The Brothers,' " *Stud Am
Fiction*, 25 (1997), 147–166.

"The Cross on the [Old] Church Tower"
Stern, Madeleine B. *Louisa May Alcott* . . . , 54–55.

"How I Went Out to Service"
Goddu, Teresa A. *Gothic America* . . . , 120–122.

"The Lady and the Woman"
Stern, Madeleine. *Louisa May Alcott* . . . , 56.
"M.L."
Klimasmith, Betsy. "Slave, Master . . . ," 118–120, 121–124, 130.

"A Marble Woman"
   Chapman, Mary. "The Masochistic Pleasures of the Gothic: Paternal
   Incest in Alcott's 'A Marble Woman,' " in Martin, Robert K., and
   Eric Savoy, Eds. *American Gothic* . . . , 191–199.
"Marion Earle; or, Only an Actress!"
   Stern, Madeleine. *Louisa May Alcott* . . . , 63–66.
"The Monk's Island"
   Stern, Madeleine. *Louisa May Alcott* . . . , 54.
"Pauline's Passion and Punishment"
   Stern, Madeleine. *Louisa May Alcott* . . . , 87.
"The Rival Prima Donnas"
   Stern, Madeleine. *Louisa May Alcott* . . . , 52–53.
"The Sisters' Trial"
   Stern, Madeleine. *Louisa May Alcott* . . . , 56–57.
"V. V.: or, Plots and Counterplots"
   Goddu, Teresa A. *Gothic America* . . . , 125–129.

IGNACIO ALDECOA

"Los bienaventurados"
   Marrero Henríquez, José M. *Documentación* . . . , 136–137.
"Pájaros y espantapájaros"
   Marrero Henríquez, José M. *Documentación* . . . , 136.

JALAL AL-E AHMAD

"The American Husband"
   Zarrin, Ali. "The Rhetoric of Self and Other in Selected Iranian Short
   Stories, 1906–1979," *Int'l Fiction R*, 24, i–ii (1997), 39–40.

CLARIBEL ALEGRÍA

"Primera comunión"
   Allen, Paula, and Wendell Aycock. "Subversion of the First Holy
   Communion in Contemporary Hispanic Fiction," *Confluencia*, 13, i
   (1997), 211–213.

SHERMAN ALEXIE

"The Lone Ranger and Tonto Fistfight in Heaven"
   Charters, Ann, and William E. Sheidley. *Resources* . . . , 5th ed., 3–4.

JACQUES-STÉPHEN ALEXIS

"Chronique d'un faux-amour"
   Mahéo, Marie-France. "Le Climat érotique: Obsession et ambiguïté

dans 'Chronique d'un faux-amour' de Jacques-Stéphen Alexis,"
Francofonia, 14, xxvii (1994), 97–105.

JAMES LANE ALLEN

"Two Gentlemen of Kentucky"
Gebhard, Caroline. "Reconstructing Southern Manhood: Race,
Sentimentality, and Camp in the Plantation Myth," in Jones, Anne
G., and Susan V. Donaldson, Eds. *Haunted Bodies* . . . , 140,
144–146.

WOODY ALLEN

"The Kugelmass Episode"
Charters, Ann, and William E. Sheidley. *Resources* . . . , 5th ed., 5–6.
"A Twenties Memory"
Bloom, James D. *The Literary Bent* . . . , 83–84.

ISABEL ALLENDE

"And of Clay Are We Created"
Baldwin, Dean. *Instructor's Resource* . . . , 214–216.
Carvalho, S. E. de. "Narration and Distance in Isabel Allende's Novels
and in *Cuentos de Eva Luna*," *Antípodas*, 6–7 (1997), 60–61.
"Dos palabras"
Carullo, Sylvia G. "Fetichismo, magia amorosa y amor erótico en dos
cuentos de Isabel Allende," *Texto Crítico*, 3, iv–v (1997), 126–128,
132.
"Niña perversa"
Carullo, Sylvia G. "Fetichismo, magia . . . ," 126, 128–132.
"The Phantom Palace"
Ford, Joh, and Marjorie Ford. *Instructor's Manual* . . . , 102–103.
"Tosca"
Koene, Jacoba. "Entre la realidad y la ficción: La parodia como arma
de subversión en 'Tosca' de Isabel Allende," *Romance Notes*, 38
(1998), 263–270.
"Walimai"
Carvalho, S. E. de. "Narration and Distance . . . ," 59–60.

DOROTHY ALLISON

"River of Names"
Charters, Ann, and William E. Sheidley. *Resources* . . . , 5th ed., 8–9.
Segrest, Mab. *My Mama's Dead Squirrel*, 129–131; rpt. in Bloom,
Harold, Ed. *Lesbian and Bisexual* . . . , 1–2.

CONCHA ALÓS

"La otra bestia"
Cook, Beverly R. "Division, Duplicity, and Duality: The Nature of the Double in Three Works by Contemporary Spanish Women Writers," *Letras Peninsulares*, 11 (1998), 665–667.

ALFREDO ALZUGARAT

"Lo que queda"
Cunha-Giabbai, Gloria da. "Variaciones sobre el olvido," *Monographic R*, 11 (1995), 334–335.

MARTIN AMIS

"Bujak and the Strong Force, or God's Dice"
Falconer, Rachel. "Bakhtin's Chronotope and the Contemporary Short Story," *So Atlantic Q*, 97 (1998), 709–712.
"The Immortals"
Falconer, Rachel. "Bakhtin's Chronotope . . . ," 718–719.
"Insight at Flame Lake"
Falconer, Rachel. "Bakhtin's Chronotope . . . ," 712–715.
"The Little Puppy That Could"
Falconer, Rachel. "Bakhtin's Chronotope . . . ," 715–718.

ALFRED ANDERSCH

"Kirschen der Freiheit"
Grimm, Gunter E. " 'Nichts als die Wahrheit': Zu Alfred Anderschs Realismus-Konzept," *Literatur für Leser*, 3 (1994), 109, 111, 112.
"Noch schöner wohnen"
Grimm, Gunter E. " 'Nichts als die Wahrheit' . . . ," 114, 115.
"Der Vater eines Mörders"
Kolk, Rainer. "*Du willst nur nicht*: Zu Alfred Anderschs 'Der Vater eines Mörders,' " *Euphorion*, 92, i (1998), 69–77.

HANS CHRISTIAN ANDERSEN

"The Emperor's New Clothes"
Ford, Joh, and Marjorie Ford. *Instructor's Manual* . . . , 5.
"The Little Mermaid"
Hees, Annelies van. "Tales of Immortality," in Pereira, Frederico, Ed. *Eleventh International* . . . , 179–180.
"The Marsh King's Daughter"
Hees, Annelies van. "Tales . . . ," 178–179.

MARGUERITE ANDERSEN

"L'Autrement pareille"
Lagrandeur, Katherine. " 'L'Autrement pareille' de Marguerite
Andersen: (s')écrire (en) silence," *Tangence*, 56 (1997), 91–101.

SHERWOOD ANDERSON

"Death in the Woods"
Charters, Ann, and William E. Sheidley. *Resources* . . . , 5th ed., 9–10.
"Hands"
Baldwin, Dean. *Instructor's Resource* . . . , 94–95.
Charters, Ann, and William E. Sheidley. *Resources* . . . , 5th ed., 12.
Ford, Joh, and Marjorie Ford. *Instructor's Manual* . . . , 33–34.

ENRIQUE ANDERSON IMBERT

"Pedro au corps léger"
Joguin, Odile. "Le fantastique ne fait plus le poids: allègement
fantastique du corps dans quelques texts contemporains," in
Marigny, Jean, Intro., *Images fantastiques du corps* . . . , 195–206.

LOU ANDREAS-SALOMÉ

"Fenitschka"
Anderson, Susan C. "Seeing Blindly: Voyeurism in Schnitzler's
'Fräulein Else' and Andreas-Salomé's 'Fenitschka,' " in Strelka,
Joseph P., Ed. *Die Seele* . . . , 14, 22–26.

ANONYMOUS

"The Charter and the Land"
Zlotnick, Susan. *Women, Writing* . . . , 186–187.
"Miss Coote's Confession; or the Voluptuous Experiences of an Old
Maid"
Heller, Tamar. "Flagellating Feminine Desire: Lesbians, Old Maids,
and New Women in 'Miss Coote's Confession,' a Victorian
Pornographic Narrative," *Victorian News*, 92 (1997), 9–15.

LAURA ANTILLANO

"La luna no es de pan-de-horno"
Rivas de Wesolowski, Luz M. "La perspectiva marginal de la historia
en la obra de Laura Antillano," *Venezuelan Lit & Arts J*, 2, i (1996),
19–21.

ROBERT ANTONI

"My Grandmother's Story of the Buried Treasure"
Patteson, Richard F. *Caribbean Passages* . . . , 148–149.

"Two-Head Fred and Tree-Foot Frieda"
Patteson, Richard F. *Caribbean Passages* . . . , 146–147.

RASHID ANWAR

"A Pilgrim's Progress"
Rahim, Habibeh. "The Mirage of Faith and Justice: Some
Sociopolitical and Cultural Themes in Post-Colonial Urdu Short
Stories," in Hawley, John C., Ed. *The Postcolonial Crescent* . . . ,
239–241.

ANWAR RIDHWAN

"Before Leaving"
Nur, Nina Z. "Crossing Cultural Boundaries at Home and Abroad: A
Comparative Study of the Short Stories of Anwar Ridhwan and
Gopal Baratham," in Zach, Wolfgang, and Ken L. Goodwin, Eds.
Nationalism vs. Internationalism . . . , 150.

"Friend"
Nur, Nina Z. "Crossing Cultural . . . ," 146–147.

"Growing Old"
Nur, Nina Z. "Crossing Cultural . . . ," 147–148.

"If That's the Way It Ends Up"
Nur, Nina Z. "Crossing Cultural . . . ," 150.

"Love of the Dragon"
Nur, Nina Z. "Crossing Cultural . . . ," 150.

"Minority"
Nur, Nina Z. "Crossing Cultural . . . ," 148–149.

"The World Is an Apartment"
Nur, Nina Z. "Crossing Cultural . . . ," 149–150.

ANJANA APPACHANA

"Her Mother"
Mohanram, Radhika. "The Problems of Reading: Mother-Daughter
Relationships and Indian Postcoloniality," in Brown-Guillory,
Elizabeth, Ed. *Women of Color* . . . , 23–24, 29, 31–33.

AHARON APPELFELD

"Kitty"
Ramras-Rauch, Gila. "Aharon Appelfeld: A Hundred Years of Jewish
Solitude," *World Lit Today*, 72 (1998), 497–498.

LOUIS ARAGON

"Les Paramètres"
Smiley, Amy. " 'Les Paramètres' du mensonge," in *Recherches croisées* . . . , 167–188.

TONY ARDIZZONE

"The Evening News"
Tamburri, Anthony J. *A Semiotic of Ethnicity* . . . , 30–32.
"The Eyes of Children"
Tamburri, Anthony J. *A Semiotic* . . . , 28–30.
"My Mother's Stories"
Tamburri, Anthony J. *A Semiotic* . . . , 24–28.
"Nonna"
Tamburri, Anthony J. *A Semiotic* . . . , 36–44.
"World Without End"
Tamburri, Anthony J. *A Semiotic* . . . , 32–36.

REINALDO ARENAS

"Adiós a mamá"
Hernández Miyares, Julio E. " 'Adiós a mamá': Un libro inédito de Reinaldo Arenas," *Círculo*, 21 (1992), 80–81.
"Algo sucede en el último balcón"
Hernández Miyares, Julio E. " 'Adiós a mamá' . . . ," 79–80.
"El Cometa Halley"
Hernández Miyares, Julio E. " 'Adiós a mamá' . . . ," 83.
"Comienza el desfile"
Luis, William. *Dance Between Two* . . . , 231–233.
"Final de un cuento"
Borland, Isabel A. *Cuban-American* . . . , 157–158.
Hernández Miyares, Julio E. " 'Adiós a mamá' . . . ," 84–85.
"La Gran Fuerza"
Hernández Miyares, Julio E. " 'Adiós a mamá' . . . ," 78–79.
"Memorias de la tierra"
Hernández Miyares, Julio E. " 'Adiós a mamá' . . . ," 85–86.
"La Torre de Cristal"
Hernández Miyares, Julio E. " 'Adiós a mamá' . . . ," 83–84.
"Traidor"
Hernández Miyares, Julio E. " 'Adiós a mamá' . . . ," 81–83.

MARCEL ARLAND

"Florence"
Guissard, Michel. "*Les Vivants* de Marcel Arland: Prolégomènes à un genre nouveau?" *Roman 20–50*, 23 (1997), 179.

"Miracle"
Guissard, Michel. "*Les Vivants . . . ,*" 179–180.
"Ombres"
Guissard, Michel. "*Les Vivants . . . ,*" 182–183.
"Rendez-vous"
Guissard, Michel. "*Les Vivants . . . ,*" 177.

ELEANOR ARNASON

"The Warlord of Saturn's Moons"
Brennan, Tom. "The Silver-Haired Maiden Lady vs. the Red-Headed Hussy or the Author's Revenge in Eleanor Arnason's 'The Warlord of Saturn's Moons,' " *New York R Sci Fiction*, 108 (August, 1997), 12–18.

[LUDWIG] ACHIM VON ARNIM

"Die Ehenschmiede"
Andermatt, Michael. "Happy-End und Katastrophe: Die Erzählschlüsse bei L. Achim von Arnim als Form romantischer Ironie," in Andermatt, Michael, Ed. *Grenzgänge . . .* , 25–27.
Wingertszahn, Christoph. " 'Schöne Seelen, lernet kochen!': Ludwig Achim von Arnims späte Reisebilder," in Andermatt, Michael, Ed. *Grenzgänge . . .* , 159–163.
"Isabella of Egypt"
Friedrichsmeyer, Sara. "Romantic Nationalism: Achim von Arnim's Gypsy Princess Isabella," in Herminghouse, Patricia, and Magda Mueller, Eds. *Gender and Germanness . . .* , 51–65.
"Mistris Lee"
Henckmann, Gisela. " 'Vielleicht beginnt nun bald die Zeit der Frauen': Zum emanzipatorischen Aspekt der Frauengestaltung und Geschlechterdifferenz im Werk Achims von Arnim," in Andermatt, Michael, Ed. *Grenzgänge . . .* , 83, 87, 88.
"Seltsames Begegnen und Wiedersehen"
Andermatt, Michael. "Happy-End . . . ," 20–21.
"Der tolle Invalide auf dem Fort Ratonneau"
Andermatt, Michael. "Happy-End . . . ," 19–21.
Bonfiglio, Thomas P. "Ironie und Modernität bei Arnim," in Andermatt, Michael, Ed. *Grenzgänge . . .* , 38–40, 40–45.

INÉS ARRENDONDO

"Las mariposas nocturnas"
Arenas Monreal, Rogelio. " 'Las mariposas nocturnas' de Inés Arrendondo: El rito del minotauro," in Herrera, Sara P., Ed. *El cuento mexicano . . .* , 298–303.

Frouman-Smith, Erica. "Women and the Problem of Domination in the Short Fiction of Inés Arrendondo," *Letras Femeninas*, 23, i–ii (1997), 164, 166–167.
"Sombra entre sombra"
Frouman-Smith, Erica. "Women . . . ," 164, 167–168.
"La Sunamita"
Frouman-Smith, Erica. "Women . . . ," 164–166.

JUAN JOSÉ ARREOLA

"Anuncio"
Mora, Carmen de. "Las confabulaciones de Juan José Arreola," in Valcárcel, Eva, Ed. *Hispanoamérica* . . . , 68.
"Apuntes de un rencoroso"
Mora, Carmen de. "Las confabulaciones . . . ," 72.
"De balística"
Mora, Carmen de. "Las confabulaciones . . . ," 75–76.
"Corrido"
Mora, Carmen de. "Las confabulaciones . . . ," 72–73.
"Es verdad os digo"
Mora, Carmen de. "Las confabulaciones . . . ," 66.
"El guardagujas"
Mora, Carmen de. "Las confabulaciones . . . ," 66–67.
"Hizo el bien mientras vivió"
Mora, Carmen de. "Las confabulaciones . . . ," 74.
"La migala"
Mora, Carmen de. "Las confabulaciones . . . ," 71.
"Monólogo del insumiso"
Mora, Carmen de. "Las confabulaciones . . . ," 75.
"Una mujer amaestrada"
Mora, Carmen de. "Las confabulaciones . . . ," 70–71.
"Pablo"
Mora, Carmen de. "Las confabulaciones . . . ," 76–77.
"Parábola del trueque"
Mora, Carmen de. "Las confabulaciones . . . ," 73.
"Parturiento montes"
Mora, Carmen de. "Las confabulaciones . . . ," 74–75.
"El prodigioso miligramo"
Mora, Carmen de. "Las confabulaciones . . . ," 67–68.
"Pueblerina"
Mora, Carmen de. "Las confabulaciones . . . ," 71–72.
"El rinoceronte"
Mora, Carmen de. "Las confabulaciones . . . ," 70.

T[IMOTHY] S[HAY] ARTHUR

"The Shipwreck"
Goodman, Nan. *Shifting the Blame* . . . , 60–61.

VICTOR ASTAF'EV

"The Shepherd and the Shepherdess"
Ziolkowski, Margaret. *Literary Exorcisms* . . . , 123–124.

MARGARET ATWOOD

"Bluebeard's Egg"
Baldwin, Dean. *Instructor's Resource* . . . , 202–204.
"Death by Landscape"
Charters, Ann, and William E. Sheidley. *Resources* . . . , 5th ed.,
14–15.
James, William C. *Locations of the Sacred* . . . , 65–66.
"Giving Birth"
Carrera Suárez, Isabel. "Towards a Female Language of Childbirth,"
in Barfoot, C. C., and Theo D'haen, Eds. *Shades of Empire* . . . ,
180–181.
Wall, Kathleen. "Representing the Other Body: Frame Narratives in
Margaret Atwood's 'Giving Birth' and Alice Munro's
'Meneseteung,' " *Canadian Lit*, 154 (Autumn, 1997), 78–82.
"Happy Endings"
Baldwin, Dean. *Instructor's Resource* . . . , 205–206.
Charters, Ann, and William E. Sheidley. *Resources* . . . , 5th ed., 16.
"Hurricane Hazel"
Rubik, Margarete. "National Identity, International Life-Styles and
Cosmopolitan Culture in Margaret Atwood's 'Significant Moments
in the Life of My Mother,' 'Hurricane Hazel' and 'Unearthing
Suite,' " *Brno Stud Engl*, 23 (1997), 145–150.
"Significant Moments in the Life of My Mother"
Rubik, Margarete. "National Identity . . . ," 145–150.
"Simmering"
Ford, Joh, and Marjorie Ford. *Instructor's Manual* . . . , 95.
"Unearthing Suite"
Rubik, Margarete. "National Identity . . . ," 145–150.

BERNARDO ATXAGA

"After Darkness I Wait for Light"
López Liquete, María Felisa. "Basque Women: Real and Imagined
Identities," in Castillo, Susan, Ed. *Engendering Identities*, 64.

"Esteban Werfell"
    López Liquete, María Felisa. "Basque . . . ," 63–64.

BERTHOLD AUERBACH

"Befehlerles"
    McInnes, Edward. "Auerbach's *Schwarzwälder Dorfgeschichten* and
    the Quest for 'German Realism' in the 1840s," in Ward, Mark G.,
    Ed. *Perspectives on German Realist . . .* , 106–107.

"Ivo, der Hajrle"
    McInnes, Edward. "Auerbach's . . . ," 104–105.

"Der Lautenbacher"
    McInnes, Edward. "Auerbach's . . . ," 107–108.

MARY HUNTER AUSTIN

"The Basket Woman"
    Harrison, Elizabeth J. "Zora Neale Hurston and Mary Hunter Austin's
    Ethnographic Fiction: New Modernist Narratives," in Harrison,
    Elizabeth J., and Shirley Peterson, Eds. *Unmanning Modernism . . .* ,
    53.

"The Return of Mr. Wills"
    Graulich, Melody. "Western Biodiversity: Rereading Nineteenth-
    Century American Women's Writing," in Kilcup, Karen L., Ed.
    Nineteenth-Century American . . . , 56.

"The Walking Woman"
    Stout, Janis P. *Through the Window . . .* , 36–37.

"White Wisdom"
    Harrison, Elizabeth J. "Zora Neale Hurston . . . ," 54–55.

FRANCISCO AYALA

"El hechizado"
    Àlvarez Ramiro, Carlos. "El uso de MacGuffin en los cuentos de
    Francisco Ayala," *Ojáncano*, 13 (1997), 58–59.

"Polar, estrella"
    Krauel, Ricardo. "Diálogo entre cine y literatura en la narrativa juvenil
    ayaliana: el caso de 'Polar, estrella,' " *Romance Lang Annual*, 8
    (1996), 529–531.

"El rapto"
    Àlvarez Ramiro, Carlos. "El uso de MacGuffin . . . ," 61–64.

"Un pez"
    Àlvarez Ramiro, Carlos. "El uso de MacGuffin . . . ," 59–61.

MARCEL AYMÉ

"Traversée de Paris"
Lloyd, Christopher. "Myths and Ironies of the Occupation: Marcel
Aymé's 'Traversée de Paris,' " in Thomas, Neil, and Françoise Le
Saux, Eds. *Myth and Its Legacy . . .*, 49–62.

VASILII AZHAEV

"The Cockroaches"
Lahusen, Thomas. *How Life Writes . . .*, 80.
"A Foreword to Life"
Lahusen, Thomas. *How Life Writes . . .*, 52, 87, 191.
"On the Seventh Day"
Lahusen, Thomas. *How Life Writes . . .*, 147–148.

MARIANO AZUELA

"The Underdogs"
Bledsoe, Penelope M. "Subject Inversion in Spanish and Narrative
Style: A Case Study of 'Los de abajo,' " in Forbes, F. William,
Teresa Méndez-Faith, Mary-Anne Vetterling, and Barbara H. Wing,
Eds. *Reflections . . .*, 35–45.
Duffey, J. Patrick. "A War of Words: Orality and Literacy in Mariano
Azuela's 'Los de abajo,' " *Romance Notes*, 38 (1998), 173–178.
Griffin, Clive. *Los de abajo*, 37–102.
———. "The Structure of 'Los de Abajo,' " *Revista Canadiense*, 6
(1981), 25–41; rpt. Foster, David W., and Daniel Altamiranda, Eds.
Twentieth-Century . . ., 25–41.
Zivley, Sherry L. "The Conclusions of Azuela's 'The Underdogs' and
Hemingway's *For Whom the Bell Tolls*," *Hemingway R*, 17, ii
(1998), 118–123.

ISAAC BABEL

"Discourse on the Tachanka"
Danow, David K. "A Poetics of Inversion: The Non-Dialogic Aspect
in Isaac Babel's *Red Calvary*," *Mod Lang R*, 86 (1991), 944–945;
rpt. Danow, David K., *Models of Narrative . . .*, 139–140.
"Guy De Maupassant"
Ford, Joh, and Marjorie Ford. *Instructor's Manual . . .*, 44–45.
"The Life and Adventures of Matthew Pavlichenko"
Danow, David K. "A Poetics . . . ," 945–946, 948–950, 951; rpt. in
his *Models of Narrative . . .*, 140–141, 145–147, 148.
"My First Goose"
Charters, Ann, and William E. Sheidley. *Resources . . .*, 5th ed., 17.

"Sandy the Christ"
Danow, David K. "A Poetics . . . ," 940–941; rpt. in his *Models of Narrative* . . . , 134–135.

INGEBORG BACHMANN

"Alles"
Treusch-Dieter, Gerburg. "Schuld und Erziehung: Sprache, Leib, Geschlecht," in Pattillo-Hess, John, and Wilhelm Petrasch, Eds. *Ingeborg Bachmann* . . . , 57–73.

"Among Murderers and Madmen"
Thorpe, Kathleen. " 'Monuments looking out upon Utopia': *The Thirtieth Year* by Ingeborg Bachmann—A Reading," in Brokoph-Mauch, Gudrun, Ed. *Thunder Rumbling* . . . , 199–201.

"Drei Wege zum See"
Pichl, Robert. "Die 'Gefällige' Prosaistin: Überlegungen zu Ingeborg Bachmanns Erzählweise im *Simultan*-Zyklus," in Pattillo-Hess, John, and Wilhelm Petrasch, Eds. *Ingeborg Bachmann* . . . , 29–30.

"Das Gebell"
Pichl, Robert. "Die 'Gefällige' . . . ," 32–34.

"Ihr glücklichen Augen"
Pichl, Robert. "Die 'Gefällige' . . . ," 31–32.

"Jugend in einer österreichischen Stadt"
Boa, Elizabeth. "Reading Ingeborg Bachmann," in Weedon, Chris, Ed. *Post-War Women's Writing* . . . , 277.

"Das Lächeln der Sphinx"
Weigel, Sigrid. "Zum Verhältnis von Philosophie und Literatur nach 1945: Benjamin, Adorno, Bachmann," *Deutsche Vierteljahrsschrift*, 70 (1996), 132–135.

"Oh Happy Eyes"
Hsu, Linda C. " 'A Favorite Selection at the Beauty Parlor?': Rereading Ingeborg Bachmann's 'Oh Happy Eyes,' " in Brokoph-Mauch, Gudrun, Ed. *Thunder Rumbling* . . . , 76–90.

"Probleme, Probleme"
Pichl, Robert. "Die 'Gefällige' . . . ," 31–32.

"Ein Schritt nach Gomorrah"
Boa, Elizabeth. "Reading . . . ," 279–280.
Lennox, Sara. "Constructing Femininity after 1945: Ingeborg Bachmann and her Readers," in Weninger, Robert, and Brigitte Rossbacher, Eds. *Wendezeiten* . . . , 180–181.

"Simultan"
Pichl, Robert. "Die 'Gefällige' . . . ," 29–30.

"A Step Towards Gomorrah"
Thorpe, Kathleen. " 'Monuments . . . ,' " 201–203.

"The Thirtieth Year"
Thorpe, Kathleen. " 'Monuments . . . ,' " 191–198.

"Undine geht"
Kosta, Barbara, and Helga Kraft. "German Women Writing after
1945," in Bullivant, Keith, Ed. *Beyond 1989* . . . , 80.
Thorpe, Kathleen. " 'Monuments . . . ,' " 204.

"Unter Mördern und Irren"
Lennox, Sara. "Constructing Femininity . . . ," 181–182.

"A Wildermuth"
Boa, Elizabeth. "Reading . . . ," 278–279.
Philipp, Frank. "The Truth About Language?—It's All Lies: Ingeborg
Bachmann's 'Ein Wildermuth,' " *MIFLC R*, 1 (1991), 90–96.
Thorpe, Kathleen. " 'Monuments . . . ,' " 203–204.

IGOR BAKHTEREV

"An Incident in 'The Crooked Stomach' "
Roberts, Graham. *The Last Soviet* . . . , 33.

"Koloborot"
Roberts, Graham. *The Last Soviet* . . . , 32–33.

"Only a Pintle"
Roberts, Graham. *The Last Soviet* . . . , 84–85.

"The Shop with a Hole in It"
Roberts, Graham. *The Last Soviet* . . . , 14.

JAMES BALDWIN

"The Outing"
de Romanet, Jerome. "Revisiting *Madeleine* and 'The Outing': James
Baldwin's Revision of Gide's Sexual Politics," *MELUS*, 22, i
(1997), 10–12.

"The Rockpile"
Ford, Joh, and Marjorie Ford. *Instructor's Manual* . . . , 72–73.

"Sonny's Blues"
Charters, Ann, and William E. Sheidley. *Resources* . . . , 5th ed.,
18–19.
Ford, Joh, and Marjorie Ford. *Instructor's Manual* . . . , 73–74.
Sherard, Tracey. "Sonny's Bebop: Baldwin's 'Blues Text' as
Intracultural Critique," *African Am R*, 32 (1998), 691–705.

J. G. BALLARD

"The Dead Astronaut"
Luckhurst, Roger. *"The Angle Between Two Walls"* . . . , 140.

"Motel Architecture"
Luckhurst, Roger. *"The Angle Between Two Walls"* . . . , 132.

"Reptile Enclosure"
Luckhurst, Roger. *"The Angle Between Two Walls"* . . . , 52–53.

"The Screen Game"
    Luckhurst, Roger. "Repetition and Unreadability: J. G. Ballard's
    Vermillion Sands," *Extrapolation*, 36 (1995), 299–300; rpt. in
    Luckhurst, Roger. *"The Angle Between Two Walls"* . . . , 174–175.

"The Secret History of World War III"
    Luckhurst, Roger. *"The Angle Between Two Walls"* . . . , 122–123.

"The Terminal Beach"
    Luckhurst, Roger. *"The Angle Between Two Walls"* . . . , 68–69.

"The Thousand Dreams of Stellavista"
    Luckhurst, Roger. *"The Angle Between Two Walls"* . . . , 133–134.

"The Watchtowers"
    Luckhurst, Roger. *"The Angle Between Two Walls"* . . . , 122.

HONORÉ DE BALZAC

"Adieu"
    Felman, Shoshana. "Women and Madness: The Critical Phallacy," in
    Warhol, Robyn R., and Diane P. Herndl, Eds. *Feminisms* . . . , 9–10,
    13–19.
    Pan, Da'an. "The Purloined Letter and the 'Purblind' Lacan: The
    Intertextual Semiotics of Poe and Lacan," *Stud Hum*, 23, i (1996),
    53–54, 61–65.

"Le Chef-d'oeuvre inconnu"
    Marin, Louis. *Cross-Readings*, 179–194.
    Strike, Norman. "Le Portrait dans 'Le Chef-d'oeuvre inconnu' de
    Balzac et *Portrait d'un inconnu* de Sarraute: Objet d'art/Sujet
    d'écriture," *French Stud Southern Africa*, 27 (1998), 78, 79–80, 86.

"Facino Cane"
    Ebguy, Jacques-David. " 'Le Récit comme vision': Balzac voyant
    dans 'Facino Cane,' " *L'Année Balzacienne*, 19 (1998), 261–283.

"La Fille aux yeux d'or"
    Sharpley-Whiting, T. Denean. " 'The Other Woman': Reading a Body
    of Differences in Balzac's 'La Fille aux yeux d'or,' " *Symposium*,
    51 (1997), 43–50.

"Louis Lambert"
    Smadja, Robert. *Corps et Roman* . . . , 37–47.

"La Maison Nucingen"
    Dupuis, Danielle. "Du 'Neveu de Rameau' à 'La Maison Nucingen,' "
    L'Année Balzacienne, 18 (1997), 221–234.

TONI CADE BAMBARA

"Gorilla, My Love"
    Baldwin, Dean. *Instructor's Resource* . . . , 180–182.

"The Drive Home"
Niemi, Robert. *Russell Banks*, 60–62.

"Firewood"
Niemi, Robert. *Russell Banks*, 143–144.

"The Fish"
Niemi, Robert. *Russell Banks*, 145–146.

"The Fisherman"
Niemi, Robert. *Russell Banks*, 136–137.

"God's Country"
Niemi, Robert. *Russell Banks*, 130–131.

"The Guinea Pig Lady"
Niemi, Robert. *Russell Banks*, 121–123.

"The Gully"
Niemi, Robert. *Russell Banks*, 146–147.

"Impasse"
Niemi, Robert. *Russell Banks*, 60.

"Indisposed"
Niemi, Robert. *Russell Banks*, 89–91.

"The Investiture"
Niemi, Robert. *Russell Banks*, 48.

"The Lie"
Niemi, Robert. *Russell Banks*, 51–52.

"The Masquerade"
Niemi, Robert. *Russell Banks*, 52–53.

"Mistake"
Niemi, Robert. *Russell Banks*, 142–143.

"My Mother's Memories, My Father's Lie, and Other True Stories"
Niemi, Robert. *Russell Banks*, 139–140.

"The Nap"
Niemi, Robert. *Russell Banks*, 48–49.

"The Neighbor"
Niemi, Robert. *Russell Banks*, 49–50.

"The New World"
Niemi, Robert. *Russell Banks*, 93–94.

"The Perfect Couple"
Niemi, Robert. *Russell Banks*, 81–83.

"Politics"
Niemi, Robert. *Russell Banks*, 133–134.

"Principles"
Niemi, Robert. *Russell Banks*, 131–132.

"Queen for a Day"
Niemi, Robert. *Russell Banks*, 138–139.

"The Right Way"
Niemi, Robert. *Russell Banks*, 134–135.

"The Rise of the Middle Class"
Niemi, Robert. *Russell Banks*, 89.

"Sarah Cole: A Type of Love Story"
Haley, Vanessa. "Russell Banks' Use of 'The Frog King' in 'Sarah Cole: A Type of Love Story,' " *Notes Contemp Lit*, 27, iii (1997), 7–10.
Niemi, Robert. *Russell Banks*, 23–24.

"Searching for Survivors (I)"
Niemi, Robert. *Russell Banks*, 57–59.

"Searching for Survivors (II)"
Niemi, Robert. *Russell Banks*, 62–63.

"A Sentimental Education"
Niemi, Robert. *Russell Banks*, 83–84.

"Success Story"
Niemi, Robert. *Russell Banks*, 140–141.

"What Noni Hubner Did Not Tell the Police about Jesus"
Niemi, Robert. *Russell Banks*, 128–129.

"With Che at Kitty Hawk"
Niemi, Robert. *Russell Banks*, 55–56.

"With Che at the Plaza"
Niemi, Robert. *Russell Banks*, 56–57.

"With Che in New Hampshire"
Niemi, Robert. *Russell Banks*, 54–55.

GOPAL BARATHAM

"Double Exposure"
Nur, Nina Z. "Crossing Cultural Boundaries at Home and Abroad: A Comparative Study of the Short Stories of Anwar Ridhwan and Gopal Baratham," in Zach, Wolfgang, and Ken L. Goodwin, Eds. *Nationalism vs. Internationalism . . .* , 152.

"Ghost"
Nur, Nina Z. "Crossing Cultural . . . ," 152.

"The Gift of Sarah Richardson"
Nur, Nina Z. "Crossing Cultural . . . ," 151.

"Island"
Nur, Nina Z. "Crossing Cultural . . . ," 152.

"People Make You Cry"
Nur, Nina Z. "Crossing Cultural . . . ," 153.

"Tomorrow's Brother"
Nur, Nina Z. "Crossing Cultural . . . ," 153.

"Ultimate Commodity"
Nur, Nina Z. "Crossing Cultural . . . ," 152–153.

"Welcome"
Nur, Nina Z. "Crossing Cultural . . . ," 151.

JULES-AMÉDÉE BARBEY D'AUREVILLY

"Le Bonheur dans le crime"
Doucette, Clarice M. "Power in Perspective: Barbey d'Aurevilly's 'Le Bonheur dans le crime,' " *Dalhousie French Stud*, 44 (1998), 55–64.

"La Vengeance d'une femme"
Cogman, P. W. M. "Criminal Conversation: Telling and Knowing in Barbey's 'La Vengeance d'une femme,' " *French Stud*, 51 (1997), 30–41.

DJUNA BARNES

"The Rabbit"
Bockting, Margaret. "The Great War and Modern Gender Consciousness: The Subversive Tactics of Djuna Barnes," *Mosaic*, 30, iii (1997), 26–30.

JULIAN BARNES

"Dragons"
Moseley, Merritt. *Understanding Julian Barnes*, 159–161.

"Experiment"
Moseley, Merritt. *Understanding Julian Barnes*, 162–163.

"Interference"
Moseley, Merritt. *Understanding Julian Barnes*, 161–162.

"One of a Kind"
Moseley, Merritt. *Understanding Julian Barnes*, 158–159.

ALLEN BARNETT

"The *Times* As It Knows Us"
Bloom, James D. *The Literary Bent* . . . , 141–144.

PÍO BAROJA Y NESSI

"El reloj"
García de Juan, Miguel Ángel. *Los cuentos* . . . , 248–249.

"El vago"
García de Juan, Miguel Ángel. *Los cuentos* . . . , 248.

PÍA BARROS

"Cartas de inocencia"
Ojeda, L. Cecilia. "Entre simulacros y enmascaramientos: 'Cuando

Santiago está a oscuras' y 'Cartas de inocencia,' de Pía Barros,"
Revista Canadiense, 23 (1998), 110–113.
"Cuando Santiago está a oscuras"
Ojeda, L. Cecilia. "Entre simulacros . . . ," 106–110.

JOHN BARTH

"Autobiography: A Self-Recorded Fiction"
Ford, Joh, and Marjorie Ford. *Instructor's Manual* . . . , 81–82.
"Menelaiad"
Nelles, William. *Frameworks* . . . , 149–152.
"On With the Story"
Charters, Ann, and William E. Sheidley. *Resources* . . . , 5th ed.,
22–23.

DONALD BARTHELME

"At the Tolstoy Museum"
Charters, Ann, and William E. Sheidley. *Resources* . . . , 5th ed., 24.
"The Balloon"
Baldwin, Dean. *Instructor's Resource* . . . , 170–172.
"The Glass Mountain"
Olsen, Lance. "Narrative Overdrive: Postmodern Fantasy,
Deconstruction, and Cultural Critique in Beckett and Barthelme,"
in Cooke, Brett, George E. Slusser, and Jaume Marti-Olivella, Eds.
The Fantastic Other . . . , 80–84.
"The Sandman"
Ford, Joh, and Marjorie Ford. *Instructor's Manual* . . . , 83.

PAULÉ BARTÓN

"Emilie Plead Choose One Egg"
Baldwin, Dean. *Instructor's Resource* . . . , 195–196.

NASREEN BASHIR

"Love's Compensation"
Rahim, Habibeh. "The Mirage of Faith and Justice: Some
Sociopolitical and Cultural Themes in Post-Colonial Urdu Short
Stories," in Hawley, John C., Ed. *The Postcolonial Crescent* . . . ,
239.

HERBERT ERNEST BATES

"Great Uncle Crow"
Baldwin, Dean. *Instructor's Resource* . . . , 155–156.

CHARLES BAUDELAIRE

"La Fanfarlo"
Houk, Deborah. "Self Construction and Sexual Identity in Nineteenth-Century French Dandyism," *French Forum*, 22 (1997), 61–62, 67, 68, 69–70.

VICKI BAUM

"Im alten Haus"
Brenner, David A. "Neglected 'Women's' Texts and Contexts: Vicki Baum's Jewish Ghetto Stories," *Women Germ Yearbook*, 13 (1997), 105.
"Rafael Gutmann"
Brenner, David A. "Neglected 'Women's' . . . ," 105–112.

MARTHA BAYLES

"The *New Yorker* Story"
Curnutt, Kirk. *Wise Economies* . . . , 205–206.

GLENDA BEAGAN

"Scream, Scream"
Baker, Simon. "The Dislocated Self: Modern Welsh Short Stories in English," in Bogaards, Winnifred M., Ed. *Literature of Region* . . . , 325.

ANN BEATTIE

"The Burning House"
Charters, Ann, and William E. Sheidley. *Resources* . . . , 5th ed., 25–26.
"Imagine a Day at the End of Your Life"
McKinstry, Susan J. "Picturing Ann Beattie," in Lounsberry, Barbara, et al., Eds. *The Tales We Tell* . . . , 32–33.
"In the White Night"
McKinstry, Susan J. "Picturing . . . ," 30.
Simmons, Philip E. *Deep Surfaces* . . . , 120–121.
"Janus"
Ford, Joh, and Marjorie Ford. *Instructor's Manual* . . . , 111–112.
"Like Glass"
McKinstry, Susan J. "Picturing . . . ," 31.
"Octascope"
Casey, Roger N. *Textual Vehicles* . . . , 158, 160.

"Parking Lot"
Casey, Roger N. *Textual Vehicles* . . . , 159, 160–161.
"Shifting"
Casey, Roger N. *Textual Vehicles* . . . , 157, 159.
McKinstry, Susan J. "Picturing . . . ," 31–32.
"A Vintage Thunderbird"
Casey, Roger N. *Textual Vehicles* . . . , 155–157.
"What Was Mine"
Simmons, Philip E. *Deep Surfaces* . . . , 122.

SIMONE DE BEAUVOIR

"Malentendu à Moscou"
Keefe, Terry. *Simone de Beauvoir*, 155–159, 164–165.

JUREK BECKER

"Die beliebteste Familiengeschichte"
Rock, David. " 'Wie ich ein Deutscher wurde': Sprachlosigkeit,
Sprache und Identität bei Jurek Becker," in Riordan, Colin, Ed.
Jurek Becker, 31–33, 40.
"Die Mauer"
Rock, David. " 'Wie ich ein . . . ," 33–36.
"Das Parkverbot"
Rock, David. "Aesthetics and Storytelling: Some Aspects of Jurek
Becker's *Erzählungen*," in Williams, Arthur, Stuart Parkes, and
Julian Preece, Eds. *Contemporary* . . . , 66–67.

SAMUEL BECKETT

"Assumption"
O'Hara, J. D. *Samuel Beckett's Hidden* . . . , 35.
"The Calmative"
Baker, Phil. *Beckett and the Mythology* . . . , 98–103.
Pilling, John. *Beckett Before Godot*, 221–227.
"A Case in a Thousand"
Baker, Phil. *Beckett and the Mythology* . . . , 1–5.
O'Hara, J. D. *Samuel Beckett's* . . . , 38–42, 56.
"Dante and the Lobster"
Acheson, James. *Samuel Beckett's Artistic* . . . , 23–26.
Charters, Ann, and William E. Sheidley. *Resources* . . . , 5th ed.,
26–28.
Pilling, John. *Beckett* . . . , 32, 99.
"Ding-Dong"
Acheson, James. *Samuel Beckett's Artistic* . . . , 26–30.

"Ping"
Baker, Phil. *Beckett and the Mythology* . . . , 90–92.
"The Smeraldina's Billet Doux"
Acheson, James. *Samuel Beckett's Artistic* . . . , 34–35.
"Walking Out"
Acheson, James. *Samuel Beckett's Artistic* . . . , 33.
"A Wet Night"
Acheson, James. *Samuel Beckett's Artistic* . . . , 29–32.
"What a Misfortune"
Acheson, James. *Samuel Beckett's Artistic* . . . , 33–34.
"Yellow"
Acheson, James. *Samuel Beckett's Artistic* . . . , 35–37.

GUSTAVO ADOLFO BÉCQUER

"The Promise"
Boudreau, H. L. "Memes: Intertextuality's Minimal Replicators," in
Brownlow, Jeanne P., and John W. Kronik, Eds. *Intertextual
Pursuits* . . . , 242–243.

RICHARD BEER-HOFMANN

"Der Tod Georgs"
Steck-Meier, Esther. "Richard Beer-Hofmann 'Der Tod Georgs'
(1900)," in Tarot, Rolf, and Gabriela Scherer, Eds. *Erzählkunst der
Vormoderne*, 400–415.

MICHEL BÉLIL

"Miroir-miroir-dis-moi-qui-est-le-plus-beau"
Morin, Lise. "Modes de représentation du réel dans la nouvelle
fantastique québécoise contemporaine," *Annales Centre
Recherches*, 19 (1994), 44–47.

JOHANNE DE BELLEFEUILLE

"Comme un gant"
Morin, Lise. "Modes de représentation du réel dans la nouvelle
fantastique québécoise contemporaine," *Annales Centre
Recherches*, 19 (1994), 47–49.

FRANCES BELLERBY

"The Green Cupboard"
Blondel, Nathalie. " 'It Goes on Happening': Frances Bellerby and the

Great War," in Raitt, Suzanne, and Trudi Tate, Eds. *Women's Fiction* . . . , 162–165.

"My Brother Martin"
Blondel, Nathalie. " 'It Goes on Happening' . . . ," 159–160.

SAUL BELLOW

"The Old System"
Weber, Donald. "Manners and Morals, Civility and Barbarism: The Cultural Contexts of *Seize the Day*," in Kramer, Michael, Ed. *New Essays* . . . , 48–51.

"Seize the Day"
Budick, Emily M. "*Yizkor* for Six Million: Mourning the Death of Civilization in Saul Bellow's 'Seize the Day,' " in Kramer, Michael, Ed. *New Essays* . . . , 93–109.
Chametzky, Jules. "Death and the Post-Modern Hero/Schlemiel: An Essay on 'Seize the Day,' " in Kramer, Michael, Ed. *New Essays* . . . , 111–123.
Girgus, Sam B. "Imaging Masochism and the Politics of Pain: 'Facing' the Word in the Cinetext of 'Seize the Day,' " in Kramer, Michael, Ed. *New Essays* . . . , 71–92.
Ranta, Jerrald. "Time in Bellow's 'Seize the Day,' " *Essays Lit*, 22 (1995), 300–315.
Weber, Donald. "Manners and Morals . . . ," 44–45, 55–64.

MARIO BENEDETTI

"Almuerzo y dudas"
Geldrich-Leffman, Hanna. "Body and Voice: The Dialogue of Marriage in the Short Stories of Mario Benedetti," *Chasqui*, 25, i (1996), 40–41.

"Cinco años de vida"
Geldrich-Leffman, Hanna. "Body and Voice . . . ," 43–44.

"Corazonada"
Tisnado, Carmen. "Mario Benedetti's 'Corazonada': Silence that Reverses Power," *Hispano*, 121 (1997), 45–52.

"Escrito en Überlingen"
Tisnado, Carmen. "Tortura y exilio, victima y victimario: Una lectura de dos cuentos de Mario Benedetti," *Alba de América*, 15 (1997), 283–285, 286, 287.

"Escuchar a Mozart"
Geldrich-Leffman, Hanna. "Body and Voice . . . ," 42.

"Gracias, vientre leal"
Geldrich-Leffman, Hanna. "Body and Voice . . . ," 41–42.

"La Guerra y la paz"
Geldrich-Leffman, Hanna. "Body and Voice . . . ," 47–48.

"Idilio"
Geldrich-Leffman, Hanna. "Body and Voice . . . ," 47.
"Los pocillos"
Geldrich-Leffman, Hanna. "Body and Voice . . . ," 45–46.
Tisnado, Carmen. "Violent Silence and Violent Discourse in 'Los pocillos,' " *Symposium*, 50 (1997), 248–258.
"Réquiem con tostadas"
Geldrich-Leffman, Hanna. "Body and Voice . . . ," 48–49.
"El retrato de Elisa"
Geldrich-Leffman, Hanna. "Body and Voice . . . ," 46.
"Sábado de gloria"
Geldrich-Leffman, Hanna. "Body and Voice . . . ," 44.
"Se acabó la rabia"
Geldrich-Leffman, Hanna. "Body and Voice . . . ," 49–50.
"Transparencia"
Geldrich-Leffman, Hanna. "Body and Voice . . . ," 47.
"Triángulo isósceles"
Geldrich-Leffman, Hanna. "Body and Voice . . . ," 42–43.
"Truth on the Rocks"
Geldrich-Leffman, Hanna. "Body and Voice . . . ," 44–45.
"Verde y sin Paula"
Tisnado, Carmen. "Tortura y exilio . . . ," 282–283, 285–286, 287.

STEPHEN VINCENT BENÉT

"The Devil and Daniel Webster"
Partenheimer, David. "Benét's 'The Devil and Daniel Webster,' " *Explicator*, 55, i (1996), 37–40.

PAZ MARQUEZ BENITEZ

"Dead Stars"
Lee, Rachel C. "Journalistic Representations of Asian Americans and Literary Responses, 1910–1920," in Cheung, King-Kok, Ed. *An Interethnic* . . . , 264–266.

ARNOLD BENNETT

"Elsie and the Child"
Squillace, Robert. *Modernism, Modernity* . . . , 35, 158–161, 184–185.

MICHA JOSEF BERDYCZEWSKI

"In Secret Thunder"
Holtzman, Avner. "Strange Fire and Secret Thunder: Between Micha

Josef Berdyczewski and Amos Oz," *Prooftexts*, 15 (1995), 154–157.

THOMAS BERNHARD

"Untergeher"
Niekerk, Carl. "Der Umgang mit dem Untergang: Projektion als erzählerisches Prinzip in Thomas Bernhards 'Untergeher,' " *Monatshefte*, 85 (1993), 464–475.

ELIZABETH BERRIDGE

"Tell It to a Stranger"
Lassner, Phyllis. *British Women Writers* . . . , 146–147.

MANU BHANDARI

"Compulsion"
Rahim, Habibeh. "The Mirage of Faith and Justice: Some Sociopolitical and Cultural Themes in Post-Colonial Urdu Short Stories," in Hawley, John C., Ed. *The Postcolonial Crescent* . . . , 236–238.

OLYMPE BHÊLY-QUENUM [AZANMADO KPOSSY GBHÊLY-HOUÉNOU]

"African Adventure"
Little, Roger. "The 'Couple Domino' in the Writings of Olympe Bhêly-Quenum," *Research African Lit*, 29, i (1998), 68–70.
"Summer Liaison"
Little, Roger. "The 'Couple Domino' . . . ," 70–73.

ANGELA BIANCHINI

"Capo d'Europa"
Jeannet, Angela M. "Exiles and Returns in Angela Bianchini's Fiction," *Italica*, 75 (1998), 95–96, 99–101.
"Gli oleandri"
Jeannet, Angela M. "Exiles . . . ," 96–97, 101–103.
"La ragazza in nero"
Jeannet, Angela M. "Exiles . . . ," 104–105, 106–109.

AMBROSE BIERCE

"An Affair of Outposts"
Schaefer, Michael W. *Just What War Is* . . . , 98.

"Chickamauga"
  Baldwin, Dean. *Instructor's Resource* . . . , 62–64.
  Schaefer, Michael W. *Just What War Is* . . . , 16, 17, 98–99.
"The Coup de Grâce"
  Schaefer, Michael W. *Just What War Is* . . . , 84, 104.
"George Thurston"
  Schaefer, Michael W. *Just What War Is* . . . , 104–105.
"A Horseman in the Sky"
  Schaefer, Michael W. *Just What War Is* . . . , 103–104.
"Jupiter Doke, Brigadier-General"
  Schaefer, Michael W. "Ambrose Bierce on the Construction of
    Military History," *War, Lit, & Arts*, 7, i (1995), 5–9.
  ———. *Just What War Is* . . . , 92–97.
"Killed at Resaca"
  Schaefer, Michael W. *Just What War Is* . . . , 122–123.
"An Occurrence at Owl Creek Bridge"
  Charters, Ann, and William E. Sheidley. *Resources* . . . , 5th ed., 29.
"One Kind of Officer"
  Schaefer, Michael W. *Just What War Is* . . . , 113–114.
"One of the Missing"
  Schaefer, Michael W. *Just What War Is* . . . , 104.
"One Officer, One Man"
  Schaefer, Michael W. *Just What War Is* . . . , 106–113.
"A Resumed Identity"
  Schaefer, Michael W. *Just What War Is* . . . , 125, 136.
"A Son of the Gods"
  Schaefer, Michael W. *Just What War Is* . . . , 115–121.

BING XIN

"The First Dinner Party"
  Lieberman, Sally T. *The Mother* . . . , 109.
"Superman"
  Lieberman, Sally T. *The Mother* . . . , 44–47.
"Two Families"
  Lieberman, Sally T. *The Mother* . . . , 139–140.

ADOLFO BIOY CASARES

"Bajo el agua"
  Pellicer, Rosa. "La trama fantástica en los últimos cuentos de A. Bioy
    Casares," *Torre*, 9 (1995), 461–462.
"El héroe de la mujeres"
  Pellicer, Rosa. "La continuación de la trama: Una nota sobre los

últimos cuentos de A. Bioy Casares," in Valcárcel, Eva, Ed. *Hispanoamérica* . . . , 104.

"Máscaras venecianas"
Pellicer, Rosa. "La continuación . . . ," 108–109.
Pellicer, Rosa. "La trama fantástica . . . ," 457.

"El navegante vuelve a su patria"
Pellicer, Rosa. "La trama fantástica . . . ," 457–458.

"Plan para una fuga al Carmelo"
Pellicer, Rosa. "La continuación . . . ," 109–110.
Pellicer, Rosa. "La trama fantástica . . . ," 459.

"La rata o una llave para la conducta"
Pellicer, Rosa. "La continuación . . . ," 107.

"Un viaje inesperado"
Pellicer, Rosa. "La continuación . . . ," 109.

ELIZABETH BISHOP

"In the Village"
Lurie, Susan. *Unsettled Subjects* . . . , 120–128, 145–146.

TERRY BISSON

"Bears Discover Fire"
Sanders, Joe. "Death, Transfiguration, and More Death in Two Stories by Terry Bisson," *New York R Sci Fiction*, 10, ii (1997), 5–6, 7–8.

"Necronauts"
Sanders, Joe. "Death . . . ," 6–8.

ALGERNON BLACKWOOD

"The Man Whom the Trees Loved"
Healy, Sharon. "Algernon Blackwood's Gentle Gothic," *Romantist*, 9–10 (1986), 62, 63.

"The Touch of Pan"
Healy, Sharon. "Algernon Blackwood's . . . ," 63.

"The Trod"
Healy, Sharon. "Algernon Blackwood's . . . ," 63.

CLARK BLAISE

"A Class of New Canadians"
Vauthier, Simone. "Une Lectrice suit 'A Class of New Canadians,' " *Études Canadiennes*, 21, i (1986), 341–348.

MAURICE BLANCHOT

"Awaiting Oblivion"
Gregg, John. "Translator's Introduction," *Awaiting Oblivion (L'Attente l'oubli)* [by Maurice Blanchot], x–xvii.

HEINRICH BÖLL

"Ende einer Dienstfahrt"
Bernáth, Árpåd. "Der strukturelle Ort des Themas 'Gewalt' in Bölls Erzählungen 'Die verlorene Ehre der Katharina Blum' und 'Ende einer Dienstfahrt' und die Erweiterung des Kunstbegriffs," in Bodi, Leslie, Günter Helmes, Egon Schwarz, and Friedrich Voit, Eds. *Weltbürger—Textwelten*, 241–261.

"Die verloren Ehre der Katharina Blum"
Bernáth, Árpåd. "Der strukturelle . . . ," 241–261.

MARITA BONNER

"High Stepper"
Allen, Carol. *Black Women Intellectuals* . . . , 107–109, 112–113.

"Nothing New"
Allen, Carol. *Black Women Intellectuals* . . . , 92–94, 98–99, 106–107.

"On the Altar"
Allen, Carol. *Black Women Intellectuals* . . . , 96–98.

"One Boy's Story"
Allen, Carol. *Black Women Intellectuals* . . . , 90–91, 103.

"One True Love"
Musser, Judith. "African American Women and Education: Marita Bonner's Response to the 'Talented Tenth,' " *Stud Short Fiction*, 34 (1997), 80–81.

"Patch Quilt"
Allen, Carol. *Black Women Intellectuals* . . . , 99–100.

"Prison Bound"
Allen, Carol. *Black Women Intellectuals* . . . , 88–89, 112.

"Reap It as You Sow It"
Allen, Carol. *Black Women Intellectuals* . . . , 117–119.

"A Sealed Pod"
Allen, Carol. *Black Women Intellectuals* . . . , 94–96, 97–98.

"Tin Can"
Allen, Carol. *Black Women Intellectuals* . . . , 116–118.
Musser, Judith. "African American Women . . . ," 81–82.

"The Whipping"
Allen, Carol. *Black Women Intellectuals* . . . , 13–14, 103–104.

ARNA W. BONTEMPS

"Saturday Night"
 Casey, Roger N. *Textual Vehicles* . . . , 131–132.
"A Summer Tragedy"
 Casey, Roger N. *Textual Vehicles* . . . , 129, 130–131.

JORGE LUIS BORGES

"Abenjacán the Bojarí, Dead in His Labyrinth"
 Pons, María C. "Las mentiras de las apariencias en Borges:
  Problematización de los conceptos historia/intriga y verosimilitud
  en 'Abenjacán el Bojarí, muerto en su laberinto,' " *Texto Crítico*, 1,
  N.S. (1995), 7–24.
"The Aleph"
 Fisher, Barbara M. *Noble Numbers* . . . , 103–112.
 Koeninger, Frieda. " 'El aleph': Sátira y parodia," *Textos*, 4, ii (1996),
  37–41.
 Mínguez, Norberto Arranz. "Análisis semiótico de la representación
  del sujeto en 'El aleph' de J. L. Borges," *Thesaurus*, 49, ii (1994),
  245–274.
 Núñez-Faraco, Humberto. "In Search of the Aleph: Memory, Truth,
  and Falsehood in Borges's Poetics," *Mod Lang R*, 92 (1997),
  613–629.
 Østergaard, Svend. *The Mathematics* . . . , 200, 201.
 Zamora, Lois P. *The Usable Past* . . . , 134–136.
"Averroes' Search"
 Martín, Marina. "Borges: Lector de un problemático Hume,"
  Cincinnati Romance R, 9 (1990), 143–153.
"Biography of Tadeo Isidoro Cruz"
 Lafon, Michel. "De *Ficciones* à *El Aleph*: Narratologie, hypertexualité
  et autobiographisme," *Variaciones Borges*, 1 (1996), 115–119.
"The Book of Sand"
 Fisher, Barbara M. *Noble Numbers* . . . , 96–97.
 Ford, Joh, and Marjorie Ford. *Instructor's Manual* . . . , 52–53.
 Merrell, Floyd. "The Writing of Forking Paths: Borges, Calvino and
  Postmodern Models of Writing," *Variaciones Borges*, 3 (1997), 65.
 Østergaard, Svend. *The Mathematics* . . . , 200, 202, 208.
"Borges and I"
 Chen, Jianguo. "The Aesthetics of the Transposition of Reality,
  Dream, and the Mirror: A Comparative Perspective on Can Xue,"
  Comp Lit Stud, 34 (1997), 370–371.
 McGuirk, Bernard. *Latin American* . . . , 174–176, 180–184.
"The Congress"
 Almeida, Ivan. " 'Le Congrès' ou la narration impossible,"
  Variaciones Borges, 1 (1996), 67–87.

Holm, Nanna, Hanne Klinting, and Mette Steenberg. "Crónica de un taller de trabajo," *Variaciones Borges*, 1 (1996), 148–149.

"The Dead Man"
Álvarez, Nicolás E. "La metaficcionalidad de la historia y del discurso narrativo de 'El muerto' de Borges," *Revista Iberoamericana*, 62 (1996), 137–148.
Holm, Nanna, Hanne Klinting, and Mette Steenberg. "Crónica . . . ," 151–152.
Klinting, Hanne. "¿Una hipálage textual? Lectura de 'El muerto,' " *Variaciones Borges*, 2 (1996), 54–67.

"Death and the Compass"
Aizenberg, Edna. *Borges, el tejedor* . . . , 116–121.
Alvarez, Nicolás E. "Construcción y desconstrucción en 'La muerte y la brújula' de Borges," *Círculo*, 27 (1998), 147–153.
Balderston, Daniel. "Fundaciones míticas en 'La muerte y la brújula,' " *Variaciones Borges*, 2 (1996), 125–136.
Bolón Pedretti, Alma. "Une éloge du leurre à propos de 'La muerte y la brújula,' " *Variaciones Borges*, 5 (1998), 86–90.
Gil, Lydia M. "La problemática de la mística judía en 'La muerte y la brújula' de Jorge Luis Borges," in Kumbier, William, and Ann Colley, Eds. *Afterimages* . . . , 175–183.
McGuirk, Bernard. *Latin American* . . . , 121, 122–131, 133–134.
Østergaard, Svend. *The Mathematics* . . . , 119.
———. "The Unconscious of Representation ('Death and the Compass')," *Variaciones Borges*, 1 (1996), 106–112.
Sarabia, Rosa. " 'La muerte y la brújula' y la parodia borgeana del género policial," *J Hispanic Philol*, 17, i (1992), 7–17.
Thau, Eric. "Implicaciones de la parodia de 'The Purloined Letter' de Edgar Allan Poe en 'La muerte y la brújula' de Jorge Luís Borges," *Mester*, 24, ii (1995), 1–12.
Yankelevich, Hector. "La Boussole de la mort: L'Écriture et le crime," *Variaciones Borges*, 5 (1998), 91–98.

"Deutsches Requiem"
Aizenberg, Edna. *Borges, el tejedor* . . . , 114–115.

"The Duel"
Matamoro, Blas. "Períodos en la obra de Borges," in Valcárcel, Eva, Ed. *Hispanoamérica* . . . , 59.

"Emma Zunz"
Aizenberg, Edna. *Borges, el tejedor* . . . , 133–139.
Dapía, Silvia G. "Why is There a Problem about Fictional Discourse?: An Interpretation of Borges's 'Theme of the Traitor and the Hero' and 'Emma Zunz,' " *Variaciones Borges*, 5 (1998), 168–175.
McGuirk, Bernard. *Latin American* . . . , 185–188, 197–202.
Morris, Herbert. "What Emma Knew: The Outrage Suffered in Jorge Luis Borges's 'Emma Zunz,' " *Indiana J Hispanic Lit*, 10–11 (1997), 165–202.

"Everything and Nothing"
Holm, Nanna, Hanne Klinting, and Mette Steenberg. "Crónica . . . ," 152.

"Examination of the Work of Herbert Quain"
Amann, Elizabeth. "Time and Creation in Borges's 'Examen de la
obra de Herbert Quain,' " *Indiana J Hispanic Lit*, 8 (1996),
145–158.
"Funes the Memorious"
Merrell, Floyd. "The Writing of Forking . . . ," 61–62.
Mortimer, Gail L. "Memory, Despair, and Welty's MacLain Twins,"
So Central R, 14, ii (1997), 37.
Østergaard, Svend. *The Mathematics* . . . , 203–204, 215.
Stewart, Jon. "Borges' Refutation of Nominalism in 'Funes el
memorioso,' " *Variaciones Borges*, 2 (1996), 68–86.
"The Garden of Forking Paths"
Baldwin, Dean. *Instructor's Resource* . . . , 139–141.
Charters, Ann, and William E. Sheidley. *Resources* . . . , 5th ed.,
30–31.
Leo de Belmont, Laura. " 'El jardín de senderos que se bifurcan,' "
Revista Lit Hispanoamericana, 34 (1997), 83–89.
Merrell, Floyd. "The Writing of Forking . . . ," 57–60.
"God's Script" [same as "The Writing of God"]
Solotorevsky, Myrna. "Estética de la totalidad y estética de la
fragmentación," *Hispamérica*, 25 (1996), 20–22.
"The Gospel According to Mark"
Hernández Palacios, Esther. "Borges, civilización y barbarie," *Texto
Crítico*, 3, N.S. (1996), 66–67.
Marval-McNair, Nora de. " 'El Evangelio según Marcos' según
Borges," *Círculo*, 24 (1995), 63–73.
Virk, Tomo. "Borges, Eliade and the Ontology of Premodern
Societies," in Valdés, María Elena de, Mario J. Valdés, and Richard
A. Young, Eds. *Latin America* . . . , 141–151.
"Guayaquil"
Díaz, Roberto Ignacio. "Borges en 'Guayaquil': Las cosas de la
historia," *Revista Hispánica Moderna*, 50, ii (1997), 315–325.
"The House of Asterión"
Lefere, Robin. " 'La casa de Asterión': Experiencia de la lectura vs.
interpretación," in Bacarisse, Pamela, Ed. *Tradición y
actualidad* . . . , 253–257.
"The Immortal"
Cordiero Gomes, Renato. "On the Legibility of the City: Text,
Labyrinth, Montage," in Valdés, María Elena de, Mario J. Valdés,
and Richard A. Young, Eds. *Latin America* . . . , 182–183.
Mansbach, Abraham. " 'El inmortal' de Borges a través de la
concepción heideggeriana de la muerte y de la individualidad,"
Revista Hispánica Moderna, 50, i (1997), 110–115.
Rodríguez-Carranza, Luz. "De la memoria al olvido, Borges y la
inmortalidad," in Collard, Patrick, Ed. *La memoria histórica* . . . ,
225–235.
"El informe de Brodie"
Hernández Palacios, Esther. "Borges . . . ," 67–68.

"La lotería de Babilonia"
Matamoro, Blas. "Períodos en la obra . . . , 57–58.
Moreiras, Alberto. "Elementos de articulación teórica para el
subalternismo latinoamericano. Candido y Borges," *Revista
Iberoamericana*, 62 (1996), 885–889.

"The Man at the Pink Corner"
Louis, Annick. "Jorge Luis Borges: La Construction d'une œuvre:
Autour de la creation du recueil *Historia universal de la infamia*,"
Variaciones Borges, 2 (1996), 149–151.

"The Mirror and the Mask"
Chartier, Roger. "Le Monument et l'événement: Parole poétique et
figures de l'écriture dans 'El espejo y la máscara' de J. L. Borges,"
Variaciones Borges, 3 (1997), 110–119.

"The Other"
Jaime-Ramírez, Helios. "La estructuración de lo fantástico en 'El libro
de arena,' de J. L. Borges," in *Coloquio Internacional . . .* ,
130–134.

"The Other Death"
Østergaard, Svend. *The Mathematics . . .* , 180–190, 196–198, 216.

"Pierre Menard, Author of *Don Quixote*"
Borinsky, Alicia. "Re-escribir y escribir: Arenas, Ménard, Borges,
Cervantes, Fray Servando," *Revista Iberoamericana*, 41, 92–93
(1975), 605–616; rpt. in Foster, David W., and Daniel Altamiranda,
Eds. *Twentieth-Century Spanish . . .* , 343–354.
Schenkel, Elmar. "The Empty Book: Borges, Babbage and
Chesterton," *Variaciones Borges*, 3 (1997), 70–72.
Toro, Alfonso de. "Posmodernidad y Latinoamérica (Con un modelo
para la narrativa posmoderna)," in Foster, David W., and Daniel
Altamiranda, Eds. *Theoretical . . .* , 239–241.
Zamora, Lois P. *The Usable Past . . .* , 128–131.

"Las previsiones de Sangiácomo" [with Bioy Casares]
Bolón Pedretti, Alma. " 'Las previsiones de Sangiácomo': La logique
de l'ajout," *Variaciones Borges*, 6 (1998), 160–170.
Klinting, Hanne. "El lector detective y el detective lector: La estrategia
interpretativa de Isidro Parodi en 'Las previsiones de
Sangiácomo,' " *Variaciones Borges*, 6 (1998), 144–159.

"Rosendo's Tale"
González, José E. *Borges and the Politics . . .* , 28.

"The Secret Miracle"
Aizenberg, Edna. *Borges, el tejedor . . .* , 112–114.
Alvarez, Nicolás E. "El discurso narrativo y la historia de 'El milagro
secreto' de Jorge Luis Borges," *Círculo*, 24 (1995), 74–79.
González, José E. *Borges and the Politics . . .* , 189.
Ruprecht, Hans-George. "L'Ecrivain et le savant: Du petit côté de
l'improbable au temps de jadis (1939, 1968)," *Variaciones Borges*,
2 (1996), 198–210.

"The Sect of the Phoenix"
 Balderston, Daniel. "The 'Fecal Dialectic': Homosexual Panic and the
  Origin of Writing in Borges," in Bergmann, Emilie L., and Paul J.
  Smith, Eds. ¿Entiendes? . . . , 37–38.
"The Shape of the Sword"
 Brant, Herbert J. "The Mask of the Phallus: Homoerotic Desire in
  Borges's 'La forma de la espada,' " Chasqui, 25 (1996), 26–38; rpt.
  Foster, David W., and Daniel Altamiranda, Eds. Twentieth-
  Century . . . , 209–222.
"The South"
 González, José E. Borges and the Politics . . . , 137–138.
"Story of the Warrior and the Captive"
 González, José E. Borges and the Politics . . . , 54–55, 69–70, 94.
 Hernández Palacios, Esther. "Borges . . . ," 60–65.
"Street Corner Man"
 González, José E. Borges and the Politics . . . , 23–32.
"Theme of the Traitor and the Hero"
 Dapía, Silvia G. "Why is There . . . ," 161–168.
 Juan-Navarro, Santiago. "Las formas secretas del tiempo: 'Tema del
  traidor y del héroe' y la metahistoria," in Forbes, F. William, Teresa
  Méndez-Faith, Mary-Anne Vetterling, and Barbara H. Wing, Eds.
  Reflections . . . , 23–33.
 Matamoro, Blas. "Períodos en la obra . . . ," 58–59.
"The Theologians"
 Holm, Nanna, Hanne Klinting, and Mette Steenberg. "Crónica . . . ,"
  150–151.
"Three Versions of Judas"
 Holm, Nanna, Hanne Klinting, and Mette Steenberg. "Crónica . . . ,"
  153–154.
"Tlön, Uqbar, Orbis Tertius"
 Almond, Ian. "Tlön, Pilgrimages and Postmodern Banality," Bull
  Hispanic Stud, 75, ii (1998), 229–235.
 Berg, Walter B. "Deconstrucciones del 'oscuro hombre de genio':
  Lectura alegórica de un cuento de Borges," in Coloquio
  Internacional . . . , 140–145.
 Clark, John R. "Idealism and Dystopia in 'Tlön, Uqbar, Orbis
  Tertius,' " Int'l Fiction R, 22 (1995), 74–79.
 Dapía, Silvia G. " 'This is Not a Universe': An Approach to Borges's
  'Tlön, Uqbar, Orbis Tertius," Chasqui, 26, ii (1997), 94–107.
 Hollis, Daniel W. The ABC-CLIO World History Companion . . . ,
  243–245.
 Juan-Navarro, Santiago. "La alquimia del verbo: 'Tlön, Uqbar, Orbis
  Tertius' de J. L. Borges y la sociedad de la Rosa-Cruz," Hispano,
  120 (1997), 68–80.
 Lunsford, Kern L. "Jorge Luis Borges's 'Tlön, Uqbar, Orbis Tertius':
  Epistemology and History; Language and Literary Creation,"

Cincinnati Romance R, 8 (1989), 101–109; rpt. Foster, David W.,
and Daniel Altamiranda, Eds. *Twentieth-Century* . . . , 199–207.
Marrero-Fente, Raúl. " 'Tlön, Uqbar, Orbis, Tertius': Los mundos
posibles de una metafísica de la ficción," in Bacarisse, Pamela, Ed.
Tradición y actualidad . . . , 259–265.

"Ulrica"
Jaime-Ramírez, Helios. "La estructuración . . . ," 134–138.

"Undr"
Jaime-Ramírez, Helios. "La estructuración . . . ," 138–141.

"The Zahir"
González, José E. *Borges and the Politics* . . . , 40–42.
Holm, Nanna, Hanne Klinting, and Mette Steenberg. "Crónica . . . ,"
149–150.

TADEUSZ BOROWSKI

"This Way to the Gas, Ladies and Gentlemen"
Charters, Ann, and William E. Sheidley. *Resources* . . . , 5th ed.,
32–33.

JUAN BOSCH

"The Woman"
Baldwin, Dean. *Instructor's Resource* . . . , 120–121.

PHYLLIS BOTTOME

"The Oblation"
Lassner, Phyllis. *British Women Writers* . . . , 224–226.

ELIZABETH BOWEN

"The Demon Lover"
Lassner, Phyllis. *British Women Writers* . . . , 155.

"The Happy Autumn Fields"
Bidney, Martin. "Nostalgic Narcissism in Comic and Tragic
Perspectives: Elizabeth Bowen's Two Fictional Reworkings of a
Tennyson Lyric," *Stud Short Fiction*, 33 (1996), 63–67.

"Mysterious Kôr"
Lassner, Phyllis. *British Women Writers* . . . , 151–154.
Parsons, Deborah L. "Souls Astray: Elizabeth Bowen's Landscape of
War," *Women*, 8, i (1997), 30–31.

"Shoes: An International Episode"
Tintner, Adeline R. *Henry James's Legacy* . . . , 230–231.

"Doña Faustina"
  Caponi, Gena D. *Paul Bowles*, 71–72.
"The Echo"
  Caponi, Gena D. *Paul Bowles*, 45–46.
"The Eye"
  Caponi, Gena D. *Paul Bowles*, 64.
"The Frozen Fields"
  Caponi, Gena D. *Paul Bowles*, 4–6.
"The Garden"
  Caponi, Gena D. *Paul Bowles*, 74–75.
"He of the Assembly"
  Caponi, Gena D. *Paul Bowles*, 94, 96.
"Here to Learn"
  Caponi, Gena D. *Paul Bowles*, 64–65.
"The Hours after Noon"
  Caponi, Gena D. *Paul Bowles*, 73.
"How Many Midnights"
  Caponi, Gena D. *Paul Bowles*, 70–71.
"Hugh Harper"
  Caponi, Gena D. *Paul Bowles*, 121–122.
"The Husband"
  Caponi, Gena D. *Paul Bowles*, 62–63.
"In Absentia"
  Caponi, Gena D. *Paul Bowles*, 126–128.
"In the Red Room"
  Caponi, Gena D. *Paul Bowles*, 124–125.
"Julian Vreden"
  Caponi, Gena D. *Paul Bowles*, 120.
"The Little House"
  Caponi, Gena D. *Paul Bowles*, 61.
"Madame and Ahmed"
  Caponi, Gena D. *Paul Bowles*, 61–62.
"Massachusetts 1932"
  Caponi, Gena D. *Paul Bowles*, 122.
"Mejdoub"
  Caponi, Gena D. *Paul Bowles*, 55–56.
  Charters, Ann, and William E. Sheidley. *Resources* . . . , 5th ed.,
    34–35.
"Midnight Mass"
  Caponi, Gena D. *Paul Bowles*, 60.
"New York 1965"
  Caponi, Gena D. *Paul Bowles*, 121.
"Pastor Dowe at Tacaté"
  Caponi, Gena D. *Paul Bowles*, 46.

"Reminders of Bouselham"
Caponi, Gena D. *Paul Bowles*, 56–57.

"Rumor and a Ladder"
Caponi, Gena D. *Paul Bowles*, 63–64.

"Tapiama"
Caponi, Gena D. *Paul Bowles*, 92–93.

"A Thousand Days for Mokhtar"
Caponi, Gena D. *Paul Bowles*, 92.

"The Time of Friendship"
Caponi, Gena D. *Paul Bowles*, 46–47.

"Under the Sky"
Caponi, Gena D. *Paul Bowles*, 69.

"Wind at Beni Midar"
Caponi, Gena D. *Paul Bowles*, 96–97.

"You Are Not I"
Caponi, Gena D. *Paul Bowles*, 71.

"You Have Left Your Lotus Pods on the Bus"
Caponi, Gena D. *Paul Bowles*, 57–58.

KAY BOYLE

"Army of Occupation"
+ Uehling, Edward M. "Tails You Lose: Kay Boyle's War Fiction," in
Elkins, Marilyn, Ed. *Critical Essays on* . . . , 136–138.

"Bitte Nehmen Sie Die Blumen"
+ Spanier, Sandra W. "The Revolution of the Word," in Elkins,
Marilyn, Ed. *Critical Essays on* . . . , 118–120.

"Episode in the Life of an Ancestor"
Clark, Suzanne. *Sentimental Modernism* . . . , 130–132; rpt. Elkins,
Marilyn, Ed. *Critical Essays on* . . . ,160–162.
+ Spanier, Sandra W. "The Revolution . . . ," 115–117.

"The Lost"
+ Uehling, Edward M. "Tails You Lose . . . ," 136, 139–141.

"Madame Tout Petit"
+ Spanier, Sandra W. "The Revolution . . . ," 112–113.

"On the Run"
Clark, Suzanne. *Sentimental Modernism* . . . , 134–136; rpt. Elkins,
Marilyn, Ed. *Critical Essays on* . . . , 164–166.
+ Spanier, Sandra W. "The Revolution . . . ," 103–104.

"Polar Bears and Others"
+ Spanier, Sandra W. "The Revolution . . . ," 117–118.

"Portrait"
+ Spanier, Sandra W. "The Revolution . . . ," 104–105.

"Spring Morning"
+ Spanier, Sandra W. "The Revolution . . . ," 106–108.

"Summer"
+ Spanier, Sandra W. "The Revolution . . . ," 113–115.
"Theme"
+ Spanier, Sandra W. "The Revolution . . . ," 110–111.
"Vacation Time"
+ Spanier, Sandra W. "The Revolution . . . ," 105–106.
"Wedding Day"
Clark, Suzanne. *Sentimental Modernism* . . . , 132–134; rpt. Elkins,
Marilyn, Ed. *Critical Essays on* . . . , 162–164.
+ Spanier, Sandra W. "The Revolution . . . ," 108–110.

OSGOOD BRADBURY

"Female Depravity: Or, the House of Death"
Siegel, Adrienne. *The Image of the American* . . . , 48–49.

RAY BRADBURY

"The Fog Horn"
Disch, Thomas M. *The Dreams Our Stuff* . . . , 81–82.

DIONNE BRAND

"I Used to Like the Dallas Cowboys"
Raiskin, Judith. "7 Days/6 Nights at 'Plantations Estates': A Critique
of Cultural Colonialism by Caribbean Writers," in Buelens, Gert,
and Ernst Rudin, Eds. *Deferring a Dream* . . . , 95–97.

"No Rinsed Blue Sky, No Red Flower Fences"
Sturgess, Charlotte. "Dionne Brand's Short Stories: Warring Forces
and Narrative Poetics," *Anglophonia*, 1 (1997), 156–157.

"Photograph"
Sturgess, Charlotte. "Dionne Brand's . . . ," 157–160.

RICHARD BRAUTIGAN

"Corporal"
Iftekharuddin, Farhat. "The New Aesthetics in Brautigan's *Revenge of
the Lawn: Stories 1962–1970*," in Kaylor, Noel H., Ed. *Creative
and Critical* . . . , 427–428.

"Partners"
Nischik, Reingard M. "Illusion, Meta-Illusion, Counter-Illusion,
Illusionism: The Function of Film in American Film Stories," in
Hebel, Udo J., and Karl Ortseifen, Eds. *Transatlantic
Encounters* . . . , 303.

"The Post Offices of Eastern Oregan"
  Iftekharuddin, Farhat. "The New Aesthetics . . . ," 420–421.
"Revenge of the Lawn"
  Iftekharuddin, Farhat. "The New Aesthetics . . . ," 423–424.
"The World War I Los Angeles Airplane"
  Iftekharuddin, Farhat. "The New Aesthetics . . . ," 424–425.

HENRY BRENT

"The Mysterious Pyramid"
  Schueller, Malini J. *U.S. Orientalisms . . .* , 81–82.

RUPERT BROOKE

"An Unusual Young Man"
  Rutherford, Jonathan. *Forever England . . .* , 64–65.

CHARLES BROCKDEN BROWN

"The Man at Home"
  Hinds, Elizabeth J. W. *Private Property . . .* , 41–44, 51, 65–66.
"Memoirs of Carwin the Biloquist"
  Hinds, Elizabeth J. W. *Private Property . . .* , 117–119, 130.

WILLIAM WELLS BROWN

"Madison Washington"
  Yarborough, Richard. "Race, Violence, and Manhood: The Masculine
  Ideal in Frederick Douglass's 'The Heroic Slave,' " in Jones, Anne
  G., and Susan V. Donaldson, Eds. *Haunted Bodies . . .* , 171–174.

GAËTAN BRULOTTE

"Le Rêve des Tomates"
  Fisher, Claudine G. "La Quête initiaque chez Gaëtan Brulotte,"
  Selecta, 14 (1993), 30–33.

GEORG BÜCHNER

"Lenz"
  Peischl, Margaret T. "Büchner's 'Lenz': A Study of Madness," *Germ
  Notes & R*, 27 (1996), 13–19.
  Walker, John. " 'Ach die Kunst! . . . Ach, die Erbärmliche

Wirklichkeit!' Suffering, Empathy, and the Relevance of Realism in Büchner's 'Lenz,' " *Forum Mod Lang Stud*, 33 (1997), 157–170.

MIKHAIL BULGAKOV

"The Blizzard"
Haber, Edythe C. *Mikhail Bulgakov* . . . , 123–124.
"Egyptian Darkness"
Haber, Edythe C. *Mikhail Bulgakov* . . . , 121–122.
"I Killed"
Haber, Edythe C. *Mikhail Bulgakov* . . . , 126–129.
"The Khan's Fire"
Haber, Edythe C. *Mikhail Bulgakov* . . . , 69–74.
"The Missing Eye"
Haber, Edythe C. *Mikhail Bulgakov* . . . , 124–125.
"Morphine"
Haber, Edythe C. *Mikhail Bulgakov* . . . , 129–133.
"No. 13 The Elpit-Workommune House"
Haber, Edythe C. *Mikhail Bulgakov* . . . , 156–160.
"On the Night of the Second"
Haber, Edythe C. *Mikhail Bulgakov* . . . , 62–66.
"The Raid (In a Magic Lantern)"
Haber, Edythe C. *Mikhail Bulgakov* . . . , 66–69.
"The Red Crown"
Haber, Edythe C. *Mikhail Bulgakov* . . . , 58–62.
"The Starry Rash"
Haber, Edythe C. *Mikhail Bulgakov* . . . , 122.
"The Steel Windpipe" [same as "The Steel Throat"]
Coulehan, John L. "Tenderness and Steadiness: Emotions in Medical Practice," *Lit & Medicine*, 14 (1995), 226–228.
Haber, Edythe C. *Mikhail Bulgakov* . . . , 119–120.
"The Unusual Adventures of a Doctor"
Haber, Edythe C. *Mikhail Bulgakov* . . . , 54–58.

HERMANN BURGER

"Blankenberg"
Pender, Malcolm. *Contemporary Images* . . . , 218, 219–221.
"Der Büchernarr"
Pender, Malcolm. *Contemporary Images* . . . , 217, 218.
"Der Leselose"
Pender, Malcolm. *Contemporary Images* . . . , 218–219.

SHARON BUTALA

"The Prize"
  Adam, Ian. "Iconicity, Space, and the Place of Sharon Butala's 'The Prize,' " *Stud Canadian Lit*, 23, i (1998), 180–183.

ROBERT OLEN BUTLER

"Jealous Husband Returns in Form of Parrot"
  Baldwin, Dean. *Instructor's Resource* . . . , 219–220.

"Letters from My Father"
  Ford, Joh, and Marjorie Ford. *Instructor's Manual* . . . , 108.

MARY BUTTS

"Speed the Plough"
  Hamer, Mary. "Mary Butts, Mothers, and War," in Raitt, Suzanne, and Trudi Tate, Eds. *Women's Fiction* . . . , 224–229.

A[NTONIA] S[USAN] BYATT

"Art Work"
  Kelly, Kathleen C. *A. S. Byatt*, 57–59.

"The Changeling"
  Campbell, Jane L. "Confecting *Sugar*: Narrative Theory and Practice in A. S. Byatt's Short Stories," *Critique*, 38 (1997), 114, 115–117.
  Kelly, Kathleen C. *A. S. Byatt*, 45–46.

"The Chinese Lobster"
  Kelly, Kathleen C. *A. S. Byatt*, 59–62.

"The Dried Witch"
  Campbell, Jane L. "Confecting *Sugar* . . . ," 111–112.
  Kelly, Kathleen C. *A. S. Byatt*, 49–51.

"In the Air"
  Campbell, Jane L. "Confecting *Sugar* . . . ," 117.
  Kelly, Kathleen C. *A. S. Byatt*, 51–52.

"The July Ghost"
  Campbell, Jane L. "Confecting *Sugar* . . . ," 109–110.
  Kelly, Kathleen C. *A. S. Byatt*, 46–48.

"Loss of Face"
  Campbell, Jane L. "Confecting *Sugar* . . . ," 111, 112–114.
  Kelly, Kathleen C. *A. S. Byatt*, 39–41.

"Medusa's Ankles"
  Kelly, Kathleen C. *A. S. Byatt*, 55–57.

"The Next Room"
  Campbell, Jane L. "Confecting *Sugar* . . . ," 111.
  Kelly, Kathleen C. *A. S. Byatt*, 48–49.

LYDIA CABRERA

"Jicotea una noche fresca"
Gutiérrez, Mariela A. *Lydia Cabrera* . . . , 170–171.

"Jicotea y el árbol de güira que nadie sembró"
Gutiérrez, Mariela A. *Lydia Cabrera* . . . , 51–52, 168–170.

"El juicio de Jicotea"
Gutiérrez, Mariela A. *Lydia Cabrera* . . . , 61, 174–175.

"Kanákaná, el aura tiñosa es sagrada, e Iroko, la ceiba, es divina"
Gutiérrez, Mariela A. *Lydia Cabrera* . . . , 95–102.

"El ladrón de boniatal"
Gutiérrez, Mariela A. *Lydia Cabrera* . . . , 165–167.

"El limo de Almendares"
Gutiérrez, Mariela A. *Lydia Cabrera* . . . , 67–71.

"La mujer de agua"
Gutiérrez, Mariela A. *Lydia Cabrera* . . . , 79–81.

"Las mujeres no podían parangonarse con las ranas"
Gutiérrez, Mariela A. *Lydia Cabrera* . . . , 78–79.

"Las mujeres se encomiendan al árbol Dagame"
Gutiérrez, Mariela A. *Lydia Cabrera* . . . , 111–124.

"Ncharriri"
Gutiérrez, Mariela A. *Lydia Cabrera* . . . , 48, 158–160.
———. "La victoria del discurso semiótico kristevano en 'Ncharriri'
de Lydia Cabrera," *Letras Femeninas*, 23, i–ii (1997), 109–127.

"Osaín de Un Pie"
Gutiérrez, Mariela A. *Lydia Cabrera* . . . , 153–155.

"Por qué . . . el algodón ciega a los pájaros"
Gutiérrez, Mariela A. *Lydia Cabrera* . . . , 186–188.

"Por qué . . . el carapacho a heridas de Jicotea"
Gutiérrez, Mariela A. *Lydia Cabrera* . . . , 196–200.

"Por qué . . . el chivo hiede"
Gutiérrez, Mariela A. *Lydia Cabrera* . . . , 75–78, 185–186.

"Por qué . . . dicen los *gangás*: Los grandes no pagan favores de
humildes"
Gutiérrez, Mariela A. *Lydia Cabrera* . . . , 192–193.

"Por qué . . . esa raya en el lomo de la jutía"
Gutiérrez, Mariela A. *Lydia Cabrera* . . . , 193–196.

"Por qué . . . Jicotea lleva a su casa a cuestas, el majá se arrastra, la
lagartija se pega a la pared"
Gutiérrez, Mariela A. *Lydia Cabrera* . . . , 182–185.

"Por qué . . . el mono perdió el fruto de su trabajo"
Gutiérrez, Mariela A. *Lydia Cabrera* . . . , 202–205.

"Por qué . . . las nariguetas de los negros están hechas de fayanca"
Gutiérrez, Mariela A. *Lydia Cabrera* . . . , 200–202.

"Por qué . . . se cerraron y volvieron a abrirse los caminos de la isla"
Gutiérrez, Mariela A. *Lydia Cabrera* . . . , 177–178.

HORTENSE CALISHER

ITALO CALVINO

"The Crow Comes Last"
McLaughlin, Martin. *Italo Calvino*, 5–8.
"If on a Winter's Night a Traveler"
Charters, Ann, and William E. Sheidley. *Resources* . . . , 5th ed., 36.
"In the Blood"
McLaughlin, Martin. *Italo Calvino*, 2–3.
"Le figlie della Luna"
McLaughlin, Martin. *Italo Calvino*, 93.
"The Memory of the World"
McLaughlin, Martin. *Italo Calvino*, 92–93.
"Mr. Palomer"
Merrell, Floyd. "The Writing of Forking . . . ," 60–61.
"The Night Driver"
McLaughlin, Martin. *Italo Calvino*, 89–90.
"Nightmare in the Prison Barracks"
McLaughlin, Martin. *Italo Calvino*, 4–5.
"Il niente e il poco"
McLaughlin, Martin. *Italo Calvino*, 97.
"The Shells and Time"
McLaughlin, Martin. *Italo Calvino*, 91–92.
"The Sky of Stone"
McLaughlin, Martin. *Italo Calvino*, 96.
"Solar Storm"
McLaughlin, Martin. *Italo Calvino*, 93–96.
"Uno dei tre è ancora vivo"
McLaughlin, Martin. *Italo Calvino*, 13–14.
"Waiting for Death in a Hotel"
McLaughlin, Martin. *Italo Calvino*, 3–4.

WADSWORTH CAMP

"The Signal Tower"
Goodman, Nan. *Shifting the Blame* . . . , 152–153.

JOHN W. CAMPBELL

"Twilight"
Landon, Brooks. *Science Fiction* . . . , 21–27.

RUBÉN M. CAMPOS

"Un cobarde"
Zaïtzeff, Serge I. "Los cuentos de Rubén M. Campos" in Herrera,
Sara P., Ed. *El cuento mexicano* . . . , 196–197.

"Un egoísta"
 Zaïtzeff, Serge I. "Los cuentos . . . ," 195.

"El entierro de la Sardina"
 Zaïtzeff, Serge I. "Los cuentos . . . ," 194.

"Fuensanta"
 Zaïtzeff, Serge I. "Los cuentos . . . ," 193–194.

"El mendigo"
 Zaïtzeff, Serge I. "Los cuentos . . . ," 192–193.

"Un noctámbulo"
 Zaïtzeff, Serge I. "Los cuentos . . . ," 192.

"El nocturno en sol"
 Zaïtzeff, Serge I. "Los cuentos . . . ," 190–191.

"El rey de copas"
 Zaïtzeff, Serge I. "Los cuentos . . . ," 189.

"Rosamunda"
 Zaïtzeff, Serge I. "Los cuentos . . . ," 194–195.

"Un suicidio"
 Zaïtzeff, Serge I. "Los cuentos . . . ," 191–192.

"El supremo don"
 Zaïtzeff, Serge I. "Los cuentos . . . ," 190.

ALBERT CAMUS

"The Adulterous Woman"
 Montgomery, Geraldine. "De la derière femme au *Premier homme*:
  Intermittences du féminin dans l'œuvre narrative de Camus," in
  Dubois, Lionel, Ed. *Albert Camus entre* . . . , 152–156.
 Rizzuto, Anthony. *Camus: Love* . . . , 55–56.
 Shahbaz, Caterina P. "La Frustration et le sens dans 'La Femme
  adultère' de Camus," *Symposium*, 50 (1997), 238–247.
 Sibelman, Simon P. "The Anguish and the Ecstasy: Camus's Use of
  Phallic Symbols in 'La Femme adultère,' " *Dalhousie French Stud*,
  45 (1998), 41–54.

"The Growing Stone"
 Horacio, Joaquim. "Exotopie: L'Enjeu dans 'La Pierre qui pousse,' "
  La Revue des Lettres Modernes, 1310–1316 (1996), 123–137.

"The Guest"
 Charters, Ann, and William E. Sheidley. *Resources* . . . , 5th ed.,
  37–38.
 McGregor, Rob R. "Camus's 'The Silent Men' and 'The Guest':
  Depictions of Absurd Awareness," *Stud Short Fiction*, 34 (1997),
  311–319.

"The Renegade"
 Greenfeld, Anne. "Laughter in Camus' 'The Stranger,' *The Fall*, and
  'The Renegade,' " *Humor*, 6 (1993), 410–413.

Howells, Valerie. " 'Le Renégat': An Ironic Re-enactment of Camus's
    Djihad?" in Cardy, Michael, George Evans, and Gabriel Jacobs,
    Eds. *Narrative Voices* . . . , 215–237.
Rizzuto, Anthony. *Camus: Love* . . . , 83–84, 85–86.

"The Silent Men"
    Baldi, Maria R. "*L'Exil et le Royaume* d'Albert Camus: Une Lecture
        de la nouvelle 'Les Muets,' " *Francofonia*, 13, xxiv (1993), 94–107.
    McGregor, Rob R. "Camus's 'The Silent Men' . . . ," 308–311.

"The Stranger"
    Abecassis, Jack I. "Camus's Pulp Fiction," *Mod Lang Notes*, 112
        (1997), 625–636, 639–640.
    Davis, Colin. "Altericide: Camus, Encounters, Reading," *Forum Mod
        Lang Stud*, 33, ii (1997), 129–134, 138–139.
    Davison, Ray. *Camus: The Challenge* . . . , 56–61, 79, 81, 84–85,
        113–114.
    Gaudard, François-C. "Concours et stylistique," *Champs du Signe*, 3
        (1992), 15–23, 26–28.
    Greenfeld, Anne. "Laughter . . . ," 404–406.
    Grégoire, Vincent. "Pour une réinterprétation du titre 'L'Etranger,' "
        Französisch Heute, 2 (1997), 3–6.
    Mino, Hiroshi. "Trois discours sur le meurtre: Meursault, Rieux et
        Clamence," *La Revue des Lettres Modernes*, 1310–1316 (1996),
        71–76, 84.
    Montgomery, Geraldine. "De la derière . . . ," 146–151.
    Riggs, Larry W. "Clerking for the Fathers: Infra-Narrative,
        Individuation, and Terminal Exile in Kafka and Camus,"
        Symposium, 50 (1996), 183–187.
    Rizzuto, Anthony. *Camus: Love* . . . , 15, 25–28, 29, 93–97.
    Rubinlicht-Proux, Anne. " 'L'Étranger' et le positivisme juridique,"
        La Revue des Lettres Modernes, 27–67.
    Shattuck, Roger. "Guilt, Justice, and Empathy in Melville and
        Camus," *Partisan R*, 63, iii (1996), 433–448.
    Strange, Alice J. "Camus's 'The Stranger,' " *Explicator*, 56, i (1997),
        36–38.

CAN XUE

"The Date"
    Chen, Jianguo. "The Aesthetics of the Transposition of Reality,
        Dream, and Mirror: A Comparative Perspective on Can Xue," *Comp
        Lit Stud*, 34 (1997), 355–356.

"Dream of the Yellow Chrysanthemum"
    Chen, Jianguo. "The Aesthetics . . . ," 354–355.

"Hut on the Mountain"
    Chen, Jianguo. "The Aesthetics . . . ," 369–370.

"Old Floating Cloud"
    Chen, Jianguo. "The Aesthetics . . . ," 366–367.

"The Skylight"
Chen, Jianguo. "The Aesthetics . . . ," 358–359.
"The Things that Happened to Me"
Chen, Jianguo. "The Aesthetics . . . ," 368–369.

ETHAN CANIN

"The Carnival Dog, the Buyer of Diamonds"
Charters, Ann, and William E. Sheidley. *Resources* . . . , 5th ed., 39.
"The Palace Thief"
Bloom, James D. *The Literary Bent* . . . , 95–97.

RAFAEL CANSINOS-ASSÉNS

"Alma-carne"
Urioste Azcorra, Carmen de. *Narrativa Andaluz* . . . , 49–51.
"La dorada"
Urioste Azcorra, Carmen de. *Narrativa* . . . , 57, 59–60.
"Las dos amigas"
Urioste Azcorra, Carmen de. *Narrativa* . . . , 51–54.
"El poderoso"
Urioste Azcorra, Carmen de. *Narrativa* . . . , 60–61.

MARIE-MAGDELEINE CARBET

"Féfé et Doudou"
Hurley, E. Anthony. "Choosing Her Own Name, or Who is Carbet?"
Coll Lang Assoc J, 41 (1998), 397–398.
"Son Amour"
Hurley, E. Anthony. "Choosing Her Own . . . ," 398–399.
"Le Troisième"
Hurley, E. Anthony. "Choosing Her Own . . . ," 399.

ALEJO CARPENTIER

"Journey Back to the Source"
Luis, William. *Dance Between Two* . . . , 192–193.

ANDRÉ CARPENTIER

"La Bouquinerie d'Outre-Temps"
Mariño Espuelas, Alicia. " 'La Bouquinerie d'Outre-Temps': Variété
de l'espace et du temps vécus ou la frontière du fantastique," *Études
Canadiennes*, 21 (1995), 225–232.

ROCH CARRIER

"La Chatte d'Espagne"
Sorin, Noëlle. "La Lisibilité sémiotique," *Revue de l'ACLA*, 18, ii
(1996), 66–80.

LEONORA CARRINGTON

"As They Rode Along the Edge"
Carroll, Rachael. " 'Something to See': Spectacle and Savagery in
Leonora Carrington's Fiction," *Critique*, 37 (1998), 155–156, 157,
159, 164.

"The Debutante"
Carroll, Rachael. " 'Something . . . ,' " 158–159.
Gambrell, Alice. *Women Intellectuals* . . . , 74–77.

"Monsieur Cyril De Guindre"
Carroll, Rachael. " 'Something . . . ,' " 158, 159, 160, 164–165.

"The Oval Lady"
Carroll, Rachael. " 'Something . . . ,' " 158, 161, 162.

"Pigeon Fly!"
Carroll, Rachael. " 'Something . . . ,' " 160–162.

"The Seventh Horse"
Carroll, Rachael. " 'Something . . . ,' " 156, 157.

"The Sisters"
Carroll, Rachael. " 'Something . . . ,' " 155, 164, 165.

"White Rabbits"
Carroll, Rachael. " 'Something . . . ,' " 162–163.

ANGELA CARTER

"Black Venus"
Day, Aidan. *Angela Carter* . . . , 179–180.
Duncker, Patricia. "Queer Gothic: Angela Carter and the Lost
Narratives of Sexual Subversion," *Critical S*, 8, i (1996), 63–65.
Gamble, Sarah. *Angela Carter* . . . , 149–150.
Travis, Molly A. *Reading Cultures* . . . , 59, 60–61.

"The Bloody Chamber"
Armitt, Lucie. "The Fragile Frames of *The Bloody Chamber*," in
Bristow, Joseph, and Trev L. Broughton, Eds. *The Infernal
Desires* . . . , 95–97.
Baldwin, Dean. *Instructor's Resource* . . . , 190–192.
Day, Aidan. *Angela Carter* . . . , 151–162.
Douglas, Paul. "Mother May I? The Use of Fairy Tales in the Fiction
of Jeff Ryman, Jane Yolen, and Angela Carter," *CEAMAG*, 9
(1996), 17–18.
Gamble, Sarah. *Angela Carter* . . . , 153–154.

Mclaughlin, Becky. "Perverse Pleasure and Fetishized Text: The Deathly Erotics of Carter's 'The Bloody Chamber,' " *Style*, 29 (1995), 405–422.

Magrs, Paul. "Boys Keep Swinging: Angela Carter and the Subject of Men," in Bristow, Joseph, and Trev L. Broughton, Eds. *The Infernal Desires . . .* , 193.

Manley, Kathleen E. B. "The Woman in Process in Angela Carter's 'The Bloody Chamber,' " *Marvels & Tales*, 12, i (1998), 71–81.

Renfroe, Cheryl. "Initiation and Disobedience: Liminal Experience in Angela Carter's 'The Bloody Chamber,' " *Marvels & Tales*, 12, i (1998), 82–94.

Roberts, Nancy. *Schools of Sympathy . . .* , 131–135.

Roemer, Danielle M. "The Contextualization of the Marquis in Angela Carter's 'The Bloody Chamber,' " *Marvels & Tales*, 12, i (1998), 95–115.

Wisker, Gina. "At Home All was Blood and Feathers: The Werewolf in the Kitchen—Angela Carter and Horror," in Bloom, Clive, Ed. *Creepers . . .* , 169–170; rpt "On Angela Carter," in Bloom, Clive, Ed. *Gothic Horror . . .* , 242–243.

———. "Revenge of the Living Doll: Angela Carter's Horror Writing," in Bristow, Joseph, and Trev L. Broughton, Eds. *The Infernal Desires . . .* , 122–123.

"The Cabinet of Edgar Allan Poe"

Hanson, Clare. " 'The Red Dawn Breaking Over Clapham': Carter and the Limits of Artifice," in Bristow, Joseph, and Trev L. Broughton, Eds. *The Infernal Desires . . .* , 61–62.

"The Company of Wolves"

Armitt, Lucie. "The Fragile Frames . . . ," 94–95.

Bruhl, Elise, and Michael Gamer. "Teaching Improprieties: *The Bloody Chamber* and the Reverent Classroom," *Marvels & Tales*, 12, i (1998), 137–142.

Charters, Ann, and William E. Sheidley. *Resources . . .* , 5th ed., 40–41.

Day, Aidan. *Angela Carter . . .* , 147–149.

Douglas, Paul. "Mother May I? . . . ," 20–21.

Gamble, Sarah. *Angela Carter . . .* , 134–135, 136–137.

Wisker, Gina. "Revenge of the Living . . . ," 125–126.

"The Courtship of Mr. Lyon"

Crunelle-Vanrigh, Anny. "The Logic of the Same and *Différance*: 'The Courtship of Mr. Lyon,' " *Marvels & Tales*, 12, i (1998), 116–132.

Day, Aidan. *Angela Carter . . .* , 135–139.

Gamble, Sarah. *Angela Carter . . .* , 133.

Pireddu, Nicoletta. "CaRterbury Tales: Romances of Disenchantment in Geoffrey Chaucer and Angela Carter," *Comparatist*, 21 (1997), 138–140.

"The Erl-King"

Armitt, Lucie. "The Fragile Frames . . . ," 93–94.

Jordan, Elaine. "Afterword," in Bristow, Joseph, and Trev L.
  Broughton, Eds. *The Infernal Desires* . . . , 217.
Magrs, Paul. "Boys Keep Swinging . . . ," 188–189.
Wisker, Gina. "At Home All . . . ," 163–165; rpt. "On Angela
  Carter," in Bloom, Clive, Ed. *Gothic Horror* . . . , 235–237.
————. "Revenge of the Living . . . ," 129–130.
"The Man Who Loved a Double Bass"
  Gamble, Sarah. *Angela Carter* . . . , 45–48.
"Master"
  Day, Aidan. *Angela Carter* . . . , 96–97.
"The Merchant of Shadows"
  Duncker, Patricia. "Queer Gothic . . . ," 66–67.
  Gamble, Sarah. *Angela Carter* . . . , 185–187.
"Overture and Incidental Music for *A Midsummer Night's Dream*"
  Peach, Linden. *Angela Carter*, 146–147.
"Peter and the Wolf"
  Gamble, Sarah. *Angela Carter* . . . , 151.
  Moss, Betty. "Desire and the Female Grotesque in Angela Carter's
    'Peter and the Wolf,' " *Marvels & Tales*, 12, i (1998), 175–191.
  Wyatt, Jean. "The Violence of Gendering: Castration Images in
    Angela Carter's *The Magic Toyshop*, *The Passion of New Eve*, and
    'Peter and the Wolf,' " *Women's Stud*, 25 (1996), 550, 551–552,
    565–566.
"Puss in Boots"
  Douglas, Paul. "Mother May I? . . . ," 19–20.
  Geoffroy-Menoux, Sophie. "Angela Carter's . . . ," 252–254.
"The Smile of Winter"
  Gamble, Sarah. *Angela Carter* . . . , 106–108.
"The Snow Child"
  Armitt, Lucie. "The Fragile Frames . . . ," 91, 94.
  Geoffroy-Menoux, Sophie. "Angela Carter's . . . ," 251–252.
  Keenan, Sally. "Angela Carter's *The Sadeian Woman*: Feminism as
    Treason," in Bristow, Joseph, and Trev L. Broughton, Eds. *The
    Infernal Desires* . . . , 136.
"A Souvenir of Japan"
  Peach, Linden. *Angela Carter*, 21, 22.
"The Tiger's Bride"
  Day, Aidan. *Angela Carter* . . . , 139–147.
  Douglas, Paul. "Mother May I? . . . ," 18–19.
  Gamble, Sarah. *Angela Carter* . . . , 133–134.
  Pireddu, Nicoletta. "CaRterbury Tales . . . ," 140–142.
"Wolf-Alice"
  Day, Aidan. *Angela Carter* . . . , 162–166.

RAYMOND CARVER

"After the Denim"
  Mullen, Bill. "A Subtle Spectacle: Televisual Culture in the Short
    Stories of Raymond Carver," *Critique*, 39 (1998), 109–110.

"The Bath"
    Mullen, Bill. "A Subtle Spectacle . . . ," 110–111.
"Bicycles, Muscles, Cigarettes"
    Simmons, Philip E. *Deep Surfaces* . . . , 117–118.
"Blackbird Pie"
    Siebert, Hilary. " 'Outside History': Lyrical Knowledge in the
        Discourse of the Short Story," in Kaylor, Noel H., Ed. *Creative and
        Critical* . . . , 35–45.
"Cathedral"
    Baldwin, Dean. *Instructor's Resource* . . . , 196–198.
    Charters, Ann, and William E. Sheidley. *Resources* . . . , 5th ed.,
        42–43.
    Ford, Joh, and Marjorie Ford. *Instructor's Manual* . . . , 93–94.
"Chef's House"
    Magee, John. "Carver's 'Chef's House,' " *Explicator*, 55, ii (1997),
        111–112.
"Distance"
    Curnutt, Kirk. *Wise Economies* . . . , 238–239.
"Errand"
    Charters, Ann, and William E. Sheidley. *Resources* . . . , 5th ed.,
        44–43.
"Fat"
    Curnutt, Kirk. *Wise Economies* . . . , 234–235.
"Feathers"
    Champion, Laurie. " 'What's to Say': Silence in Raymond Carver's
        'Feathers,' " *Stud Short Fiction*, 34 (1997), 193–201.
"Gazebo"
    Curnutt, Kirk. *Wise Economies* . . . , 240–241.
"Intimacy"
    Curnutt, Kirk. *Wise Economies* . . . , 241.
    Ford, Joh, and Marjorie Ford. *Instructor's Manual* . . . , 92–93.
"Menudo"
    Simmons, Philip E. *Deep Surfaces* . . . , 109–110.
"Mr. Coffee and Mr. Fixit"
    Mullen, Bill. "A Subtle Spectacle . . . ," 108–109.
"One More Thing"
    Simmons, Philip E. *Deep Surfaces* . . . , 114.
"A Serious Talk"
    Simmons, Philip E. *Deep Surfaces* . . . , 111, 112–113.
"So Much Water So Close to Home"
    Curnutt, Kirk. *Wise Economies* . . . , 233–234.
    Simmons, Philip E. *Deep Surfaces* . . . , 115–117.
"Tell the Women We're Going"
    Siebert, Hilary. "Social Critique and Story Technique in the Fiction

of Raymond Carver," in Lounsberry, Barbara, et al., Eds. *The Tales We Tell* . . . , 24–27.

"What Do You Do in San Francisco?"
Curnutt, Kirk. *Wise Economies* . . . , 238.

"What We Talk About When We Talk About Love"
Charters, Ann, and William E. Sheidley. *Resources* . . . , 5th ed., 46–47.

"Where I'm Calling From"
Curnutt, Kirk. *Wise Economies* . . . , 236–237, 242–243.

"Whoever Was Using This Bed"
Curnutt, Kirk. *Wise Economies* . . . , 235, 236.

"Will You Please Be Quiet, Please?"
Bethea, Arthur F. "Carver's 'Will You Please Be Quiet, Please?' "
Explicator, 56, iii (1998), 132–134.

"Why Don't You Dance?"
Mullen, Bill. "A Subtle Spectacle . . . ," 106–108.

ALICE CARY

"Mrs. Walden's Confidant"
Fick, Thomas H. "Maternal Iconography and Nation Building in Alice Cary's 'Mrs. Walden's Confidant,' " *Stud Am Fiction*, 25 (1997), 131–146.

ROSARIO CASTELLANOS

"Álbum de familia"
López González, Aralia. "Tradición y nueva poética en un cuento de Rosario Castellanos," in Herrera, Sara P., Ed. *El cuento mexicano* . . . , 350–359.

"Las amistades efímeras"
Domenella, Ana R. " 'Yo soy una memoria' indias, ladinas y comitecas en los cuentos de Rosario Castellanos," *Texto Crítico*, 3, iv-v (1997), 100.

"Cuidad real"
Domenella, Ana R. " 'Yo soy una memoria' . . . ," 98–100.

"Modesta Gómez"
Domenella, Ana R. " 'Yo soy una memoria' . . . ," 94–96.

"La tregua"
Domenella, Ana R. " 'Yo soy una memoria' . . . ," 93–94.

"Vals Capricho"
Domenella, Ana R. " 'Yo soy una memoria' . . . ," 96–98.

WILLA CATHER

"Alexander's Bridge"
  Lindemann, Marilee. "Introduction," *Alexander's Bridge* [by Willa Cather], x–xi, xvi–xviii, xix–xxii, xxiv, xxvi–xxxiii.

"Behind the Singer Tower"
  Goodman, Nan. *Shifting the Blame* . . . , 114.

"The Marriage of Phaedra"
  Stich, K. P. "Woman as Enemy: Willa Cather's 'The Marriage of Phaedra,' " *Mod Lang Stud*, 24, ii (1994), 38–47.

"On the Divide"
  Warner, Nicholas O. *Spirits of America* . . . , 213–214.

"Paul's Case"
  Charters, Ann, and William E. Sheidley. *Resources* . . . , 5th ed., 49–50.
  Saari, Rob. " 'Paul's Case': A Narcissistic Personality Disorder, 301.81," *Stud Short Fiction*, 34 (1997), 389–395.

"The Professor"
  Murphy, John J. "The Modernist Conversion of Willa Cather's Professor," in Barnstone, Aliki, Michael T. Manson, and Carol J. Singley, Eds. *The Calvinist Roots* . . . , 54–58, 64–66, 67, 69, 70.

"The Song of the Lark"
  Nealon, Christopher. "Affect-Genealogy: Feeling and Affiliation in Willa Cather," *Am Lit*, 69 (1997), 11–16.

"Tom Outland's Story"
  Goldberg, Jonathan. "Strange Brothers," *Stud Novel*, 28 (1996), 325–332; rpt. in Sedgwick, Eve K., Ed. *Novel Gazing* . . . , 468–476.

RAYMOND CHANDLER

"Blackmailers Don't Shoot"
  Hiney, Tom. *Raymond Chandler* . . . , 80–82.

"The Curtain"
  Baldwin, Dean. *Instructor's Resource* . . . , 129–131.

"Do You Terribly Mind Being Seduced"
  Hiney, Tom. *Raymond Chandler* . . . , 225.

"The King in Yellow"
  Hiney, Tom. *Raymond Chandler* . . . , 96–97.

"Mandarin's Jade"
  Hiney, Tom. *Raymond Chandler* . . . , 86.

"Marlowe Takes on the Syndicate"
  Hiney, Tom. *Raymond Chandler* . . . , 274.

"The Pencil"
  Tate, James O. "Raymond Chandler's Pencil," in Delamater, Jerome H., and Ruth Prigozy, Eds. *The Detective* . . . , 27–34.

"Red Wind"
  Hiney, Tom. *Raymond Chandler* . . . , 95.
"Smart Aleck Kill"
  Hiney, Tom. *Raymond Chandler* . . . , 83–84, 94.

SUZY MCKEE CHARNAS

"The Unicorn Tapestry"
  Hollinger, Veronica. "Fantasies of Absence: The Postmodern
  Vampire," in Gordon, Joan, and Veronica Hollinger, Eds. *Blood
  Read* . . . , 200–201, 205.

FRANÇOIS-RENÉ DE CHATEAUBRIAND

"Atala"
  Bailey, Caroline. "Beneath the Surface of 'Atala': 'Le Crocodile au
  Fond du Bassin,' " *French Stud*, 51, ii (1997), 138–154.
  Wang, Ban. "Writing, Self, and the Other: Chateaubriand and His
  'Atala,' " *French Forum*, 22 (1997), 133–148.
  Williams, Timothy J. "The Chalice as a Key Symbol in the Death
  Scene of 'Atala,' " *Romance Notes*, 38 (1997), 37–43.
"René"
  Glaudes, Pierre. "René: Le Mal de l'infini," *Magazine Litteraire*, 366
  (1998), 48–51.

GEORGES-OLIVIER CHÂTEAUREYNAUD

"Newton go home"
  Joguin, Odile. "Le fantastique ne fait plus le poids: allègement
  fantastique du corps dans quelques texts contemporains," in
  Marigny, Jean, Intro. *Images fantastiques du corps*, 195–206.

MARIE CHAUVET

"The Vultures"
  Chancy, Myriam J. A. *Framing Silence* . . . , 148–154.

FRAY ANGELICO CHAVEZ

"The Angel's New Wings"
  Padilla, Genaro M. "A Reassessment of Fray Angelico Chavez's
  Fiction," in Bloom, Harold, Ed. *Hispanic-American Writers*, 127.
"The Bell That Sang Again"
  Padilla, Genaro M. "A Reassessment . . . ," 122–123.

"The Lean Years"
  Padilla, Genaro M. "A Reassessment . . . ," 124–127.
"Wake for Don Corino"
  Padilla, Genaro M. "A Reassessment . . . ," 123–124.

JOHN CHEEVER

"Clancy and the Tower of Babel"
  Ford, Joh, and Marjorie Ford. *Instructor's Manual* . . . , 60–61.
"The Five-Forty-Eight"
  Ford, Joh, and Marjorie Ford. *Instructor's Manual* . . . , 61–62.
"The Swimmer"
  Charters, Ann, and William E. Sheidley. *Resources* . . . , 5th ed.,
    51–53.
"Torch Song"
  Spilka, Mark. *Eight Lessons* . . . , 291–306.

ANTON CHEKHOV

"About Love"
  Callow, Philip. *Chekhov: The Hidden Ground*, 286–287.
"An Anonymous Story"
  Callow, Philip. *Chekhov* . . . , 207–208.
"Anyuta"
  Callow, Philip. *Chekhov* . . . , 51–52.
"Ariadne"
  Callow, Philip. *Chekhov* . . . , 235–236.
"At a Country House"
  Callow, Philip. *Chekhov* . . . , 219–220.
"An Attack of Nerves"
  Hutchings, Stephen C. *Russian Modernism* . . . , 68, 98–99, 101.
  Sherbinin, Julie W. de. *Chekhov and Russian* . . . , 85–87, 114.
"The Bet"
  Ford, Joh, and Marjorie Ford. *Instructor's Manual* . . . , 27–28.
"The Bishop"
  Callow, Philip. *Chekhov* . . . , 352–356.
  Hutchings, Stephen C. *Russian Modernism* . . . , 87, 95.
  Sherbinin, Julie W. de. *Chekhov and Russian* . . . , 143–144.
"The Black Monk"
  Callow, Philip. *Chekhov* . . . , 215–217.
"A Boring Story"
  Flath, Carol A. "The Limits to the Flesh: Searching for the Soul in
    Chekhov's 'A Boring Story,' " *Slavic & East European J*, 41
    (1997), 272–286.
  Hutchings, Stephen C. *Russian Modernism* . . . , 89–91.

"The Huntsman"
  Callow, Philip. *Chekhov* . . . , 61–62.

"In the Autumn"
  Sherbinin, Julie W. de. *Chekhov and Russian* . . . , 56–58.

"In the Cart"
  Callow, Philip. *Chekhov* . . . , 275–277.

"In the Ravine"
  Baxter, Charles. *Burning Down the House* . . . , 179–184.
  Callow, Philip. *Chekhov* . . . , 326–330.

"The Kiss"
  Callow, Philip. *Chekhov* . . . , 91–93.
  Hutchings, Stephen C. *Russian Modernism* . . . , 2–5, 96–97, 98.

"The Lady"
  Sherbinin, Julie W. de. *Chekhov and Russian* . . . , 68–74.

"The Lady with the Dog" [same as "The Lady with the Lapdog," "The
Lady with the Pet Dog," "The Lady with the Small Dog"]
  Baldwin, Dean. *Instructor's Resource* . . . , 76–78.
  Callow, Philip. *Chekhov* . . . , 313–316.
  Charters, Ann, and William E. Sheidley. *Resources* . . . , 5th ed., 56.
  Hutchings, Stephen C. *Russian Modernism* . . . , 94, 97–98, 107–109.
  Siemens, Elena. "A Tempest in a Tea Cup: Mikhalkov's *Dark Eyes*
    and Chekhov's 'The Lady with the Dog,' " in Clayton, J. Douglas,
    Ed. *Chekhov Then* . . . , 260, 261–262, 263–264.
  Zviniatskovsky, Vladimir. "Two Ladies With Two Dogs and Two
    Gentlemen (Joyce Carol Oats and Chekhov)," in Clayton, J.
    Douglas, Ed. *Chekhov Then* . . . , 126–134.

"Man in a Shell"
  Callow, Philip. *Chekhov* . . . , 284–285.

"Maria Ivanova"
  Sherbinin, Julie W. de. *Chekhov and Russian* . . . , 58–59.

"My Life"
  Callow, Philip. *Chekhov* . . . , 252–254.
  Sherbinin, Julie W. de. *Chekhov and Russian* . . . , 125–142.

"The Name-Day Party"
  Hutchings, Stephen C. *Russian Modernism* . . . , 99–102.

"On Holy Night"
  Sherbinin, Julie W. de. *Chekhov and Russian* . . . , 20–21.

"On the Road"
  Callow, Philip. *Chekhov* . . . , 93–94.

"Peasants"
  Callow, Philip. *Chekhov* . . . , 262–265.
  Sherbinin, Julie W. de. *Chekhov* . . . ," 10, 74–83.

"Peasant Women"
  Sherbinin, Julie W. de. *Chekhov and Russian* . . . , 89–105.

CHEN BAICHEN

GEORGE CHESNEY

"The Battle of Dorking"
Clarke, I. F. "Great SF Short Fiction, 3: 'The Battle of Dorking' by
George Chesney," *Foundation*, 70 (1997), 82–83.

CHARLES CHESNUTT

"Aunt Mimy's Son"
Duncan, Charles. *The Absent Man* . . . , 59–60, 64–66.

"The Averted Strike"
Goodman, Nan. *Shifting the Blame* . . . , 127–129.

"A Bad Night"
Duncan, Charles. *The Absent Man* . . . , 35–36.

"Baxter's Procrustes"
Duncan, Charles. *The Absent Man* . . . , 167–176.
Wonham, Henry B. *Charles W. Chesnutt* . . . , 70–74.

"The Bouquet"
Duncan, Charles. *The Absent Man* . . . , 148–150.

"Cartwright's Mistake"
Duncan, Charles. *The Absent Man* . . . , 57–59.

"Cicely's Dream"
Duncan, Charles. *The Absent Man* . . . , 122–123, 124.

"The Conjurer's Revenge"
Wonham, Henry B. *Charles W. Chesnutt* . . . , 28–32.

"Dave's Neckliss"
Titus, Mary. "The Dining Room Door Swings Both Ways: Food, Race,
and Domestic Space in the Nineteenth-Century South," in Jones,
Anne G., and Susan V. Donaldson, Eds. *Haunted Bodies* . . . ,
252–253.
Wonham, Henry B. " 'The Curious Psychological Spectacle of a Mind
Enslaved': Charles W. Chesnutt and Dialect Fiction," *Mississippi Q*,
51 (1997–1998), 59–62.
———. *Charles W. Chesnutt* . . . , 44–47.

"The Doll"
Duncan, Charles. *The Absent Man* . . . , 110–113.
Wonham, Henry B. *Charles W. Chesnutt* . . . , 65–66.

"The Goophered Grapevine"
Duncan, Charles. *The Absent Man* . . . , 99–106.
Osinubi, Viktor. "African American Writers and the Use of Dialect in
Literature: The Foregrounding of Ethnicity," *J Commonwealth &
Postcolonial Stud*, 4, i (1996), 69–70.
Slote, Ben. "Listening to 'The Goophered Grapevine,' and Hearing
Raisins Sing," *Am Lit Hist*, 6 (1994), 684–694; rpt. Wonham, Henry
B. *Charles W. Chesnutt* . . . , 143–153.
Wonham, Henry B. *Charles W. Chesnutt* . . . , 11–18.

————. "Plenty of Room for Us All? Participation and Prejudice in Charles Chesnutt's Dialect Tales," *Stud Am Fiction*, 26 (1998), 133–136.

"A Grass Widow"
Duncan, Charles. *The Absent Man . . .* , 68–76.

"The Gray Wolf's Ha'nt"
Wonham, Henry B. *Charles W. Chesnutt . . .* , 37–40.

"Her Virginia Mammy"
Duncan, Charles. *The Absent Man . . .* , 115–121.
Wonham, Henry B. *Charles W. Chesnutt . . .* , 61–63.

"Hot-Foot Hannibal"
Wonham, Henry B. *Charles W. Chesnutt . . .* , 40–44.

"Lonesome Ben"
Wonham, Henry B. *Charles W. Chesnutt . . .* , 51–54.
————. "Plenty of Room . . . ," 142–144.

"The Marked Tree"
Duncan, Charles. *The Absent Man . . .* , 96–98.

"Mars Jeems's Nightmare"
Duncan, Charles. *The Absent Man . . .* , 90–91.
Wonham, Henry B. *Charles W. Chesnutt . . .* , 22–27.
————. "Plenty of Room . . . ," 137–142.

"A Matter of Principle"
Duncan, Charles. *The Absent Man . . .* , 141–143, 146–147.

"The Passing of Grandison"
Duncan, Charles. *The Absent Man . . .* , 159–165.
Wonham, Henry B. *Charles W. Chesnutt . . .* , 63–64.

"Po' Sandy"
Duncan, Charles. *The Absent Man . . .* , 92–93.
Titus, Mary. "The Dining Room . . . ," 253.
Wonham, Henry B. *Charles W. Chesnutt . . .* , 18–22.
Yaeger, Patricia. "Faulkner's 'Greek Amphora Priestess': Verbena and Violence in *The Unvanquished*," in Kartiganer, Donald M., and Ann J. Abadie, Eds. *Faulkner and Gender . . .* , 200–201, 202.

"The Shadow of My Past"
Duncan, Charles. *The Absent Man . . .* , 37–46.

"The Sheriff's Children"
Charters, Ann, and William E. Sheidley. *Resources . . .* , 5th ed., 58–59.
Wonham, Henry B. *Charles W. Chesnutt . . .* , 60–61.

"Sis' Becky's Pickaninny"
Richardson, Brian. *UnLikely Stories . . .* , 147–148.
Wonham, Henry B. *Charles W. Chesnutt . . .* , 33–37.

"Stryker's Waterloo"
Goodman, Nan. *Shifting the Blame . . .* , 131–132.

"Tobe's Tribulations"
    Wonham, Henry B. *Charles W. Chesnutt* . . . , 49–51.
"Uncle Wellington's Wives"
    Duncan, Charles. *The Absent Man* . . . , 143–146.
    Wonham, Henry B. *Charles W. Chesnutt* . . . , 66–68.
"A Victim of Heredity"
    Wonham, Henry B. " 'The Curious . . . ,' " 62–64.
    ———. *Charles W. Chesnutt* . . . , 47–49.
"Walter Knox's Record"
    Duncan, Charles. *The Absent Man* . . . , 152.
"The Web of Circumstance"
    Ford, Joh, and Marjorie Ford. *Instructor's Manual* . . . , 24–25.
    Wonham, Henry B. *Charles W. Chesnutt* . . . , 68–69.
"The Wife of His Youth"
    Duncan, Charles. *The Absent Man* . . . , 125–135.
    Marcus, Lisa. " 'Of One Blood': Reimaging American Genealogy in
        Pauline Hopkins's *Contending Forces*," in Reesman, Jeanne C., Ed.
        Speaking the Other . . . , 134–137.
    Sundquist, Eric J. *To Wake the Nations* . . . , 298–301; rpt. Wonham,
        Henry B. *Charles W. Chesnutt* . . . , 139–141.
    Wonham, Henry B. " 'The Curious . . . ,' " 65–68.
    ———. *Charles W. Chesnutt* . . . , 57–60.

G[ILBERT] K[EITH] CHESTERTON

"The Angry Street"
    Schenkel, Elmar. "The Empty Book: Borges, Babbage and
        Chesterton," *Variaciones Borges*, 3 (1997), 76–77.
"The Blast of the Book"
    Schenkel, Elmar. "The Empty Book . . . ," 74–76, 78–79.
"The Blue Cross"
    Gavrell, Kenneth. "The Worst 'Great' Detective Story," *Clues*, 18, i
        (1997), 39–41.

LYDIA MARIA CHILD

"The Quadroons"
    Sollors, Werner. *Neither Black Nor White* . . . , 202–208, 210–211.

KATE CHOPIN

"After the Winter"
    Koloski, Bernard. *Kate Chopin: A Study* . . . , 50–51.
"At the 'Cadian Ball' "
    Beer, Janet. *Kate Chopin, Edith Wharton* . . . , 60.
    Koloski, Bernard. *Kate Chopin: A Study* . . . , 22–22.

"At Chênière Caminada"
  Beer, Janet. *Kate Chopin, Edith Wharton* . . . , 52–54.
  Koloski, Bernard. *Kate Chopin: A Study* . . . , 48–49.
"Athénaïse"
  Beer, Janet. *Kate Chopin, Edith Wharton* . . . , 31–32, 42–45.
  Koloski, Bernard. *Kate Chopin: A Study* . . . , 36–40.
  Morgan-Proux, Catherine. "Athena or Goose? Kate Chopin's Ironical
    Treatment of Motherhood in 'Athénaïse,' " *Southern Stud*, 4, iv
    (1993), 325–340.
"La Belle Zoraïdé"
  Beer, Janet. *Kate Chopin, Edith Wharton* . . . , 26–28.
  Koloski, Bernard. *Kate Chopin: A Study* . . . , 27–29.
"The Bênitous' Slave"
  Beer, Janet. *Kate Chopin, Edith Wharton* . . . , 70–71.
"Beyond the Bayou"
  Green, Suzanne D. "Fear, Freedom and the Perils of Ethnicity:
    Otherness in Kate Chopin's 'Beyond the Bayou' and Zora Neale
    Hurston's 'Sweat,' " *Southern Stud*, 5, iii–iv (1994), 115–120.
  Koloski, Bernard. *Kate Chopin: A Study* . . . , 68–69.
"Boulôt and Boulotte"
  Beer, Janet. *Kate Chopin, Edith Wharton* . . . , 82–83.
"Charlie"
  Koloski, Bernard. *Kate Chopin: A Study* . . . , 77–79.
"Croque Mitaine"
  Beer, Janet. *Kate Chopin, Edith Wharton* . . . , 87–88.
"Désirée's Baby"
  Baldwin, Dean. *Instructor's Resource* . . . , 70–72.
  Beer, Janet. *Kate Chopin, Edith Wharton* . . . , 36–37.
  Charters, Ann, and William E. Sheidley. *Resources* . . . , 5th ed.,
    61–62.
  Elfenbein, Anna S. *Women on the Color* . . . , 126–131; rpt in Koloski,
    Bernard. *Kate Chopin: A Study* . . . , 115–120.
  Koloski, Bernard. *Kate Chopin: A Study* . . . , 24–26.
"Doctor Chevalier's Lie"
  Beer, Janet. *Kate Chopin, Edith Wharton* . . . , 74–77.
"A Dresden Lady in Dixie"
  Beer, Janet. *Kate Chopin, Edith Wharton* . . . , 32–36.
"The Falling in Love of Fedora"
  Koloski, Bernard. *Kate Chopin: A Study* . . . , 61–63.
"The Godmother"
  Beer, Janet. *Kate Chopin, Edith Wharton* . . . , 14–17.
"A Harbinger"
  Beer, Janet. *Kate Chopin, Edith Wharton* . . . , 77–78.
"Her Letters"
  Beer, Janet. *Kate Chopin, Edith Wharton* . . . , 45–48.
  Koloski, Bernard. *Kate Chopin: A Study* . . . , 63–65.

"Ripe Figs"
  Beer, Janet. *Kate Chopin, Edith Wharton* . . . , 87.
  Koloski, Bernard. *Kate Chopin: A Study* . . . , 31–32.
"A Rude Awakening"
  Shaker, Bonnie J. " 'Lookin' Jis' Like W'ite Folks': Coloring Locals
    in Kate Chopin's 'A Rude Awakening,' " *Louisiana Lit*, 14, ii
    (1997), 116–125.
"A Sentimental Soul"
  Koloski, Bernard. *Kate Chopin: A Study* . . . , 49–50.
"A Shameful Affair"
  Beer, Janet. *Kate Chopin, Edith Wharton* . . . , 48–50.
"The Storm"
  Beer, Janet. *Kate Chopin, Edith Wharton* . . . , 60–62.
  Ford, Joh, and Marjorie Ford. *Instructor's Manual* . . . , 21–22.
  Koloski, Bernard. *Kate Chopin: A Study* . . . , 75–77.
  + Seyersted, Per. "[On 'The Storm']," in Koloski, Bernard. *Kate
    Chopin: A Study* . . . , 145–148.
"The Story of an Hour"
  Charters, Ann, and William E. Sheidley. *Resources* . . . , 5th ed., 63.
  Koloski, Bernard. *Kate Chopin: A Study* . . . , 3–4.
"Tante Cat'rinette"
  Koloski, Bernard. *Kate Chopin: A Study* . . . , 40–41.
"A Turkey Hunt"
  Beer, Janet. *Kate Chopin, Edith Wharton* . . . , 85–86.
"Two Portraits"
  Beer, Janet. *Kate Chopin, Edith Wharton* . . . , 58–59.
  Koloski, Bernard. *Kate Chopin: A Study* . . . , 61.
"Two Summers and Two Souls"
  Beer, Janet. *Kate Chopin, Edith Wharton* . . . , 51–52.
"A Very Fine Fiddle"
  Beer, Janet. *Kate Chopin, Edith Wharton* . . . , 84–85.
"A Visit to Avoyelles"
  Koloski, Bernard. *Kate Chopin: A Study* . . . , 22.
"A Vocation and a Voice"
  Koloski, Bernard. *Kate Chopin: A Study* . . . , 54–58.

AGATHA CHRISTIE

"The Case of the Perfect Maid"
  Baldwin, Dean. *Instructor's Resource* . . . , 106–108.

SANDRA CISNEROS

"Beautiful and Cruel"
  Spencer, Laura G. "Fairy Tales and Opera: The Fate of the Heroine in

the Work of Sandra Cisneros," in Reesman, Jeanne C., Ed. *Speaking the Other* . . . , 281–282.

"*Bien* Pretty"
  Christie, John S. *Latino Fiction* . . . , 89–90.
  Griffin, Susan E. "Resistance and Reinvention in Sandra Cisneros' *Woman Hollering Creek*," in Brown, Julie, Ed. *Ethnicity* . . . , 93–94.

"Eyes of Zapata"
  Zamora, Lois P. *The Usable Past* . . . , 169–170.

"La Fabulosa: A Texas Operetta"
  Spencer, Laura G. "Fairy Tales . . . ," 282–287.

"The House on Mango Street"
  Adeleke, Joseph A. "Female Stereotypes in Chicano/a Literature: A Study of Six Modern Novels" in Adebayo, Aduke, Ed. *Feminism and Black Women's* . . . , 238–240.
  Charters, Ann, and William E. Sheidley. *Resources* . . . , 5th ed., 65–67.
  Griffin, Susan E. "Resistance . . . ," 87–88, 90.
  Kaup, Monika. "The Architecture of Ethnicity in Chicana Literature," *Am Lit*, 69 (1997), 385–392.
  Kelly, Margot. "A Minor Revolution: Chicano/a Composite Novels and the Limits of Genre," in Brown, Julie, Ed. *Ethnicity* . . . , 70–75.
  Kuribayashi, Tomoko. "The Chicana Girl Writes Her Way In and Out: Space and Bilingualism in Sandra Cisneros' 'The House on Mango Street,' " in Kuribayashi, Tomoko, and Julie Tharp, Eds. *Creating Safe Space* . . . , 165–177.
  Spencer, Laura G. "Fairy Tales . . . ," 279–282.
  Valdés, María Elena de. "In Search of Identity in Cisneros's 'The House on Mango Street,' " *Canadian R Am Stud*, 23, i (1992), 55–72; rpt., expanded, in her *The Shattered Mirror* . . . , 162–182.

"Little Miracles, Kept Promises"
  Griffin, Susan E. "Resistance . . . ," 92–93.
  Herrera-Sobek, María. "Social Protest, Folklore, and Feminist Ideology in Chicana Prose and Poetry," in Preston, Cathy L., Ed. *Folklore, Literature* . . . , 109–111.
  McCracken, Ellen. "Toward a Comparative Text Grammar of Visual and Verbal Semiosis: Material Religious Culture and Chicana Fiction," in Rauch, Irmengard, and Gerald F. Carr, Eds. *Semiotics Around the World* . . . , 717–720.
  Pérez, Laura E. "Spirit Glyphs: Reimaging Art and Artist in the Work of Chicana *Tlamatinime*," *Mod Fiction Stud*, 44 (1998), 52–53.
  Zamora, Lois P. *The Usable Past* . . . , 165–166, 167–169.

"The Monkey Garden"
  Ford, Joh, and Marjorie Ford. *Instructor's Manual* . . . , 121–122.

"Never Marry a Mexican"
  Gonzalez, Maria. "Love and Conflict: Mexican American Women Writers as Daughters," in Brown-Guillory, Elizabeth, Ed. *Women of Color* . . . , 164–166.

Smith, Paula J. "Changing the Backdrop: Portraiture in Sandra
Cisneros' 'Never Marry a Mexican,' " *Revista de Estudios
Hispánicos*, 23 (1996), 249–262.

"One Holy Night"
Christie, John S. *Latino Fiction* . . . , 135.

"Red Clowns"
Herrera-Sobek, María. "The Politics of Rape: Sexual Transgression in
Chicana Fiction," in St. Joan, Jacqueline, and Annette B.
McElhiney, Eds. *Beyond Portia* . . . , 222–223.

"Tepeyac"
Christie, John S. *Latino Fiction* . . . , 84–85.

"Woman Hollering Creek"
Doyle, Jacqueline. "Haunting the Borderlands: La Llorona in Sandra
Cisneros's 'Woman Hollering Creek,' " in Roberson, Susan L., Ed.
Women, America . . . , 62–78.
García, Alesia. "Politics and Indigenous Theory in Leslie Marmon
Silko's 'Yellow Woman' and Sandra Cisneros' 'Woman Hollering
Creek,' " in Preston, Cathy L., Ed. *Folklore, Literature* . . . , 16–19.
Herrera-Sobek, María. "Social Protest . . . ," 108–109.
Gonzalez, Maria. "Love and Conflict . . . ," 168–169.
Griffin, Susan E. "Resistance . . . ," 87–92.
Rocard, Marcienne. "L'Écriture délibérément métissée de Sandra
Cisneros dans *Woman Hollering Creek*," *Annales Centre
Recherches*, 19 (1994), 144–145.
Zamora, Lois P. *The Usable Past* . . . , 164, 172.

CLARÍN [LEOPOLDO ALAS]

"Benedictino"
Miller, Stephen. "De la cuentística de Alas y Pardo Bazán en los años
noventa, con referencia a Galdós," *Romance Q*, 45 (1998), 36–42.

AUSTIN CLARKE

"Canadian Experience"
Clarke, George E. "Clarke vs. Clarke: Tory Elitism in Austin Clarke's
Short Fiction," *West Coast Line*, 22 (1997), 117.

"How He Does It"
Coleman, Daniel. *Masculine Migrations* . . . , 29–41, 45–51.

"A Man"
Coleman, Daniel. *Masculine Migrations* . . . , 29–45, 47–51.

"The Motor Car"
Clarke, George E. "Clarke vs. Clarke . . . ," 117–118.

"Not So Old, But Oh So Professional"
Clarke, George E. "Clarke vs. Clarke . . . ," 118–119.

HUGH CLIFFORD

"In the Heart of Kalamantan"
  Dryden, Linda. "Conrad and Hugh Clifford: An 'Irreproachable
  Player on the Flute' and 'A Ruler of Men,' " *Conradian*, 23, i
  (1998), 55–69.

JOSEPH BECKHAM COBB

"The Legend of Black Creek"
  Piacentino, Ed. " 'Sleepy Hollow' Comes South: Washington Irving's
  Influence on Old Southwestern Humor," *Southern Lit J*, 30, i
  (1997), 32–35.

J. M. COETZEE

"In the Heart of the Country"
  Briganti, Chiara. " 'A Bored Spinster with a Locked Diary': The
  Politics of Hysteria in 'In the Heart of the Country,' " *Research
  African Lit*, 25, ii (1994), 33–49; rpt. Kossew, Sue, Ed. *Critical
  Essays on . . .* , 84–97.
  Macaskill, Brian. "Charting J. M. Coetzee's Middle Voice: 'In the
  Heart of the Country,' " *Contemp Lit*, 35 (1994), 441–475; rpt.
  Kossew, Sue, Ed. *Critical Essays on . . .* , 66–82.
  Manus, Vicki B. " 'In the Heart of the Country': A Voice in a
  Vacuum," *Commonwealth Essays & Stud*, 19, i (1996), 60–70.
  Sheckels, Theodore F. *The Lion . . .* , 203–212.

"The Narrative of Jacobus Coetzee"
  Manus, Vicki B. "The Colonialist Subject in 'The Narrative of
  Jacobus Coetzee' by J. M. Coetzee," *Commonwealth Essays &
  Stud*, 18, i (1995), 42–47.

ANITA SCOTT COLEMAN

"The Brat"
  Young, Mary E. "Anita Scott Coleman: A Neglected Harlem
  Renaissance Writer," *Coll Lang Assoc J*, 40 (1997), 282–283.

"Cross Crossings Cautiously"
  Young, Mary E. "Anita Scott Coleman . . . ," 272–273.

". . . G'Long, Old White Man's Gal . . ."
  Young, Mary E. "Anita Scott Coleman . . . ," 274–276.

"El Tisico"
  Young, Mary E. "Anita Scott Coleman . . . ," 285–286.

"The Hand that Fed"
  Young, Mary E. "Anita Scott Coleman . . . ," 274.

"Jack Arrives"
  Young, Mary E. "Anita Scott Coleman . . . ," 285.

"The Little Grey House"
 Young, Mary E. "Anita Scott Coleman . . . ," 278.
"Love's Power"
 Young, Mary E. "Anita Scott Coleman . . . ," 276–277.
"The Nettleby's New Year"
 Young, Mary E. "Anita Scott Coleman . . . ," 280–281.
"Phoebe and Peter Up North"
 Young, Mary E. "Anita Scott Coleman . . . ," 279.
"Phoebe Goes to a Lecture"
 Young, Mary E. "Anita Scott Coleman . . . ," 279–280.
"Rich Man, Poor Man"
 Young, Mary E. "Anita Scott Coleman . . . ," 277–278.
"Three Dogs and a Rabbit: A Story of Passing and Memory"
 Young, Mary E. "Anita Scott Coleman . . . ," 284–285.
"Two Old Women A-Shopping Go! A Story of Man, Marriage and Poverty"
 Young, Mary E. "Anita Scott Coleman . . . ," 277.

MARYSE CONDE

"Three Women in Manhattan"
 Anim-Addo, Joan. "Audacity and Outcome: Writing African-
 Caribbean Womanhood," in Anim-Addo, Joan, Ed. *Framing the
 Word* . . . , 210–211.

CYRIL CONNOLLY

"Bond Strikes Camp"
 Woods, Gregory. *A History of Gay* . . . , 241.

ELIZABETH CONNOR

"The Apple"
 Balzano, Wanda. "Elizabeth Connor's 'The Apple': Between Eve and
 Prometheus," in Serpillo, Giuseppe, and Donatella Badin, Eds. *The
 Classical World* . . . ," 133–138.

JOSEPH CONRAD

"Amy Foster"
 Hooper, Myrtle. " 'Oh, I Hope He Won't Talk': Narrative and Silence
 in 'Amy Foster,' " *Conradian*, 21, ii (1996), 51–64.
 Israel, Nico. "Exile, Conrad, and 'La Différence Essentielle des
 Races,' " *Novel*, 30 (1997), 365–376.

Kaplan, Carola M. "Conrad the Pole: Definitively Not 'One of Us,' " in Kurczaba, Alex S., Ed. *Conrad and Poland*, 145–148, 196–197, 200–202, 205.

Yim, Sung-Kyun. "Distancing and Mystifying: Conrad's Narrative Technique in 'Amy Foster' and 'The Lagoon,' " *J Engl Lang & Lit*, 42, iv (1996), 828–831.

"Because of the Dollars"

Billy, Ted. *A Wilderness of Words* . . . , 182–194.

"Il Conde"

Billy, Ted. *A Wilderness of Words* . . . , 203–210.

"The End of the Tether"

Billy, Ted. *A Wilderness of Words* . . . , 194–203.

Kerr, Douglas. "Conrad and the 'Three Ages of Man': 'Youth,' 'The Shadow-Line,' 'The End of the Tether,' " *Conradian*, 23, ii (1998), 35–37, 40–43.

Stape, J. H. " 'One Can Learn Something from Balzac': Conrad and Balzac," in Moore, Gene M., Owen Knowles, and J. H. Stape, Eds. *Conrad: Intertexts* . . . , 108–112.

"Falk"

Billy, Ted. *A Wilderness of Words* . . . , 27–37.

Jaudel, Philippe. " 'Falk,' ou l'animal humain," *La Revue des Lettres Modernes*,1342–1348 (1998), 65–79.

"Heart of Darkness"

Baldwin, Dean. *Instructor's Resource* . . . , 79–82.

Banerjee, A. "The Politicization of 'Heart of Darkness,' " *Lit Criterion*, 27, iii (1992), 19–22.

Bell, Michael. *Literature, Modernism* . . . , 149, 154–155.

Bender, Todd K. *Literary Impressionism* . . . , 6, 7, 10, 11–12, 52–53, 60, 141.

Beyer, Manfred. "The Sepulchral City Revisited: Joseph Conrad: 'Heart of Darkness,' " *Connotations*, 7, iii (1997–1998), 273–289.

Billy, Ted. *A Wilderness of Words* . . . , 69–77.

Bivona, Daniel. *British Imperial Literature* . . . , 106–111.

Brannigan, John. *New Historicism* . . . , 133–154.

Charters, Ann, and William E. Sheidley. *Resources* . . . , 5th ed., 68–69.

Cole, Sarah. "Conradian Alienation and Imperial Intimacy," *Mod Fiction Stud*, 44 (1998), 257–270.

+ Collins, Harold R. "Africans in 'Heart of Darkness,' " in Swisher, Clarice, Ed. *Readings on* . . . , 133–142.

Collins, Tracy J. R. "Eating, Food, and Starvation References in Conrad's 'Heart of Darkness,' " *Conradiana*, 30 (1998), 152–160.

Cousineau, Thomas. " 'Heart of Darkness': The Outsider Demystified," *Conradiana*, 30 (1998), 140–151.

Curtler, Hugh M. "Achebe on Conrad: Racism and Greatness in 'Heart of Darkness,' " *Conradiana*, 29 (1997), 30–40.

D'Amelio-Martiello, Nadia. "Dentelles étincelantes ajourant le tissu de la nuit cosmique: 'Heart of Darkness' de Conrad et *Darkness*

Visible de Golding,"*La Revue des Lettres Modernes*, 1342–1348 (1998), 21–42.

Deena, Seodial. "Racism and Cultural Imperialism in Conrad's 'Heart of Darkness,' " *Ufahamu*, 25, i (1997), 130–155.

Fothergill, Anthony. "Signs, Interpolations, Meanings: Conrad and the Politics of Utterance," *Conradian*, 22, i-ii (1997), 44–46.

Gaggi, Silvio. *From Text to Hypertext . . .* , 35–42.

Gibson, Andrew. "Ethics and Unrepresentability in 'Heart of Darkness,' " *Conradian*, 22, i-ii (1997), 113–137.

Hagen, Susan. "Gender, Intelligence, and Good Sex in 'Heart of Darkness,' " *Furman Stud*, 37 (1995), 45–54.

Hayes, Peter. "Conrad, Male Tyranny, and the Idealization of Women," *ArielE*, 28, iii (1997), 106–109.

Hendershot, Cyndy. *The Animal Within . . .* , 148–163.

Heywood, Leslie. "Gendered Restraints: 'Heart of Darkness' and the Anorexic Logic of Literary Modernism," in Rado, Lisa, Ed. *Modernism . . .* , 357–372.

Hochschild, Adam. "Mr. Kurtz, I Presume," *New Yorker* (14 April, 1997), 40–47.

Humphries, Reynold. "Conrad avec Freud et Lacan: Les enjeux de la représentation dans 'Heart of Darkness,' "*La Revue des Lettres Modernes*, 1342–1348 (1998), 7–19.

Johnson, A. James M. "Victorian Anthropology, Racism, and 'Heart of Darkness,' " *ArielE*, 28, iv (1997), 120–126.

Kaplan, Carola M. "Colonizers, Cannibals, and the Horror of Good Intentions in Joseph Conrad's 'Heart of Darkness,' " *Stud Short Fiction*, 34 (1997), 323–333.

Koushki, Mahmood M. "The Colonialist Bias in Conrad's 'Heart of Darkness,' " *Panjab Univ Research Bull*, 24, ii (1993), 125–132.

Lehan, Richard. *The City in Literature . . .* , 99–101, 102–103.

Lewis, Pericles. " 'His Sympathies Were in the Right Place': 'Heart of Darkness' and the Discourse of National Character," *Nineteenth-Century Lit*, 53 (1998), 211–244.

Lloyd, Tom. *Crises of Realism . . .* , 172–187.

Lord, Ursula. *Solitude Versus Solidarity . . .* , 60–67, 93–95, 97, 101–143.

Meyer, Rosalind S. " ' . . . inside like a kernal?': Literary Sources of 'Heart of Darkness,' " *Mod Lang R*, 93 (1998), 330–332.

Middleton, Tim. "Re-reading Conrad's 'Complete Man': Constructions of Masculine Subjectivity in 'Heart of Darkness' and *Lord Jim*," in Carabine, Keith, Owen Knowles, and Paul Armstrong, Eds. *Conrad, James . . .* , 265–269.

Najder, Zdzisław. *Conrad in Perspective . . .* , 58–59, 136, 144, 184, 193–194, 204–205.

Navarette, Susan J. *The Shape . . .* , 135, 202–204, 206, 207–211, 214–227.

Nettels, Elsa. "Unread Words: The Power of Letters in the Fiction of Henry James and Joseph Conrad," in Carabine, Keith, Owen Knowles, and Paul Armstrong, Eds. *Conrad, James . . .* , 69–70.

Rangarajan, Sudarsan. "Conrad's 'Heart of Darkness,' " *Explicator*, 56, iii (1998), 139–140.

Rasson, Luc. " 'Chacun sa place': L'Anticolonialisme dans 'Heart of Darkness' (1899) et *Voyage au bout de la nuit*," in Buisine, Alain, and Norbert Dodille, Eds. *L'Exotisme*, 267–280.

Scannell, James M. "The Method Is Unsound: The Aesthetic Dissonance of Colonial Justification in Kipling, Conrad, and Greene," *Style*, 30 (1996), 414–417.

+ Schwarz, Daniel R. "Marlow's Role in 'Heart of Darkness,' " in Swisher, Clarice, Ed. *Readings on . . .* , 122–132.

——. *Reconfiguring Modernism . . .* , 79–97, 156–157.

Sens, Jean-Mark. " 'Heart of Darkness': Sub-line & Sublime, the Exotic Immensity," *Cahiers Victoriens et Edouardiens*, 44 (1996), 127–134.

Sinaiko, Herman L. *Reclaiming the Canon . . .* , 126–141.

Stone, Carole, and Fawzia Afzal-Khan. "Gender, Race, and Narrative Structure: A Reappraisal of Joseph Conrad's 'Heart of Darkness,' " *Conradiana*, 29 (1997), 221, 223–234.

+ Straus, Nina P. "The Exclusion of the Intended from Secret Sharing in Conrad's 'Heart of Darkness,' " in Roberts, Andrew M., Ed. *Joseph Conrad*, 171–188.

Taylor, Derek. "Conrad's 'Heart of Darkness,' " *Explicator*, 56, iv (1998), 195–198.

Wallenstein, Jimmy. " 'Heart of Darkness': The Smoke-and-Mirrors Defense," *Conradiana*, 29 (1997), 205–220.

Walker, Stanwood. "The 'Advanced Guard' in the Colonies: Ibsen's Thomas Stockmann and Conrad's Kurtz," *Conradiana*, 30 (1998), 53–63.

Watt, Ian. *Conrad in the . . .* , 148–149, 154–155, 158–160, 163, 164–169, 174, 176–180, 188–196, 198–201, 205–253.

West, Russell. "Navigation and Nomadism: The Two Languages of 'Heart of Darkness,' " *L'Epoque Conradienne*, 23 (1997), 103–120.

+ White, Allon. "Joseph Conrad and the Rhetoric of Enigma," in Roberts, Andrew M., Ed. *Joseph Conrad*, 235–246.

Yim, Harksoon. "Necessary Interaction of Realism and Myth in Conrad's 'Heart of Darkness,' " *Pubs Arkansas Philol Assoc*, 21, ii (1994), 71–85.

"The Idiots"

Billy, Ted. *A Wilderness of Words . . .* , 163–171.

Erdinast-Vulcan, Daphna. " 'Signifying Nothing': Conrad's 'Idiots' and the Anxiety of Modernism,"*La Revue des Lettres Modernes*, 1342–1348 (1998), 82–83, 89–90.

Moore, Gene M. "Conrad's 'The Idiots' and Maupassant's 'La Mère aux monstres,' " in Moore, Gene M., Owen Knowles, and J. H. Stape, Eds. *Conrad: Intertexts . . .* , 52, 53–54, 55–56.

"The Informer"

Billy, Ted. *A Wilderness of Words . . .* , 108–121.

Hampson, Robert. "Storytellers and Storytelling in 'The Partner,' 'The Informer,' 'The Lesson of the Master' and *The Sacred Fount*,"

in Carabine, Keith, Owen Knowles, and Paul Armstrong, Eds.
Conrad, James . . . , 137–141.

"The Inn of the Two Witches"
Billy, Ted. *A Wilderness of Words* . . . , 137–148.

"Karain"
Billy, Ted. *A Wilderness of Words* . . . , 121–129.
Dryden, Linda. " 'Karain': Constructing the Romantic Subject,"
L'Epoque Conradienne, 23 (1997), 30–49.
Gogwilt, Christopher. "Conrad's Alien Genealogies: Joseph Conrad's
'Karain: A Memory,' Pramoedya Ananta Toer, and Postcolonial
American Perspectives," *Western Hum R*, 52, ii (1998), 96–109.
Krajka, Wieslaw. "Making Magic as Cross-cultural Encounter: The
Case of Conrad's 'Karain: A Memory,' " in Carabine, Keith, Owen
Knowles, and Paul Armstrong, Eds. *Conrad, James* . . . , 245–259.

"The Lagoon"
Billy, Ted. *A Wilderness of Words* . . . , 171–176.
Yim, Sung-kyun. "Distancing and Mystifying . . . ," 831–836.

"An Outcast of the Islands"
Watt, Ian. *Conrad in the* . . . , 72–73.

"An Outpost of Progress"
Billy, Ted. *A Wilderness of Words* . . . , 63–69.
Gikandi, Simon. "Race and the Modernist Aesthetic," in Youngs, Tim,
Ed. *Writing and Race*, 153–155.
Paccaud-Huguet, Josiane. "The Master Discourse and the Irreverent
Tongue in 'An Outpost of Progress,' " *L'Epoque Conradienne*, 22
(1996), 94–114.
Watt, Ian. *Conrad in the* . . . , 175–176.

"The Partner"
Billy, Ted. *A Wilderness of Words* . . . , 129–137.
Hampson, Robert. "Storytellers . . . ," 124–127.

"The Planter of Malata"
Billy, Ted. *A Wilderness of Words* . . . , 150–163.
Renner, Stanley. " 'The Planter of Malata,' the Love Song of Geoffrey
Renouard, and the Questions of Conrad's Artistic Integrity,"
Conradiana, 30 (1998), 3–23.

"Prince Roman"
Najder, Zdzisław. *Conrad in Perspective* . . . , 59, 206.

"The Return"
Billy, Ted. *A Wilderness of Words* . . . , 176–180.

"The Secret Sharer"
Billy, Ted. *A Wilderness of Words* . . . , 20–27.
Dilworth, Thomas. "Conrad's 'The Secret Sharer,' " *Explicator*, 56, i
(1997), 30–33.
Ford, Joh, and Marjorie Ford. *Instructor's Manual* . . . , 22–25.
Jones, Michael P. *Conrad's Heroism* . . . , 101, 102, 103, 104, 105,
106–107, 107–112; rpt. in Swisher, Clarice, Ed. *Readings on* . . . ,
85–93.

Levenson, Michael. "Secret History in 'The Secret Sharer,' " in Schwarz, Daniel R., Ed. *Joseph Conrad* . . . , 163–174.

Miller, J. Hillis. "Sharing Secrets," in Schwarz, Daniel R., Ed. *Joseph Conrad* . . . , 232–252.

Miller, Norma. "All Is Vanity Under the Sun: Conrad's Floppy Hat as Biblical Allusion," *Conradiana*, 30 (1998), 64–67.

Paccaud-Huguet, Josiane. "Reading Shadows into Lines: Conrad with Lacan," *Conradian*, 22, i-ii (1997), 152–154.

Phelan, James. "Sharing Secrets," in Schwarz, Daniel R., Ed. *Joseph Conrad* . . . , 128–144.

Ruppel, Richard. "Joseph Conrad and the Ghost of Oscar Wilde," *Conradian*, 23, i (1998), 24.

Schwarz, Daniel R. " 'The Secret Sharer' as an Act of Memory," in Schwarz, Daniel R., Ed. *Joseph Conrad* . . . , 95–111.

Scott, Bonnie K. "Intimacies Engendered in Conrad's 'The Secret Sharer,' " in Schwarz, Daniel R., Ed. *Joseph Conrad* . . . , 197–210.

"The Shadow Line"

Billy, Ted. *A Wilderness of Words* . . . , 37–52.

Kerr, Douglas. "Conrad and the 'Three . . . ,' " 32–35, 39–40.

Paccaud-Huguet, Josiane. " 'Another Turn of the Racking Screw': The Poetics of Disavowal in 'The Shadow Line,' " in Carabine, Keith, Owen Knowles, and Paul Armstrong, Eds. *Conrad, James* . . . , 147–170.

———. "Reading Shadows . . . ," 147–152, 155–177.

"A Smile of Fortune"

Billy, Ted. *A Wilderness of Words* . . . , 80–92.

"The Tale"

Kingsbury, Celia M. " 'Infinities of Absolution': Reason, Rumor, and Duty in Joseph Conrad's 'The Tale,' " *Mod Fiction Stud*, 44 (1998), 715–729.

"Typhoon"

Billy, Ted. *A Wilderness of Words* . . . , 92–105.

"Youth"

Billy, Ted. *A Wilderness of Words* . . . , 54–63.

Epstein, Hugh. "The Duality of 'Youth': Some Literary Contexts," *Conradian*, 21, ii (1996), 1–14.

Kerr, Douglas. "Conrad and the 'Three . . . ,' " 31–32, 38–39.

Watt, Ian. *Conrad in the* . . . , 133–134, 176.

HIBER CONTERIS

"Manhattan-Tango"

Cunha-Giabbai, Gloria da. "Variaciones sobre el olvido," *Monographic R*, 11 (1995), 328–331.

ROSE TERRY COOKE

"How Celia Changed Her Mind"

Kilcup, Karen L. " 'Essays in Invention': Transformations of Advice

in Nineteenth-Century American Women's Writing," in Kilcup,
Karen L., Ed. *Nineteenth-Century American* . . . , 199, 200.
"Miss Beulah's Bonnet"
Fetterley, Judith. " 'Not in the Least American': Nineteenth-Century
Literary Regionalism as UnAmerican Literature," in Kilcup, Karen
L., Ed. *Nineteenth-Century American* . . . , 22–24, 27.
Kilcup, Karen L. " 'Essays in Invention': . . . ," 196–197.
"Too Late"
Campbell, Donna M. *Resisting Regionalism* . . . , 33–35.

J. CALIFORNIA COOPER

"The Big Day"
Jablon, Madelyn. "Womanist Storytelling: The Voice of the
Vernacular" in Brown, Julie, Ed. *Ethnicity* . . . , 50–54.
"Femme Fatale"
Jablon, Madelyn. "Womanist Storytelling . . . ," 56–59.

ROBERT COOVER

"The Babysitter"
Baldwin, Dean. *Instructor's Resource* . . . , 172–174.

JULIO CORTÁZAR

"Apocalypse at Solentiname"
Larsen, Neil. "Cortázar and Postmodernity: New Interpretive
Liabilities," in Alonso, Carlos J., Ed. *Julio Cortázar* . . . , 71, 73.
Luciani, Frederick. "The Man in the Car / in the Trees / behind the
Fence: From Cortázar's 'Blow-up' to Oliver Stone's *JFK*," in
Alonso, Carlos J., Ed. *Julio Cortázar* . . . , 195–198.
Moreiras, Alberto. " 'Apocalypse at Solentiname' as Heterological
Production," in Alonso, Carlos J., Ed. *Julio Cortázar* . . . , 157–178.
"Las armas secretas"
Carmosino, Roger. "Forma y funciones del doble en tres cuentos de
Cortázar: 'La noche boca arriba,' 'Las armas secretas,' y 'El otro
cielo,' " *Texto Crítico*, 2, N.S. (1995), 86–87.
"Axolotl"
Amar Sánchez, Ana María. "Between Utopia and Inferno (Julio
Cortázar's Version)," trans. M. Elizabeth Ginway, in Alonso, Carlos
J., Ed. *Julio Cortázar* . . . , 28–30.
Barrientos, Juan J. "Tres explicaciones ajolotescas en una," *Revista
de la Universidad Nacional Autónoma de México*, 494 (1992),
21–25.
+ Bennett, Maurice J. "A Dialogue of Gazes: Metamorphosis and
Epiphany in Julio Cortázar's 'Axolotl,' " in Foster, David W., and
Daniel Altamiranda, Eds. *Twentieth-Century Spanish* . . . , 109–114.

McNab, Pamela. "Julio Cortázar's 'Axolotl': Literary Archaeology of the Unreal," *Int'l Fiction R*, 24, i-ii (1997), 12–22.
"Bestiary"
McNab, Pamela J. "Shifting Symbols in Cortázar's 'Bestiario,' " *Revista Hispánica Moderna*, 50, ii (1997), 335–346.
"Blow-up"
Llácer, Eusebio. "Relaciones espacio-temporales en tres cuentos de Cortázar: 'La autopista del sur,' 'Las babas del diablo,' 'Cartas de mamá,' " *Escritura*, 19, xxxvii-xxxviii (1994), 54–55.
Luciani, Frederick. "The Man in the Car . . . ," 186–187.
Zavala, Lauro. "Realidades múltiples en la lectura de Julio Cortázar," *Texto Crítico*, 2, N.S. (1995), 71–79.

"Cambio de luces"
Schmidt-Cruz, Cynthia. "What Does Luciana Want? Reclaiming the Female Consciousness in Cortázar's 'Cambio de luces,' " *Hispanic R*, 65 (1997), 415–430.

"Continuidad de los parques"
Charters, Ann, and William E. Sheidley. *Resources . . .* , 5th ed., 71–72.
Lunn, Patricia V. "The Grammar of Technique: Inside 'Continuidad de los parques,' " *Hispania*, 80 (1997), 227–233.
Zavala, Lauro. "Realidades múltiples . . . ," 68–71.

"Diario para un cuento"
Kovach-Allen, K. "The Dark Side of Cortázar's Humor," in Forbes, F. William, Teresa Méndez-Faith, Mary-Anne Vetterling, and Barbara H. Wing, Eds. *Reflections . . .* , 127–130.

"The Gates of Heaven"
Franco, Jean. "Comic Stripping: Cortázar in the Age of Mechanical Reproduction," in Alonso, Carlos J., Ed. *Julio Cortázar . . .* , 40–44.

"Graffiti"
Roemer, Danielle M. "Graffiti as Story and Act," in Preston, Cathy L., Ed. *Folklore, Literature . . .* , 22–28.

"The Idol of the Cyclades"
Pellón, Gustavo. "Cortázar and the Idolatry of Origins," in Alonso, Carlos J., Ed. *Julio Cortázar . . .* , 126–127.

"Intelligence in Flames"
Lindstrom, Naomi. *The Social Conscience . . .* , 108.

"La isla a mediodía"
Cappello, Jean F. "Science as Story: Julio Cortázar and Schrödinger's Cat," *Revista de Estudios Hispánicos*, 31 (1997), 41–60.
Pellón, Gustavo. "Cortázar and the Idolatry . . . ," 125–126.

"Letters from Mama"
Llácer, Eusebio. "Relaciones . . . ," 55–58.

"Little Black Cat's Neck"
Prieto, René. "Cortázar's Closet," in Alonso, Carlos J., Ed. *Julio Cortázar . . .* , 79–81.

"Lugar llamado Kindberg"
Young, Richard A. "La lectura intertextual y 'Lugar llamado Kindberg,' de Julio Cortázar," in *Coloquio Internacional* . . . , 201–211.

"Meeting"
González, Aníbal. " 'Press Clippings' and Cortázar's Ethics of Writing," in Alonso, Carlos J., Ed. *Julio Cortázar* . . . , 240–241.

"La noche boca arriba"
Amar Sánchez, Ana María. "Between Utopia . . . ," 25–28.
Amícola, José. " 'La noche boca arriba' como encrucijada literaria," *Revista Iberoamericana*, 63 (1997), 459–466.
Carmosino, Roger. "Forma y . . . ," 83–85.
Prieto, René. "Cortázar's Closet," 81–83.
Wasserman, Martin. "Julio Cortázar's 'The Night Face Up': Literary Support for Federn's Ideas on Anesthetic Dreams," *Revista/Review Interamericana*, 25, i–iv (1995), 116–127.

"No One Should Be Blamed"
Kovach-Allen, K. "The Dark Side . . . ," 124.
Prieto, René. "Cortázar's Closet," 77–79.

"Orientation of Cats"
Lohafer, Susan. "Preclosure in an 'Open' Story: Julio Cortázar's 'Orientation of Cats,' " in Kaylor, Noel H., Ed. *Creative and Critical* . . . , 215–234.

"El otro cielo"
Carmosino, Roger. "Forma y . . . ," 87–91.
López de Espinosa, Susana. "El conde de Lautreamont en 'El otro cielo' de Julio Cortázar," in Frugoni de Fritzsche, Teresita, Ed. *Primeras Jornadas* . . . , 43–50.
McGuirk, Bernard. *Latin American* . . . , 142–147, 148, 149–152.

"Pequeña historia tendiente a ilustrar lo precario de la estabilidad dentro de la cual creemos existir, o sea que las leyes podrían ceder terreno a las excepciones, azares o improbabilidades, ahí te quiero ver"
Kovach-Allen, K. "The Dark Side . . . ," 124–126.

"Press Clippings"
González, Aníbal. " 'Press Clippings' . . . ," 238–253.

"The Pursuer"
Sommer, Doris. "Pursuing a Perfect Present," in Alonso, Carlos J., Ed. *Julio Cortázar* . . . , 211–230.

"Reunión con un círculo rojo"
Rodríguez Pasqués, Petrona D. de. "Elementos vampíricos en el pintor Jacobo Borges y en el cuento de Cortázar 'Reunión con un círculo rojo,' " in Frugoni de Fritzsche, Teresita, Ed. *Primeras Jornadas* . . . , 38–41.

"The Southern Throughway"
Llácer, Eusebio. "Relaciones . . . ," 51–54.

"Texto en un libreta"
Kovach-Allen, K. "The Dark Side . . . ," 126–127.

RAFAEL COURTOISIE

"La caída del muro"
　　Younoszai, Bárbara. "El sur como el otro sumergido en la
　　marginalidad," *Alba de América*, 15 (1997), 246–253.

MIA COUTO

"The Birds of God"
　　Long-Innes, Chesca. "The Psychopathology of Post-Colonial
　　Mozambique: Mia Couto's *Voices Made Night*," *Am Imago*, 55, i
　　(1998), 174–175.
"The Fire"
　　Long-Innes, Chesca. "The Psychopathology . . . ," 164–166.
"The Girl with a Twisted Future"
　　Long-Innes, Chesca. "The Psychopathology . . . ," 172–174.
"How Ascolino Do Perpetuo Socorro Lost His Spouse"
　　Long-Innes, Chesca. "The Psychopathology . . . ," 161–162.
"How Old Jossias was Saved from the Waters"
　　Long-Innes, Chesca. "The Psychopathology . . . ," 168.
"The Tale of the Two who Returned from the Dead"
　　Long-Innes, Chesca. "The Psychopathology . . . ," 176–177.
"The Talking Raven's Last Warning"
　　Long-Innes, Chesca. "The Psychopathology . . . ," 163–164.
"The Whales of Quissico"
　　Long-Innes, Chesca. "The Psychopathology . . . ," 168–170.

STEPHEN CRANE

"The Blue Hotel"
　　Waldmeir, Joseph J. *"Miss Tina Did It"* . . . , 14–20.
"The Bride Comes to Yellow Sky"
　　Robertson, Michael. *Stephen Crane, Journalism* . . . , 121.
　　Teague, David W. *The Southwest* . . . , 80–88.
"An Experiment in Luxury"
　　Robertson, Michael. *Stephen Crane* . . . , 101–103.
"An Experiment in Misery"
　　Derrick, Scott S. *Monumental Anxieties* . . . , 184, 185.
　　Robertson, Michael. *Stephen Crane* . . . , 95–101.
"Four Men in a Cave"
　　Derrick, Scott S. *Monumental Anxieties* . . . , 186.
"George's Mother"
　　Derrick, Scott S. *Monumental Anxieties* . . . , 175–176, 183–184.
"A Ghoul's Accountant"
　　Derrick, Scott S. *Monumental Anxieties* . . . , 186.

CHRIS CRUTCHER

DAI FANG

Subversive Discourse in Wang Anyi's Four Tales of Sexual Transgression," in Yingjin Zhang, Ed. *China in a Polycentric World* . . . , 96.

SIMIN DANISHVAR

"The Accident"
Talattof, Kamran. "Iranian Women's Literature: From Pre-Revolutionary Social Discourse to Post-Revolutionary Feminism," *Int'l J Middle East Stud*, 29 (1997), 536.

"The Iranians' New Year"
Zarrin, Ali. "The Rhetoric of Self and Other in Selected Iranian Short Stories, 1906–1979," *Int'l Fiction R*, 24, i-ii (1997), 38–39.

"The Playhouse"
Talattof, Kamran. "Iranian Women's . . . ," 536.

"To Whom Can I Say Hello?"
Talattof, Kamran. "Iranian Women's . . . ," 536, 550–551.

ELLA D'ARCY

"The Pleasure-Pilgrim"
Tintner, Adeline R. *Henry James's Legacy* . . . , 306–307.

RUBÉN DARÍO

"The Bourgeois King"
Aching, Gerard. *The Politics* . . . , 152–153.

"The Pipe's Smoke"
Salgado, María A. "Rubén Darío's Short Stories: Autobiography, Fantasy and the Fantastic," in Sullivan, C. W., Ed. *The Dark Fantastic* . . . , 15–18.

"The Ruby"
Baldwin, Dean. *Instructor's Resource* . . . , 59–61.

"The Spectre"
Salgado, María A. "Rubén Darío's Short . . . ," 18–19.

"El velo de la reina Mab"
Burgos, Fernando. "Actuación, fantasia y poética en los cuentos de *Azul*," *Torre*, 1, i-ii (1996), 101–111.

KAMALA DAS

"A Doll for the Child Prostitute"
Herk, Aritha van. "Instructions from Our Mothers: A Loving Matricide," in Barfoot, C. C., and Theo D'haen, Eds. *Shades of Empire* . . . , 201–202.

AVRAM DAVIDSON

"The Beasts of the Elysian Fields"
  Wessells, Henry. " 'A Place That You Can Put Your Arms Around':
  Avram Davidson's Jack Limekiller Stories," *Foundation*, 69 (1997),
  46–47.

"Bloody Man"
  Wessells, Henry. " 'A Place . . . ,' " 48–49.

"A Far Country"
  Wessells, Henry. " 'A Place . . . ,' " 54–55.

"A Good Night's Sleep"
  Wessells, Henry. " 'A Place . . . ,' " 50–51.

"Limekiller at Large"
  Wessells, Henry. " 'A Place . . . ,' " 53–54.

"Manatee Gal, Ain't You Coming Out Tonight"
  Wessells, Henry. " 'A Place . . . ,' " 49–50.

"There Beneath the Silky-Tree and Whelmed in Deeper Gulphs Than
Me"
  Wessells, Henry. " 'A Place . . . ,' " 51–53.

ELSPETH DAVIE

"Accompanist"
  Poggi, Valentina. "Vision and Space in Elspeth Davie's Fiction," in
  Gifford, Douglas, and Dorothy McMillan, Eds. *A History . . .* ,
  533–534.

"Counter Movement"
  Poggi, Valentina. "Vision and Space . . . ," 527–528.

"A Field in Space"
  Poggi, Valentina. "Vision and Space . . . ," 528–529.

"Promise"
  Poggi, Valentina. "Vision and Space . . . ," 535.

"Space"
  Poggi, Valentina. "Vision and Space . . . ," 529–530.

"The Stroke"
  Poggi, Valentina. "Vision and Space . . . ," 528.

LYDIA DAVIS

"A Few Things Wrong with Me"
  Baldwin, Dean. *Instructor's Resource . . .* , 187–188.

REBECCA HARDING DAVIS

"Blind Tom"
  Thomson, Rosemarie G. "Crippled Girls and Lame Old Women:

Sentimental Spectacles of Sympathy in Nineteenth-Century American Women's Writing," in Kilcup, Karen L., Ed. *Nineteenth-Century American* . . . , 136–138.

"A Faded Leaf of History"

Pfaelzer, Jean. "Nature, Nurture, and Nationalism: 'A Faded Leaf of History,' " in Kilcup, Karen L., Ed. *Nineteenth-Century American* . . . , 112–127.

"Life in the Iron Mills"

Curnutt, Kirk. "Direct Addresses, Narrative Authority, and Gender in Rebecca Harding Davis's 'Life in the Iron Mills,' " *Style*, 28 (Summer, 1994), 146–168; rpt. in his *Wise Economies* . . . , 83–84, 87–100.

Doriani, Beth M. "New England Calvinism and the Problem of the Poor in Rebecca Harding Davis's 'Life in the Iron Mills," in Schuldiner, Michael, Ed. *Studies in Puritan* . . . , 205–208, 209–217.

Hughes, Sheila H. "Between Bodies of Knowledge There Is a Great Gulf Fixed: A Liberationist Reading of Class and Gender in 'Life in the Iron Mills,' " *Am Q*, 49 (1997), 113–135.

Pfaelzer, Jean. "Engendered Nature/Denatured History: 'The Yares of Black Mountain,' " in Reesman, Jeanne C., Ed. *Speaking the Other* . . . , 236–238.

"The Yares of Black Mountain"

Pfaelzer, Jean. "Engendered Nature/Denatured . . . ," 229–236, 240–241.

JOHN WILLIAM DE FOREST

"The First Time Under Fire"

Schaefer, Michael W. *Just What War Is* . . . , 27–35, 68–69, 101–102.

BEATRIZ DE LA GARZA

"The Candy Vendor's Boy"

Garza-Falcón, Leticia M. *Gente Decente* . . . , 225–227.

"The Kid from the Alamo"

Garza-Falcón, Leticia M. *Gente Decente* . . . , 232–235.

"Temporary Residents"

Garza-Falcón, Leticia M. *Gente Decente* . . . , 219–225.

WALTER DE LA MARE

"A. B. O."

Navarette, Susan J. *The Shape* . . . , 62–67, 79–80, 84–87, 88–89, 94–97, 100–109.

DON DELILLO

"Spaghetti and Meatballs"
Gardaphé, Fred L. "(Ex)Tending or Escaping Ethnicity: Don DeLillo and Italian/American Literature," in Giordano, Paolo A., and Anthony J. Tamburri, Eds. *Beyond the Margin* . . . , 138–140.
"Take the 'A' Train"
Gardaphé, Fred L. "(Ex)Tending . . . ," 135–138.
"Videotape"
Charters, Ann, and William E. Sheidley. *Resources* . . . , 5th ed., 76.

FRIEDRICH CHRISTIAN DELIUS

"Der Sonntag, an dem ich Weltmeister wurde"
Sanna, Simonetta. "Sprachpuzzle und Selbstfindung: Delius' 'Der Sonntag, an dem ich Weltmeister wurde,' " trans. Claudia Spang, in Durzak, Manfred, and Hartmut Steinecke, Eds. *F. C. Delius* . . . , 163–180.
Vieregg, Axel. "Zur Erzählweise von Delius in 'Der Sonntag, an dem ich Weltmeister wurde,' " in Durzak, Manfred, and Hartmut Steinecke, Eds. *F. C. Delius* . . . , 143–162.
"Der Spaziergang von Rostock nach Syrakus"
Brodersen, Momme. "Von Seume zu Ernest Bloch: Einige Assoziationen zu Paul Gompitz' Italienreise," in Durzak, Manfred, and Hartmut Steinecke, Eds. *F. C. Delius* . . . , 221–224.
Steinecke, Hartmut. "Spraziergang mit Seume: Delius' Erzählung 'Der Spaziergang von Rostock nach Syrakus,' " in Durzak, Manfred, and Hartmut Steinecke, Eds. *F. C. Delius* . . . , 207–217.

LESTER DEL REY

"Helen O'Loy"
Disch, Thomas M. *The Dreams Our Stuff* . . . , 10–11.

MARIA DERMOÛT

"The Buddha Ring"
Beekman, E. M. *Troubled Pleasures* . . . , 476.
"The Chest"
Beekman, E. M. *Troubled Pleasures* . . . , 487–488.

MAHASWETA DEVI

"Draupadi"
Collu, Gabrielle. "Unleashing Kali: Anger as Resistance in South

Asian Women's Writing," in Bogaards, Winnifred M., Ed. *Literature of Region* . . . , 409–410.
"Stanadayini"
Shetty, Sandhya. "(Dis)figuring the Nation: Mother, Metaphor, Metonymy," *Differences*, 7, iii (1995), 66–73.
"The Witch-Hunt"
Kelleher, Margaret. *The Feminization* . . . , 207–210.

JUNOT DÍAZ

"Fiesta"
Charters, Ann, and William E. Sheidley. *Resources* . . . , 5th ed., 77–78.

PALOMA DÍAZ-MÁS

"El rapto del Santo Grial"
Bellver, Catherine G. "Humor and the Resistance to Meaning in 'El rapto del Santo Grial,' " *Romanic R*, 87, i (1996), 145–155.

MANUEL DÍAZ RODRÍGUEZ

"Celos"
Mora, Gabriela. "Modernismo decadentista: *Confidencias de psiquis* de Manuel Díaz Rodríguez," *Revista Iberoamericana*, 63 (1997), 271–272.
"Fetichismo"
Mora, Gabriela. "Modernismo . . . ," 269–270.
"Flor de voluptuosidad"
Mora, Gabriela. "Modernismo . . . ," 266–269.
"Mi secreto"
Mora, Gabriela. "Modernismo . . . ," 272–273.
"Tic"
Mora, Gabriela. "Modernismo . . . ," 270–271.

PHILIP K. DICK

"The Golden Man"
Attebery, Brian. "Super Men," *Sci-Fiction Stud*, 25 (1998), 61, 72–74.

CHARLES DICKENS

"A Christmas Carol"
Erickson, Lee. "The Primitive Keynesianism of Dickens's 'A Christmas Carol,' " *Stud Lit Imagination*, 30, i (1997), 51–64.

Higbie, Robert. *Dickens and Imagination*, 69–71.
Lerner, Laurence. *Angels and Absences* . . . , 114–116.
Waters, Catherine. *Dickens and the Politics* . . . , 74–78, 80–82.
Yoon, Hye-Joon. *Physiognomy of Capital* . . . , 116–119.
"Dr. Marigold's Prescriptions"
    Lerner, Laurence. *Angels and Absences* . . . , 116–117.
"George Silverman's Explanation"
    McKnight, Natalie J. *Suffering Mothers* . . . , 49–50.
"A Holiday Romance"
    Higbie, Robert. *Dickens and Imagination*, 157–158.
"Mugby Junction"
    Yoon, Hye-Joon. *Physiognomy of Capital* . . . , 119–121.
"The Perils of Certain English Prisoners"
    Peck, John. *War, the Army* . . . , 81–84.
"The Signalman"
    Korte, Barbara. *Body Language* . . . , 53–55, 81–82.
    Tytler, Graeme. "Charles Dickens's 'The Signalman': A Case of
        Partial Insanity?" *Hist Psychiatry*, 8 (1997), 424–431.
"The Wreck of the Golden Mary"
    Lerner, Laurence. *Angels and Absences* . . . , 117–118.

MODIKWE DIKOBE

"The Marabi Dance"
    Sheckels, Theodore F. *The Lion* . . . , 70–76.

BLAGA DIMITROVA

"Elmaz"
    Scholz, Hannelore. " 'Life from Its Very Beginning at Its End': The
        Unhomely Boundaries in the Works of Bulgarian Author Blaga
        Dimitrova," trans. Elizabeth Naylor, in Brinker-Gabler, Gisela, and
        Sidonie Smith, Eds. *Writing New Identities* . . . , 260–261.

ISAK DINESEN [BARONESS KAREN BLIXEN]

"The Blue Jar"
    Charters, Ann, and William E. Sheidley. *Resources* . . . , 5th ed., 79.
"The Dreamers"
    Lee, Judith. "Freed from Certainty: Toward a Feminist Theory of the
        Fantastic," in Cooke, Brett, George E. Slusser, and Jaume Marti-
        Olivella, Eds. *The Fantastic Other* . . . , 268–274.
    Sodowsky, Gargi R., and Roland Sodowsky. "Myriad Possibilities in
        Isak Dinesen's 'The Dreamers': An Existential Interpretation," in
        Kaylor, Noel H., Ed. *Creative and Critical* . . . , 329–340.

"The Ghost Horses"
  Branson, Stephanie R. "Banishing the Nightmare: Lawrence's 'The
    Rocking Horse Winner' and Dinesen's 'The Ghost Horses,' " *Short
    Story*, 2, ii (1992), 42–50.

DING LING

"Miss Sophie's Diary"
  Findeisen, Raoul D. "*Kairos* or the Due Time: On Date and Dates in
    Modern Chinese Literature," in Findeisen, Raoul D., and Robert H.
    Gassmann, Eds. *Autumn Floods* . . . , 239–240.
  McDougall, Bonnie S., and Kam Louie. *The Literature of China* . . . ,
    132–133.
  Wang, Shunzhu. "The Double-Voiced Feminine Discourses in Ding
    Ling's 'Miss Sophie's Diary' and Zora Neale Hurston's *Their Eyes
    Were Watching God*," *Tamkang R*, 28, i (1997), 137–138, 140–142,
    144–148, 153–154, 155.
"A Suicide's Diary"
  Findeisen, Raoul D. "*Kairos* or the Due Time . . . ," 240–241.
"When I Was in Xia Village"
  McDougall, Bonnie S., and Kam Louie. *The Literature of China* . . . ,
    214–215.

BIRAGO DIOP

"Les Mamelles"
  Harrow, Kenneth W. "Bessie Head and Death: Change on the
    Margins," in Barfoot, C. C., and Theo D'haen, Eds. *Shades of
    Empire* . . . , 175–177.

CHITRA BANERJEE DIVAKARUNI

"Doors"
  Leach, Laurie. "Conflict over Privacy in Indo-American Short
    Fiction," in Brown, Julie, Ed. *Ethnicity* . . . , 198, 199–201.

ALFRED DÖBLIN

"Der Dritte"
  Kyora, Sabine. "Zum Paradox in Döblins frühen Erzählungen," in
    Sander, Gabriele, Ed. *Internationales Alfred-Döblin-
    Kolloquium* . . . , 65–70.
"Die Ermordung einer Butterblume"
  Marx, Reiner. "Literatur und Zwangsneurose—Eine
    Gegenübertragungs-Improvisation zu Alfred Döblins früher

Erzählung 'Die Ermordung einer Butterblume,' " in Sander,
Gabriele, Ed. *Internationales Alfred-Döblin-Kolloquium* . . . ,
50–60.
"Die Tänzerin und der Leib"
Keck, Annette. "Lektüren der Frauen: Zur De(kon)struktion
literarischer Sinnbildungskonzepte im Frühwerk Alfred Döblins,"
in Sander, Gabriele, Ed. *Internationales Alfred-Döblin-
Kolloquium* . . . , 71–81.

E. L. DOCTOROW

"Willi"
Williams, John. *Fictions as False* . . . , 129–130.

MARY MAPES DODGE

"Sunday Afternoon in a Poor-House"
Thomson, Rosemarie G. "Crippled Girls and Lame Old Women:
Sentimental Spectacles of Sympathy in Nineteenth-Century
American Women's Writing," in Kilcup, Karen L., Ed. *Nineteenth-
Century American* . . . , 132–134, 135.

JOSÉ DONOSO

"Chatanooga Choo-choo"
Pérez, Janet. "Masks, Gender Expectations, Machismo and [Criss]
Cross-Gender Writing in the Fiction of José Donoso," *Hispano*, 119
(1997), 54.

HILDA DOOLITTLE [H.D.]

"Kora and Ka"
Tate, Trudi. "HD's War Neurotics," in Raitt, Suzanne, and Trudi Tate,
Eds. *Women's Fiction* . . . , 248–252.
———. *Modernism, History and the First* . . . , 20–25.

JOHN DOS PASSOS

"An Aesthete's Nightmare"
Nanney, Lisa. *John Dos Passos*, 40–41.
"The Almeh"
Casey, Janet G. *Dos Passos* . . . , 62–64.
Nanney, Lisa. *John Dos Passos*, 42–43.
"The Cardinal's Grapes"
Nanney, Lisa. *John Dos Passos*, 43–44.

FYODOR DOSTOEVSKY

FREDERICK DOUGLASS

"The Heroic Slave"
   Yarborough, Richard. "Race, Violence, and Manhood: The Masculine
   Ideal in Frederick Douglass's 'The Heroic Slave,' " in Jones, Anne
   G., and Susan V. Donaldson, Eds. *Haunted Bodies* . . . , 166–178.

ARTHUR CONAN DOYLE

"The Adventure of the Beryl Coronet"
   Kestner, Joseph A. *Sherlock's Men* . . . , 84–85.
   Rye, Marilyn. "Profession and Performance: The Work Ethic of
   Sherlock Holmes," in Putney, Charles R., Joseph A. C. King, and
   Sally Sugarman, Eds. *Sherlock Holmes*
   . . . , 72–73.
"The Adventure of Black Peter"
   Kestner, Joseph A. *Sherlock's Men* . . . , 145–147.
"The Adventure of the Blanched Soldier"
   Kestner, Joseph A. *Sherlock's Men* . . . , 194–198.
   Otis, Laura. "The Empire Bites Back: Sherlock Holmes as an Imperial
   Immune System," *Stud Twentieth-Century Lit*, 22 (1998), 38–39.
"The Adventure of the Blue Carbuncle"
   Baldwin, Dean. *Instructor's Resource* . . . , 68–69.
"The Adventure of the Bruce-Partington Plans"
   Kestner, Joseph A. *Sherlock's Men* . . . , 171–173.
"The Adventure of the Cardboard Box"
   Kestner, Joseph A. *Sherlock's Men* . . . , 109–110.
"The Adventure of Charles Augustus Milverton"
   Belsey, Catherine. "Constructing the Subject: Deconstructing the
   Text," in Warhol Robyn R., and Diane P. Herndl, Eds.
   Feminisms . . . , 604–606.
   Kestner, Joseph A. *Sherlock's Men* . . . , 147–148.
   Maertens, James W. "Masculine Power and the Ideal Reasoner:
   Sherlock Holmes, Technician-Hero," in Putney, Charles R., Joseph
   A. C. King, and Sally Sugarman, Eds. *Sherlock Holmes* . . . ,
   316–317.
"The Adventure of the Copper Beeches"
   Kestner, Joseph A. *Sherlock's Men* . . . , 92–94.
"The Adventure of the Creeping Man"
   Kestner, Joseph A. *Sherlock's Men* . . . , 191–194.
"The Adventure of the Crooked Man"
   Kestner, Joseph A. *Sherlock's Men* . . . , 102–104.
"The Adventure of the Dancing Men"
   Kestner, Joseph A. *Sherlock's Men* . . . , 36–37, 133–136.

"The Adventure of the Retired Colourman"
Kestner, Joseph A. *Sherlock's Men* . . . , 182–183.

"The Adventure of the Second Stain"
Kestner, Joseph A. *Sherlock's Men* . . . , 150–151.

"The Adventure of Shoscombe Old Place"
Kestner, Joseph A. *Sherlock's Men* . . . , 184–186.

"The Adventure of the Six Napoleons"
Kestner, Joseph A. *Sherlock's Men* . . . , 142–143.

"The Adventure of the Solitary Cyclist"
Kestner, Joseph A. *Sherlock's Men* . . . , 144–145.

"The Adventure of the Speckled Band"
Dadlez, E. M. *What's Hecuba to Him?* . . . , 148–149.
Hendershot, Cyndy. *The Animal Within* . . . , 139–148.
Kestner, Joseph A. *Sherlock's Men* . . . , 90–92.
Krasner, James. "Watson Falls Asleep: Narrative Frustration and
Sherlock Holmes," *Engl Lit Transition*, 40 (1997), 428–429.
Levine, Michael G. "The Vanishing Point . . . ," 252–254.
Schmitt, Cannon. *Alien Nation* . . . , 1–3, 157–159, 166–168.
Tatlow, Antony. "Interpretation and the Unconscious of the Text,"
Tamkang R, 26, iii (1996), 83–84.

"The Adventure of the Stockbroker's Clerk"
Kestner, Joseph A. *Sherlock's Men* . . . , 102.

"The Adventure of the Sussex Vampire"
Hendershot, Cyndy. "The Restoration of the Angel: Female
Vampirism in Doyle's 'The Adventure of the Sussux Vampire,' "
Victorian News, 89 (1996), 10–14.
Kestner, Joseph A. *Sherlock's Men* . . . , 183–184.

"The Adventure of the Three Gables"
Kestner, Joseph A. *Sherlock's Men* . . . , 188–189.

"The Adventure of the Three Garridebs"
Kestner, Joseph A. *Sherlock's Men* . . . , 190–191.

"The Adventure of the Three Students"
Kestner, Joseph A. *Sherlock's Men* . . . , 136–137.

"The Adventure of the Veiled Lodger"
Kestner, Joseph A. *Sherlock's Men* . . . , 181–182.

"The Adventure of Wisteria Lodge"
Kestner, Joseph A. *Sherlock's Men* . . . , 169–171.
Otis, Laura. "The Empire Bites . . . ," 54–55.

"The Adventure of the Yellow Face"
Kestner, Joseph A. *Sherlock's Men* . . . , 110–112.

"The Boscombe Valley Mystery"
Kestner, Joseph A. *Sherlock's Men* . . . , 81–83.
Kitts, Thomas M. "Unlikely Kinsmen: Holmes and Iago," in Putney,
Charles R., Joseph A. C. King, and Sally Sugarman, Eds. *Sherlock
Holmes* . . . , 220.

"A Case of Identity"
Kestner, Joseph A. *Sherlock's Men* . . . , 88–90.
Kromm, Sandra. "A Feminist Appraisal . . . ," 279–281.
Rye, Marilyn. "Profession and Performance . . . ," 67–68.

"The Disappearance of Lady Frances Carfax"
Kestner, Joseph A. *Sherlock's Men* . . . , 169–170.

"The Final Problem"
Kestner, Joseph A. *Sherlock's Men* . . . , 113–115.
Levine, Michael G. "The Vanishing Point . . . ," 254–255.

"The Five Orange Pips"
Kestner, Joseph A. *Sherlock's Men* . . . , 83–84.
Levine, Michael G. "The Vanishing Point . . . ," 260–268.
Rifelj, Carol. " 'Knowledge of Literature—Nil?' Sherlock Holmes the
Reader," *Clues*, 18, ii (1997), 11–16.

"His Last Bow"
Kestner, Joseph A. *Sherlock's Men* . . . , 173–175.

"The Hound of the Baskervilles"
Kestner, Joseph A. *Sherlock's Men* . . . , 122–130.
Raubicheck, Walter. " 'The Hound of the Baskervilles': Doyle,
Holmes, and the Unconscious," in Putney, Charles R., Joseph A. C.
King, and Sally Sugarman, Eds. *Sherlock Holmes* . . . , 287–295.

"The Man with the Twisted Lip"
Kestner, Joseph A. *Sherlock's Men* . . . , 95–97.
Krasner, James. "Watson Falls Asleep . . . ," 431.

"The Musgrave Ritual"
Kestner, Joseph A. *Sherlock's Men* . . . , 107–109.
Krasner, James. "Watson Falls Asleep . . . ," 426–428, 429–430,
433–434.

"The Red-Headed League"
Kestner, Joseph A. *Sherlock's Men* . . . , 86–88.
Krasner, James. "Watson Falls Asleep . . . ," 430–431.
Sweeney, Susan Elizabeth. "The Other Side of the Coin in Arthur
Conan Doyle's 'The Red-Headed League,' " in Putney, Charles R.,
Joseph A. C. King, and Sally Sugarman, Eds. *Sherlock Holmes* . . . ,
37–63.
van der Linde, Gerhard. "Shaped in the Image . . . ," 161–162.

"The Resident Patient"
Krasner, James. "Watson Falls Asleep . . . ," 431–432.

"A Scandal in Bohemia"
Kestner, Joseph A. *Sherlock's Men* . . . , 75–78.
Krasner, James. "Watson Falls Asleep . . . ," 434–435.
Kromm, Sandra. "A Feminist Appraisal . . . ," 270–271.
Maertens, James W. "Masculine Power and the Ideal Reasoner:
Sherlock Holmes, Technician-Hero," in Putney, Charles R., Joseph
A. C. King, and Sally Sugarman, Eds. *Sherlock Holmes* . . . , 308,
309.
Owen, Kathleen B. " 'The Game's Afoot': Predecessors and Pursuits

of a Postmodern Detective Novel," in Delamater, Jerome H., and
Ruth Prigozy, Eds. *Theory and Practice* . . . , 78–79.
Prchal, Timothy R. "An Ideal Helpmate: The Detective Character as
(Fictional) Object and Ideal Imago," in Delamater, Jerome H., and
Ruth Prigozy, Eds. *Theory and Practice* . . . , 32.
Sullivan, Mary Rose. "Sherlock Holmes and Sam Spade: Brothers
under the Skin," in Putney, Charles R., Joseph A. C. King, and Sally
Sugarman, Eds. *Sherlock Holmes* . . . , 177–178.

"The Sign of Four"
Kestner, Joseph A. *Sherlock's Men* . . . , 57–73.
Lehan, Richard. *The City in Literature* . . . , 85, 88–91.
Rye, Marilyn. "Profession and Performance . . . ," 67.

"A Study in Scarlet"
Kestner, Joseph A. *Sherlock's Men* . . . , 46–57.
Lehan, Richard. *The City in Literature* . . . , 86, 87–88.
Rye, Marilyn. "Profession and Performance . . . ," 66–67.
Weimer, Christopher B. "A Cervantine Reading of Conan Doyle:
Interpolated Narrative in 'A Study in Scarlet,' " in Putney, Charles
R., Joseph A. C. King, and Sally Sugarman, Eds. *Sherlock
Holmes* . . . , 201–209.

"The Terror of Blue John Gap"
Seed, David. "Eruptions of the Primitive into the Present: *The Jewel
of Seven Stars* and *The Lair of the White Worm*," in Hughes,
William, and Andrew Smith, Eds. *Bram Stoker* . . . , 197–199.

ROBERT DRAKE

"Mr. Marcus and the Overhead Bridge"
Perkins, James A. "Robert Drake: The Railroad as Metaphor," in
Folks, Jeffrey J., and James A. Perkins, Eds. *Southern Writers* . . . ,
109–110.

"A Ticket as Long as Your Arm"
Perkins, James A. "Robert Drake . . . ," 110–111.

"The Tower and the Pear Tree"
Perkins, James A. "Robert Drake . . . ," 111.

ANNETTE VON DROSTE-HÜLSHOFF

"Die Judenbuche"
Helfer, Martha B. " 'Wer wagt es eitlen Blutes Drang zu messen?':
Reading Blood in Annette von Droste-Huelshoff's 'Die
Judenbuche,' " *Germ Q*, 71 (1998), 228–252.
Huszai, Villö D. "-Denken Sie Sich, der Mergel ist unschuldig an dem
Morde—Zu Droste-Huelshoffs Novelle 'Die Judenbuche,' "
Zeitschrift für Deutsche Philologie, 116 (1997), 481–499.
Pickar, Gertrud B. "Die 'Bauernhochzeit' in Droste's 'Die

Judenbuche': A Contemporary Reading," in Bodi, Leslie, Günter
Helmes, Egon Schwarz, and Friedrich Voit, Eds.
Weltbürger—Textwelten, 68–92.
"Ledwina"
Kontje, Todd. *Women, the Novel . . .* , 130–135.
Sazaki, Kristina R. "The Crippled Text/Woman: Annette von Droste-
Hülshoff's 'Ledwina,' " *Monatshefte*, 89 (1997), 168–181.

ANDRE DUBUS

"Adultery"
Ferriss, Lucy. "Andre Dubus: 'Never Truly Members,' " in Folks,
Jeffrey J., and James A. Perkins, Eds. *Southern Writers . . .* ,
230–232.
————. " 'Never Truly Members': Andre Dubus's Patriarchal
Catholicism," *So Atlantic R*, 62, ii (1997), 43–47, 52–53.
"Anna"
Miner, Madonne. " 'Jumping from one heart to another': How Andre
Dubus Writes about Women," *Critique*, 39 (1997), 19–24.
"A Father's Story"
Ferriss, Lucy. " 'Never Truly Members' . . . ," 40–41.
"Leslie in California"
Miner, Madonne. " 'Jumping from one . . . ,' " 19, 24–27.
"Molly"
Ferriss, Lucy. "Andre Dubus . . . ," 232–236.
————. " 'Never Truly Members' . . . ," 47–52.
"Rose"
Miner, Madonne. " 'Jumping from one . . . ,' " 19, 27–30.

ANNE DUDEN

"Das Judasschaf"
Bird, Stephanie. "Desire and Complicity in Anne Duden's 'Das
Judasschaf,' " *Mod Lang R*, 93 (1998), 741–753.
Littler, Margaret. "Diverging Trends in Feminine Aesthetics: Anne
Duden and Brigitte Kronauer," in Williams, Arthur, Stuart Parkes,
and Julian Preece, Eds. *Contemporary . . .* , 163–164, 167–171.
Meusinger, Annette. "The Wired Mouth: On the Positionality of
Perception in Anne Duden's 'Opening of the Mouth' and 'Das
Judasschaf,' " *Women Germ Yearbook*, 13 (1997), 191–198,
200–201.
"Opening of the Mouth"
Meusinger, Annette. "The Wired . . . ," 190–192, 195–201.
"Tag und Nacht"
Bossinade, Johanna. "Original Differentiation: The Poetics of Anne

Duden," in Weedon, Chris, Ed. *Post-War Women's* . . . , 131–133, 136–148.

"Übergang"
Bossinade, Johanna. "Original Differentiation . . . ," 109–110.

DAPHNE DU MAURIER

"Don't Look Now"
Horner, Avril, and Sue Zlosnik. *Daphne du Maurier* . . . , 173–183.

PAUL LAURENCE DUNBAR

"The Lynching of Jube Benson"
Jones, Gayl. *Liberating Voices* . . . , 59–63; rpt. Wall, Cheryl A., Ed.
Zora Neale Hurston . . . , 156–160.

MARGUERITE DURAS

"Albert of the Capitals"
Watts, Philip. *Allegories of the Purge* . . . , 189.

"L'Amant"
Angelini, Eileen M. "Look Who's Talking: A Study of Narrative Voice in Marguerite Duras' 'L'Amant,' " *Cincinnati Romance R*, 14 (1995), 172–181.
Martín, Annabel. "Narrative and the Politics of Identity," *Selecta*, 13 (1992), 40–41.
Naturel, Mireille. "Ailleurs et altérité dans trios romans contemporains: 'L'Amant,' *Le Chercheur d'or, La Goutte d'or,*" *Etudes Francophones*, 13, i (1998), 29–33.
Rowley, Hazel. "That Black Limousine on the Mekong: Marguerite Duras' Chinese Puzzle," *Auto/Bio Stud*, 12, i (1997), 108–110, 113–115.
Solomon, Julie. " 'J'ai un visage détruit': Pleasures of Self-Portraiture in Marguerite Duras's 'L'Amant,' " *Australian J French Stud*, 34 (1997), 100–114.

"L'Homme assis dans le couloir"
Felka, Rike. "Das Begehren, markiert zu werden: Über Marguerite Duras und Elfriede Jelinek," in Härle, Gerhard, Maria Kalveram, and Wolfgang Popp, Eds. *Erkenntniswunsch* . . . , 217–219, 224.

"Monsieur X, Here Called Pierre Rabier"
Watts, Philip. *Allegories of the Purge* . . . , 189–193.

FRIEDRICH DÜRRENMATT

"Der Auftrag"
Crockett, Roger A. *Understanding* . . . , 182–188.
Plouffe, Bruce. *The Post-War Novella* . . . , 100–151.

"The Coup"
    Plouffe, Bruce. *The Post-War Novella* . . . , 152–175.
"Die Falle"
    Crockett, Roger A. *Understanding* . . . , 14–15.
"Grieche sucht Griechin"
    Crockett, Roger A. *Understanding* . . . , 72–79.
"Der Hund"
    Crockett, Roger A. *Understanding* . . . , 16–17.
"Minotaurus: Eine Ballade"
    Crockett, Roger A. *Understanding* . . . , 176–178.
"Mondfinsternis"
    Crockett, Roger A. *Understanding* . . . , 81–82.
"Die Panne"
    Crockett, Roger A. *Understanding* . . . , 93–95.
"Pilatus"
    Crockett, Roger A. *Understanding* . . . , 15–16.
"Der Sturz"
    Crockett, Roger A. *Understanding* . . . , 167–171.
"Der Tunnel"
    Crockett, Roger A. *Understanding* . . . , 17.

STUART DYBEK

"Death of the Rightfielder"
    Febles, Jorge. "Dying Players: Ramírez's 'El centerfielder' and
        Dybek's 'Death of the Rightfielder,' " *Confluencia*, 12, i (1996),
        157, 163–165.

EDITH EATON [SUI SIN FAR]

"Its Wavering Image"
    Lee, Rachel C. "Journalistic Representations of Asian Americans and
        Literary Responses, 1910–1920," in Cheung, King-Kok, Ed. *An
        Interethnic* . . . , 266–269.
    Roh-Spaulding, Carol. " 'Wavering' Images: Mixed-Race Identity in
        the Stories of Edith Eaton/Sui Sin Far," in Brown, Julie, Ed.
        Ethnicity . . . , 169–172.
"The Sing-Song Woman"
    Roh-Spaulding, Carol. " 'Wavering' Images . . . ," 164–166.
"The Smuggling of Tie Co"
    Roh-Spaulding, Carol. " 'Wavering' Images . . . ," 166–167.
"The Story of One White Woman Who Married a Chinese"
    Roh-Spaulding, Carol. " 'Wavering' Images . . . ," 167–169.

MARIA VON EBNER-ESCHENBACH

"Das Beste"
Brokoph-Mauch, Gudrun. " 'Die Frauen haben nichts als die Liege':
Variationen zum Thema Liebe in den Erzählungen der Marie von
Ebner-Eschenbach," in Strelka, Joseph P., Ed. *Des Mitleids
tiefe* . . . , 59–60.

"Erste Beichte"
Brokoph-Mauch, Gudrun. " 'Die Frauen . . . ,' " 73–75.

"Erste Trennung"
Brokoph-Mauch, Gudrun. " 'Die Frauen . . . ,' " 60–64, 71.

"Krambambuli"
Bauer, Werner M. "Falsche Analogie: Vermenschlichung und
Säkularisation in den Tiergeschichten der Marie von Ebner-
Eschenbach," in Strelka, Joseph P., Ed. *Des Mitleids tiefe* . . . ,
121–136, 142.

"Ein Lied"
Brokoph-Mauch, Gudrun. " 'Die Frauen . . . ,' " 73–75.

"Maslans Frau"
Brokoph-Mauch, Gudrun. " 'Die Frauen . . . ,' " 69–72.

"Ein Original"
Brokoph-Mauch, Gudrun. " 'Die Frauen . . . ,' " 73–75.

"Oversberg"
Pawlowa, Nina. "Der Konflikt als Grundstruktur in der Novellistik von
Marie von Ebner-Eschenbach und Jeremias Gotthelf," in Strelka,
Joseph P., Ed. *Des Mitleids tiefe* . . . , 157–161.

"Die Resel"
Brokoph-Mauch, Gudrun. " 'Die Frauen . . . ,' " 66–67.

"Die Sünderin"
Brokoph-Mauch, Gudrun. " 'Die Frauen . . . ,' " 67–69.

"Das tägliche Leben"
Brokoph-Mauch, Gudrun. " 'Die Frauen . . . ,' " 62–64.

"Unverbesserlich"
Brokoph-Mauch, Gudrun. " 'Die Frauen . . . ,' " 75–76.

"Wieder der Alte"
Brokoph-Mauch, Gudrun. " 'Die Frauen . . . ,' " 64–66, 72.

ESTEBAN ECHEVERRÍA

"The Matador"
Cabañas, Miguel A. "Generos al matadero: Esteban Echeverría y la
cuestión de los tipos literarios," *Revista de Crítica*, 24, xlviii (1998),
133–147.

UMBERTO ECO, WITH GIUSEPPE PONTIGGIA, GIANNI RIOTTA, AND ANTONIO TABUCCHI

"The Pharaoh's Curse"
  Bondanella, Peter. *Umberto Eco* . . . , 197–199.

JOSEPH VON EICHENDORFF

"Aus dem Leben eines Taugenichts"
  Cronjäger, Christine. "The Romantic Image of Nature in Joseph von
    Eichendorff's 'Aus dem Leben eines Taugenichts' and Washington
    Irving's 'Rip Van Winkle,' " in Wright, Will, and Steven Kaplan,
    Eds. *The Image of Nature* . . . , 127–129.

KURT EISNER

"The Firefly"
  Gurganus, Albert E. "A German Socialist's African *Märchen*: Kurt
    Eisner as *Aufklärer*," *J Black Stud*, 23 (1992), 214–217.

GEORGE ELIOT [MARY ANN EVANS]

"Amos Barton"
  Alley, Henry. *The Quest for Anonymity* . . . , 32–35.
"Brother Jacob"
  Hughes, Kathryn. *George Eliot: The Last* . . . , 238–239.
  Robertson, Linda K. *The Power of Knowledge* . . . , 32, 129–130.
"Janet's Repentance"
  Alley, Henry. *The Quest* . . . , 37–39.
  Barrat, Alain. "The Picture and the Message in George Eliot's *Scenes
    of Clerical Life*: The Thematic Function of the Rural Setting,"
    George Eliot-George Henry Lewes Stud, 30–31 (1996), 51–52,
    53–54.
  Judd, Catherine. *Bedside Seductions* . . . , 138–139, 143, 150.
  Logan, Deborah A. *Fallenness in Victorian* . . . , 22–23, 137–145.
  Robertson, Linda K. *The Power* . . . , 71, 87, 91, 128–129.
  Spilka, Mark. *Eight Lessons* . . . , 20–36.
  Weisser, Susan O. *A "Craving Vacancy"* . . . , 121–126.
"The Lifted Veil"
  Bull, Malcolm. "Mastery and Slavery in 'The Lifted Veil,' " *Essays
    Crit*, 48 (1998), 244–261.
  Flint, Kate. "Blood, Bodies, and 'The Lifted Veil,' " *Nineteenth-
    Century Lit*, 51 (1997), 455–473.
  Hughes, Kathryn. *George Eliot: The Last* . . . , 220–221.
  Robertson, Linda K. *The Power* . . . , 48–49.
  Wood, Jane. "Scientific Rationality and Fanciful Fiction: Gendered

Discourse in 'The Lifted Veil,' " *Women's Writing*, 3, ii (1996), 161–176.

"Mr. Gilfil's Love Story"
Alley, Henry. *The Quest* . . . , 31–32, 35–37.
Robertson, Linda K. *The Power* . . . , 121.
Thompson, Andrew. *George Eliot and Italy* . . . , 50, 51, 54–67.
Weisser, Susan O. *A "Craving Vacancy"* . . . , 118–121.

GEORGE ELLIOT

"An Act of Piety"
Lynch, Gerald. " 'To Keep What Was Good and Pass It On': George Elliott's Small Town Memorial, *The Kissing Man*," *Stud Canadian Lit*, 22, i (1997), 75–77.

"The Kissing Man"
Lynch, Gerald. " 'To Keep . . . ,' " 77–79.

"A Leaf for Everything Good"
Lynch, Gerald. " 'To Keep . . . ,' " 74–75, 79–81.

"The Listeners"
Lynch, Gerald. " 'To Keep . . . ,' " 83–84.

"A Room, a Light for Love"
Lynch, Gerald. " 'To Keep . . . ,' " 81–83.

"You'll Get the Rest of Him Soon"
Lynch, Gerald. " 'To Keep . . . ,' " 84–86.

"The Way Back"
Lynch, Gerald. "The One and the Many: Canadian Short Story Cycles," in Lounsberry, Barbara, et al., Eds. *The Tales We Tell* . . . , 41–42.
Lynch, Gerald. " 'To Keep . . . ,' " 88–90.

RALPH ELLISON

"Battle Royal"
Charters, Ann, and William E. Sheidley. *Resources* . . . , 5th ed., 80–81.

"King of the Bingo Game"
Ford, Joh, and Marjorie Ford. *Instructor's Manual* . . . , 64–65.

ENCHI FUMIKO

"Days of Hunger"
Ruch, Barbara. "Beyond Absolution: Enchi Fumiko's *The Waiting Years* and *Masks*," in Miller, Barbara S., Ed. *Masterworks of Asian* . . . , 443–444.

NAZLI ERAY

"Monte Kristo"
Bertram, Carel. "Restructuring the House, Restructuring the Self:
Renegotiating the Meanings of Place in the Turkish Short Story,"
in Arat, Zehra F., Ed. *Deconstructing Images* . . . , 268–269.

LOUISE ERDRICH

"American Horse"
Palmer, Linda. "Healing Ceremonies: Native American Stories of
Cultural Survival," in Brown, Julie, Ed. *Ethnicity* . . . , 110.
"Fleur"
Ford, Joh, and Marjorie Ford. *Instructor's Manual* . . . , 123–124.
"The Leap"
Ford, Joh, and Marjorie Ford. *Instructor's Manual* . . . , 124–125.
"The Red Convertible"
Charters, Ann, and William E. Sheidley. *Resources* . . . , 5th ed.,
83–84.
"Snares"
Baldwin, Dean. *Instructor's Resource* . . . , 210–211.

AHMED ESSOP

"Betrayal"
Sheckels, Theodore F. *The Lion* . . . , 55.
"Black and White"
Sheckels, Theodore F. *The Lion* . . . , 57.
"Gerty's Brother"
Sheckels, Theodore F. *The Lion* . . . , 57–58.
"The Hajji"
Sheckels, Theodore F. *The Lion* . . . , 53–55.
"The Notice"
Sheckels, Theodore F. *The Lion* . . . , 58–59.
"Two Sisters"
Sheckels, Theodore F. *The Lion* . . . , 55–57.

ALICE MAUDE EWELL

"Miss Tom and Peepsie"
Scheick, William J. "Introduction: Female Legacy, Narrative Agency
and Identity in Alice Maude Ewell's Fiction," in Scheick, William
J., Ed. *Alice Maude Ewell's* . . . , 9–14.

"A Woman's Fancy"
Scheick, William J. "Introduction . . . ," 15–23.

VANCE EWING

"Beelzebub"
Clark, Daniel A., and P. Andrew Miller. "Variations on the Plantation
Romance: Five Stories by Southern Women Writers," *Stud Popular
Culture*, 19, ii (1996), 112–114.
"An Old Whistle"
Clark, Daniel A., and P. Andrew Miller. "Variations . . . ," 107–109.
"A Promise Fulfilled"
Clark, Daniel A., and P. Andrew Miller. "Variations . . . ," 110–111.

HANS FALLADA

"Der Apparat der Liebe"
Ulrich, Roland. "Gefängnis als ästhetischer Erfahrungsraum bei
Fallada," in Müller-Waldeck, Gunnar, and Roland Ulrich, Eds. *Hans
Fallada* . . . , 138–139.
"Wandervögel"
Thöming Jürgen C. "Hans Fallada als verlorener Sohn Johannes
Gäntschow," in Müller-Waldeck, Gunnar, and Roland Ulrich, Eds.
Hans Fallada . . . , 190–191.

FANG JI

"The Visitor"
McDougall, Bonnie S., and Kam Louie. *The Literature of China* . . . ,
247–248.

BEVERLY FARMER

"A Drop of Water"
Hammett, Kristin. "Beverly Farmer: A Retrospective," *Southerly*, 56,
i (1996), 97–98.
"Home Time"
Hammett, Kristin. "Beverly Farmer . . . ," 95–96.
"Vase with Red Fishes"
Hammett, Kristin. "Beverly Farmer . . . ," 100–101.
"A Woman with Black Hair"
Hammett, Kristin. "Beverly Farmer . . . ," 95.

J[AMES] G[ORDON] FARRELL

"The Pussycat Who Fell in Love with the Suitcase"
Crane, Ralph J., and Jennifer Livett. *Troubled Pleasures* . . . , 137–149.

JAMES T. FARRELL

"Boyhood"
Fanning, Charles. "Introduction: James T. Farrell and Short Fiction,"
Chicago Stories [by James T. Farrell], xxv–xxvi.
"The Buddies"
Fanning, Charles. "Introduction . . . ," xxiv.
"A Front-Page Story"
Fanning, Charles. "Introduction . . . ," xxiv–xxv.
"Helen, I Love You"
Fanning, Charles. "Introduction . . . ," xxiii.
"Kilroy Was Here"
Fanning, Charles. "Introduction . . . ," xxvii–xxviii.
"Looking 'Em Over"
Fanning, Charles. "Introduction . . . ," xxiii–xxiv.
"The Scarecrow"
Fanning, Charles. "Introduction . . . ," xxiii.

WILLIAM FAULKNER

"Ad Astra"
Duvall, John N. "Faulkner's Crying Game: Male Homosexual Panic,"
in Kartiganer, Donald M., and Ann J. Abadie, Eds. *Faulkner and
Gender* . . . , 55–57.
"Afternoon of a Cow"
Duvall, John N. "Faulkner's Crying . . . ," 66–69.
"All the Dead Pilots"
Duvall, John N. "Faulkner's Crying . . . ," 58–60.
"And Now What's To Do?"
Polk, Noel. "Faulkner: The Artist as Cuckold," in Kartiganer, Donald
M., and Ann J. Abadie, Eds. *Faulkner and Gender* . . . , 33–34.
"The Artist"
Hönnighausen, Lothar. *Faulkner* . . . , 93–94.
"Artist at Home"
Hönnighausen, Lothar. *Faulkner* . . . , 88–93.
Polk, Noel. "Faulkner: The Artist . . . ," 36–39.
"Barn Burning"
Ford, Joh, and Marjorie Ford. *Instructor's Manual* . . . , 49–50.
Matthews, John T. "Faulkner and Proletarian Literature," in

Kartiganer, Donald M., and Ann J. Abadie, Eds. *Faulkner in Cultural . . .* , 172–174.

"The Bear"

MacKethan, Lucinda H. "The Grandfather Clause: Reading the Legacy from 'The Bear' to *Song of Solomon*," in Kolmerten, Carol A., Stephen M. Ross, and Judith B. Wittenberg, Eds. *Unflinching Gaze . . .* , 92–102, 103, 105–106, 107, 108–110, 112.

Özdemir, Erinç. "The Thematic and Structural Function of Time in William Faulkner's 'The Bear,' " *J Am Stud Turkey*, 3 (1996), 95–105.

Wallach, Rick. "Moby Bear: Thematics and Structural Concordances Between William Faulkner's 'The Bear' and Herman Melville's *Moby Dick*," *Southern Lit J*, 30, i (1997), 43–54.

Wang, Jennie. *Novelistic Love . . .* , 142–155, 158–161.

"Black Music"

Hönnighausen, Lothar. *Faulkner . . .* , 81–82, 84.

"Carcassonne"

Hönnighausen, Lothar. *Faulkner . . .* , 83–88.

"A Courtship"

Polk, Noel. "Faulkner: The Artist . . . ," 28–29.

"Delta Autumn"

Fowler, Doreen. *Faulkner . . .* , 155–159.

Singal, Daniel J. *William Faulkner . . .* , 275–276.

Wang, Jennie. "Romantic Love and Its Repudiation of Cultural Legacy: Faulkner's Silver Horn in 'Delta Autumn,' " *Short Story*, 4, ii, N.S. (1996), 85–102; rpt. in her *Novelistic Love . . .* , 141, 173–187.

"Divorce in Naples"

Parker, Robert D. "Sex and Gender, Feminine and Masculine: Faulkner and the Polymorphous Exchange of Cultural Binaries," in Kartiganer, Donald M., and Ann J. Abadie, Eds. *Faulkner and Gender . . .* , 79–81.

"Doctor Martino"

Boyd, Molly. "William Faulkner's 'Doctor Martino,' " *Southern Q*, 34, ii (1996), 39–49.

"Dry September"

Baldwin, Dean. *Instructor's Resource . . .* , 115–117.

Donaldson, Susan V. "Making a Spectacle: Welty, Faulkner, and Southern Gothic," *Mississippi Q*, 50 (1997), 572–573.

Jones, Anne G. " 'Like a Virgin': Faulkner, Sexual Cultures, and the Romance of Resistance," in Kartiganer, Donald M., and Ann J. Abadie, Eds. *Faulkner in Cultural . . .* , 44–45.

"Evangeline"

Batty, Nancy E. "Riff, Refrain, Reframe: Toni Morrison's Song of Absalom," in Kolmerten, Carol A., Stephen M. Ross, and Judith B. Wittenberg, Eds. *Unflinching Gaze . . .* , 85–87.

"The Fire and the Hearth"
Fowler, Doreen. *Faulkner* . . . , 162–164.
Godden, Richard. "Agricultural Adjustment, Revenants, Remnants, and Counter-Revolution in Faulkner's 'The Fire and the Hearth,' " *Faulkner J*, 12, ii (1997), 41–55.
Rowe, John C. *At Emerson's Tomb* . . . , 240–243.
Singal, Daniel J. *William Faulkner* . . . , 266–272.
Wang, Jennie. *Novelistic Love* . . . , 164–168.
Weinstein, Philip M. "Mister: The Drama of Black Manhood in Faulkner and Morrison," in Kartiganer, Donald M., and Ann J. Abadie, Eds. *Faulkner and Gender* . . . , 282–283.

"Go Down, Moses"
Fowler, Doreen. *Faulkner* . . . , 159–163, 164–166.
Singal, Daniel J. *William Faulkner* . . . , 272–275.
Wang, Jennie. *Novelistic Love* . . . , 187–189.

"The Hill" [earlier version of "Nympholepsy"]
Hönnighausen, Lothar. *Faulkner* . . . , 193, 268.

"Honor"
Parker, Robert D. "Sex and Gender . . . ," 89–92.

"A Justice"
Gray, Richard. " 'Implacable and Brooding Image': William Faulkner and Southern Landscape," in D'haen, Theo, and Hans Bertens, Eds. *"Writing" Nation* . . . , 134–137.

"Lo!"
Wadlington, Warwick. "The Guns of *Light in August*: War and Peace in the Second Thirty Years War," in Kartiganer, Donald M., and Ann J. Abadie, Eds. *Faulkner in Cultural* . . . , 135–136.

"Nympholepsy" [originally "The Hill"]
Hönnighausen, Lothar. *Faulkner* . . . , 188, 193, 200.

"An Odor of Verbena"
Schaller, Barry R. *A Vision of American* . . . , 40–44.
Yaeger, Patricia. "Faulkner's 'Greek Amphora Priestess': Verbena and Violence in *The Unvanquished*," in Kartiganer, Donald M., and Ann J. Abadie, Eds. *Faulkner and Gender* . . . , 208–209, 221–225.

"Old Man"
Lester, Cheryl. "*If I Forget Thee, Jerusalem* and the Great Migration: History in Black and White," in Kartiganer, Donald M., and Ann J. Abadie, Eds. *Faulkner in Cultural* . . . , 201–203.

"The Old People"
Wang, Jennie. *Novelistic Love* . . . , 171–173.

"Out of Nazareth"
Hönnighausen, Lothar. *Faulkner* . . . , 185, 193, 195.

"Pantaloon in Black"
Rowe, John C. *At Emerson's Tomb* . . . , 236–237.
Singal, Daniel J. *William Faulkner* . . . , 264–266.
Wang, Jennie. *Novelistic Love* . . . , 168–171.

"Red Leaves"
  Gray, Richard. " 'Implacable . . . ,' " 133–134.

"A Rose for Emily"
  Bourdieu, Pierre. "A Reflecting Story," trans. Richard Nice, in Roth,
    Michael S., Ed. *Rediscovering History* . . . , 371–377.
  Caesar, Judith. " 'Miss Leonora When Last Seen': Why Americans
    Run Away From Home," *Stud Short Fiction*, 34 (1997), 450–452,
    455–457.
  Charters, Ann, and William E. Sheidley. *Resources* . . . , 5th ed.,
    85–86.
  Ford, Joh, and Marjorie Ford. *Instructor's Manual* . . . , 47–48.
  O'Bryan-Knight, Jean. "From Spinster to Eunuch: William Faulkner's
    'A Rose for Emily' and Mario Vargas Llosa's *Los cachorros*,"
    Comp Lit Stud, 34 (1997), 328–347.
  Yağcioğlu, Semiramis. "Language, Subjectivity and Ideology in 'A
    Rose for Emily,' " *J Am Stud Turkey*, 2 (1995), 50–58.

"Skirmish at Sartoris"
  Doyle, Don H. "Faulkner's History: Sources and Interpretation," in
    Kartiganer, Donald M., and Ann J. Abadie, Eds. *Faulkner in
    Cultural* . . . , 26–27.
  Jones, Anne G. " 'Like a Virgin' . . . ," 53.
  Yaeger, Patricia. "Faulkner's . . . ," 214–221.

"The Tall Men"
  Singal, Daniel J. *William Faulkner* . . . , 276–277.

"That Evening Sun"
  Charters, Ann, and William E. Sheidley. *Resources* . . . , 5th ed.,
    87–88.

"There Was a Queen"
  Lahey, Michael E. "Narcissa's Love Letters: Illicit Space and the
    Writing of Female Identity in 'There Was a Queen,' " in Kartiganer,
    Donald M., and Ann J. Abadie, Eds. *Faulkner and Gender* . . . ,
    160–178.

"Tomorrow"
  Evans, Ron. "Faulkner's 'Tomorrow,' " *Explicator*, 56, ii (1998),
    95–99.

"Was"
  Wang, Jennie. *Novelistic Love* . . . , 162–164.

"Wash"
  Matthews, John T. "Faulkner and Proletarian . . . ," 170–172.

JESSIE REDMON FAUSET

"Double Trouble"
  Allen, Carol. *Black Women Intellectuals* . . . , 72–73.

"The Sleeper Wakes"
  Allen, Carol. *Black Women Intellectuals* . . . , 60–62.

FENG YUANJUN

"After the Separation"
  Lieberman, Sally T. *The Mother* . . . , 121–122.
"Fond Mother"
  Lieberman, Sally T. *The Mother* . . . , 122–124.
"Separation"
  Lieberman, Sally T. *The Mother* . . . , 119–121.

MARIE FÉRAUD

"Oh, the Poor Old Man"
  Rosello, Mireille. *Declining the Stereotype* . . . , 86, 87–95, 96–100.
"Les Ray Ban"
  Rosello, Mireille. *Declining* . . . , 47–56.

CRISTINA FERNÁNDEZ CUBAS

"Con Agata en Estambul"
  Pérez, Janet. "Cristina Fernández Cubas: Narrative Unreliability and
    the Flight from Clarity, or, the Quest for Knowledge in the Fog,"
    Hispano, 122, ii (1998), 33.
"El lugar"
  Pérez, Janet. "Cristina Fernández Cubas . . . ," 33, 35.
"La mujer de verde"
  Pérez, Janet. "Cristina Fernández Cubas . . . ," 32, 33.
"Mundo"
  Pérez, Janet. "Cristina Fernández Cubas . . . ," 31, 32, 33, 35, 36.

ROSARIO FERRÉ

"Cuando las mujeres quieren a los hombres"
  Cornejo-Parriego, Rosalía. "*Racialización* colonial y diferencia
    femenina en 'Love story' de Poniatowska y 'Cuando las mujeres
    quieren a los hombres' de Ferré," *Afro-Hispanic R*, 16, ii (1997),
    11–17.
  Puleo, Gustavo C. "Rosario Ferré: Nueva voz en el cuento
    puertorriqueño," *Cincinnati Romance R*, 12 (1993), 172–175.
  Shaw, Donald L. *The Post-Boom* . . . , 127–129.
"Isolda en el espejo"
  Murphy, Marie. "Rosario Ferré en el espejo: Defiance and
    Inversions," *Hispanic R*, 65 (1997), 146–149.
"El libro envenenado"
  Shaw, Donald L. *The Post-Boom* . . . , 135–137.
"Mercedes-Benz 220 SL"
  Shaw, Donald L. *The Post-Boom* . . . , 125–127.

"La muñeca menor"
Franco, Jean. "Self-Destructing Heroines," *Minnesota R*, 22 (1984),
111–112; rpt. in Foster, David W., and Daniel Altamiranda, Eds.
Twentieth-Century Spanish . . . , 275–276.
Shaw, Donald L. *The Post-Boom* . . . , 123–125.

"Sleeping Beauty"
Franco, Jean. "Self-Destructing Heroines," 112–113; in Foster, David
W., and Daniel Altamiranda, Eds. *Twentieth-Century Spanish* . . . ,
276–277.
Shaw, Donald L. *The Post-Boom* . . . , 129–130.

TIMOTHY FINDLEY

"Bragg and Minna"
Brydon, Diana. *Timothy Findley*, 133.

"Dust"
Brydon, Diana. *Timothy Findley*, 9, 135.

"A Gift of Mercy"
Brydon, Diana. *Timothy Findley*, 134.

"Hilton Agonistes"
Brydon, Diana. *Timothy Findley*, 136.

"Madonna of the Cherry Trees"
Brydon, Diana. *Timothy Findley*, 135–136.

"Stones"
Brydon, Diana. *Timothy Findley*, 133–134.

"What Mrs. Felton Knew"
Brydon, Diana. *Timothy Findley*, 131–132.

F. SCOTT FITZGERALD

"The Baby Party"
Ford, Joh, and Marjorie Ford. *Instructor's Manual* . . . , 46–47.

"Babylon Revisited"
Baldwin, Dean. *Instructor's Resource* . . . , 110–112.
Charters, Ann, and William E. Sheidley. *Resources* . . . , 5th ed., 89.
Cowart, David. " 'Babylon Revisited': The Tragedy of Charlie
Wales," *Cahiers de la Nouvelle*, 3 (1984), 21–27.
Kennedy, J. Gerald. "Figuring the Damage: Fitzgerald's 'Babylon
Revisited' and Hemingway's 'The Snows of Kilimanjaro,' " in
Kennedy, J. Gerald, and Jackson R. Bryer, Eds. *French
Connections* . . . , 318–327.
Zhang, Aiping. *Enchanted Places* . . . , 62, 74–76.

"Basil and Cleopatra"
Zhang, Aiping. *Enchanted Places* . . . , 99, 104.

"Boil Some Water—Lots of It"
Zhang, Aiping. *Enchanted Places* . . . , 157, 159.

"The Bridal Party"
　　Zhang, Aiping. *Enchanted Places* . . . , 70–76.

"Crazy Sunday"
　　Margolies, Alan. "The Maturing of F. Scott Fitzgerald," *Twentieth Century Lit*, 43 (1997), 86.

"Dalyrimple Goes Wrong"
　　Jolliff, William G. "The Damnation of Bryan Dalyrimple—and Theron Ware: F. Scott Fitzgerald's Debt to Harold Frederic," *Stud Short Fiction*, 35 (1998), 87–90.

"The Dance"
　　Margolies, Alan. "The Maturing . . . ," 89–90.

"The Diamond as Big as the Ritz"
　　Rand, William E. "The Structure of the Outsider in the Short Fiction of Richard Wright and F. Scott Fitzgerald," *Coll Lang Assoc J*, 40 (1996), 232–233, 234–237, 238, 240, 242–243, 244–245.

"Forging Ahead"
　　Zhang, Aiping. *Enchanted Places* . . . , 98–99.

"The Freshest Boy"
　　Zhang, Aiping. *Enchanted Places* . . . , 127.

"The Hotel Child"
　　Margolies, Alan. "The Maturing . . . ," 85.
　　Tintner, Adeline R. *Henry James's Legacy* . . . , 319–320.

"The Jelly Bean"
　　Zhang, Aiping. *Enchanted Places* . . . , 41–42.

"The Lees of Happiness"
　　Zhang, Aiping. *Enchanted Places* . . . , 42.

"Majesty"
　　Zhang, Aiping. *Enchanted Places* . . . , 125–126.

"A New Leaf"
　　Zhang, Aiping. *Enchanted Places* . . . , 61–62.

"One Trip Abroad"
　　Zhang, Aiping. *Enchanted Places* . . . , 60–61.

"The Scandal Detectives"
　　Zhang, Aiping. *Enchanted Places* . . . , 95.

"A Snobbish Story"
　　Gale, Robert L. "Fitzgerald's 'A Snobbish Story,' " *Explicator*, 55, iii (1997), 154.

GUSTAVE FLAUBERT

"Hérodias"
　　Berg, William J., and Laurey K. Martin. *Gustave Flaubert*, 22–27.

"The Legend of Saint Julian"
　　Aykanian, Nancy. "Flaubert's 'Medieval Trifle': 'La Légende de saint Julien l'Hospitalier,' " *Romance R*, 6, i (1996), 70–84.

Berg, William J., and Laurey K. Martin. *Gustave Flaubert*, 18–22, 26–27.

"A Simple Heart"
Baldwin, Dean. *Instructor's Resource* . . . , 52–55.
Berg, William J., and Laurey K. Martin. *Gustave Flaubert*, 14–18, 26–27.
Cervo, Nathan A. "Flaubert's 'Un Coeur simple,' " *Explicator*, 55, ii (1997), 80–81.
Charters, Ann, and William E. Sheidley. *Resources* . . . , 5th ed., 91–92.
Le Juez, Brigitte. "Représentations de femmes d'interiéur dans 'Un Coeur simple' de Gustave Flaubert," *Women French Stud*, 5 (1997), 19–26.
Reynolds, James M. "Flaubert's 'Un Coeur Simple,' " *Explicator*, 55, i (1996), 26–29.
Schwartz, Hillel. *The Culture* . . . , 144, 149, 153.

"Quidquid Volueris"
Diamond, Marie J. "Flaubert's 'Quidquid Volueris': The Colonial Father and the Poetics of Hysteria," *SubStance*, 85 (1998), 71–87.

GEORGE FLEMING [CONSTANCE FLETCHER]

"The Next House"
Tintner, Adeline R. *Henry James's Legacy* . . . , 41–42.

BRANQUINHO DA FONSECA

"O Barão"
Sternberg, Ricardo da S. L. "Alterity in 'O Barão,' " *Luso-Brazilian R*, 34, i (1997), 95–104.

THEODOR FONTANE

"Grete Minde"
Jensen, Birgit A. "Die Entfachung der kindlichen Vitalität in Theodor Fontanes 'Grete Minde,' " *Germ Life & Letters*, 50 (1997), 339–353.

PESI FONUA

"Mateuteu (Be Prepared)"
Flanagan, Kathleen. "Refractions on the Pacific Rim: Tongan Writers' Responses to Transnationalism," *World Lit Today*, 72 (1998), 92.

"The Point of No Return"
Flanagan, Kathleen. "Refractions . . . ," 92.

"Sun and Rain"
    Flanagan, Kathleen. "Refractions . . . ," 91–92.
"Tidal Wave"
    Flanagan, Kathleen. "Refractions . . . ," 91.

RICHARD FORD

"Children"
    Folks, Jeffrey J. "Richard Ford: Postmodern Cowboys," in Folks,
        Jeffrey J., and James A. Perkins, Eds. *Southern Writers* . . . ,
        216–217.
"Communist"
    Folks, Jeffrey J. "Richard Ford . . . ," 221–223.
"Empire"
    Folks, Jeffrey J. "Richard Ford . . . ," 219–220.
"Great Falls"
    Folks, Jeffrey J. "Richard Ford . . . ," 215–216.
"Optimists"
    Folks, Jeffrey J. "Richard Ford . . . ," 221.
"Rock Springs"
    Folks, Jeffrey J. "Richard Ford . . . ," 214–215.
"Winterkill"
    Folks, Jeffrey J. "Richard Ford . . . ," 220–221.

E. M. FORSTER

"Arthur Snatchfold"
    Bredbeck, Gregory W. " 'Queer Superstitions': Forster, Carpenter,
        and the Illusion of (Sexual) Identity," in Martin, Robert K., and
        George Piggford, Eds. *Queer Forster*, 50–51.
    Lane, Christopher. "Betrayal and Its Consolations in *Maurice*, 'Arthur
        Snatchfold,' and 'What Does It Matter? A Morality,' " in Martin,
        Robert K., and George Piggford, Eds. *Queer Forster*, 174–178,
        187–188.
"The Eternal Moment"
    Caporaletti, Silvana. "The Thematization of Time in E. M. Forster's
        'The Eternal Moment' and Joyce's 'The Dead,' " *Twentieth Century
        Lit*, 43 (1997), 408, 409–411, 411–414, 417.
"The Life to Come"
    Lane, Christopher. "Betrayal . . . ," 187–188.
"Little Imber"
    Martin, Robert K. " 'It Must Have Been the Umbrella': Forster's
        Queer Begetting," in Martin, Robert K., and George Piggford, Eds.
        Queer Forster, 272–273.

"Luigi Cornaro"
Piggford, George. "Camp Sites: Forster and the Biographies of Queer
Bloomsbury," in Martin, Robert K., and George Piggford, Eds.
Queer Forster, 106.

"The Machine Stops"
Caporaletti, Silvana. "Science as Nightmare: 'The Machine Stops' by
E. M. Forster," *Utopian Stud*, 8, ii (1997), 32–46.
Landon, Brooks. *Science Fiction* . . . , 11–21.
Seabury, Marcia Bundy. "Images of a Networked Society: E. M.
Forster's 'The Machine Stops,' " *Stud Short Fiction*, 34 (1997),
61–71.

"My Own Centenary"
Martin, Robert K., and George Piggford. "Introduction: Queer,
Forster?" in Martin, Robert K., and George Piggford, Eds. *Queer
Forster*, 5.

"The Obelisk"
Bredbeck, Gregory W. " 'Queer Superstitions' . . . ," 51.
Lane, Christopher. "Betrayal . . . ," 187.

"The Other Boat"
Dorland, Tamera. " 'Contrary to the Prevailing Current'?
Homoeroticism and the Voice of Maternal Law in 'The Other
Boat,' " in Martin, Robert K., and George Piggford, Eds. *Queer
Forster*, 193–219. [See also *Style*, 29 (1995), 474–497.]
Lane, Christopher. "Betrayal . . . ," 187.

"Other Kingdom"
Ferguson, Suzanne. "Local Color and the Function of Setting in the
English Short Story," in Kaylor, Noel H., Ed. *Creative and
Critical* . . . , 24–25.

"The Other Side of the Hedge"
Bristow, Joseph. "*Fratrum Societati*: Forster's Apostolic
Dedications," in Martin, Robert K., and George Piggford, Eds.
Queer Forster, 120–121.

"Ralph and Tony"
Martin, Robert K. " 'It Must Have . . . ,' " 258–260.

"The Road from Colonus"
Doloff, Steven. "More Classical Roots for Forster's 'The Road from
Colonus,' " *Notes & Queries*, 45 (1998), 233–234.

"The Story of a Panic"
Martin, Robert K., and George Piggford. "Introduction . . . ," 4–5.

"What Does It Matter? A Morality"
Lane, Christopher. "Betrayal . . . ," 179–186.

MARY WILKINS FREEMAN

"Arethusa"
Reichardt, Mary R. *Mary Wilkins Freeman* . . . , 81–83.

"The Balking of Christopher"
Reichardt, Mary R. *Mary Wilkins Freeman* . . . , 90–92.
"The Balsam Fir"
Reichardt, Mary R. *Mary Wilkins Freeman* . . . , 83–84.
"Brakes and White Vi'lets"
Mann, Susan G. "A House of One's Own: The Subversion of 'True Womanhood' in Mary E. Wilkins Freeman's Short Fiction," *Colby Q*, 34 (1998), 49.
"The Cat"
Reichardt, Mary R. *Mary Wilkins Freeman* . . . , 78–79.
"Christmas Jenny"
Mann, Susan G. "A House . . . ," 45, 48.
"A Church Mouse"
Elrod, Eileen R. "Rebellion, Restraint, and New England Religion: The Ambivalent Feminism of Mary Wilkins Freeman," in Schuldiner, Michael, Ed. *Studies in Puritan* . . . , 241.
"A Conflict Ended"
Camfield, Gregg. *Necessary Madness* . . . , 141–144, 148.
Reichardt, Mary R. *Mary Wilkins Freeman* . . . , 38–40.
"Evelina's Garden"
Reichardt, Mary R. *Mary Wilkins Freeman* . . . , 65–66.
"A Gatherer of Simples"
Mann, Susan G. "Gardening as 'Women's Culture' in Mary E. Wilkins Freeman's Short Fiction," *New England Q*, 71 (1998), 46–47.
"The Great Pine"
Reichardt, Mary R. *Mary Wilkins Freeman* . . . , 84–85.
"An Honest Soul"
Reichardt, Mary R. *Mary Wilkins Freeman* . . . , 54–57.
"An Independent Thinker"
Elrod, Eileen R. "Rebellion, Restraint . . . ," 242.
"The Jester"
Reichardt, Mary R. *Mary Wilkins Freeman* . . . , 101–102.
"Juliza"
Reichardt, Mary R. *Mary Wilkins Freeman* . . . , 26–31.
"Life-Everlastin' "
Reichardt, Mary R. *Mary Wilkins Freeman* . . . , 49–53.
"The Little Maid at the Door"
Reichardt, Mary R. *Mary Wilkins Freeman* . . . , 60–62.
"The Long Arm"
Behling, Laura. "Detective Deviation in Mary E. Freeman's 'The Long Arm,' " *Am Lit Realism*, 31 (1998), 75–89.
Reichardt, Mary R. *Mary Wilkins Freeman* . . . , 74–76.
Shaw, S. Bradley. "New England Gothic by the Light of Common

Day: Lizzie Borden and Mary E. Wilkins Freeman's 'The Long
Arm,' " *New England Q*, 70 (1997), 211–236.
"The Lost Ghost"
Reichardt, Mary R. *Mary Wilkins Freeman* . . . , 70–71.
"Louisa"
Cutter, Martha J. "Mary E. Wilkins Freeman's Two New England
Nuns," *Colby Q*, 26 (1990), 213–217, 220–225; rpt. Reichardt,
Mary R. *Mary Wilkins Freeman* . . . , 179–183, 186–192.
"Luella Miller"
Reichardt, Mary R. *Mary Wilkins Freeman* . . . , 72–73.
"A Mistaken Charity"
Mann, Susan G. "Gardening . . . ," 47–48.
―――. "A House . . . ," 48.
"A Moral Exigency"
Reichardt, Mary R. *Mary Wilkins Freeman* . . . , 35–38.
"A New England Nun"
Barnstone, Aliki. "Houses within Houses: Emily Dickinson and Mary
Wilkins Freeman's 'A New England Nun,' " *Centennial R*, 28
(1984), 129–135; rpt. Reichardt, Mary R. *Mary Wilkins
Freeman* . . . , 167–171.
Camfield, Gregg. *Necessary Madness* . . . , 148–149.
Cutter, Martha J. "Mary E. Wilkins Freeman's . . . ," 213–220; rpt.
Reichardt, Mary R. *Mary Wilkins Freeman* . . . , 179–186.
Fienberg, Lorne. "Mary E. Wilkins Freeman's 'Soft Diurnal
Commotion': Women's Work and Strategies of Containment," *New
England Q*, 62 (1989), 483–488, 503–504; rpt. Reichardt, Mary R.
Mary Wilkins Freeman . . . , 173–177.
Mann, Susan G. "A House . . . ," 48.
+Pryse, Majorie. "An Uncloistered 'New England Nun,' " in
Reichardt, Mary R. *Mary Wilkins Freeman* . . . , 159–166.
Reichardt, Mary R. *Mary Wilkins Freeman* . . . , 33–35.
"An Object of Love"
Reichardt, Mary R. *Mary Wilkins Freeman* . . . , 21–26.
"The Old Maid Aunt"
Reichardt, Mary R. *Mary Wilkins Freeman* . . . , 99–100.
"Old Woman Magoun"
Reichardt, Mary R. *Mary Wilkins Freeman* . . . , 96–97.
"On the Walpole Road"
Elrod, Eileen R. "Rebellion, Restraint . . . ," 242–243.
"The Outside of the House"
Reichardt, Mary R. *Mary Wilkins Freeman* . . . , 106–107.
"The Parrot"
Reichardt, Mary R. *Mary Wilkins Freeman* . . . , 79–81.
"A Poetess"
Camfield, Gregg. *Necessary Madness* . . . , 145–157.

Campbell, Donna M. *Resisting Regionalism* . . . , 27–28.
Reichardt, Mary R. *Mary Wilkins Freeman* . . . , 45–48.
"The Reign of the Doll"
Reichardt, Mary R. *Mary Wilkins Freeman* . . . , 92–93.
"The Revolt of Mother"
Baldwin, Dean. *Instructor's Resource* . . . , 64–66.
Charters, Ann, and William E. Sheidley. *Resources* . . . , 5th ed.,
93–94.
Cheung, Kai-chong. "Female Rebellion: Old Style and New," in
Akiyama, Masayuki, and Yiu-nam Leung, Eds. *Crosscurrents* . . . ,
201–203.
Elrod, Eileen R. "Rebellion, Restraint . . . ," 238–240, 248.
Reichardt, Mary R. *Mary Wilkins Freeman* . . . , 42–43.
"The Revolt of Sophia Lane"
Reichardt, Mary R. *Mary Wilkins Freeman* . . . , 89–90.
"Sarah Edgewater"
Reichardt, Mary R. *Mary Wilkins Freeman* . . . , 105–106.
"The School-Teacher's Story"
Reichardt, Mary R. *Mary Wilkins Freeman* . . . , 69–70.
"The Secret"
Reichardt, Mary R. *Mary Wilkins Freeman* . . . , 97–99.
"The Selfishness of Amelia Lamkin"
Reichardt, Mary R. *Mary Wilkins Freeman* . . . , 93–95.
"The Southwest Chamber"
Reichardt, Mary R. *Mary Wilkins Freeman* . . . , 71–72.
"A Symphony in Lavender"
Mann, Susan G. "A House . . . ," 44, 48.
"Two Old Lovers"
Campbell, Donna M. *Resisting Regionalism* . . . , 68–69.
"A Village Singer"
Camfield, Gregg. *Necessary Madness* . . . , 137–139.
Campbell, Donna M. *Resisting Regionalism* . . . , 27.
Elrod, Eileen R. "Rebellion, Restraint . . . ," 241–242.
Reichardt, Mary R. *Mary Wilkins Freeman* . . . , 43–45.

CARLOS FUENTES

"Aura"
Gallo, Marta. "Proyección de 'La cena' de Alfonso Reyes en 'Aura'
de Carlos Fuentes," in Herrera, Sara P., Ed. *El cuento mexicano* . . . ,
237–256.
Montero, Bernal H. " 'Aura': Seducción y Lectura," *Antípodas*, 8–9
(1996–1997), 44–55.
Pérez, Genaro J. "La configuración de elementos góticos en
'Constancia,' *Aura* y 'Tlactocatzine, del jardín de Flandes' de
Carlos Fuentes," *Hispania*, 80 (1997), 16–17.

Veeder, William. "James and Fame Enduring," *Henry James R*, 19 (1998), 265–267, 269–270, 272–273, 274, 277.
Zubizarreta, John. "The Intertextual Intrigue of Carlos Fuentes's 'Aura,' " *MIFLC R*, 1 (1991), 139–148.
"Constancia"
    Pérez, Genaro J. "La configuración . . . ," 14–16.
"Mother's Day"
    + Valdés, María Elena de. *The Shattered Mirror . . .* , 53–60.
    Van Delden, Maarten. *Carlos Fuentes . . .* , 154–161.
"Sons of the Conquerer"
    Helmuth, Chalene. *The Postmodern Fuentes*, 129–130.
"These Were Palaces"
    Baldwin, Dean. *Instructor's Resource . . .* , 192–194.
"Tlactocatzine, del jardín de Flandes"
    Pérez, Genaro J. "La configuración . . . ," 17–18.
"The Two Americas"
    Helmuth, Chalene. *The Postmodern Fuentes*, 131–132.
"The Two Shores"
    Helmuth, Chalene. *The Postmodern Fuentes*, 130–131.
    Jay, Paul. "Translation, Invention, Resistance: Rewriting the Conquest in Carlos Fuentes's 'The Two Shores,' " *Mod Fiction Stud*, 43 (1997), 405–408, 413–431.

FUKAZAWA SHICHIRÔ

"Narayama-Bushikô"
    Siganos, André. "L'Écriture de la montagne," *Revue de Littérature Comparée*, 3 (July–Sept., 1998), 355–367.

HENRY BLAKE FULLER

"Carl Carlsen's Progress"
    Szuberla, Guy. " 'Carl Carlesen's Progress' and Henry Blake Fuller's Silences," *Am Lit Realism*, 31 (1998), 12–23.

FÜRUZAN [TOTAL NAME]

"The Girl from the Provinces"
    Bertram, Carel. "Restructuring the House, Restructuring the Self: Renegotiating the Meanings of Place in the Turkish Short Story," in Arat, Zehra F., Ed. *Deconstructing Images . . .* , 265–266, 267–268.

ILYAS AHMAD GADDI

"Aren't You My Sister Salma"
    Rahim, Habibeh. "The Mirage of Faith and Justice: Some

Sociopolitical and Cultural Themes in Post-Colonial Urdu Short
Stories," in Hawley, John C., Ed. *The Postcolonial Crescent* . . . ,
235–236.

ERNEST J. GAINES

"Bloodline"
Carmean, Karen. *Ernest J. Gaines* . . . , 148–151.
"Just Like a Tree"
Carmean, Karen. *Ernest J. Gaines* . . . , 152–155.
"A Long Day in November"
Carmean, Karen. *Ernest J. Gaines* . . . , 138–142.
"The Sky Is Gray"
Baldwin, Dean. *Instructor's Resource* . . . , 159–161.
Carmean, Karen. *Ernest J. Gaines* . . . , 142–145.
"Three Men"
Carmean, Karen. *Ernest J. Gaines* . . . , 145–148.

MARY GAITSKILL

"Tiny, Smiling Daddy"
Charters, Ann, and William E. Sheidley. *Resources* . . . , 5th ed.,
95–96.

TESS GALLAGHER

"Rain Flooding Your Campfire"
Charters, Ann, and William E. Sheidley. *Resources* . . . , 5th ed.,
97–98.

MAVIS GALLANT

"1993"
Charters, Ann, and William E. Sheidley. *Resources* . . . , 5th ed., 99.

GAO XIAOSHENG

"Li Shunda Builds a House"
McDougall, Bonnie S., and Kam Louie. *The Literature of China* . . . ,
374–375.

GUY GARCIA

"La Promesa"
Christie, John S. *Latino Fiction* . . . , 166–167.

GABRIEL GARCÍA MÁRQUEZ

"El avión de la bella durmiente"
Méndez, José L. "Los peregrinos extraviados: Reflexiones sobre 'Las cosas extrañas que le suceden a los latinoamericanos en Europa,' " *Torre*, 10, i–ii (1996), 160–161.

"Balthazar's Marvelous Afternoon"
Fajardo-Acosta, Fidel. "Art, Economics, Religion and Society: A Vision of Redemption in Gabriel García Márquez's 'La prodigiosa tarde de Baltazar,' " *Hispanic J*, 17, i (1996), 31–43.

"Buen viaje, señor presidente"
Camacho Delgado, José M. "De Tormes a Aracataca: Una interpretación de 'Buen viaje, señor presidente,' " *Revista de Estudios Colombianos*, 17 (1997), 10–13.
Méndez, José L. "Los peregrinos extraviados . . . ," 163–164.
Pérez, Henry. "Democratic President or Dictator? The Nature of the Presidency in García Márquez's 'Buen viaje, señor presidente,' " *Pubs Arkansas Philol Assoc*, 22, ii (1996), 65–75.

"Chronicle of a Death Foretold"
Pettey, John C. "Nietzsche's *Birth of Tragedy* and Euripides's *Bacchae* as Sources for the Apollonian and Dionysian Aspects of García Márquez's 'Chronicle of a Death Foretold,' " *Hispano*, 121 (1997), 21–34.
Rendon, Mario. "The Latino and His Culture: 'Chronicle of a Death Foretold' by García Márquez," *Am J Psychoanalysis*, 54 (1994), 345–358.
Solotorevsky, Myrna. "Estética de la totalidad y estética de la fragmentación," *Hispamérica*, 25 (1996), 26–34.
Zamora, Lois P. *The Usable Past* . . . , 59–67.

"Funerales de la Mamá Grande"
+ Castillo, Debra A. "The Storyteller and the Carnival Queen: 'Funerales de la Mamá Grande,' " in Foster, David W., and Daniel Altamiranda, Eds. *Twentieth-Century Spanish* . . . , 185–195.

"The Handsomest Drowned Man in the World"
Ford, Joh, and Marjorie Ford. *Instructor's Manual* . . . , 79–80.

"María dos Prazeres"
Méndez, José L. "Los peregrinos extraviados . . . ," 163, 164.

"Monologue of Isabel Watching It Rain in Macondo"
Baldwin, Dean. *Instructor's Resource* . . . , 150–152.

"One Day After Saturday"
Rama, Angel. "Un novelista de la violencia americana," in Simón Martínez, Pedro, Ed. *Sobre García Márquez*, 55–56, 58; rpt. "A Chronicler of American Violence," in Fiddian, Robin, Ed., *García Márquez*, 43–44, 46.

"La santa"
Méndez, José L. "Los peregrinos extraviados . . . ," 162–163.

"A Very Old Man with Enormous Wings"
Charters, Ann, and William E. Sheidley. *Resources* . . . , 5th ed.,
100–101.
Penuel, Arnold M. "The Contingency of Reality in García Márquez's
'Un señor muy viejo con unas alas enormes," *Romance Notes*, 38
(1998), 191–197.

FRANCISCO GARCÍA PAVÓN

"Los andamios"
Belmonte Serrano, José. "Cuento, luego existo: *La Guerra de los dos
mil años*, de Francisco García Pavón," *Boletín de la Biblioteca de
Menéndez Pelayo*, 72 (1996), 265–266.
"El avión en paz"
Belmonte Serrano, José. "Cuento, luego existo . . . ," 264–265.
"El cementerio capitoné"
Belmonte Serrano, José. "Cuento, luego existo . . . ," 263–264.
"La Fiesta Nacional"
Belmonte Serrano, José. "Cuento, luego existo . . . ," 265.
"Muerte y blancura de Baudelio Perona Cepeda"
Belmonte Serrano, José. "Cuento, luego existo . . . ," 260–261.

DIANE GARDNER

"The Land Girl"
Lassner, Phyllis. *British Women Writers* . . . , 134–136.

JOHN GARDNER

"The Art of Living"
Nutter, Ronald G. *A Dream of Peace* . . . , 208–212.
"Come on Back"
Nutter, Ronald G. *A Dream of Peace* . . . , 18, 185–187.
"The Library Horror"
Nutter, Ronald G. *A Dream of Peace* . . . , 40–41.
"Redemption"
Nutter, Ronald G. *A Dream of Peace* . . . , 9–10, 12–17, 19–20, 23–25.

HELEN GARNER

"Cosmo Cosmolino"
Kelly, Philippa. "Transgressive Spaces: Helen Garner's *Cosmo
Cosmolino*," *Westerly*, 40, i (1995), 21–25.
"Recording Angel"
Kelly, Philippa. "Transgressive . . . ," 20–21.

HUGH GARNER

"One-Two-Three Little Indians"
Ware, Tracy. "Race and Conflict in Garner's 'One-Two-Three Little Indians' and Laurence's 'The Loons,' " *Stud Canadian Lit*, 23, ii (1998), 72–75.

ELENA GARRO

"El árbol"
San Pedro, Teresa A. "Suicida / Fratricida / Deicida / Mujer en el cuento de Elena Garro 'El árbol,' " in Hernández de López, Ana M., Ed. *Narrativa hispanoamericana* . . . , 57–70.

ANDREW P. GASKELL

"The Big Game"
Crawford, Scott A. G. M. "A National Ethos in Three Dimensions: Rugby in Contemporary New Zealand Fiction," *Arete*, 4, i (1986), 59–61.

ELIZABETH CLEGHORN GASKELL

"Cousin Phillis"
Pettitt, Clare. " 'Cousin Holman's Dresser': Science, Social Change, and the Pathologized Female in Gaskell's 'Cousin Phillis,' " *Nineteenth-Century Lit*, 52 (1998), 471–489.
"The Doom of the Griffiths"
Stitt, Megan P. *Metaphors of Change* . . . , 34–40.
"Lizzie Leigh"
Logan, Deborah A. *Fallenness in Victorian* . . . , 76–82.
"The Well of Pen-Morfa"
Logan, Deborah A. *Fallenness* . . . , 71–76.

THÉOPHILE GAUTIER

"Arria Marcella, souvenir de Pompeii"
Brix, Michel. "Résurrection du passé et creation romantique: A propos d' 'Arria Marcella,' " *Bull de la Soc Théophile Gautier*, 18 (1996), 227–237.
Cussac, Héléne. "L'Espace pompéien dans 'Arria Marcella,' " *Francofonia*, 34 (1998), 137–150.
Montoro-Araque, Mercedes. "De l'inertie corporelle à la vivification de la Pierre: L'unité du 'corps fantastique' feminine chez Théophile Gautier," in Marigny, Jean, Intro., *Images fantastiques du corps*, 77–79.

"La Cafetière"
  Montoro-Araque, Mercedes. "De l'inertie . . . ," 70–71.
"Jettatura"
  Fischer, Dominique D. " 'Jettatura': La Comédie de l'impensable ou
    les masques du demon descriptif," *Bull de la Soc Théophile
    Gautier*, 18 (1996), 271–285.
  Met, Philippe. "Fantastique et herméneutique: Le Clair-obscur des
    signes dans 'Jettatura,' " *Bull de la Soc Théophile Gautier*, 20
    (1998), 73–96.
"La Morte amoureuse"
  Montoro-Araque, Mercedes. "De l'inertie . . . ," 73–74.
"Omphale ou la tapisserie amoureuse"
  Montoro-Araque, Mercedes. "De l'inertie . . . ," 71–73.
"La Pied de momie"
  Montoro-Araque, Mercedes. "De l'inertie . . . ," 75–76.

GE FEI

"A Flock of Brown Birds"
  Zhang, Xudong. *Chinese Modernism* . . . , 172–183.
"Green-Yellow"
  Zhang, Xudong. *Chinese Modernism* . . . , 191–199.
"The Lost Boat"
  Zhang, Xudong. *Chinese Modernism* . . . , 183–190.
"Recollection of Mr. Wuyou"
  Zhang, Xudong. *Chinese Modernism* . . . , 164–169.

MARTHA GELLHORN

"Portrait of a Lady"
  Tintner, Adeline R. *Henry James's Legacy* . . . , 331–332.

WILLIAM GIBSON

"The Gernsback Continuum"
  Stevens, Tyler. "The Sinister Fruitiness' of Machines: *Neuromancer*,
    Internet Sexuality, and the Turing Test," *Stud Novel*, 28 (1996),
    420–423; rpt. [under the name of Tyler Curtain] in Sedgwick, Eve
    K., Ed. *Novel Gazing* . . . , 135–137.

CHARLOTTE PERKINS GILMAN

"Ad'line"
  Knight, Denise D. *Charlotte Perkins Gilman* . . . , 36–38.

"Bee Wise"
   Beer, Janet. *Kate Chopin, Edith Wharton* . . . , 175–176.
   Knight, Denise D. *Charlotte Perkins Gilman* . . . , 80–81.

"The Boys and the Butter"
   Knight, Denise D. *Charlotte Perkins Gilman* . . . , 73.

"The Chair of English"
   Knight, Denise D. *Charlotte Perkins Gilman* . . . , 71.

"Circumstances Alter Cases"
   Knight, Denise D. *Charlotte Perkins Gilman* . . . , 39–41.

"Clifford's Tower"
   Knight, Denise D. *Charlotte Perkins Gilman* . . . , 30–32.

"The Cottagette"
   Knight, Denise D. *Charlotte Perkins Gilman* . . . , 67.

"A Day's Berryin' "
   Knight, Denise D. *Charlotte Perkins Gilman* . . . , 35–36.

"Dr. Clair's Place"
   Knight, Denise D. *Charlotte Perkins Gilman* . . . , 56–57.

"An Extinct Angel"
   Knight, Denise D. *Charlotte Perkins Gilman* . . . , 27–28.

"The Giant Wistaria"
   Knight, Denise D. *Charlotte Perkins Gilman* . . . , 18–23.
   + Scharnhorst, Gary. "['The Giant Wistaria']," in Knight, Denise D.,
   Charlotte Perkins Gilman . . . , 166–173.

"The Girl in the Pink Hat"
   Beer, Janet. "Charlotte Perkins Gilman and Women's Health: 'The
   Long Limitation,' " in Gough, Val, and Jill Rudd, Eds. *A Very
   Different Story* . . . , 65–66.

"Her Doll"
   Knight, Denise D. *Charlotte Perkins Gilman* . . . , 83–84.

"Her Memories"
   Beer, Janet. *Kate Chopin, Edith Wharton* . . . , 191.
   Knight, Denise D. *Charlotte Perkins Gilman* . . . , 79–80.

"His Mother"
   Knight, Denise D. *Charlotte Perkins Gilman* . . . , 71–72.

"An Honest Woman"
   Cutter, Martha J. "Of Metatexts, Metalanguages, and Possible Worlds:
   The Metanarrative in C. P. Gilman's Late Short Fiction," *Am Lit
   Realism*, 31 (1998), 45–47.

"The Hypnotizer"
   Knight, Denise D. *Charlotte Perkins Gilman* . . . , 54.

"Improving on Nature"
   Beer, Janet. *Kate Chopin, Edith Wharton* . . . , 159–161.

"Joan's Defender"
   Knight, Denise D. *Charlotte Perkins Gilman* . . . , 73–74.

Peyser, Thomas. *Utopia & Cosmopolis* . . . , 74–77.
Siegel, Jennifer S. "Charlotte Perkins (Stetson) Gilman's 'The Yellow
    Wallpaper': Fiction 'With a Purpose' and the Need to Know the
    Real Story," *CEA Critic*, 59, iii (1997), 44–57.
Smith, Evans L. "Myths of Poesis, Hermeneusis, and Psychogenesis:
    Hoffmann, Tagore, and Gilman," *Stud Short Fiction*, 34 (1997),
    230–232.
Wiesenthal, Chris. *Figuring Madness* . . . , 23–40.
Wolfreys, Julian. *The Rhetoric* . . . , 75–84.

GEORGE GISSING

"The House of Cobwebs"
    Ferguson, Suzanne. "Local Color and the Function of Setting in the
    English Short Story," in Kaylor, Noel H., Ed. *Creative and
    Critical* . . . , 27–28.

ANATOLII GLADILIN

"A Rehearsal on Friday"
    Ziolkowski, Margaret. *Literary Exorcisms* . . . , 13, 23, 29.

ERNEST GLANVILLE

"Abe Pike and the Honey-Bird"
    MacKenzie, Craig. "Artfulness in the Early South African Oral-Style
    Story: Ernest Glanville's 'Abe Pike' Tales," *J So African Stud*, 23,
    iv (1997), 548.
"End of the Scouting"
    MacKenzie, Craig. "Artfulness . . . ," 548–549.
"A Kaffir's Play"
    MacKenzie, Craig. "Artfulness . . . ," 549–550.
"Uncle Abe's Big Shoes"
    MacKenzie, Craig. "Artfulness . . . ," 546, 547.

ELLEN GLASGOW

"Dare's Gift"
    Goodman, Susan. *Ellen Glasgow: A Biography*, 146–147.
"The Shadowy Third"
    Goodman, Susan. *Ellen Glasgow: A Biography*, 146.

SUSAN GLASPELL

"A Jury of Her Peers"
    Baldwin, Dean. *Instructor's Resource* . . . , 91–93.

NIKOLAI GOGOL

"The Diary of a Madman"
Gasperetti, David. *The Rise of the Russian* . . . , 195–196.
Waszink, Paul M. "The King Knocks: Writers and Readers in Gogol's 'Diary of a Madman,' " *Russian Lit*, 41, i (1997), 61–92.

"The Nose"
Doležel, Lubomír. *Heterocosmica* . . . , 162.

"The Overcoat"
Ayers, Carolyn J. "Analytical Mimesis in the Russian Tale and Gogol's 'The Overcoat,' " in Scholz, Bernhard F., Ed. *Mimesis: Studien* . . . , 265–269.
Baldwin, Dean. *Instructor's Resource* . . . , 39–41.
Charters, Ann, and William E. Sheidley. *Resources* . . . , 5th ed., 105–106.
Doležel, Lubomír. *Heterocosmica* . . . , 161–162.
Gasperetti, David. *The Rise* . . . , 161, 194, 196–197.
Meletinsky, Eleazar M. *The Poetics of Myth*, 265.

WILLIAM GOLDING

"The Inheritors"
Shepherd, Valerie. *Literature about Language*, 10–31.

PEDRO A. GÓMEZ VALDERRAMA

"¡Tierra!"
Díaz, Luis Correa. "El grito colombino de '¡Tierra!' en el relato de Pedro Gómez Valderrama," *Thesaurus*, 49, i (1994), 92–109.

ALLEGRA GOODMAN

"And Also Much Cattle"
Cronin, Gloria L. "Immersions in the Postmodern: The Fiction of Allegra Goodman," in Halio, Jay L., and Ben Siegel, Eds. *Daughters of Valor* . . . , 254–255.

"Fait"
Cronin, Gloria L. "Immersions . . . ," 253–254.

"Fannie Mae"
Cronin, Gloria L. "Immersions . . . ," 265.

"Fantasy Rose"
Cronin, Gloria L. "Immersions . . . ," 261.

"Further Ceremony"
Cronin, Gloria L. "Immersions . . . ," 255–256.

"Mosquitoes"
Cronin, Gloria L. "Immersions . . . ," 262–263.

"One Down: A Story"
   Cronin, Gloria L. "Immersions . . . ," 265.
"Onionskin"
   Cronin, Gloria L. "Immersions . . . ," 256–258.
"Oral History"
   Cronin, Gloria L. "Immersions . . . ," 252–253.
"The Persians"
   Cronin, Gloria L. "Immersions . . . ," 261–262.
"Retrospective"
   Cronin, Gloria L. "Immersions . . . ," 255.
"Sarah"
   Cronin, Gloria L. "Immersions . . . ," 263–265.
"The Succession"
   Cronin, Gloria L. "Immersions . . . ," 251.
"Total Immersion"
   Cronin, Gloria L. "Immersions . . . ," 251–252.
"Variant Text"
   Cronin, Gloria L. "Immersions . . . ," 249–250.
"The Wedding of Henry Markowitz"
   Cronin, Gloria L. "Immersions . . . ," 259–261.
"Wish List"
   Cronin, Gloria L. "Immersions . . . ," 250–251.
"Young People"
   Cronin, Gloria L. "Immersions . . . ," 258–259.

NADINE GORDIMER

"Ah, Woe is Me"
   Narang, Harish. "Literature and Society in South Africa (Changing
   Sub-Text in the Stories of Nadine Gordimer)," *Panjab Univ
   Research Bull*, 24, i (1993), 61–63.
"A Chip of the Glass Ruby"
   Narang, Harish. "Literature and Society . . . ," 65–67.
"Country Lovers"
   Charters, Ann, and William E. Sheidley. *Resources . . .* , 5th ed., 108.
"Crimes of Conscience"
   Ford, Joh, and Marjorie Ford. *Instructor's Manual . . .* , 70–71.
"The Lion on the Freeway"
   Sheckels, Theodore F. *The Lion . . .* , xi, xiii.
"Once Upon a Time"
   Froelich, Vera P., and Jennifer Halle. "Gordimer's 'Once Upon a
   Time,' " *Explicator*, 56, iv (1998), 213–215.
"The Smell of Death and Flowers"
   Narang, Harish. "Literature and Society . . . ," 63–65.

"Something for the Time Being"
Shepherd, Valerie. *Literature about Language*, 146–164.
"Spoils"
Baldwin, Dean. *Instructor's Resource . . .* , 217–219.

ANGÉLICA GORODISCHER

"Los embriones del violeta"
Juzyn-Amestoy, Olga. "La narrativa fantástica de Angélica
Gorodischer: La mirada 'femenina' y los límites del deseo," *Letras
Femeninas, Número Extraordinario Conmemorativo: 1974–1994*,
87–96.

JUANA MANUELA GORRITI

"El emparedado"
Barrera, Trinidad. "La fantasía de Juana Manuela Gorriti,"
Hispamérica, 25, lxxiv (1996), 109–110.
"El fantasma de un rencor"
Barrera, Trinidad. "La fantasía . . . ," 110.
"Quien escucha su mal oye"
Barrera, Trinidad. "La fantasía . . . ," 106–109.
"Una visita infernal"
Barrera, Trinidad. "La fantasía . . . ," 110.
"Yerbas y alfileres"
Barrera, Trinidad. "La fantasía . . . ," 110–111.

REMY DE GOURMONT

"Le Magnolia"
Stableford, Brian. "*Sang* for Supper: Notes on the Metaphorical Use
of Vampires in *The Empire of Fear* and *Young Blood*," in Gordon,
Joan, and Veronica Hollinger, Eds. *Blood Read . . .* , 69–70.

WILLIAM GOYEN

"The Children of Old Somebody"
Zamora, Lois P. *The Usable Past . . .* , 115–116.
"The Fair Sister"
Horvath, Brooke. "Misreading (in) 'The Fair Sister,' " in Horvath,
Brooke, Irving Malin, and Paul Ruffin, Eds. *A Goyen
Companion . . .* , 29–43.
"Ghost and Flesh, Water and Dirt"
Zamora, Lois P. *The Usable Past . . .* , 114–115.

"In the Icebound Hothouse"
Kuehl, John. "Goyen's Garden," in Horvath, Brooke, Irving Malin, and Paul Ruffin, Eds. *A Goyen Companion* . . . , 85–88, 91–94, 95–96.

"Palm"
Malin, Irving. "Palm Reading," in Horvath, Brooke, Irving Malin, and Paul Ruffin, Eds. *A Goyen Companion* . . . , 125–130.

"Precious Door"
Kuehl, John. "Goyen's Garden," 89–90.

"Spain"
Strandberg, Victor. "*In a Farther Country*: The Goyen-McCullers Freak Show," in Horvath, Brooke, Irving Malin, and Paul Ruffin, Eds. *A Goyen Companion* . . . , 140, 143–144, 146–149.

"Tongues of Men and of Angels"
Repusseau, Patrice. "El Mudo Speaking: A Winged Victory in 'Tongues of Men and of Angels,' " in Horvath, Brooke, Irving Malin, and Paul Ruffin, Eds. *A Goyen Companion* . . . , 98–99, 101–102, 112–114, 114–115, 121.

PATRICIA GRACE

"Between Earth and Sky"
Carrera Suárez, Isabel. "Towards a Female Language of Childbirth," in Barfoot, C. C., and Theo D'haen, Eds. *Shades of Empire* . . . , 185–186.

"At the River"
Baldwin, Dean. *Instructor's Resource* . . . , 184–185.

KATHERINE WHYTE GRANT

"Moileag"
Bateman, Meg. "Women's Writing in Scottish Gaelic Since 1750," in Gifford, Douglas, and Dorothy McMillan, Eds. *A History* . . . , 671–672.

HENRY GREEN

"The Lull"
Deeming, David. "Henry Green's War: 'The Lull' and the Postwar Demise of Green's Modernist Aesthetic," *Mod Fiction Stud*, 44 (1998), 867–873, 875–877.

JULIEN GREEN

"Christine"
O'Dwyer, Michael. *Julien Green* . . . , 28–30, 31.

"Les Clefs de la mort"
O'Dwyer, Michael. *Julien Green* . . . , 28, 29, 30–33.
"Léviathan"
O'Dwyer, Michael. *Julien Green* . . . , 25–28.
"Voyageur sur la terre"
O'Dwyer, Michael. *Julien Green* . . . , 33–35.

GRAHAM GREENE

"A Day Saved"
Merivale, Patricia. "Gumshoe Gothics: 'The Man of the Crowd' and His Followers," in Prier, A., and Gerald Gillespie, Eds. *Narrative Ironies*, 173–174.

FREDERICK PHILIP GROVE [FELIX PAUL GREVE]

"Snow"
New, W. H. "A Geography of 'Snow': Reading Notes," *Stud Canadian Lit*, 23, i (1998), 52–74.

ALBERTO GUERRA

"Espejo de paciencia"
Alvarez, José B. "(Re)escritura de la violencia: El individuo frente la historia en la cuentística novísima cubana," *Chasqui*, 26, ii (1997), 91–92.

JOÃO GUIMARÃES ROSA

"Seqüência"
McGuirk, Bernard. *Latin American* . . . , 252–255.
"The Third Bank of the River"
McGuirk, Bernard. *Latin American* . . . , 247–250.

ROMESH GUNESEKERA

"Batik"
Burnett, Paula. "The Captives and the Lion's Claw: Reading Romesh Gunesekera's *Monkfish Moon*," *J Commonwealth Lit*, 32, ii (1997), 6–7, 9–10.
"Captives"
Burnett, Paula. "The Captives . . . ," 10–12, 12–13.
"A House in the Country"
Burnett, Paula. "The Captives . . . ," 7–8.

"Monkfish Moon"
Burnett, Paula. "The Captives . . . ," 8, 12.

MADAN GUPTA

"A Mother's Prayer"
Rahim, Habibeh. "The Mirage of Faith and Justice: Some
Sociopolitical and Cultural Themes in Post-Colonial Urdu Short
Stories," in Hawley, John C., Ed. *The Postcolonial Crescent* . . . ,
241–242.
"The Rapist"
Rahim, Habibeh. "The Mirage of Faith . . . ," 243–244.

H. RIDER HAGGARD

"Hunter Quatermain's Story"
Baldwin, Dean. *Instructor's Resource* . . . , 61–62.

THOMAS CHANDLER HALIBURTON

"Sayings and Doings in Cumberland"
New, W. H. *Land Sliding* . . . , 193–194.

ANNA FIELDING HALL [SAME AS MRS. S. C. HALL]

"Lilly O'Brien"
Ferguson, Suzanne. "Local Color and the Function of Setting in the
English Short Story," in Kaylor, Noel H., Ed. *Creative and
Critical* . . . , 11–12.

RADCLYFFE HALL

"Miss Ogilvy Finds Herself"
Buck, Claire. " 'Still Some Obstinate Emotion Remains': Radclyffe
Hall and the Meanings of Service," in Raitt, Suzanne, and Trudi
Tate, Eds. *Women's Fiction* . . . , 181–188.

HAN SHAOGONG

"Pa Pa Pa"
McDougall, Bonnie S., and Kam Louie. *The Literature of China* . . . ,
406–407.

PETER HANDKE

"Das Feuer"
  Pilipp, Frank. "In Defense of Kafka: The Case of Peter Handke," in Pilipp, Frank, Ed. *The Legacy of Kafka* . . . , 137–144.
"Langsame Heimkehr"
  Sokel, Walter H. "Das Apokalyptische und dessen Vermeidung: Zum Zeitbegriff im Erzählwerk Handkes," in Bodi, Leslie, Günter Helmes, Egon Schwarz, and Friedrich Voit, Eds. *Weltbürger—Textwelten*, 280–285.

BARRY HANNAH

"Bats Out of Hell Division"
  Weston, Ruth D. "Debunking Some Illusions About Self and Story in the Surfiction of Barry Hannah," in Kaylor, Noel H., Ed. *Creative and Critical* . . . , 296–297.
"Evening of the Yarp: A Report by Roonswent Dover"
  Weston, Ruth D. "Debunking . . . ," 298–299.
"Scandale d'Estime"
  Weston, Ruth D. "Debunking . . . ," 293–295.
"The Spy of Loog Root"
  Weston, Ruth D. "Debunking . . . ," 299–300.
"Two Things, Dimly, Were Going at Each Other"
  Weston, Ruth D. "Debunking . . . ," 300–301.

MAURITS HANSEN

"Luren"
  Sjåvik, Jan. "A Rhetorical Approach to Three Norwegian Short Stories," *Selecta*, 14 (1993), 80–81.

THOMAS HARDY

"Barbara of the House of Grebe"
  Gilmartin, Sophie. *Ancestry and Narrative* . . . , 227–228.
"The Duke's Reappearance"
  Ray, Martin. "Thomas Hardy's 'The Duke's Reappearance,' " *Notes & Queries*, 43 (1997), 435–436.
"The Fiddler of the Reels"
  Daleski, H. M. *Thomas Hardy* . . . , 21–22.
"Squire Petrick's Lady"
  Derry, Stephen. "Vandyke and Hardy's 'Squire Petrick's Lady,' " *Notes & Queries*, 45 (1998), 226–227.
"The Three Strangers"
  Ferguson, Suzanne. "Local Color and the Function of Setting in the

English Short Story," in Kaylor, Noel H., Ed. *Creative and Critical* . . . , 16–18.

"The Unconquerable" [written with Florence Dugdale]
Tintner, Adeline R. *Henry James's Legacy* . . . , 156–158.

FRANCES ELLEN WATKINS HARPER

"The Two Offers"
Rosenthal, Debra J. "Deracialized Discourse: Temperance and Racial Ambiguity in Harper's 'The Two Offers' and *Sowing and Reaping*," in Reynolds, David S., and Debra J. Rosenthal, Eds. *The Serpent* . . . , 157–158, 160–162.

GEORGE WASHINGTON HARRIS

"Parson Bullen's Lizards (Retribution)"
Camfield, Gregg. *Necessary Madness* . . . , 122, 124–126.

JIM HARRISON

"Brown Dog"
Johnson, Robert. "Brown Dog's Insight: The Fiction of Jim Harrison," *Notes Contemp Lit*, 27, i (1997), 2–4.

"The Seven-Ounce Man"
Johnson, Robert. "Brown Dog's . . . ," 2–4.

BRET HARTE

"The Luck of Roaring Camp"
Nissen, Axel. "The Feminization of Roaring Camp: Bret Harte and *The American Woman's Home*," *Stud Short Fiction*, 34 (1997), 379–388.
Stevens, J. David. " 'She war a woman': Family Roles, Gender, and Sexuality in Bret Harte's Western Fiction," *Am Lit*, 69 (1997), 573–576.

"Miggles"
Stevens, J. David. " 'She war a woman' . . . ," 576–580.

"The Poet of Sierra Flat"
Stevens, J. David. " 'She war a woman' . . . ," 585–589.

"Tennessee's Partner"
Stevens, J. David. " 'She war a woman' . . . ," 580–585.

WILHELM HAUFF

"Jud Suess"
Chase, Jeffersons. "The Wandering Court Jew and The Hand of God:

Wilhelm Hauff's 'Jud Suess' as Historical Figure," *Mod Lang R*, 93 (1998), 724–740.

ELIZABETH HAUPTMANN

"Auf der Suche nach Nebeneinnahmen"
Führich, Angelika. " 'Dieses Chicago, das haben Männer aufgebaut?'
Elizabeth Hauptmanns Kurzprosa der zwanziger Jahre," *Brecht Yearbook*, 21 (1996), 93–95.

"Happy End"
Führich, Angelika. " 'Dieses Chicago . . . ,' " 94–95.

"Julia ohne Romeo"
Führich, Angelika. " 'Dieses Chicago . . . ,' " 89–92.

"Er soll dein Herr sein"
Führich, Angelika. " 'Dieses Chicago . . . ,' " 91–95.

GERHART HAUPTMANN

"Der Apostel"
Fattori, Anna. "Gerhart Hauptmann 'Der Apostel' (1890)," in Tarot, Rolf, and Gabriela Scherer, Eds. *Erzählkunst der Vormoderne*, 282–303.

NATHANIEL HAWTHORNE

"The Ambitious Guest"
Marshall, Ian. *Story Line* . . . , 209–213.

"The Artist of the Beautiful"
Warner, Nicholas O. *Spirits of America* . . . , 137, 138.

"The Birthmark"
Hendershot, Cyndy. *The Animal Within* . . . , 86–91.

"Circe's Palace"
Warner, Nicholas O. *Spirits of America* . . . , 128–129.

"The Celestial Railroad"
Met, Pierre. "Un Rêve de Hawthorne: 'The Celestial Railroad,' " in Pereira, Frederico, Ed. *Eleventh International* . . . , 181–186.

"David Swan: A Fantasy"
Warner, Nicholas O. *Spirits of America* . . . , 130–131.

"Egotism; or, The Bosom-Serpent"
Alkana, Joseph. *The Social Self* . . . , 44–47.
Gatta, John. *American Madonna* . . . , 14.

"Fancy's Show-Box"
Warner, Nicholas O. *Spirits of America* . . . , 138.

"Fire Worship"
　　Allison, John. "Conservative Architecture: Hawthorne in Melville's 'I and My Chimney,' " *So Central R*, 13, i (1996), 20.

"The Gentle Boy"
　　Alkana, Joseph. *The Social Self . . .* , 66–67.
　　Colacurcio, Michael J. *Doctrine and Difference . . .* , 187.

"The Great Carbuncle"
　　Marshall, Ian. *Story Line . . .* , 214–224.

"The Great Stone Face"
　　Alkana, Joseph. *The Social Self . . .* , 42–44.
　　Marshall, Ian. *Story Line . . .* , 205–207.

"The Hollow of the Three Hills"
　　Johnston, Paul K. "Playing at Work: Nathaniel Hawthorne's Triple Thinking in 'The Hollow of the Three Hills,' " *Nathaniel Hawthorne R*, 23, ii (1997), 2–3, 4, 5–7.

"The Maypole of Merry Mount"
　　Ford, Joh, and Marjorie Ford. *Instructor's Manual . . .* , 8–9.

"The Minister's Black Veil"
　　Birk, John F. "Hawthorne's Mister Hooper: The Veil of Ham?" *Prospects*, 21 (1996), 3–6.
　　Danow, David K. *Models of Narrative . . .* , 91–99.
　　Randall, Dale B. J. "Image-Making and Image-Breaking: Seeing 'The Minister's Black Veil' through a Miltonic Glass, Darkly," *Resources Am Lit Stud*, 23, i (1997), 19–20, 22–25.
　　Stouck, David, and Janet Giltrow. " 'A Confused and Doubtful Sound of Voices': Ironic Contingencies in the Language of Hawthorne's Romances," *Mod Lang R*, 92 (1997), 563, 564, 565–566, 567, 570–571.

"My Kinsman, Major Molineux"
　　Baldwin, Dean. *Instructor's Resource . . .* , 31–33.
　　Charters, Ann, and William E. Sheidley. *Resources . . .* , 5th ed., 109–110.
　　Covici, Pascal. *Humor and Revelation . . .* , 28–36.
　　Sarbu, Aladár. *The Reality of Appearances . . .* , 69–70.

"Passages from a Relinquished Work"
　　Curnutt, Kirk. *Wise Economies . . .* , 48, 51.

"Peter Goldthwaite's Treasure"
　　Allison, John. "Conservative Architecture . . . ," 19, 21.

"Rappaccini's Daughter"
　　Brown, Gillian. "Hawthorne's Endangered Daughters," *Western Hum R*, 50–51, iv–i (1997), 328–331.
　　Gatta, John. *American Madonna . . .* , 13, 14.
　　Hendershot, Cyndy. *The Animal Within . . .* , 91–96.
　　Ringel, Faye. "Genetic Experimentation: Mad Scientists and the Beast" in Sullivan, C. W., Ed. *The Dark Fantastic . . .* , 41–42.
　　Roger, Patricia M. "Taking a Perspective: Hawthorne's Concept of

Language and Nineteenth-Century Language Theory," *Nineteenth-Century Lit*, 51 (1997), 447–453.

Stouck, David, and Janet Giltrow. " 'A Confused . . . ,' " 564, 565, 567, 568–570.

"Wakefield"

Curnutt, Kirk. *Wise Economies* . . . , 43–55.

Danow, David K. *Models of Narrative* . . . , 71, 72, 74–75.

Polk, Noel. "Welty, Hawthorne, and Poe: Men of the Crowd and the Landscape of Alienation," *Mississippi Q*, 50 (1997), 554–557.

Sarbu, Aladár. *The Reality of Appearances* . . . , 71–72.

Swope, Richard. "Approaching the Threshold(s) in Postmodern Detective Fiction: Hawthorne's 'Wakefield' and Other Missing Persons," *Critique*, 39 (1998), 209–211.

Zamora, Lois P. *The Usable Past* . . . , 94–95.

"Young Goodman Brown"

Alkana, Joseph. *The Social Self* . . . , 47–48, 50–54.

Burleson, Donald R. "Sabbats: Hawthorne/Wharton," *Stud Weird Fiction*, 12 (1993), 12–16.

Charters, Ann, and William E. Sheidley. *Resources* . . . , 5th ed., 111–112.

Ford, Joh, and Marjorie Ford. *Instructor's Manual* . . . , 7–8.

Martin, Terry J. *Rhetorical Deception* . . . , 19–31.

Sarbu, Aladár. *The Reality of Appearances* . . . , 70–71.

Stouck, David, and Janet Giltrow. " 'A Confused . . . ,' " 565, 566–568.

ELIZABETH HAY

"Crossing the Snow Line"

Paillot, Patricia. "Correspondances et esthétique des contraires dans 'Crossing the Snow Line' d'Elizabeth Hay," *Annales Centre Recherches*, 19 (1994), 63–68.

JOHN HAY

"The Foster Brothers"

Thomas, Brook. *American Literary Realism* . . . , 182–183.

BESSIE HEAD

"The Cardinals"

Cloete, Nettie. "Exile, Gender and Prejudice: Bessie Head and the Problem of Oppression," in Bogaards, Winnifred M., Ed. *Literature of Region* . . . , 314–315.

"The Collector of Treasures"

Harrow, Kenneth W. "Bessie Head and Death: Change on the

Margins," in Barfoot, C. C., and Theo D'haen, Eds. *Shades of Empire* . . . , 177–178.

Ingersoll, Earl G. "Reconstructing Masculinity in the Postcolonial World of Bessie Head," *ArielE*, 29, iii (1998), 109–115.

Matsikidze, Isabella. "The Postnationalistic Phase: A Poetics of Bessie Head's Fiction," *Bucknell R*, 37, i (1993), 132.

"The Deep River: A Story of Ancient Tribal Migration"
Ingersoll, Earl G. "Reconstructing . . . ," 97–99.

"Heaven Is Not Closed"
Harrow, Kenneth W. "Bessie Head . . . ," 165–171.

"Life"
Charters, Ann, and William E. Sheidley. *Resources* . . . , 5th ed., 114.
Harrow, Kenneth W. "Bessie Head . . . ," 172–175.
Ingersoll, Earl G. "Reconstructing . . . ," 106–109.

"The Lovers"
Ingersoll, Earl G. "Reconstructing . . . ," 103–104.

"A Period of Darkness"
Ingersoll, Earl G. "Reconstructing . . . ," 101–103.

"A Power Struggle"
Ingersoll, Earl G. "Reconstructing . . . ," 99–101.

"Property"
Ingersoll, Earl G. "Reconstructing . . . ," 104–106.

"Snapshots of a Wedding"
Ford, Joh, and Marjorie Ford. *Instructor's Manual* . . . , 89–90.
Harrow, Kenneth W. "Bessie Head . . . ," 174–175.

JOHANN PETER HEBEL

"Die Drei Diebe"
Geisenhansluecke, Achim. "Vor dem Gesetz der Dichtung: Hebel und Kafka," *Germ R*, 73 (1998), 300–302.

"Wie der Zundelfrieder eines Tages aus dem Gefaengnis entwich und gluecklich ueber die Grenzen kam"
Geisenhansluecke, Achim. "Vor dem . . . ," 299–302, 304.

ANNE HÉBERT

"Aurélien, Clara, Mademoiselle et le Lieutenant anglais"
Pestre de Almeida, Lilian. "Une Douloureuse Éclipse amoureuse dans le paysage québécois: Analyse du dernier récit d'Anne Hébert," *Francofonia*, 33 (1997), 91–103.

"Le Printemps de Catherine"
Knight, Kelton W. "Memory, the Imperfect Mirror: A Study of Anne Hébert's 'Le Printemps de Catherine,' " *Selecta*, 13 (1992), 14–16.

SADEQ HEDAYAT

"Abu Nasr's Throne"
Zarrin, Ali. "The Rhetoric of Self and Other in Selected Iranian Short
Stories, 1906–1979," *Int'l Fiction R*, 24, i-ii (1997), 37–38.

CHRISTOPH HEIN

"Die Familiengruft"
Jackman, Graham. " 'Unverhofftes Wiedersehen': Narrative
Paradigms in Christoph Hein's *Nachtfahrt und früher Morgen* and
Exekution eines Kalbes," *Germ Life & Letters*, 51 (1998), 405.
"Kein Seeweg nach Indien"
Roth, David. "Christoph Hein und Jurek Becker: Zwei Krititsche
Autoren aus der DDR ueber die Wende und zum Vereinten
Deutschland," *Germ Life & Letters*, 50 (1997), 185–188.
"Unverhofftes Wiedersehen"
Jackman, Graham. " 'Unverhofftes Wiedersehen' . . . ," 405–406.
"Die Vergewaltigung"
Jackman, Graham. " 'Unverhofftes Wiedersehen' . . . ," 406–407.

HEINRICH HEINE

"Aus den Memoiren des Herren von Schnabelewopski"
Schirmeisen, Andreas. "Heines 'Aus den Memoiren des Herren von
Schnabelewopski': Eine parodistische Negation des
Bildungsromans?" *Heine Jahrbuch*, 35 (1996), 66–78.
"The Rabbi of Bacherach"
Bauer, Barbara. "Nicht alle Hebräer sind dürr und freudlos: Heinrich
Heines Ideen zur Reform des Judentums in der Erzählung 'Der
Rabbi von Bacherach,' " *Heine Jahrbuch*, 35 (1996), 23–51.
Hermand, Jost. "Heinrich Heine's Ghetto Tale 'The Rabbi of
Bacherach' is Published," trans. James Steakley, in Gilman, Sander
L., and Jack Zipes, Eds. *Yale Companion* . . . , 152–157.
Lutz, Edith. "Der Held in mehrfacher Gestalt: Der 'Rabbi von
Bacherach' als Held des mythischen Zirkels," *Heine Jahrbuch*, 35
(1996), 57–64.

ROBERT HEINLEIN

"Solution Unsatisfactory"
Disch, Thomas M. *The Dreams Our Stuff* . . . , 83–84.

LILIANA HEKER

"Dios"
Corpa Vargas, Mirta. *Los cuentos de* . . . , 70–71.

JOSEPH HELLER

"The Polar Bear in the Ice Box"
Craig, David M. *Tilting at Mortality* . . . , 26.

"Room for Renoir"
Craig, David M. *Tilting at Mortality* . . . , 260.

"A Scientific Fact"
Craig, David M. *Tilting at Mortality* . . . , 122.

"A Simple Mission"
Craig, David M. *Tilting at Mortality* . . . , 260–261.

"The Sound of Asthma"
Craig, David M. *Tilting at Mortality* . . . , 261.

"World Full of Great Cities"
Craig, David M. *Tilting at Mortality* . . . , 36–37.

"Young Girl on a Train"
Craig, David M. *Tilting at Mortality* . . . , 36.

ERNEST HEMINGWAY

"After the Storm"
Leff, Leonard J. *Hemingway and His Conspirators* . . . , 152.

"An Alpine Idyll"
Busch, Frieder. "Too Long, Or Not Too Long: Ernest Hemingway's Alpenidyll," in Hebel, Udo J., and Karl Ortseifen, Eds. *Transatlantic Encounters* . . . , 257–268.
Leff, Leonard J. *Hemingway* . . . , 34.

"The Battler"
Clifford, Stephen P. *Beyond the Heroic "I"* . . . , 161–166.

"Big Two-Hearted River"
Curnutt, Kirk. *Wise Economies* . . . , 7–8.
Doležel, Lubomír. *Heterocosmica* . . . , 43–48.
Waldmeir, Joseph J. *"Miss Tina Did It"* . . . , 53–68.

"The Butterfly and the Tank"
Watson, William B. "The Other Paris Years of Ernest Hemingway: 1937 and 1938," in Kennedy, J. Gerald, and Jackson R. Bryer, Eds. *French Connections* . . . , 150–152.

"A Canary for One"
Carter, Steven. "Hemingway's 'A Canary for One,' " *Explicator*, 55, iii (1997), 154–155.
Leff, Leonard J. *Hemingway* . . . , 48.
Tintner, Adeline R. *Henry James's Legacy* . . . , 315–317.

"Cat in the Rain"
Clifford, Stephen P. *Beyond the Heroic 'I'* . . . , 167–170.
Davison, Richard A. "Hemingway, Steinbeck, and the Art of the Short Story," *Steinbeck Q*, 21, iii-iv (1988), 79–80.
Felty, Darren. "Spatial Confinement in Hemingway's 'Cat in the Rain,' " *Stud Short Fiction*, 34 (1997), 363–369.

Lindsay, Clarence. "Risking Nothing: American Romantics in 'Cat in the Rain,' " *Hemingway R*, 17, i (1997), 15–27.

"The Chauffeurs of Madrid"
Watson, William B. "The Other Paris . . . ," 146–148.

"A Clean, Well-Lighted Place"
Monteiro, George. "Grace, Good Works, and the Hemingway Ethic," in Barnstone, Aliki, Michael T. Manson, and Carol J. Singley, Eds. *The Calvinist . . .* , 81–82.
Olson, Barbara K. *Authorial Divinity . . .* , 47–48.

"The Denunciation"
Watson, William B. "The Other Paris . . . ," 149–150.

"The Doctor and the Doctor's Wife"
Comley, Nancy R., and Robert Scholes. "Reading 'Up in Michigan,' " in Smith, Paul, Ed. *New Essays . . .* , 35–36.
Olson, Barbara K. *Authorial Divinity . . .* , 41–42.

"The End of Something"
Clifford, Stephen P. *Beyond the Heroic 'I' . . .* , 160–161.
Comley, Nancy R., and Robert Scholes. "Reading . . . ," 36–38.
Waldmeir, Joseph J. *"Miss Tina Did It" . . .* , 48–49.

"Fathers and Sons"
Beegel, Susan F. "Second Growth: The Ecology of Loss in 'Fathers and Sons,' " in Smith, Paul, Ed. *New Essays . . .* , 75–110.

"Fifty Grand"
Leff, Leonard J. *Hemingway . . .* , 23.

"The Gambler, the Nun, and the Radio"
Bond, Adrian. "Being Operated On: Hemingway's 'The Gambler, the Nun, and the Radio,' " *Stud Short Fiction*, 34 (1997), 371–378.

"God Rest You Merry, Gentlemen"
Brenner, Gerry. "(S)Talking Game: Dialogically Hunting Hemingway's Domestic Hunters," *Hemingway R*, 16, ii (1997), 41.

"Hills Like White Elephants"
Charters, Ann, and William E. Sheidley. *Resources . . .* , 5th ed., 115–116.
Curnutt, Kirk. *Wise Economies . . .* , 159–172.
Ford, Joh, and Marjorie Ford. *Instructor's Manual . . .* , 50–51.
Olson, Barbara K. *Authorial Divinity . . .* , 43–44.
Smith, Paul. "Introduction: Hemingway and the Practical Reader," in Smith, Paul, Ed. *New Essays . . .* , 15–16.

"Homage to Switzerland"
Aykroyd, Lucas. " 'Homage to Switzerland' as Monodrama: A Microcosm of Hemingway's Autobiographically Inspired Fiction," *Hemingway R*, 17, i (1997), 38–48.

"Indian Camp"
Coulehan, John L. "Tenderness and Steadiness: Emotions in Medical Practice," *Lit & Medicine*, 14 (1995), 222, 227.

"The Killers"
  Carter, Steven. "Rosencrantz and Guildenstern Are Alive: A Note on Al and Max in Hemingway's 'The Killers,' " *Hemingway R*, 17, i (1997), 68–71.
  Curnutt, Kirk. *Wise Economies* . . . , 7, 12–13, 160.
  Leff, Leonard J. *Hemingway* . . . , 47–48.
  Nelles, William. *Frameworks* . . . , 45–48.
  Olson, Barbara K. *Authorial Divinity* . . . , 42–44.
  Smith, Paul. "Introduction . . . ," 9–10.
  Waldmeir, Joseph J. *"Miss Tina Did It"* . . . , 41–51.

"Landscape with Figures"
  Watson, William B. "The Other Paris . . . ," 153–154.

"The Mother of a Queen"
  Brenner, Gerry. "(S)Talking Game . . . ," 40.

"Night Before Battle"
  Watson, William B. "The Other Paris . . . ," 152–153.

"Nobody Ever Dies"
  Watson, William B. "The Other Paris . . . ," 154–155.

"Now I Lay Me"
  Phelan, James. "Nick's Strange Monologue, Hemingway's Powerful Lyric, and the Reader's Disconcerting Experience," in Smith, Paul, Ed. *New Essays* . . . , 47–72.

"The Old Man and the Sea"
  Foulke, Robert. *The Sea Voyage* . . . , 131–136.
  Lockerbie, D. Bruce. *Dismissing God* . . . , 201–202.
  Monteiro, George. "Grace, Good Works . . . ," 86–87.

"Old Man at the Bridge"
  Watson, William B. "The Other Paris . . . ," 147–148.

"One Reader Writes"
  Smith, Paul. "Introduction . . . ," 12–14.

"A Pursuit Race"
  Nolan, Charles J. "Hemingway's Puzzling Pursuit Race," *Stud Short Fiction*, 34 (1997), 481–491.
  Olson, Barbara K. *Authorial Divinity* . . . , 46.

"The Sea Change"
  Brenner, Gerry. "(S)Talking Game . . . ," 41.
  Curnutt, Kirk. *Wise Economies* . . . , 169–170.
  Olson, Barbara K. *Authorial Divinity* . . . , 46–47.

"The Short Happy Life of Francis Macomber"
  Baldwin, Dean. *Instructor's Resource* . . . , 124–126.
  Brenner, Gerry. "(S)Talking Game . . . ," 35–36, 38.
  Fusco, Andrea de. "Discussing 'Macomber' in the Undergraduate Writing Seminar: What We Talk about When We Talk about Hemingway," *Hemingway R*, 17, i (1997), 72–79.
  Olson, Barbara K. *Authorial Divinity* . . . , 51–54.
  O'Meara, Lauraleigh. "Shooting Cowards, Critics, and Failed Writers:

F. Scott Fitzgerald and Hemingway's Francis Macomber,"
Hemingway R, 16, ii (1997), 27–28, 32.

"The Snows of Kilimanjaro"
Bloom, James D. *The Literary Bent* . . . , 83, 116–117.
Brenner, Gerry. "(S)Talking Game . . . ," 40.
Friedman, Norman. "Harry or Ernest?: The Unresolved Ambiguity in 'The Snows of Kilimanjaro,' " in Kaylor, Noel H., Ed. *Creative and Critical* . . . , 359–373.
Kennedy, J. Gerald. "Figuring the Damage: Fitzgerald's 'Babylon Revisited' and Hemingway's 'The Snows of Kilimanjaro,' " in Kennedy, J. Gerald, and Jackson R. Bryer, Eds. *French Connections* . . . , 327–337.
Larsen, Richard B. "Imaginary Heaven, African Hell in 'The Snows of Kilimanjaro,' " *J Assoc Interdisciplinary Stud Arts*, 2, ii (1997), 45–51.
Moddelmog, Debra A. "Re-Placing Africa in 'The Snows of Kilimanjaro': The Intersecting Economies of Capitalist-Imperialism and Hemingway Biography," in Smith, Paul, Ed. *New Essays* . . . , 119–124.
Monteiro, George. "Grace, Good Works . . . ," 82–85.
Olson, Barbara K. *Authorial Divinity* . . . , 50–51.
O'Meara, Lauraleigh. "Shooting Cowards, Critics, and Failed Writers: F. Scott Fitzgerald and Hemingway's Francis Macomber," *Hemingway R*, 16, ii (1997), 27–29, 32.
Spilka, Mark. *Eight Lessons* . . . , 212–216, 218–222.

"Soldier's Home"
Carter, Steven. " 'It Was All a Lie Both Ways': Krebs's Zero Summer," *Lubelskie Materialy Neofilologiczne*, 20 (1996), 7–14.
Curnutt, Kirk. " 'In the temps de Gertrude': Hemingway, Stein, and the Scene of Instruction at 27, rue de Fleurus," in Kennedy, J. Gerald, and Jackson R. Bryer, Eds. *French Connections* . . . , 124–125.
Leff, Leonard J. *Hemingway* . . . , 12.
McKenna, John J., and David M. Raabe. "Using Temperament Theory to Understand Conflict in Hemingway's 'Soldier's Home,' " *Stud Short Fiction*, 34 (1997), 203–213.
Waldmeir, Joseph J. *"Miss Tina Did It"* . . . , 58–59, 60.

"Summer People"
Hen, Judy. "Stut Is No 'Slut': Righting the Wrong in Ernest Hemingway's Misprinted 'Summer People,' " *Hemingway R*, 16, ii (1997), 19–25.

"Ten Indians"
Wadden, Paul. "Barefoot in the Hemlocks: Nick Adams' Betrayal of Love in 'Ten Indians,' " *Hemingway R*, 16, ii (1997), 3–18.

"The Three-Day Blow"
Losada, Luis A. "Not So Precise: 'The Three-Day Blow' and Baseball Again," *Hemingway R*, 16, ii (1997), 77–81.
Waldmeir, Joseph J. *"Miss Tina Did It"* . . . , 48–49.

"Today is Friday"
    Monteiro, George. "Grace, Good Works . . . ," 75–77.
"Under the Ridge"
    Watson, William B. "The Other Paris . . . ," 155–156.
"Up in Michigan"
    Clifford, Stephen P. *Beyond the Heroic 'I'* . . . , 153–159.
    Comley, Nancy R., and Robert Scholes. "Reading . . . ," 19–24,
        41–44.
    Leff, Leonard J. *Hemingway* . . . , 9–11.
"A Very Short Story"
    Comley, Nancy R., and Robert Scholes. "Reading . . . ," 31–32.
"A Way You'll Never Be"
    Leff, Leonard J. *Hemingway* . . . , 158.
"Wine of Wyoming"
    Leff, Leonard J. *Hemingway* . . . , 133–134.

AMY HEMPEL

"In the Cemetery Where Al Jolson Is Buried"
    Charters, Ann, and William E. Sheidley. *Resources* . . . , 5th ed., 117.

JOSEPHINE HERBST

"A Bad Blow"
    Wiedemann, Barbara. *Josephine Herbst's* . . . , 50–53.
"As a Fair Young Girl"
    Wiedemann, Barbara. *Josephine Herbst's* . . . , 53–56, 60, 71, 130.
"A Dreadful Night"
    Wiedemann, Barbara. *Josephine Herbst's* . . . , 62–64.
"Dry Sunday in Connecticut"
    Wiedemann, Barbara. *Josephine Herbst's* . . . , 33–37, 60, 132.
"The Elegant Mr. Gason"
    Wiedemann, Barbara. *Josephine Herbst's* . . . , 27–31, 60, 109, 132.
"The Embalmer's Holiday"
    Wiedemann, Barbara. *Josephine Herbst's* . . . , 98–100.
"The Enemy"
    Wiedemann, Barbara. *Josephine Herbst's* . . . , 88–93, 130.
"The Golden Egg"
    Wiedemann, Barbara. *Josephine Herbst's* . . . , 46–50, 53, 60, 71.
"The Golden Harvest"
    Wiedemann, Barbara. *Josephine Herbst's* . . . , 76, 84–88, 132.
"The Governor Does Not Come"
    Wiedemann, Barbara. *Josephine Herbst's* . . . , 79–80, 82, 88.

"Happy Birthday"
Wiedemann, Barbara. *Josephine Herbst's* . . . , 31–33.

"The Hunter of Doves"
Wiedemann, Barbara. *Josephine Herbst's* . . . , 98, 111–112, 113–127, 132.

"I Hear You, Mr. and Mrs. Brown"
Wiedemann, Barbara. *Josephine Herbst's* . . . , 56–59.

"I Saw Your Light"
Wiedemann, Barbara. *Josephine Herbst's* . . . , 64–66.

"Just Like a Ship"
Wiedemann, Barbara. *Josephine Herbst's* . . . , 98, 100–102.

"The Last Word"
Wiedemann, Barbara. *Josephine Herbst's* . . . , 106–109, 130.

"Leave Me Out of the Picture"
Wiedemann, Barbara. *Josephine Herbst's* . . . , 125–127, 130.

"A Man of Steel"
Wiedemann, Barbara. *Josephine Herbst's* . . . , 67–71, 130.

"A New Break"
Wiedemann, Barbara. *Josephine Herbst's* . . . , 59–61, 70–71.

"Once a Year"
Wiedemann, Barbara. *Josephine Herbst's* . . . , 41–44, 45, 60.

"Pennsylvania Idyl"
Wiedemann, Barbara. *Josephine Herbst's* . . . , 39–40, 45, 60.

"She Showed the Cloven Hoof"
Wiedemann, Barbara. *Josephine Herbst's* . . . , 66–67.

"Summer Boarders"
Wiedemann, Barbara. *Josephine Herbst's* . . . , 37–39, 130.

"A Summer with Yorick"
Wiedemann, Barbara. *Josephine Herbst's* . . . , 102–106.

"The Top of the Stairs"
Wiedemann, Barbara. *Josephine Herbst's* . . . , 74–76, 79, 82, 131.

"A Very Successful Man"
Wiedemann, Barbara. *Josephine Herbst's* . . . , 76–80, 82, 131.

"You Can Live Forever"
Wiedemann, Barbara. *Josephine Herbst's* . . . , 41, 76, 81–82, 84, 88, 131.

FELISBERTO HERNÁNDEZ

"El cocodrilo"
Juzyn-Amestoy, Olga. "El acto representativo: 'El cocodrilo' de Felisberto Hernández," in Forbes, F. William, Teresa Méndez-Faith, Mary-Anne Vetterling, and Barbara H. Wing, Eds. *Reflections* . . . , 107–119.

"El corazón verde"
Márquez Aguayo, César A. "Ritual y Memoria en *Nadie encendía las lámparas*," *Torre de Papel*, 7, ii (1997), 16, 30–32.

"Mamma's Tree"
Graziano, Frank. *The Lust of Seeing* . . . , 37, 191–194.

"Menos Julia"
Márquez Aguayo, César A. "Ritual y Memoria . . . ," 28–29.

"My First Concert"
Graziano, Frank. *The Lust of Seeing* . . . , 102–103.

"My First Teacher"
Graziano, Frank. *The Lust of Seeing* . . . , 149–150.

"The Usher"
Graziano, Frank. *The Lust of Seeing* . . . , 133–148, 155–158, 160–161, 163.

HERMANN HESSE

"Siddharta"
Tusken, Lewis W. *Understanding Herman Hesse*, 98–107.

PAUL HEYSE

"Andrea Delfin"
Mullan, Boyd. "Death in Venice: The Tragedy of a Man and a City in Paul Heyse's 'Andrea Delfin,' " *Colloquia Germanica*, 29 (1997), 97–114.

"Auf Tod und Leben"
Burns, Barbara. "Heyse and Storm on the Slippery Slope: Two Differing Approaches to Euthenasia," *Germ Life & Letters*, 51 (1998), 29–42.

FERNAND HIBBERT

"Orphise"
Romain, Guerda. "Before Black Was Beautiful: The Representation of Women in the Haitian National Novel," *French R*, 71 (1997), 60–61.

AIDAN HIGGINS

"Killachter Meadow"
Mahony, Christina H. *Contemporary Irish* . . . , 215–216.

PATRICIA HIGHSMITH

"The Black House"
Harrison, Russell. *Patricia Highsmith*, 132–135.
"Blow It"
Harrison, Russell. *Patricia Highsmith*, 129–131.
"Broken Glass"
Harrison, Russell. *Patricia Highsmith*, 120–123.
"A Clock Ticks at Christmas"
Harrison, Russell. *Patricia Highsmith*, 127–129.
"The Network"
Harrison, Russell. *Patricia Highsmith*, 117–120.
"Old Folks at Home"
Harrison, Russell. *Patricia Highsmith*, 131–132.
"The Terrors of Basket-Weaving"
Harrison, Russell. *Patricia Highsmith*, 123–127.

CHARLES HOWARD HINTON

"The Persian King"
Clarke, Bruce. "A Scientific Romance: Thermodynamics and the
Fourth Dimension in Charles Howard Hinton's 'The Persian
King,' " *Weber Stud*, 14, i (1997), 62–74.

MARY ANNE HOARE

"A Sketch of Famine"
Kelleher, Margaret. *The Feminization* . . . , 65–66, 70.

EDWARD D. HOCH

"The Faceless Thing"
Spoto, Mary T. "Needing Burial: Horror and Reconciliation in Edward
D. Hoch's 'The Faceless Thing,' " *Stud Weird Fiction*, 20 (1997),
13–18.

JACK HODGINS

"The Concert Stages of Europe"
Grady, Wayne. "Creatures of Clay: *The Barclay Family Theatre*," in
Struthers, J. R. (Tim), Ed. *On Coasts* . . . , 171–172.
"The Lepers' Squint"
Grady, Wayne. "Creatures of Clay . . . ," 174–175.
"Separating"
Kenneally, Michael. "The Internationalism of Jack Hodgins's

Regional Imagination," in Zach, Wolfgang, and Ken L. Goodwin,
Eds. *Nationalism vs. Internationalism* . . . , 320–321.
Struthers, J. R. (Tim). "Visionary Realism: Jack Hodgins, *Spit
Delaney's Island*, and the Redemptive Imagination," in Struthers,
J. R. (Tim), Ed. *On Coasts* . . . , 72–76.

"Spit Delaney's Island"
Kenneally, Michael. "The Internationalism . . . ," 322–323.
Struthers, J. R. (Tim). "Visionary Realism . . . ," 76–81.

"The Sumo Revisions"
Grady, Wayne. "Creatures of Clay . . . ," 175.
Mandel, Ann. "Fiction as Invasion: *The Barclay Family Theatre*," in
Struthers, J. R. (Tim), Ed. *On Coasts* . . . , 165–166.

BRENT HODGSON

"Sally the Birthday Girl"
Falconer, Rachel. "Bakhtin's Chronotope and the Contemporary
Short Story," *So Atlantic Q*, 97 (1998), 721–723.

E[RNEST] T[HEODOR] A[MADEUS] HOFFMANN

"Die Abenteuer der Silvester-Nacht"
McGlathery, James M. *E. T. A. Hoffmann*, 67–69.

"Der Artushof"
McGlathery, James M. *E. T. A. Hoffmann*, 70–71.

"Aus dem Leben eines bekannten Mannes"
McGlathery, James M. *E. T. A. Hoffmann*, 96–97.

"Die Automate"
McGlathery, James M. *E. T. A. Hoffmann*, 65–66.
Schwartz, Hillel. *The Culture* . . . , 134.

"Der Baron von B."
McGlathery, James M. *E. T. A. Hoffmann*, 94.

"Die Bergwerke zu Falun"
McGlathery, James M. *E. T. A. Hoffmann*, 91–92.
Smith, Evans L. "Myths of Poesis, Hermeneusis, and Psychogenesis:
Hoffmann, Tagore, and Gilman," *Stud Short Fiction*, 34 (1997),
227–228, 233–234.

"Die Brautwahl"
McGlathery, James M. *E. T. A. Hoffmann*, 88–89.

"Datura fastuosa"
McGlathery, James M. *E. T. A. Hoffmann*, 110.

"Doge und Dogaresse"
McGlathery, James M. *E. T. A. Hoffmann*, 84–85.

"Don Juan"
McGlathery, James M. *E. T. A. Hoffmann*, 61–63.

"Die Doppelgänger"
McGlathery, James M. *E. T. A. Hoffmann*, 109–110.

"Eine Spukgeschichte"
McGlathery, James M. *E. T. A. Hoffmann*, 100–101.

"Der Elementargeist"
McGlathery, James M. *E. T. A. Hoffmann*, 108–109.

"Erscheinungen"
McGlathery, James M. *E. T. A. Hoffmann*, 82–83.

"Die Fermate"
McGlathery, James M. *E. T. A. Hoffmann*, 69–70.

"Ein Fragment aus dem Leben dreier Freunde"
McGlathery, James M. *E. T. A. Hoffmann*, 77–78.

"Das Fräulein von Scuderi"
McGlathery, James M. *E. T. A. Hoffmann*, 97–99.

"Das fremde Kind"
McGlathery, James M. *E. T. A. Hoffmann*, 121–122.

"Die Geheimnisse"
McGlathery, James M. *E. T. A. Hoffmann*, 103–104.

"Das Gelübde"
McGlathery, James M. *E. T. A. Hoffmann*, 80–81.

"Die Genesung"
McGlathery, James M. *E. T. A. Hoffmann*, 112.

"Der goldne Topf"
Hildebrandt, Alexandra. "Die 'Sprache' der Enurese: Analerotische
Phantasien in E. T. A. Hoffmanns Kunstmärchen 'Der golden
Topf,' " *Confronto Letterario*, 13, xxvi (1996), 618–621, 623–631.
McGlathery, James M. *E. T. A. Hoffmann*, 114–118.
Meletinsky, Eleazar M. *The Poetics of Myth*, 267–269.
Snider, Daren. "Students, Snakes and Witches: Defining the Subject
in Hoffmann's 'Golden Pot,' " *Utah Foreign Lang R*, n.v.
(1992–1993), 118–125.

"Haimatochare"
McGlathery, James M. *E. T. A. Hoffmann*, 99.

"Ignaz Denner"
McGlathery, James M. *E. T. A. Hoffmann*, 66–67.

"Irrungen"
McGlathery, James M. *E. T. A. Hoffmann*, 101–102.

"Die Jesuiterkirche in G."
McGlathery, James M. *E. T. A. Hoffmann*, 73–74.

"Der Kampf der Sänger"
McGlathery, James M. *E. T. A. Hoffmann*, 83–84.

"Klein Zaches genannt Zinnober"
McGlathery, James M. *E. T. A. Hoffmann*, 122–124.

"Die Königsbraut"
McGlathery, James M. *E. T. A. Hoffmann*, 127–129.

"Der Magnetiseur"
McGlathery, James M. *E. T. A. Hoffmann*, 63–65.
"Das Majorat"
McGlathery, James M. *E. T. A. Hoffmann*, 79–80.
"Die Marquise de la Pivardiere"
McGlathery, James M. *E. T. A. Hoffmann*, 104–105.
"Meister Floh"
McGlathery, James M. *E. T. A. Hoffmann*, 129–132.
"Meister Johannes Wacht"
McGlathery, James M. *E. T. A. Hoffmann*, 111–112.
"Meister Martin der Küfner und seine Gesellen"
McGlathery, James M. *E. T. A. Hoffmann*, 86–87.
"Nachricht von den neuesten Schicksalen des Hundes Berganza"
McGlathery, James M. *E. T. A. Hoffmann*, 50–52.
"Nußknacker und Mausekönig"
McGlathery, James M. *E. T. A. Hoffmann*, 118–121.
"Das öde Haus"
McGlathery, James M. *E. T. A. Hoffmann*, 78–79.
"Prinzessin Brambilla"
McGlathery, James M. *E. T. A. Hoffmann*, 124–127.
Meletinsky, Eleazar M. *The Poetics . . .* , 268–269.
"Rat Krespel"
McGlathery, James M. *E. T. A. Hoffmann*, 75–77, 94.
"Die Räuber"
McGlathery, James M. *E. T. A. Hoffmann*, 105–106.
"Ritter Gluck"
McGlathery, James M. *E. T. A. Hoffmann*, 59–61.
Neubauer, John. "Mimeticism and Intertextuality in 'Ritter Gluck,' "
    in Prier, A., and Gerald Gillespie, Eds. *Narrative Ironies*, 239–251.
"Das Sanctus"
McGlathery, James M. *E. T. A. Hoffmann*, 74–75.
"Der Sandmann"
Allen, Richard. "Reading Kleist and Hoffmann," in Bygrave, Stephen,
    Ed. *Romantic Writings*, 259–266.
Baldwin, Dean. *Instructor's Resource . . .* , 28–29.
Becker, Allienne. "Hoffmann's Fantastic Sandman," in Sullivan,
    C. W., Ed. *The Dark Fantastic . . .* , 23–31.
Castein, Hanne. " 'Zerrbilder des Lebens': E. T. A. Hoffmann's 'Der
    Sandmann' and the Robot Heritage," *Pubs Engl Goethe Soc*, 67
    (1997), 43–54.
Johnson, Steven. *Interface Culture . . .* , 173–176.
McGlathery, James M. *E. T. A. Hoffmann*, 71–73.
Wagenknecht, David. "Reading Organ Speech in 'The Sandman,'
    Hamlet and Freud's Theoretical Language," *Colloquium
    Helveticum*, 25 (1997), 150, 158–162, 164–165.

"Signor Formica"
McGlathery, James M. *E. T. A. Hoffmann*, 94–95, 127.
"Spielerglück"
McGlathery, James M. *E. T. A. Hoffmann*, 92–94.
"Der unheimliche Gast"
McGlathery, James M. *E. T. A. Hoffmann*, 89–91, 92.
"Vampirismus"
McGlathery, James M. *E. T. A. Hoffmann*, 106–107.
"Des Vetters Eckfenster"
McGlathery, James M. *E. T. A. Hoffmann*, 20, 146–147.
"Der Zusammenhang der Dinge"
McGlathery, James M. *E. T. A. Hoffmann*, 95–96.

HUGO VON HOFMANNSTHAL

"Soldatengeschichte"
Nehring, Wolfgang. "Religiosität und Religion im Werk Hugo von
Hofmannsthals," in Auckenthaler, Karlheinz F., Ed. *Numinoses und
Heiliges . . .* , 82–83.

LINDA HOGAN

"Making Do"
Hansen, Elaine T. *Mother Without Child . . .* , 155–156.

BARBARA HONIGMANN

"Bonsoir, Madame Benhamou"
Remmler, Karen. "Reclaiming Space: Jewish Women in Germany
Today," in Brinker-Gabler, Gisela, and Sidonie Smith, Eds. *Writing
New Identities . . .* , 179.
"Double Grave"
Remmler, Karen. "The 'Third Generation' of Jewish-German Writers
After the Shoah Emerges in Germany and Austria," in Gilman,
Sander L., and Jack Zipes, Eds. *Yale Companion . . .* , 803–804.

HUGH HOOD

"A Green Child"
Ivison, Douglas. " 'A Reader's Guide to the Intersection of Time and
Space': Urban Spatialization in Hugh Hood's *Around the
Mountain*," *Stud Canadian Lit*, 23, i (1998), 240–242.
"Looking Down from Above"
Ivison, Douglas. " 'A Reader's Guide . . . ,' " 244–245.

"The Village Inside"
    Ivison, Douglas. " 'A Reader's Guide . . . ,' " 243–244.

MARY HOOD

"After Moore"
    Aiken, David. "Mary Hood: The Dark Side of the Moon," in Folks,
        Jeffrey J., and James A. Perkins, Eds. *Southern Writers* . . . , 24, 25.
"And Venus Is Blue"
    Aiken, David. "Mary Hood . . . ," 27–28.
"Finding the Chain"
    Aiken, David. "Mary Hood . . . ," 29–30.
"The Goodwife Hawkins"
    Aiken, David. "Mary Hood . . . ," 26–27.

PAULINE ELIZABETH HOPKINS

"Bro'r Abr'm Jimson's Wedding"
    McCaskill, Barbara. " 'To Labor . . . and Fight on the Side of Good':
        Spirit, Class, and Nineteenth-Century American Women's Writing,"
        in Kilcup, Karen L., Ed. *Nineteenth-Century American* . . . ,
        167–174.
"The Mystery Within Us"
    Schrager, Cynthia D. "Pauline Hopkins and William James: The New
        Psychology and the Politics of Race," in Abel, Elizabeth, Barbara
        Christian, and Helene Moglen, Eds. *Female Subjects* . . . , 309–310.
"Talma Gordon"
    Marcus, Lisa. " 'Of One Blood': Reimagining American Genealogy
        in Pauline Hopkins's *Contending Forces*," in Reesman, Jeanne C.,
        Ed. *Speaking the Other* . . . , 135–139.
    Nickerson, Catherine R. *The Web of Iniquity* . . . , 190–194.
    Sollors, Werner. *Neither Black Nor White* . . . , 72–74.

PAUL HORGAN

"The Devil in the Desert"
    Labrie, Ross. *The Catholic Imagination* . . . , 74–76.
"To the Castle"
    Labrie, Ross. *The Catholic Imagination* . . . , 76–77.

WILLIAM DEAN HOWELLS

"The Critical Bookstore"
    Bardon, Ruth. "Introduction," *Selected Short Stories* . . . [by William
        Dean Howells], 198–200.

EPELI HUA'OFA

LANGSTON HUGHES

"Thank You, M'am"
Charters, Ann, and William E. Sheidley. *Resources* . . . , 5th ed., 118–119.

KERI HULME

"King Bait"
Nabholz, Ann-Catherine. "Animals in Keri Hulme's *Te Kaihua/The Windeater*: Reflections on Biocentric Egalitarianism," *Commonwealth*, 20 (1998), 43–46.

"One Whale Singing"
Carrera Suárez, Isabel. "Towards a Female Language of Childbirth," in Barfoot, C. C., and Theo D'haen, Eds. *Shades of Empire* . . . , 186–187.
Nabholz, Ann-Catherine. "Animals in . . . ," 50–53.

"A Tally of the Souls of Sheep"
Nabholz, Ann-Catherine. "Animals in . . . ," 46–50.

"The Windeater"
Carrera Suárez, Isabel. "Towards a Female . . . ," 187–188.

WILLIAM HUMPHREY

"Apple of Discord"
Almon, Bert. *William Humphrey* . . . , 424–430.

"The Ballad of Jesse Neighbours"
Almon, Bert. *William Humphrey* . . . , 193–197.

"Buck Fever"
Almon, Bert. *William Humphrey* . . . , 420–421.

"The Dead Language"
Almon, Bert. *William Humphrey* . . . , 412–413.

"Dead Weight"
Almon, Bert. *William Humphrey* . . . , 423–424.

"Dolce Far' Niente"
Almon, Bert. *William Humphrey* . . . , 341–342.

"An Eye for an Eye"
Almon, Bert. *William Humphrey* . . . , 422.

"The Fauve"
Almon, Bert. *William Humphrey* . . . , 62–64.

"A Fresh Snow"
Almon, Bert. *William Humphrey* . . . , 71–72.

"A Good Indian"
Almon, Bert. *William Humphrey* . . . , 198–199.

"A Home Away from Home"
Almon, Bert. *William Humphrey* . . . , 201–204.

THOMAS HÜRLIMANN

FANNIE HURST

"T.B."
Ravitz, Abe C. *Imitations* . . . , 63–65.
"A Ticket to Life"
Ravitz, Abe C. *Imitations* . . . , 151.
"White Apes"
Ravitz, Abe C. *Imitations* . . . , 145–147.

ZORA NEALE HURSTON

"Black Death"
Gambrell, Alice. *Women Intellectuals* . . . , 116–118.
Gates, Henry L, and Sieglinde Lemke. "Introduction," *The Complete Stories* [by Zora Neale Hurston], xvi–xvii.
"The Bone of Contention"
Lurie, Susan. *Unsettled Subjects* . . . , 38–39, 54–57.
"The Conscience of the Country"
Gates, Henry L, and Sieglinde Lemke. "Introduction," xxi–xxii.
Peters, Pearlie M.F. *The Assertive Women in* . . . , 81–88.
"Drenched in Light"
Gates, Henry L, and Sieglinde Lemke. "Introduction," xii–xiv.
Samuels, Wilfred D. "The Light at Daybreak: Heterosexual Relationships in Hurston's Short Stories," in Cronin, Gloria L., Ed. *Critical Essays* . . . , 241–242.
"The Gilded Six-Bits"
Baldwin, Dean. *Instructor's Resource* . . . , 127–129.
Charters, Ann, and William E. Sheidley. *Resources* . . . , 5th ed., 120–121.
Gates, Henry L, and Sieglinde Lemke. "Introduction," xvii–xix.
Jones, Gayl. *Liberating Voices* . . . , 63–69; rpt. Wall, Cheryl A., Ed. *Zora Neale Hurston* . . . , 160–166.
Peters, Pearlie M.F. *The Assertive Women in* . . . , 89–95.
Rodgers, Lawrence R. *Canaan Bound* . . . , 93–94.
"High John De Conquer"
Gates, Henry L, and Sieglinde Lemke. "Introduction," xix–xxi.
"Hoodoo in America"
Gambrell, Alice. *Women Intellectuals* . . . , 116–118.
"Hurricane"
Samuels, Wilfred D. "The Light . . . ," 249–251.
"John Redding Goes to Sea"
Peters, Pearlie M.F. *The Assertive Women in* . . . , 24–25.
Samuels, Wilfred D. "The Light . . . ," 241, 242–243.
"Magnolia Flower"
Gates, Henry L, and Sieglinde Lemke. "Introduction," xv–xvi.
"Mule Bones"
Peters, Pearlie M.F. *The Assertive Women in* . . . , 97–104.

"Muttsy"
Samuels, Wilfred D. "The Light . . . ," 251–252.
"Spunk"
Gates, Henry L, and Sieglinde Lemke. "Introduction," xiv–xv.
Samuels, Wilfred D. "The Light . . . ," 244–246.
"Story in Harlem Slang"
Peters, Pearlie M.F. *The Assertive Women in* . . . , 97–104.
Samuels, Wilfred D. "The Light . . . ," 251–252.
"Sweat"
Charters, Ann, and William E. Sheidley. *Resources* . . . , 5th ed., 122.
Green, Suzanne D. "Fear, Freedom and the Perils of Ethnicity:
Otherness in Kate Chopin's 'Beyond the Bayou' and Zora Neale
Hurston's 'Sweat,' " *Southern Stud*, 5, iii–iv (1994), 107–115.
+Hemenway, Robert E. "From *Zora Neale Hurston: A Literary
Biography*," in Wall, Cheryl A., Ed. *Zora Neale Hurston* . . . ,
149–152.
Lowe, John. *Jump at the Sun* . . . , 52–79; rpt. Wall, Cheryl A., Ed.
Zora Neale Hurston . . . , 182–192.
Samuels, Wilfred D. "The Light . . . ," 247–248.
+Seidel, Kathryn L. "The Artist in the Kitchen: The Economics of
Creativity in Hurston's 'Sweat,' " in Wall, Cheryl A., Ed. *Zora
Neale Hurston* . . . , 169–181.
Wall, Cheryl A. "Introduction," in Wall, Cheryl A., Ed. *Zora Neale
Hurston* . . . , 7–13.

GEORGES HYVERNAUD

"The Cattle Car"
Desné, Roland. "Afterword," *The Cattle Car* [by Georges
Hyvernaud], 150–156.

JORGE IBARGÜENGOITIA

"La mujer que no"
Bubnova, Tatiana. "El impostor ante el espejo: Ibargüengoitia y su
interlocutor en *La Ley de Herodes*," in Herrera, Sara P., Ed. *El
cuento mexicano* . . . , 325, 326–327.
"¿Quién se lleva a Blanca?"
Bubnova, Tatiana. "El impostor . . . ," 331–332.
"La vela perpetua"
Bubnova, Tatiana. "El impostor . . . ," 325, 327–331.

YUSUF IDRIS

"Al-Amaliyya al-Kubrâ"
Wise, Renate. "Subverting Holy Scriptures: The Short Stories of

Curnutt, Kirk. *Wise Economies* . . . , 27–33, 38, 40, 124.
+ Fetterley, Judith. "Palpable Designs: An American Dream: 'Rip Van Winkle," in Warhol Robyn R., and Diane P. Herndl, Eds. *Feminisms* . . . , 502–508.
Ford, Joh, and Marjorie Ford. *Instructor's Manual* . . . , 5–7.
Gardner, Jared. *Master Plots* . . . , 81–82.
Kuczynski, Peter. "Intertextuality in 'Rip Van Winkle': Irving's Use of Büsching's Folk-Tale *Peter Klaus* in an Age of Transition," in Gassenmeier, Michael, Petra Bridzun, Jens M. Gurr, and Frank E. Pointner, Eds. *British Romantics* . . . , 301–315.
Pryse, Marjorie. "Origins of American . . . , 22–23.

"The Specter Bridegroom"
Hönnighausen, Lothar. "The American Interest in German Romanticism: Washington Irving, John Pendleton Kennedy, and Gottfried August Bürger's 'Lenore'—A Cultural Studies Approach," in Hebel, Udo J., and Karl Ortseifen, Eds. *Transatlantic Encounters* . . . , 105–109, 113.

FAZIL ABDULOVICH ISKANDER

"Belshazzar's Feasts"
Ziolkowski, Margaret. *Literary Exorcisms* . . . , 24, 32, 35.

SHIRLEY JACKSON

"The Lottery"
Baldwin, Dean. *Instructor's Resource* . . . , 141–143.
Charters, Ann, and William E. Sheidley. *Resources* . . . , 5th ed., 124–125.

"The Tooth"
Willingham-Sirmans, Karen, and Mary Lowe-Evans. "Jackson's 'The Tooth,' " *Explicator* 55, ii (1997), 96–97.

VIOLET JACOB

"The Debatable Land"
Anderson, Carol. "Tales of Her Own Countries: Violet Jacob," in Gifford, Douglas, and Dorothy McMillan, Eds. *A History* . . . , 340–351.

W[ILLIAM] W[YMARK] JACOBS

"The Brown Man's Servant"
Hoppenstad, Gary. "British *Noir*: The Crime Fiction of W. W. Jacobs," *J Pop Culture*, 32, i (1998), 159.
Prince, Gerald. "Narratology and Genre: The Case of 'The Monkey's

Paw,' " in Cooke, Brett, George E. Slusser, and Jaume Marti-Olivella, Eds. *The Fantastic Other* . . . , 101–109.

"Captain Roberts"
Hoppenstad, Gary. "British *Noir* . . . ," 155, 156, 161.

"His Brother's Keeper"
Hoppenstad, Gary. "British *Noir* . . . ," 153–154, 155, 161.

"In the Library"
Hoppenstad, Gary. "British *Noir* . . . ," 152–153, 155, 161.

"The Interruption"
Hoppenstad, Gary. "British *Noir* . . . ," 154, 155, 161.

"The Lost Ship"
Hoppenstad, Gary. "British *Noir* . . . ," 157, 158, 161.

"The Monkey's Paw"
Hoppenstad, Gary. "British *Noir* . . . ," 151–152, 158–159.

"Over the Side"
Hoppenstad, Gary. "British *Noir* . . . ," 159, 160, 161.

LAURA JACOBSON

"The Wooing of Rachael Schlipsky"
Kilcup, Karen L. " 'Essays in Invention': Transformations of Advice in Nineteenth-Century American Women's Writing," in Kilcup, Karen L., Ed. *Nineteenth-Century American* . . . , 198–199.

MOHAMMAD ALI JAMALZADEH

"The Friendship of Auntie Bear"
Zarrin, Ali. "The Rhetoric of Self and Other in Selected Iranian Short Stories, 1906–1979," *Int'l Fiction R*, 24, i–ii (1997), 36–37.

C[YRIL] L[IONEL] R[OBERT] JAMES

"La Divina Pastora"
Nielsen, Aldon L. *C. L. R. James* . . . , 18–20.

"The Star that Would Not Shine"
Nielsen, Aldon L. *C. L. R. James* . . . , 22–23.

"Triumph"
Nielsen, Aldon L. *C. L. R. James* . . . , 23–25.

"Turner's Prosperity"
Nielsen, Aldon L. *C. L. R. James* . . . , 21.

HENRY JAMES

"Abasement of the Northmores"
Tintner, Adeline R. *Henry James's Legacy* . . . , 156.

"The Altar of the Dead"
Stevens, Hugh. *Henry James and Sexuality*, 155–163.
———. "Homoeroticism, Identity, and Agency in James's Late
Tales," in Buelens, Gert, Ed. *Enacting History* . . . , 138–144.
Tintner, Adeline R. *Henry James's Legacy* . . . , 241–242.
Ward, Geoff. " 'The Strength of Applied Irony,': James's 'The Altar
of the Dead,' " in Reeve, N. H., Ed. *Henry James* . . . , 63–70.
Westervelt, Linda A. *Beyond Innocence* . . . , 30–34.

"The Aspern Papers"
Foster, Dennis A. *Sublime Enjoyment* . . . , 68–80.
Hadley, Tessa. " 'The Aspern Papers': Henry James's 'Editorial
Heart,' " *Cambridge Q*, 26 (1997), 314–324.
Mengham, Rod. "Wall to Wall: Figuring 'The Aspern Papers,' " in
Reeve, N. H., Ed. *Henry James* . . . , 41–59.
Miller, J. Hillis. "History, Narrative, and Responsibility: Speech Acts
in 'The Aspern Papers,' " *Textual Practice*, 9 (1995), 243–267; rpt.
in Buelens, Gert, Ed. *Enacting History* . . . , 193–209.
Reesman, Jeanne C. " 'The Deepest Depths of the Artificial':
Attacking Women and Reality in 'The Aspern Papers,' " *Henry
James R*, 19 (1998), 148–165.
Salmon, Richard. *Henry James and* . . . , 91–105.
———. "The Right to Privacy/The Will to Knowledge: Henry James
and the Ethics of Biographical Enquiry," in Gould, Warwick, and
Thomas E. Staley, Eds. *Writing the Lives* . . . , 144–147.
Thomas, Brook. *American Literary Realism* . . . , 16, 53–54, 72–80,
81, 88, 284.
Veeder, William. "James and Fame Enduring," *Henry James R*, 19
(1998), 268–269, 270–271, 274–277.
Waldmeir, Joseph J. *"Miss Tina Did It"* . . . , 29–39.

"The Author of 'Beltraffio' "
Monk, Leland. "A Terrible Beauty Is Born: Henry James,
Aestheticism, and Homosexual Panic," in Foster, Thomas, Carol
Siegel, and Ellen E. Berry, Eds. *Bodies of Writing* . . . , 247–265.
Treitel, Ilona. "Absence as Metaphor in Henry James's 'The Author
of "Beltraffio,' " " *Stud Short Fiction*, 34 (1997), 171–181.

"The Beast in the Jungle"
Brown, Arthur A. "Henry James and Immortality: 'The Beast in the
Jungle' and 'Is There a Life After Death,' " *Colby Q*, 34 (1998),
245–249.
Buelens, Gert. "In Possession of a Secret: Rhythms of Mastery and
Surrender in 'The Beast in the Jungle,' " *Henry James R*, 19 (1998),
17–35.
Heyns, Michiel W. "The Double Narrative of 'The Beast in the
Jungle': Ethical Plot, Ironical Plot, and the Play of Power," in
Buelens, Gert, Ed. *Enacting History* . . . , 109–124.
Westervelt, Linda A. *Beyond Innocence* . . . , 31–34.

"The Beldonald Holbein"
Salmon, Richard. *Henry James and* . . . , 165–166.

"The Birthplace"
Tanner, Tony. " 'The Birthplace,' " in Reeve, N. H., Ed. *Henry James* . . . , 77–94.

"Broken Wings"
Robertson, Michael. *Stephen Crane, Journalism* . . . , 42–43.

"Daisy Miller"
Bell, Ian F. A. "Displays of the Female: Formula and Flirtation in 'Daisy Miller,' " in Reeve, N. H., Ed. *Henry James* . . . , 17–40.
Weisbuch, Robert. "Henry James and the Idea of Evil," in Freedman, Jonathan, Ed. *The Cambridge* . . . , 105–111.

"A Day of Days"
Southward, David. "Flirtations in Early James," *Mod Lang R*, 93 (1998), 513–516.

"The Death of the Lion"
DaRosa, Marc. "Henry James, Anonymity, and the Press: Journalistic Modernity and the Decline of the Author," *Mod Fiction Stud*, 43 (1997), 826–828, 830, 835–849, 853.
Robertson, Michael. *Stephen Crane* . . . , 43–44.
Rowe, John C. *The Other Henry James*, 112–118.
Salmon, Richard. *Henry James and* . . . , 107–108, 110–111, 112–115.

"The Figure in the Carpet"
Miller, J. Hillis. *Reading Narrative*, 98–104.

"Flickerbridge"
Salmon, Richard. *Henry James and* . . . , 138–139.

"Fordham Castle"
Stevens, Hugh. *Henry James and Sexuality*, 118–119.

"Four Meetings"
Waldmeir, Joseph J. *"Miss Tina Did It"* . . . , 4–5.

"Georgina's Reasons"
Johanningsmeier, Charles. "Henry James's Dalliance with the Newspaper World," *Henry James R*, 19 (1998), 43–44, 45, 47, 49.

"The Given Case"
Dawson, Melanie. "The Literature of Reassessment: James's *Collier*'s Fiction," *Henry James R*, 19 (1998), 233–234.

"Glasses"
Poole, Adrian. "Through 'Glasses' Darkly," in Reeve, N. H., Ed. *Henry James* . . . , 1–16.

"The Great Good Place"
Veeder, William. "James and the Limitations of Self-Therapy," in Reeve, N. H., Ed. *Henry James* . . . , 173–187.

"In the Cage"
Stevens, Hugh. *Henry James and Sexuality*, 151–152.

"John Delavoy"
Salmon, Richard. *Henry James and* . . . , 111–114.

"Paste"
  Charters, Ann, and William E. Sheidley. *Resources* . . . , 5th ed., 127.
  Ford, Joh, and Marjorie Ford. *Instructor's Manual* . . . , 16–17.

"The Point of View"
  Robertson, Michael. *Stephen Crane* . . . , 49–50.

"Poor Richard"
  Southward, David. "Flirtations . . . ," 506–508.

"The Private Life"
  Salmon, Richard. *Henry James and* . . . , 89–91.

"The Pupil"
  Bell, Millicent. "The Unmentionable Subject in 'The Pupil,' " in
    Freedman, Jonathan, Ed. *The Cambridge* . . . , 139–150.
  Horne, Philip. "The Master and the 'Queer Affair' of 'The Pupil,' "
    in Reeve, N. H., Ed. *Henry James* . . . , 123–133.

"The Real Right Thing"
  Dawson, Melanie. "The Literature . . . ," 235–236.

"The Real Thing"
  Schwartz, Hillel. *The Culture* . . . , 322, 324.

"The Romance of Certain Old Clothes"
  Rochette-Crawley, Susan. "Between Two Streams: The Romance
    Tradition and Naturalism in Two Early Stories by Henry James," in
    Kaylor, Noel H., Ed. *Creative and Critical* . . . , 439–442.

"A Round of Visits"
  Stevens, Hugh. *Henry James and Sexuality*, 153–155.

"Sir Dominick Ferrand"
  Salmon, Richard. *Henry James and* . . . , 84–86.
  ———. "The Right to . . . ," 138–140.

"Sir Edmund Orme"
  Brown, Arthur A. "Ghosts and the Nature of Death in Literature:
    Henry James's 'Sir Edmund Orme,' " *Am Lit Realism*, 31 (1998),
    60–70.

"The Special Type"
  Dawson, Melanie. "The Literature . . . ," 234–235.

"The Story of a Year"
  Heyns, Michiel W. "The Double Narrative of 'The Beast in the
    Jungle': Ethical Plot, Ironical Plot, and the Play of Power," in
    Buelens, Gert, Ed. *Enacting History* . . . , 109–110.
  Kaufman, Marjorie. "He Knew That *He* Knew . . . ," 158–162.

"A Tragedy of Error"
  Rochette-Crawley, Susan. "Between Two . . . ," 432–437.
  Southward, David. "Flirtations . . . ," 490–492.

"Travelling Companions"
  Staiger, Jeff. "The Fall as Conversion: Catholicism and the American
    Girl in James's 'Travelling Companions,' " *Henry James R*, 18
    (1997), 127–139.

"The Turn of the Screw"
Banerjee, Jacqueline. "The Legacy of Anne Brontë in Henry James's 'The Turn of the Screw,' " *Engl Stud*, 78 (1997), 533–540, 542.
Boehm, Beth A. "A Postmodern Turn of 'The Turn of the Screw' " *Henry James R*, 19 (1998), 248–254.
Dawson, Melanie. "The Literature . . . ," 232–233.
Haviland, Beverly. *Henry James's Last* . . . , 28, 38.
Navarette, Susan J. *The Shape* . . . , 112–117, 122–135, 235.
Schwarz, Daniel R. "Manet, James's 'The Turn of the Screw' and the Voyeuristic Imagination," *Henry James R*, 18 (1997), 1–21.
――――. *Reconfiguring Modernism* . . . , 52–53, 64–73, 77–78.
Wiesenthal, Chris. *Figuring Madness* . . . , 108–138.
Woods, Gregory. *A History of Gay* . . . , 326–329.

"Washington Square"
Bell, Millicent. "From 'Washington Square' to The Spoils of Poynton: Jamesian Metamorphosis," in Reeve, N. H., Ed. Henry James . . . , 95–113.

M. R. JAMES

"Canon Alberic's Scrap-book"
MacCulloch, Simon. "The Toad in the Study: M. R. James, H. P. Lovecraft, and Forbidden Knowledge," *Stud Weird Fiction*, 20 (1997), 5–7.

"Casting the Runes"
MacCulloch, Simon. "The Toad in the . . . ," 7–9.

"Count Magnus"
MacCulloch, Simon. "The Toad in the Study: M. R. James, H. P. Lovecraft, and Forbidden Knowledge (Part Two)," *Stud Weird Fiction*, 21 (1997), 19–20.

"Lost Hearts"
MacCulloch, Simon. "The Toad in the . . . ," 4–5.

"Martin's Close"
MacCulloch, Simon. "The Toad in the . . . ," 10.

"The Mezzotint"
MacCulloch, Simon. "The Toad in the . . . (Part Two)," 23–24, 25–26.

"Oh, Whistle, and I'll Come to You, My Lad"
Cowlishaw, Brian. " 'A Warning to the Curious': Victorian Science and the Awful Unconscious in M. R. James's Ghost Stories," *Victorian News*, 94 (1998), 37–38.
MacCulloch, Simon. "The Toad in the . . . (Part Two)," 21–23.

"The Residence at Whitminster"
MacCulloch, Simon. "The Toad in the . . . ," 11.

ELFRIEDE JELINER

"Lust"
Felka, Rike. "Das Begehren, markiert zu werden: Über Marguerite

Duras und Elfriede Jelinek," in Härle, Gerhard, Maria Kalveram, and Wolfgang Popp, Eds. *Erkenntniswunsch* . . . , 217–219, 224–225.

GISH JEN

"Birthmates"
 Feddersen, R. C. "From Story to Novel and Back Again: Gish Jin's Developing Art of Short Fiction," in Kaylor, Noel H., Ed. *Creative and Critical* . . . , 352–358.

"In the American Society"
 Charters, Ann, and William E. Sheidley. *Resources* . . . , 5th ed., 128–129.

"What Means Switch"
 Feddersen, R. C. "From Story . . . ," 351.

"The White Umbrella"
 Feddersen, R. C. "From Story . . . ," 350–351.

SARAH ORNE JEWETT

"An Autumn Holiday"
 Neinstein, Raymond L. "Loaded Guns: Place and Women's Place in Nineteenth-Century New England," in D'haen, Theo, and Hans Bertens, Eds. *"Writing" Nation* . . . , 89–91.

"The Foreigner"
 Davis, Cynthia J. "Making the Strange(r) Familiar: Sarah Orne Jewett's 'The Foreigner,' " in Inness, Sherrie A., and Diana Royer, Eds. *Breaking Boundaries* . . . , 88–108.
 Fetterley, Judith. " 'Not in the Least American': Nineteenth-Century Literary Regionalism as UnAmerican Literature," in Kilcup, Karen L., Ed. *Nineteenth-Century American* . . . , 29–30.

"The Town Poor"
 Thomson, Rosemarie G. "Crippled Girls and Lame Old Women: Sentimental Spectacles of Sympathy in Nineteenth-Century American Women's Writing," in Kilcup, Karen L., Ed. *Nineteenth-Century American* . . . , 134–136.

"A White Heron"
 Charters, Ann, and William E. Sheidley. *Resources* . . . , 5th ed., 130–131.
 Curnutt, Kirk. *Wise Economies* . . . , 101–115.
 Fetterley, Judith. "Theorizing Regionalism: Celia Thaxter's *Among the Isles of Shoals*," in Inness, Sherrie A., and Diana Royer, Eds. *Breaking Boundaries* . . . , 40–41.
 Ford, Joh, and Marjorie Ford. *Instructor's Manual* . . . , 17–18.
 Meisenheimer, D. K. "Regionalist Bodies/Embodied Regions: Sarah

Orne Jewett and Zitkala-Ša," in Inness, Sherrie A., and Diana
Royer, Eds. *Breaking Boundaries* . . . , 111–112, 114.
Neinstein, Raymond L. "Loaded Guns . . . ," 91–94.

RUTH PRAWER JHABVALA

"In the Mountains"
Baldwin, Dean. *Instructor's Resource* . . . , 185–187.
"The Widow"
Usha, V. T. "Ruth Prawer Jhabvala's 'The Widow': Reading the
Subtext," *Lit Criterion*, 27, i–ii (1992), 133–137.

JIANG ZILONG

"Manager Qiao Assumes Office"
McDougall, Bonnie S., and Kam Louie. *The Literature of China* . . . ,
387–388.

A. YEMISI JIMOH

"Peace Be Still"
Jablon, Madelyn. "Womanist Storytelling: The Voice of the
Vernacular" in Brown, Julie, Ed. *Ethnicity* . . . , 54–55.

NICK JOAQUIN

"Balikbayan"
Binongo, José N. G. "Incongruity, Mathematics, and Humor in
Joaquinesquerie," *Philippine Stud*, 41 (1993), 487.
"Going to Jerusalem"
Binongo, José N. G. "Incongruity . . . ," 484–485.
"Gotita de Dragon"
Binongo, José N. G. "Incongruity . . . ," 501–502.
"How Love Came to Juan Tamad"
Binongo, José N. G. "Incongruity . . . ," 498–501.
"Lechonito the Holy Innocent"
Binongo, José N. G. "Incongruity . . . ," 488–489.
"The Order of Melchizedek"
Sharrad, Paul. "Unsettling Promise: The Revenant in Post-Colonial
Writing," in Delrez, Marc, and Bénédicte Ledent, Eds. *The
Contact* . . . , 348–350.
"The Traveling Salesman and the Split Woman"
Binongo, José N. G. "Incongruity . . . ," 486, 487–488.

Illusionism: The Function of Film in American Film Stories," in
Hebel, Udo J., and Karl Ortseifen, Eds. *Transatlantic
Encounters* . . . , 299–300.

JAMES JONES

"A Bottle of Cream"
   Carter, Steven R. *James Jones* . . . , 151–152.

"Greater Love"
   Carter, Steven R. *James Jones* . . . , 110–112.

"The Ice-Cream Headache"
   Carter, Steven R. *James Jones* . . . , 85, 88–91.

"Just Like the Girl"
   Carter, Steven R. *James Jones* . . . , 127–129.

"The King"
   Carter, Steven R. *James Jones* . . . , 85, 86–87.

"None Sing so Wildly"
   Carter, Steven R. *James Jones* . . . , 147–148, 149–151.

"Secondhand Man"
   Carter, Steven R. *James Jones* . . . , 126–127.

"Sunday Allergy"
   Carter, Steven R. *James Jones* . . . , 148–149.

"The Tennis Game"
   Carter, Steven R. *James Jones* . . . , 127, 129–130.

"Two Legs for the Two of Us"
   Carter, Steven R. *James Jones* . . . , 147, 148.

"The Valentine"
   Carter, Steven R. *James Jones* . . . , 85, 87–88.

"The Way It Is"
   Carter, Steven R. *James Jones* . . . , 84, 85–86.

NEIL JORDAN

"A Love"
   Mahony, Christina H. *Contemporary Irish* . . . , 241–242.

"Night in Tunisia"
   Mahony, Christina H. *Contemporary Irish* . . . , 240–241.
   Pramaggiore, Maria. "The Celtic Blue Note: Jazz in Neil Jordan's
      'Night in Tunisia,' *Angel* and *The Miracle*," *Screen*, 39 (1998),
      280–283.

"Skin"
   Mahony, Christina H. *Contemporary Irish* . . . , 241.

HIMĀMŚU JOŚĪ

"Choti'i' "
  Damsteegt, Theo. "A Man and a Woman: An Analysis of a Modern
    Hindi Short Story," in Meij, Dick van der, Ed. *India and
    Beyond* . . . , 55–70.

JAMES JOYCE

"After the Race"
  Coleman, George L. "Sense Deprivation in 'After the Race' and a
    'Painful Case,' " in Hart, Clive, C. George Sandulescu, Bonnie K.
    Scott, and Fritz Senn, Eds. *Images of Joyce*, 362–368.
  Kelly, Joseph. *Our Joyce: From Outcast* . . . , 45.

"Araby"
  Baldwin, Dean. *Instructor's Resource* . . . , 87–89.
  Bašić, Sonja. "A Book of Many Uncertainties: Joyce's *Dubliners*," in
    Bosinelli, Rosa M. B., and Harold F. Mosher, Eds. *ReJoycing* . . . ,
    32–33.
  Charters, Ann, and William E. Sheidley. *Resources* . . . , 5th ed.,
    134–135.
  Ford, Joh, and Marjorie Ford. *Instructor's Manual* . . . , 34–35.
  Fuhrel, Robert. "The Quest of Joyce and O'Connor in 'Araby' and
    'The Man of the House,' " in Evans, Robert C., and Richard Harp,
    Eds. *Frank O'Connor* . . . , 173–187.
  Ingersoll, Earl G. "The Seasons and Times of *Dubliners*," *Notes Mod
    Irish Lit*, 10 (1998), 32–33.

"The Boarding House"
  Baccolini, Raffaella. " 'She Had Become a Memory': Women as
    Memory in James Joyce's *Dubliners*," in Bosinelli, Rosa M. B., and
    Harold F. Mosher, Eds. *ReJoycing* . . . , 149–152.
  Bašić, Sonja. "A Book of Many . . . ," 24–26.
  Ford, Joh, and Marjorie Ford. *Instructor's Manual* . . . , 35–36.
  Hedberg, Johannes. "Humour in *Dubliners*—A Passed-Over
    Element," in Hart, Clive, C. George Sandulescu, Bonnie K. Scott,
    and Fritz Senn, Eds. *Images of Joyce*, 397–398.
  Kelly, Joseph. *Our Joyce: From Outcast* . . . , 60.
  Mosher, Harold. "The Unnarrated in *Dubliners*," in Hart, Clive, C.
    George Sandulescu, Bonnie K. Scott, and Fritz Senn, Eds. *Images
    of Joyce*, 417–418.

"Clay"
  Kelly, Joseph. *Our Joyce: From Outcast* . . . , 48.

"Counterparts"
  Nash, John. "Counterparts before the Law: Mimicry and Exclusion,"
    in Brannigan, John, Geoff Ward, and Julian Wolfreys, Eds.
    Re:Joyce . . . , 3–16.
  Spilka, Mark. *Eight Lessons* . . . , 188–200.
  Williams, Trevor L. "No Cheer for 'the Gratefully Oppressed':

Riquelme, John P. "Joyce's 'The Dead': The Dissolution of the Self and the Police," in Bosinelli, Rosa M. B., and Harold F. Mosher, Eds. *ReJoycing* . . . , 123–141.

Williams, Trevor L. *Reading Joyce* . . . , 91–96.

Yee, Cordell D. K. *The Word According to* . . . , 25–26, 95–97.

"An Encounter"

Kelly, Joseph. *Our Joyce: From Outcast* . . . , 45.

Norris, Margot. "A Walk on the Wild(e) Side: The Doubled Reading of 'An Encounter,' " in Valente, Joseph, Ed. *Quare Joyce*, 19–33.

Woods, Gregory. *A History of Gay* . . . , 329–330.

"Eveline"

Baccolini, Raffaella. " 'She Had Become . . . ,' " 156–158.

Bock, Martin. "Syphilisation and Its Discontents: Somatic Indications of Psychological Ills in Joyce and Lowry," in McCarthy, Patrick A., and Paul Tiessen, Eds. *Joyce/Lowry* . . . , 131.

Brown, Suzanne H. "The Chronotope of the Short Story: Time, Character, and Brevity," in Kaylor, Noel H., Ed. *Creative and Critical* . . . , 199–202, 204–208.

Ehrlich, Heyward. "Socialism, Gender . . . ," 96–98.

Kelly, Joseph. *Our Joyce: From Outcast* . . . , 37–38.

Shepherd, Valerie. *Literature about Language*, 88–92.

Williams, Trevor L. *Reading Joyce* . . . , 75–78.

Yee, Cordell D. K. *The Word According to* . . . , 34–35.

"Grace"

Bašić, Sonja. "A Book of Many . . . ," 20–22.

Corcoran, Marlena G. "Language, Character . . . ," 171–173.

Hedberg, Johannes. "Humour in *Dubliners* . . . ," 402–403.

Kane, Jean. "Imperial Pathologies: Medical Discourse and Drink in *Dubliners'* 'Grace,' " *Lit & Medicine*, 14 (1995), 191–209.

Kelly, Joseph. *Our Joyce: From Outcast* . . . , 47–48.

Rice, Thomas J. *Joyce, Chaos* . . . , 31–36.

Williams, Trevor L. *Reading Joyce* . . . , 86–87.

"Ivy Day"

Brian, Michael. " 'A Very Fine Piece of Writing': An Etymological, Dantean, and Gnostic Reading of Joyce's 'Ivy Day in the Committee Room,' " in Bosinelli, Rosa M. B., and Harold F. Mosher, Eds. *ReJoycing* . . . , 206–227.

Hedberg, Johannes. "Humour in *Dubliners*—A Passed-Over Element," in Hart, Clive, C. George Sandulescu, Bonnie K. Scott, and Fritz Senn, Eds. *Images of Joyce*, 400–401.

Kelly, Joseph. *Our Joyce: From Outcast* . . . , 54–56.

"A Little Cloud"

Hedberg, Johannes. "Humour in *Dubliners* . . . ," 398–400.

Kelly, Joseph. *Our Joyce: From Outcast* . . . , 45–46.

Linguanti, Elsa. "Joyce's 'The Dead' . . . ," 117–118.

Mosher, Harold F. "Clichés and Repetition in *Dubliners*: The Example of 'A Little Cloud,' " in Bosinelli, Rosa M. B., and Harold F. Mosher, Eds. *ReJoycing* . . . , 54–59, 61–63.

Yee, Cordell D. K. *The Word According to* . . . , 95.

"A Mother"
Hedberg, Johannes. "Humour in *Dubliners* . . . ," 401.
Kelly, Joseph. *Our Joyce: From Outcast* . . . , 47.
Leonard, Garry. "The Masquerade of Gender: Mrs. Kearney and the 'Moral Umbrella,' " in Wawrzycka Jolanta W., and Marlena G. Corcoran, Eds. *Gender in Joyce*, 133–149.

"A Painful Case"
Baccolini, Raffaella. " 'She Had Become . . . ,' " 152–154.
Coleman, George L. "Sense Deprivation in . . . ," 362, 368–370.
Linguanti, Elsa. "Joyce's 'The Dead' . . . ," 118–119.
Malamud, Randy. "Durkheimian Sensibilities in Joyce: Anomie and the Social Suicide," in Hart, Clive, C. George Sandulescu, Bonnie K. Scott, and Fritz Senn, Eds. *Images of Joyce*, 127–137.
Rice, Thomas J. "The Geometry . . . ," 45.
Weaver, Jack W. *Joyce's Music and Noise* . . . , 19–21.
Williams, Trevor L. "No Cheer . . . ," 101–104.
————. *Reading Joyce* . . . , 68–71.

"The Sisters"
Bašić, Sonja. "A Book of Many . . . ," 19–20, 22–24, 28.
Bock, Martin. "Syphilisation and Its . . . ," 127–130.
Hedberg, Johannes. "Humour in *Dubliners* . . . ," 393–395.
Kelly, Joseph. *Our Joyce: From Outcast* . . . , 36–37.
Linguanti, Elsa. "Joyce's 'The Dead' . . . ," 114, 115, 116, 117, 118.
Pearce, Sandra M. " 'Umbrellas Re-covered': A Note Uncovering Joyce's Sign of Sterility in *Dubliners*, *Exiles*, and *Ulysses*," *Colby Q*, 33 (1997), 202–203.
Yee, Cordell D. K. *The Word According to* . . . , 25, 29–33, 79, 94.

"Two Gallants"
Bašić, Sonja. "A Book of Many . . . ," 31–32.
Fisher-Seidel, Therese. " 'The Story of the Injured Lady': Gender and Intertextuality in *Dubliners*," in Hart, Clive, C. George Sandulescu, Bonnie K. Scott, and Fritz Senn, Eds. *Images of Joyce*, 386–387.
Hedberg, Johannes. "Humour in *Dubliners* . . . ," 395–397.
Kelly, Joseph. *Our Joyce: From Outcast* . . . , 48–50.
Williams, Trevor L. *Reading Joyce* . . . , 78–81.

FRANZ KAFKA

"Advocates"
Thiher, Allen. "The Legacy of Kafka's Short Fiction: Knowledge of the Impossibility of Knowledge," in Pilipp, Frank, Ed. *The Legacy* . . . ," 205–206.

"The Animal in the Synagogue"
Wasserman, Martin. "Kafka's 'The Animal in the Synagogue': His Marten as a Special Biblical Memory," *Stud Short Fiction*, 34 (1997), 241–245.

"Before the Law"
Fisch, Harold. *New Stories for Old* . . . , 96–97.
Geisenhansluecke, Achim. "Vor dem Gesetz der Dichtung: Hebel und Kafka," *Germ R*, 73 (1998), 303–307.
Gölz, Sabine I. *The Split Scene of Reading* . . . , 133–141.
Reffet, Michel. "Die religiöse Dimension in der deutschen Prager Literatur: Franz Kafka 'Vor dem Gesetz,' Franz Werfel 'Der veruntreute Himmel,' " in Auckenthaler, Karlheinz F., Ed. *Numinoses und Heiliges* . . . , 169–184, 186–187.
Thiher, Allen. "The Legacy. . . ," 201–202.

"The Bridge"
Thiher, Allen. "The Legacy . . . ," 204.

"The Burrow"
Barzel, Hillel. "Kafka's Jewish Identity: A Contemplative World-View," in Schrader, Hans J., Elliott M. Simon, and Charlotte Wardi, Eds. *The Jewish Self-Portrait*. . . , 102–103.
Thiher, Allen. "The Legacy . . . ," 209–210.

"The Cares of a Family Man"
Parlej, Piotr. *The Romantic Theory* . . . , 262–264.

"A Country Doctor"
Doležel, Lubomír. *Heterocosmica* . . . , 188–189.
McGurk, Patricia. "Cracking the Code in 'A Country Doctor': Kafka, Freud, and Homotextuality," in Pereira, Frederico, Ed. *Eleventh International* . . . , 111–118.
Thiher, Allen. "The Legacy . . . ," 201.

"A Crossbreed"
Doležel, Lubomír. *Heterocosmica* . . . , 188.

"Description of a Struggle"
Goebel, Rolf J. "Paris, Capital of Modernity: Kafka and Benjamin," *Monatshefte*, 90 (1998), 445–464.
Woods, Gregory. *A History of Gay* . . . , 227–228.

"Erstes Leid"
Vollmer, Hartmut. "Die Verzweiflung des Artisten—Franz Kafkas Erzählung 'Erstes Leid,'—eine Parabel kuenstlerischer Grenzerfahrung," *Deutsche Vierteljahrsschrift*, 72 (1998), 126–146.

"The Giant Mole" [originally "The Village School Teacher"]
Thiher, Allen. "The Legacy . . . ," 207–209.

"A Hunger Artist"
Charters, Ann, and William E. Sheidley. *Resources* . . . , 5th ed., 139–140.
Gilman, Sander L. "Kafka Goes to Camp," in Gilman, Sander L., and Jack Zipes, Eds. *Yale Companion* . . . , 431–432.

"The Hunter Gracchus"
Blamberger, Günter. "Kafka's Death Images," in Debatin, Bernhard, Timothy R. Jackson, and Daniel Steuer, Eds. *Metaphor and Rational Discourse*, 242–248.

"In Our Synagogue"
Barzel, Hillel. "Kafka's Jewish . . . ," 98.

"In the Penal Colony"
Bishop, Ryan, and Walter Spitz. "The Sentence," *Lang & Lit*, 17 (1992), 19–37.
Holquist, Michael. "Metropole and Penal Colony: Two Models of Comparison," in Franci, Giovanna, Ed. *Remapping the Boundaries* . . . , 31–38.
Netto, Jeffrey A. "Violence and the Scene of Writing: Deconstruction, Psychoanalysis and Technologies of Inscription," in Wright, Will, and Steven Kaplan, Eds. *The Image of Violence* . . . , 353–354.
Porush, David. " 'The Hacker We Call God': Transcendent Writing Machines in Kafka and Pynchon," *Pynchon Notes*, 34–35 (1994), 129–147.
Riggs, Larry W. "Clerking for the Fathers: Infra-Narrative, Individuation, and Terminal Exile in Kafka and Camus," *Symposium*, 50 (1996), 182–183.

"Investigations of a Dog"
Barzel, Hillel. "Kafka's Jewish . . . ," 98–100.
Thiher, Allen. "The Legacy . . . ," 210–214.

"The Judgment"
Hart, Heidi. "Kafka and the Problem of Authentic Selfhood," *Utah Foreign Lang R*, n.v. (1991–1992), 100–104.
Riggs, Larry W. "Clerking for . . . ," 180–181.
Speirs, Ronald, and Beatrice Sandberg. *Franz Kafka*, 12.

"The Metamorphosis"
Charters, Ann, and William E. Sheidley. *Resources* . . . , 5th ed., 141–142.
Hahn, Hannelore. " 'La metamorfosis (Die Verwandlung)' de Franz Kafka y 'El túnel' de Ernesto Sábato," *Círculo*, 24 (1995), 80–85.
Meletinsky, Eleazar M. *The Poetics of Myth*, 315, 320–321, 325–326.
Natanson, Maurice. *The Erotic Bird* . . . , 105–126.
Speirs, Ronald, and Beatrice Sandberg. *Franz Kafka*, 24.
Zhou, Jianming. "Zur Bedeutung von Literarischen Motiven im Kulturaustausch," *Germ R*, 71 (1996), 50–51, 54–56, 58–59, 61–65, 67–68, 70–71.

"The New Advocate"
Thiher, Allen. "The Legacy . . . ," 199–200.

"An Old Manuscript" [same as "An Old Page"]
Goebel, Rolf J. "Kafka's 'An Old Manuscript' and the European Discourse on Ch'ing Dynasty China," in Hsia, Adrian, Ed. *Kafka and China*, 97–111.

"The Refusal"
Thiher, Allen. "The Legacy . . . ," 205.

"Report to an Academy"
Ford, Joh, and Marjorie Ford. *Instructor's Manual* . . . , 38–39.
Riggs, Larry W. "Clerking for . . . ," 182.

"The Silence of the Sirens"
  Gölz, Sabine I. *The Split Scene of Reading* . . . , 161–182.
"The Stoker"
  Speirs, Ronald, and Beatrice Sandberg. *Franz Kafka*, 37–38.
"Up in the Gallery"
  Pilipp, Frank. "In Defense of Kafka: The Case of Peter Handke," in
    Pilipp, Frank, Ed. *The Legacy of Kafka* . . . , 137–144.
"A Visit to a Mine"
  Thiher, Allen. "The Legacy . . . ," 202–203.

LONNY KANEKO

"The Shoyu Kid"
  Streamas, John. "The Invention of Normality in Japanese American
    Internment Narratives," in Brown, Julie, Ed. *Ethnicity* . . . ,
    133–136.

ZEYNEP KARABEY

"Silence"
  Bertram, Carel. "Restructuring the House, Restructuring the Self:
    Renegotiating the Meanings of Place in the Turkish Short Story,"
    in Arat, Zehra F., Ed. *Deconstructing Images* . . . , 270–271.

JORGE KATTÁN ZABLAH

"Milagros, milagros y más milagros"
  Leal, Luis. "La ironia, hilo conductor en los cuentos de Jorge Kattán
    Zablah," *Alba de América*, 15 (1997), 324–325.

KAWABATA YASUNARI

"Immortality"
  Baldwin, Dean. *Instructor's Resource* . . . , 161–162.

JONATHAN KEATES

"La Dolce Prospettiva"
  Tintner, Adeline R. *Henry James's Legacy* . . . , 435–436.

GOTTFRIED KELLER

"Clothes Make the Man"
  Goetschel, Willi. "Love, Sex, and Other Utilities: Keller's Unsettling

Account," in Prier, A., and Gerald Gillespie, Eds. *Narrative Ironies*, 230.

"Eugenia"
Downing, Eric. "Double Takes: Genre and Gender in Keller's *Sieben Legenden*," *Germ R*, 73 (1998), 229–236.

"The Forger of His Own Fortune"
Goetschel, Willi. "Love, Sex . . . ," 230–231.

"The Lost Smile"
Goetschel, Willi. "Love, Sex . . . ," 232–234.

"Mirror, the Cat"
Goetschel, Willi. "Love, Sex . . . ," 227–229.

"The Misused Love Letter"
Goetschel, Willi. "Love, Sex . . . ," 231.

"Mrs. Regel Amrain and Her Youngest Son"
Goetschel, Willi. "Love, Sex . . . ," 227.

"Pankraz the Sulker"
Goetschel, Willi. "Love, Sex . . . ," 226.

"The Three Righteous Comb-Makers"
Dürr, Volker. " 'Nun sag, wie hast du's mit der Religion?' Gottfried Keller's Critique of Reformed Protestantism in *Meretlein* and Later Narratives," *Colloquia Germanica*, 29 (1996), 126–128.
Goetschel, Willi. "Love, Sex . . . ," 227.

"Das verlorene Lachen"
Dürr, Volker. " 'Nun sag . . . ," 129–132.

"A Village Romeo and Juliet"
Goetschel, Willi. "Love, Sex . . . ," 226–227.
Johnston, Otto W. "Chromatic Symbolism in Gottfried Keller's *Romeo und Julia auf dem Dorfe*," in Stephan, Alexander, Ed. *Themes and Structures . . .* , 154–163.

JAMES PATRICK KELLY

"Think Like a Dinosaur"
Duncan, Andy. "Think Like a Humanist: James Patrick Kelly's 'Think Like a Dinosaur' as a Satiric Rebuttal to Tom Godwin's 'The Cold Equations,' " *New York R Sci Fiction*, 8, xciv (1996), 1, 8–11.

JESSIE KESSON

"Railway Journey"
Murray, Isobel. "Jessie Kesson," in Gifford, Douglas, and Dorothy McMillan, Eds. *A History . . .* , 484–486.

DANIIL KHARMS [DANIIL INVANOICH YUVACHEV]

"The Artist and the Watch"
Roberts, Graham. *The Last Soviet . . .* , 93.

"Blue Notebook No. 10"
Roberts, Graham. *The Last Soviet* . . . , 136–137.
"The Career of Ivan Yakovlevich"
Roberts, Graham. *The Last Soviet* . . . , 90.
"The Connection"
Roberts, Graham. *The Last Soviet* . . . , 90–91.
"Knights"
Roberts, Graham. *The Last Soviet* . . . , 34–35.
"Mashkin Killed Koshkin"
Roberts, Graham. *The Last Soviet* . . . , 88–89.
"The Old Woman"
Roberts, Graham. *The Last Soviet* . . . , 39–44.
"On Equilibrium"
Roberts, Graham. *The Last Soviet* . . . , 91–92, 135.
"On Phenomena and Existences No. 2"
Roberts, Graham. *The Last Soviet* . . . , 135–136.
"They Call Me the Capuchin"
Roberts, Graham. *The Last Soviet* . . . , 34–35.

ALEXANDER KIELLAND

"Karen"
Sjåvik, Jan. "A Rhetorical Approach to Three Norwegian Short Stories," *Selecta*, 14 (1993), 81.

KIM WŎNJU

"Awakening"
Yung-Hee Kim. "From Subservience to Autonomy: Kim Wŏnju's 'Awakening,' " *Korean Stud*, 21 (1997), 10–17.

JAMAICA KINCAID

"At the Bottom of the River"
Baldwin, Dean. *Instructor's Resource* . . . , 189–190.
"Girl"
Charters, Ann, and William E. Sheidley. *Resources* . . . , 5th ed., 144.
"Poor Visitor"
Ford, Joh, and Marjorie Ford. *Instructor's Manual* . . . , 114–115.

GRACE KING

"A Crippled Hope"
Robison, Lori. " 'Why, Why Do We Not Write Our Side?' Gender and

Southern Self-Representation in Grace King's *Balcony Stories*," in
Inness, Sherrie A., and Diana Royer, Eds. *Breaking Boundaries* . . . ,
65–69.
"The Story of a Day"
Robison, Lori. " 'Why, Why Do We . . . ,' " 64–65.

MAXINE HONG KINGSTON

"No Name Woman"
Richardson, Brian. *UnLikely Stories* . . . , 152–153.

W[ILLIAM] P[ATRICK] KINSELLA

"Shoeless Joe Jackson Comes to Iowa"
Charters, Ann, and William E. Sheidley. *Resources* . . . , 5th ed.,
145–146.

RUDYARD KIPLING

"At the End of the Passage"
Bivona, Daniel. *British Imperial Literature* . . . , 73–80.
Hai, Ambreen. "On Truth and Lie in a Colonial Sense: Kipling's Tales
of Tale-Telling," *ELH*, 64 (1997), 604–606.
"Baa Baa, Black Sheep"
Daniel, Anne M. "Kipling's Use of Verse and Prose in 'Baa Baa,
Black Sheep,' " *Stud Engl Lit 1500–1900*, 37 (1997), 857–875.
"The Big Drunk Draf"
Peck, John. *War, the Army* . . . , 148–149.
" 'The Biggest Liar in Asia' (By One Who Knows Him)"
Hai, Ambreen. "On Truth . . . ," 604–606.
"Black Jack"
Peck, John. *War, the Army* . . . , 162–163.
"The Bronckhorst Divorce-Case"
Scannell, James M. "The Method Is Unsound: The Aesthetic
Dissonance of Colonial Justification in Kipling, Conrad, and
Greene," *Style*, 30 (1996), 412–413.
"The Captive"
Peck, John. *War, the Army* . . . , 161–162.
"The Comprehension of Private Copper"
Holden, Philip. "Halls of Mirrors: Mimicry and Ambivalence in
Kipling's Boer War Short Stories," *ArielE*, 28, iv (1997), 94–95,
96, 98–99, 102–103, 104, 105, 106–107.
Peck, John. *War, the Army* . . . , 162.
"The Conversion of Aurelian McGoggin"
Bivona, Daniel. *British Imperial Literature* . . . , 69–70.

HEINRICH VON KLEIST

Brown, Robert H. "Fear of Social Change in Kleist's 'Erdbeben in Chili,' " *Monatshefte*, 84 (1992), 447–458.
"Der Findling"
Brown, Hilda M. *Heinrich von Kleist* . . . , 195–205.
Newman, Gail M. "Family Violence in Heinrich von Kleist's 'Der Findling,' " *Colloquia Germanica*, 29 (1996), 287–302.
"Die Heilige Cäcilie oder Die Gewalt der Musik"
Brown, Hilda M. *Heinrich von Kleist* . . . , 161–179.
Brueggeman, Diethelm. " 'Die heilige Cäcilie als Paradigma fuer Kleists Hermetik," *Deutsche Vierteljahrsschrift*, 72 (1998), 592–599, 603–607, 610–636.
"Die Marquise von O——"
Allan, Seán. " '. . . auf einen Lasterhaften war ich gefasst, aber auf keinen—Teufel': Heinrich von Kleist's 'Die Marquise von O——,' " *Germ Life & Letters*, 50 (1997), 307–322.
Brown, Hilda M. *Heinrich von Kleist* . . . , 206–222.
Murphy, Harriet. "Theatres of Emptiness: The Case of Kleist's 'Marquise von O——,' " *Oxford Germ Stud*, 24 (1995), 80–111.
"Michael Kohlhaas"
Brown, Hilda M. *Heinrich von Kleist* . . . , 97–128.
Moraru, Christian. "The Reincarnated Plot: E. L. Doctorow's *Ragtime*, Heinrich von Kleist's 'Michael Kohlhaas,' and the Spectacle of Modernity," *Comparatist*, 21 (1997), 92–93, 97, 103–105.
Müller, Gernot. " 'Schmutz zugleich und Glanz': Zu einer mutmaßlichen Gemäldeallusion Kleists und ihrem Reflex im 'Michael Kohlhaas,' " in Anderson, Bo, and Gernot Müller, Eds. *Kleine Beiträge* . . . , 179, 186–192.
Sussman, Henry S. "Kleist's 'Michael Kohlhaas' and Postmodernity, with Some Thoughts on Franz Kafka," *J Kafka Soc Am*, 18, ii (1994), 37–49.
Zeuch, Ulrike. "Die 'praktische Notwendigkeit des moralischen Imperativs'—der Vernunft unbegreiflich? Zu Heinrich von Kleists Konsequenzen aus der inhaltlichen Leere eines formalen Prinzips," *Das Achtzehnte Jahrhundert*, 21, i (1997), 90–99, 102–103.
"Die Verlobung in St. Domingo"
Allen, Richard. "Reading Kleist and Hoffmann," in Bygrave, Stephen, Ed. *Romantic Writings*, 251–259.
Brown, Hilda M. *Heinrich von Kleist* . . . , 179–194.
"Der Zweikampf"
Brown, Hilda M. *Heinrich von Kleist* . . . , 129–144.
Krüger-Fürhoff, Irmela M. "Den verwundeten Körper lesen: Zur Hermeneutik physischer und ästhetischer Grenzverletzungen im Kontext von Kleists 'Zweikampf,' " *Kleist-Jahrbuch*, n.v. (1998), 21–22, 25–36.

VLADY KOCIANCICH

"Los falsos límites"
Dellepiane, Angela B. "The Short Stories and Novels of Vlady Kociancich," *Letras Femeninas*, 22, i–ii (1996), 78.

"La extranjera"
Dellepiane, Angela B. "The Short Stories . . . ," 82.
"Leila"
Dellepiane, Angela B. "The Short Stories . . . ," 81–82.
"Todos los caminos"
Dellepiane, Angela B. "The Short Stories . . . ," 82–83.

KOJIMA NOBUO

"The Rifle"
Goossen, Theodore W. "Introduction," in Goossen, Theodore, Ed. *The Oxford Book* . . . , xxix–xxx.

NANCY KRESS

"Margin of Error"
Landon, Brooks. *Science Fiction* . . . , 173–174.

BRIGITTE KRONAUER

"A Day That Didn't End Hopelessly After All"
Ittner, Jutta. "Jigsaw Puzzles: Female Perception and Self in Brigitte Kronauer's 'A Day That Didn't End Hopelessly After All,' " *Women Germ Yearbook*, 13 (1997), 171–187.
"Day with Interruption and Opponent"
Ittner, Jutta. "My Self, My Body, My World: Homemaking in the Fiction of Brigitte Kronauer," in Wiley, Catherine, and Fiona R. Barnes, Eds. *Homemaking* . . . , 56–58.
"The Miracle of a Hypothesis"
Ittner, Jutta. "My Self . . . ," 58–59, 61.
"A Sort of Achievement According to Nature"
Ittner, Jutta. "My Self . . . ," 62.

OLGA KUCHKINA

"The Philosopher and the Maiden"
Efimov, Nina. "Crime and Punishment in Ol'ga Kuckina's 'Filosof I Devka,' " in Efimov, Nina A., Christine D. Tomei, and Richard L. Chapple, Eds. *Critical Essays* . . . , 84–93.

SHRAWAN KUMAR

"Me Without My Mask"
Rahim, Habibeh. "The Mirage of Faith and Justice: Some

Sociopolitical and Cultural Themes in Post-Colonial Urdu Short
Stories," in Hawley, John C., Ed. *The Postcolonial Crescent* ... ,
233–235.

HENRY KUTTNER

"The Piper's Son"
Attebery, Brian. "Super Men," *Sci-Fiction Stud*, 25 (1998), 68.
"The Voice of the Lobster"
Russell, W. M. S. "Great SF Short Fiction, 2: 'The Voice of the
Lobster' by Henry Kuttner," *Foundation*, 70 (1997), 80–81.

TOMMASO LANDOLFI

"Gogol's Wife"
Schwartz, Hillel. *The Culture* ... , 127.

HERNÁN LARA ZAVALA

"Después del amor"
Brescia, Pablo A. J. "Hernán Lara Zavala: *Después del amor* ... y de
otras cuentos," in Herrera, Sara P., Ed. *El cuento mexicano* ... ,
489–491.
"El dilema de Genoveva Montanaro"
Brescia, Pablo A. J. "Hernán Lara Zavala ... ," 484–486.
"Perla ante el espejo"
Brescia, Pablo A. J. "Hernán Lara Zavala ... ," 486–489.

RING LARDNER

"Haircut"
Blythe, Hal, and Charlie Sweet. "Lardner's 'Haircut,' " *Explicator*,
55, iv (1997), 219–221.

NELLA LARSEN

"Passing"
Butler, Judith. "Passing, Queering: Nella Larsen's Psychoanalytic
Challenge," in Abel, Elizabeth, Barbara Christian, and Helene
Moglen, Eds. *Female Subjects* ... , 267–281.
Haviland, Beverly. "Passing from Paranoia to Plagiarism: The Abject
Authorship of Nella Larsen," *Mod Fiction Stud*, 43 (1997),
300–302.
Johnson, Barbara. *The Feminist Difference* ... , 158–160.
Sisney, Mary F. "The View from the Outside: Black Novels of

Manners," in Bowers, Bege K., and Barbara Brothers, Eds. *Reading and Writing* . . . , 177–179; rpt. in Felton, Sharon, and Michelle C. Loris, Eds. *The Critical Response* . . . , 68–70.

Sullivan, Neil. "Nella Larsen's 'Passing' and the Fading Subject," *African Am R*, 32 (1998), 373–386.

"Quicksand"

Clemmen, Yves W. A. "Nella Larsen's 'Quicksand': A Narrative of Difference," *Coll Lang Assoc J*, 40 (1997), 458–466.

Johnson, Barbara. *The Feminist Difference* . . . , 37–60.

———. "The Quicksands of the Self: Nella Larsen and Heinz Kohut," in Abel, Elizabeth, Barbara Christian, and Helene Moglen, Eds. *Female Subjects* . . . , 252–265.

Roberts, Kimberley. "The Clothes Make the Woman: The Symbolics of Prostitution in Nella Larsen's 'Quicksand' and Claude McKay's *Home to Harlem*," *Tulsa Stud Women's Lit*, 16 (1997), 112–118.

Sisney, Mary F. "The View from the Outside . . . ," 175–177; rpt. in Felton, Sharon, and Michelle C. Loris, Eds. *The Critical Response* . . . , 67–68.

"Sanctuary"

Haviland, Beverly. "Passing . . . ," 305–306.

ROBERTO LUIS LASTRE

"El día de cartas"

Alvarez, José B. "(Re)escritura de la violencia: El individuo frente la historia en la cuentística novísima cubana," *Chasqui*, 26, ii (1997), 87–89.

MARGARET LAURENCE

"Horses of the Night"

New, W. H. *Land Sliding* . . . , 158–159.

"The Loons"

Ware, Tracy. "Race and Conflict in Garner's 'One-Two-Three Little Indians' and Laurence's 'The Loons,' " *Stud Canadian Lit*, 23, ii (1998), 75–80.

"The Mask of the Bear"

Charters, Ann, and William E. Sheidley. *Resources* . . . , 5th ed., 147–148.

"To Set Our House in Order"

Baldwin, Dean. *Instructor's Resource* . . . , 175–178.

MARY LAVIN

"An Akoulina of the Irish Midlands"

Corcoran, Neil. *After Yeats and Joyce* . . . , 77–78.

"The Becker Wives"
> Neary, Michael. "Flora's Answer to the Irish Question: A Study of Mary Lavin's 'The Becker Wives,' " *Twentieth Century Lit*, 42 (1996), 516–525.

"Trastevere"
> Tallone, Giovanna. " 'Terra Incognita': Mary Lavin's Italian Stories," in Serpillo, Giuseppe, and Donatella Badin, Eds. *The Classical World* . . . , 104, 105–107.

"Villa Violetta"
> Tallone, Giovanna. " 'Terra Incognita' . . . ," 104–105, 106–107.

D. H. LAWRENCE

"The Blind Man"
> Becket, Fiona. *D. H. Lawrence* . . . , 18–19.
> Monk, Ray. "Devilish Repressions: Bertrand Russell's Use of Fiction as Autobiography," in Gould, Warwick, and Thomas E. Staley, Eds. *Writing the Lives* . . . , 255–257.
> Rosenbaum, S. P. *Aspects of Bloomsbury* . . . , 49–51.
> Tate, Trudi. *Modernism, History and the First* . . . , 104–109.
> Wussow, Helen. *The Nightmare of History* . . . , 87–88.

"The Captain's Doll"
> Wussow, Helen. *The Nightmare* . . . , 137–140.

"England, My England"
> Bell, Michael. *Literature, Modernism* . . . , 117–118.

"A Fragment of Stained Glass"
> Michelucci, Stefania. "The Functional Aspect of the Wood in the Shorter Fiction by D. H. Lawrence," *British & Am Stud*, 1, i (1996), 53–54.

"Glad Ghosts"
> Ellis, David. *D. H. Lawrence* . . . , 275–276.

"The Horsedealer's Daughter"
> Bell, Michael. *Literature, Modernism* . . . , 97–111.

"Jimmy and the Desperate Woman"
> Ellis, David. *D. H. Lawrence* . . . , 165–167.

"The Ladybird"
> Wussow, Helen. *The Nightmare* . . . , 136–137.

"The Last Laugh"
> Ellis, David. *D. H. Lawrence* . . . , 156–157.

"Monkey Nuts"
> Wussow, Helen. *The Nightmare* . . . , 82–83.

"The Mortal Coil"
> Wussow, Helen. *The Nightmare* . . . , 89–90.

"Mother and Daughter"
> Ellis, David. *D. H. Lawrence* . . . , 415–416.

"Odour of Chrysanthemums"
  Charters, Ann, and William E. Sheidley. *Resources* . . . , 5th ed.,
    149–150.
  Clifford, Stephen P. *Beyond the Heroic 'I'* . . . , 47–49.
  Ferguson, Suzanne. "Local Color and the Function of Setting in the
    English Short Story," in Kaylor, Noel H., Ed. *Creative and
    Critical* . . . , 21–23.
"The Princess"
  Clifford, Stephen P. *Beyond the Heroic 'I'* . . . , 274–275, 276–287.
"The Prussian Officer"
  Baldwin, Dean. *Instructor's Resource* . . . , 89–91.
  Michelucci, Stefania. "The Functional . . . ," 55.
"The Rocking-Horse Winner"
  Branson, Stephanie R. "Banishing the Nightmare: Lawrence's 'The
    Rocking Horse Winner' and Dinesen's 'The Ghost Horses,' " *Short
    Story*, 2, ii (1992), 41–50.
  Charters, Ann, and William E. Sheidley. *Resources* . . . , 5th ed., 152.
  Ellis, David. *D. H. Lawrence* . . . , 280, 281.
  Ford, Joh, and Marjorie Ford. *Instructor's Manual* . . . , 40–41.
"St. Mawr"
  Poplawski, Paul. "Lawrence's Satiric Style: Language and Voice in
    'St. Mawr,' " in Eggert, Paul, and John Worthen, Eds. *Lawrence
    and Comedy*, 158–178.
"Samson and Delilah"
  Díaz-Medrano, Conchita. "Narrative Voice and Point of View in D. H.
    Lawrence's 'Samson and Delilah,' " *Essays Lit*, 22 (1995), 87–96.
"The Shades of Spring"
  Michelucci, Stefania. "The Functional . . . ," 52–53.
"Tickets, Please"
  Wussow, Helen. *The Nightmare* . . . , 80–82.
"Two Blue Birds"
  Ellis, David. *D. H. Lawrence* . . . , 300–301.
"The White Stocking"
  Spilka, Mark. *Eight Lessons* . . . , 153–166.
"Wintry Peacock"
  Ford, Joh, and Marjorie Ford. *Instructor's Manual* . . . , 39–40.
  Wussow, Helen. *The Nightmare* . . . , 83–85.
"The Woman Who Rode Away"
  Ellis, David. *D. H. Lawrence* . . . , 187–188.
  Sargent, M. Elizabeth. "The Wives, the Virgins, and Isis: Lawrence's
    Exploration of Female Will in Four Late Novellas of Spiritual
    Quest," *D. H. Lawrence R*, 26 (1997), 230–235.

DAVID LEAVITT

"Gravity"
  Ford, Joh, and Marjorie Ford. *Instructor's Manual* . . . , 127–128.

"We Meet at Last"
Charters, Ann, and William E. Sheidley. *Resources* . . . , 5th ed.,
154–155.

JEAN-MARIE GUSTAVE LE CLÉZIO

"Pawana"
Thibault, Bruno. " 'Awaité Pawana': J. M. G. Le Clézio's Vision of
the Sacred," *World Lit Today*, 71 (1997), 723–729.

VERNON LEE [VIOLET PAGET]

"Amour Dure"
Zorn, Christa. "Aesthetic Intertextuality as Cultural Critique: Vernon
Lee Rewrites History through Walter Pater's 'La Gioconda,"
Victorian News, 91 (1997), 4–10.
"The Doll"
Navarette, Susan J. *The Shape* . . . , 155–160, 164–169, 170–176.
"Lady Tal"
Tintner, Adeline R. *Henry James's Legacy* . . . , 17–18.
"A Wicked Voice"
Navarette, Susan J. *The Shape* . . . , 150–153.

JOSEPH SHERIDAN LE FANU

"Carmilla"
Auerback, Nina. "My Vampire, My Friend: The Intimacy Dracula
Destroyed," in Gordon, Joan, and Veronica Hollinger, Eds. *Blood
Read* . . . , 11–12.
"Green Tea"
Hendershot, Cyndy. *The Animal Within* . . . , 100–105.

GERTRUD VON LE FORT

"The Song at the Scaffold"
La Chevallerie, Eleanore von. "Gertrud von Le Fort and the Fear of
Blanche de la Force," *Renascence*, 48 (1995), 12–22.

URSULA K. LE GUIN

"Buffalo Gals Won't You Come Out Tonight"
Armbruster, Karla. " 'Buffalo Gals, Won't You Come Out Tonight': A
Call for Boundary-Crossing in Ecofeminist Literary Criticism," in
Gaard, Greta, and Patrick D. Murphy, Eds. *Ecofeminist
Literary* . . . , 106–115.

Helford, Elyce R. "Going 'Native': Le Guin, Misha, and the Politics of Speculative Literature," *Foundation*, 71 (1997), 77–81.
"The Day Before the Revolution"
Donawerth, Jane. *Frankenstein's Daughters* . . . , 91–92.
"The Ones Who Walk Away from Omelas"
Charters, Ann, and William E. Sheidley. *Resources* . . . , 5th ed., 156.

MURRAY LEINSTER

"First Contact"
Landon, Brooks. *Science Fiction* . . . , 72–74.

BOB LEMAN

"The Pilgrimage of Clifford M."
Carter, Margaret L. "The Vampire as Alien in Contemporary Fiction," in Gordon, Joan, and Veronica Hollinger, Eds. *Blood Read* . . . , 41–42.

MONFOON LEONG

"New Year for Fong Wing"
Wang, Qun. "Asian American Short Stories: Dialogizing the Asian American Experience," in Brown, Julie, Ed. *Ethnicity* . . . , 119–120.

NIKOLAI LESKOV

"The Hour of God's Will"
Sperrle, Irmhild C. "Leskov, Tolstoy, and the Three Questions," *Tolstoy Stud J*, 10 (1998), 63–79.

DORIS LESSING

"The Black Madonna"
Baldwin, Dean. *Instructor's Resource* . . . , 165–167.
"How I Finally Lost My Heart"
Ford, Joh, and Marjorie Ford. *Instructor's Manual* . . . , 65–67.
"The Mother of the Child in Question"
Ford, Joh, and Marjorie Ford. *Instructor's Manual* . . . , 67–68.
"The Old Chief Mshlanga"
Charters, Ann, and William E. Sheidley. *Resources* . . . , 5th ed., 157–158.

GEORGE HENRY LEWES

"Metamorphoses"
Handley, Graham. "G. H. Lewes, 'Metamorphoses' and George
Eliot," *George Eliot-George Henry Lewes Stud*, 28–29 (1995),
50–56.

MERIDEL LE SUEUR

"The Dark of Time"
Mickenberg, Julia. "Writing the Midwest: Meridel Le Sueur and the
Making of a Radical Regional Tradition," in Inness, Sherrie A., and
Diana Royer, Eds. *Breaking Boundaries . . .* , 157–158.

PRIMO LEVI

"His Own Blacksmith"
Wilson, Rita. "Primo Levi: The Craft of Narration," in Gitay,
Yehoshua, Ed. *Literary Responses . . .* , 35.

MEYER LEVIN

"After All I Did For Israel"
Furman, Andrew. *Israel Through the Jewish-American . . .* , 37–38.
"Maurie Finds His Medium"
Furman, Andrew. *Israel Through the Jewish-American . . .* , 24–26.

SINCLAIR LEWIS

"Number Seven to Sagapoose"
Di Renzo, Anthony. "Introduction," *If I Were Boss . . .* [by Sinclair
Lewis], xxxiii.
"The Whisperer"
Di Renzo, Anthony. "Introduction," xxv–xxvi.

WYNDHAM LEWIS

"The Death of the Ankou"
Edwards, Paul. "Wyndham Lewis's Narrative of Origins: 'The Death
of Ankou,' " *Mod Lang R*, 92 (1997), 22–35.

THOMAS LIGOTTI

"Les Fleurs"
Joshi, S. T. "Thomas Ligotti: The Escape from Life," *Stud Weird
Fiction*, 12 (1993), 35.

"The Last Feast of Harlequin"
Joshi, S. T. "Thomas Ligotti . . . ," 35.

SHIRLEY GEOK-LIN LIM

"Flight"
Manuel, Dolores de. "Imagined Homecomings: Strategies for Reconnection in the Writing of Asian Exiles," in Kain, Geoffrey, Ed. *Ideas of Home* . . . , 43–44.

LING SHUHUA

"After Drinking"
McDougall, Bonnie S. "Dominance and Disappearance: A Post-Feminist Review of Fiction by Mao Dun and Ling Shuhua," in Findeisen, Raoul D., and Robert H. Gassmann, Eds. *Autumn Floods* . . . , 294–295.

"The Embroidered Pillows"
McDougall, Bonnie S. "Dominance . . . ," 295–296.

"The Eve of the Mid-Autumn Festival"
McDougall, Bonnie S. "Dominance . . . ," 298–299.

"Goodbye"
McDougall, Bonnie S. "Dominance . . . ," 296–297.

"It's Said That Something Like This Did Happen"
McDougall, Bonnie S. "Dominance . . . ," 300–301.

"The Lucky One"
McDougall, Bonnie S., and Kam Louie. *The Literature of China* . . . , 122–123.

"Madam"
McDougall, Bonnie S. "Dominance . . . ," 299–300.

"Waiting"
McDougall, Bonnie S. "Dominance . . . ," 301.

"Women"
McDougall, Bonnie S., and Kam Louie. *The Literature of China* . . . , 123.

OSMAN LINS

"The Confused"
Nunes, Benedito. "Narration in Many Voices," trans. Linda Ledford-Miller, *R Contemp Fiction*, 15, iii (1995), 202.

"Hahn's Pentagon"
Nunes, Benedito. "Narration . . . ," 198–199, 200.

"Lost and Found"
Nunes, Benedito. "Narration . . . ," 201.

CLARICE LISPECTOR

"Evolution of Myopia"
Ford, Joh, and Marjorie Ford. *Instructor's Manual* . . . , 78–79.

"El huevo y la gallina"
Russotto, Márgara. "Encantamiento y compassion: Un estudio de 'El huevo y la gallina,' " *Inti*, 43–44 (1996), 167–175.

"The Smallest Woman in the World"
Charters, Ann, and William E. Sheidley. *Resources* . . . , 5th ed., 159–160.

LIU XINWU

"The Class Teacher"
McDougall, Bonnie S., and Kam Louie. *The Literature of China* . . . , 391–392.

SYLVIA LIZÁRRAGA

"Silver Lake Road"
Herrera-Sobek, María. "The Politics of Rape: Sexual Transgression in Chicana Fiction," in St. Joan, Jacqueline, and Annette B. McElhiney, Eds. *Beyond Portia* . . . , 220–221.

JACK LONDON

"All Gold Canyon"
Baskett, Sam. "Mythic Dimensions of 'All Gold Canyon,' " *Jack London J*, 2 (1995), 10–24.

"The Apostate"
Simpson, Mark. "Travel's Disciplines," *Canadian R Am Stud*, 26, ii (1996), 89–91.

"By the Turtle of Tasman"
Berkove, Lawrence I. "London's Developing Conceptions of Masculinity," *Jack London J*, 3 (1996), 121–126.

"The Chinago"
Riedl, Gary, and Thomas R. Tietze. "Misinterpreting the Unreadable: Jack London's 'The Chinago' and 'The Whale Tooth,' " *Stud Short Fiction*, 34 (1997), 508–513, 518.

"The House of Pride"
Berkove, Lawrence I. "London's Developing . . . ," 119–121, 125.

"The Red One"
Kirsch, James. "Jack London's Quest: 'The Red One,' " *Psychological Perspectives*, 11 (1980), 143–154; rpt. Nuernberg, Susan M., Ed. *The Critical Response* . . . , 206–216.

"The Strength of the Strong"
  Lovett-Graff, Bennett. "Prehistory as Posthistory: The Socialist
    Science Fiction of Jack London," *Jack London J*, 3 (1996), 91–95.

"The Sun-Dog Trial"
  Cassuto, Leonard. "Chasing the Lost Signifier Down 'The Sun-Dog
    Trial,' " *Jack London J*, 2 (1995), 64–72.

"To Build a Fire"
  Adams, George R. "Why the Man Dies in 'To Build a Fire,' " in
    Nuernberg, Susan M., Ed. *The Critical Response* . . . , 27–36.
  Charters, Ann, and William E. Sheidley. *Resources* . . . , 5th ed., 161.
  +Labor, Earle, and King Hendricks. "Jack London's Twice-Told
    Tale," in Nuernberg, Susan M., Ed. *The Critical Response* . . . ,
    9–16.
  +May, Charles E. " 'To Build a Fire': Physical Fiction and
    Metaphysical Critics," in Nuernberg, Susan M., Ed. *The Critical
    Response* . . . , 22–26.
  +Mellard, James M. "Dramatic Mode and Tragic Structure in 'To
    Build a Fire,' " in Nuernberg, Susan M., Ed. *The Critical
    Response* . . . , 17–21.
  +Peterson, Clell. "The Theme of Jack London's 'To Build a Fire,' "
    in Nuernberg, Susan M., Ed. *The Critical Response* . . . , 3–8.
  Reesman, Jeanne C. " 'Never Travel Alone': Naturalism, Jack London,
    and the White Silence," *Am Lit Realism*, 29, ii (1997), 40–46.

"The Whale Tooth"
  Riedl, Gary, and Thomas R. Tietze. "Misinterpreting . . . ," 513–518.

"When the World Was Young"
  Petersen, Per Serritslev. "The Dr. Jekyll and Mr. Hyde Motif in Jack
    London's Science Fiction: Formula and Intertextuality in 'When the
    World Was Young,' " *Jack London J*, 3 (1996), 105–116.

JOHN LUTHER LONG

"Madame Butterfly"
  Schueller, Malini J. *U.S. Orientalisms* . . . , 199–200.

AUGUSTUS BALDWIN LONGSTREET

"A Sage Conversation"
  Pryse, Marjorie. "Origins of American Literary Regionalism: Gender
    in Irving, Stowe, and Longstreet," in Inness, Sherrie A., and Diana
    Royer, Eds. *Breaking Boundaries* . . . , 31.

ROBERTO LÓPEZ MORENO

"Señor Dios"
  Negrín, Edith. "La crítica al poder desde la ciudad perdida: 'Yo se lo

dije al presidente,' de Roberto López Moreno," in Herrera, Sara P.,
Ed. *El cuento mexicano* . . . , 425–426.
"Yo se lo dije al presidente"
Negrín, Edith. "La crítica . . . ," 428–237.

VIOLETA LÓPEZ SURIA

"La barra"
Bertrán, Dorian L. "Percances de ocupación en Katherine Mansfield
y Violeta López Suria," *Revista de Estudios Hispánicos*, 22 (1995),
365–367, 373–378.

JEAN LORRAIN

"The Glass of Blood"
Stableford, Brian. "*Sang* for Supper: Notes on the Metaphorical Use
of Vampires in *The Empire of Fear* and *Young Blood*," in Gordon,
Joan, and Veronica Hollinger, Eds. *Blood Read* . . . , 70–72.
"L'un d'eux"
Ziegler, Robert. "The Narrative Masks of Jean Lorrain," *Selecta*, 15
(1994), 32–33.

DAVID WONG LOUIE

"The Mover"
Cheung, King-kok. "Of Men and Men: Reconstructing Chinese
American Masculinity," in Stanley, Sandra K., Ed. *Other
Sisterhoods* . . . , 188–189.
"Pangs of Love"
Cheung, King-kok. "Of Men and Men . . . ," 185–187.

H. P. LOVECRAFT

"The Call of Cthulhu"
Garrett, Michael. "Death Takes a Dive: Poe's 'The City in the Sea'
and Lovecraft's 'The Call of Cthulhu,' " *Lovecraft Stud*, 35 (Fall,
1996), 22–24.
"The Dunwich Horror"
Schnabel, William. "Le Corps fantastique chez Lovecraft," in
Marigny, Jean, Intro., *Images fantastiques du corps*, 107–108, 114.
"The Haunter of the Dark"
MacCulloch, Simon. "The Toad in the Study: M. R. James, H. P.
Lovecraft, and Forbidden Knowledge (Part Two)," *Stud Weird
Fiction*, 21 (1997), 18–20.

"He"
Faig, Kenneth W. "Lovecraft's 'He,' " *Lovecraft Stud*, 37 (Fall, 1997), 17–25.

"The Outsider"
Montelone, Paul. "The Inner Significance of 'The Outsider,' " *Lovecraft Stud*, 35 (Fall, 1996), 9–21.

"The Shadow over Innsmouth"
Lovett-Graff, Bennett. "Shadows over Lovecraft: Reactionary Fantasy and Immigrant Eugenics," *Extrapolation*, 38 (1997), 173–192.

"The White Ship"
Montelone, Paul. " 'The White Ship': A Schopenhauerian Odyssey," *Lovecraft Stud*, 36 (Spring, 1997), 2–14.

MALCOLM LOWRY

"Ghostkeeper"
Bond, Greg. "Malcolm Lowry's 'history of someone's imagination': A Critical Reassessment of *Dark as the Grave Wherein My Friend is Laid*," *Malcolm Lowry R*, 40 (1997), 80–81.

LU LING [XU SIYU]

"The Battle of the Lowlands"
McDougall, Bonnie S., and Kam Louie. *The Literature of China* . . . , 239.

LU XÜN [LU HSÜN OR CHOU SHU-JEN]

"Diary of a Madman"
Charters, Ann, and William E. Sheidley. *Resources* . . . , 5th ed., 163–164.
Hockx, Michel. "Mad Women and Mad Men: Intraliterary Contact in Early Republican Literature," in Findeisen, Raoul D., and Robert H. Gassmann, Eds. *Autumn Floods* . . . , 316–318.
Huters, Theodore. "The Stories of Lu Xun," in Miller, Barbara S., Ed. *Masterworks of Asian* . . . , 313–315.
Lieberman, Sally T. *The Mother* . . . , 193–194.
Lyell, William A. "Down the Road that Mei Took: Women in Yin Fu's Work," in Findeisen, Raoul D., and Robert H. Gassmann, Eds. *Autumn Floods* . . . , 336–337.
McDougall, Bonnie S., and Kam Louie. *The Literature of China* . . . , 83–84, 94–96.

"In the Wineshop"
Lieberman, Sally T. *The Mother* . . . , 88–91.

"The Loner"
Yin, Xiaoling. "Lu Xun's Parallel to Walter Benjamin: The

Consciousness of the Tragic in 'The Loner,' " *Tamkang R*, 26, iii (1996), 53–68.

"The New Year's Sacrifice"
Huters, Theodore. "The Stories . . . ," 315–318.
Lieberman, Sally T. *The Mother* . . . , 196–202.
McDougall, Bonnie S., and Kam Louie. *The Literature of China* . . . , 98.
Richardson, Brian. *UnLikely Stories* . . . , 151.

"Story in a Teacup"
McDougall, Bonnie S., and Kam Louie. *The Literature of China* . . . , 96.

"The Story of Hair"
Findeisen, Raoul D. *"Kairos* or the Due Time: On Date and Dates in Modern Chinese Literature," in Findeisen, Raoul D., and Robert H. Gassmann, Eds. *Autumn Floods* . . . , 226–227.

"Tomorrow"
Lieberman, Sally T. *The Mother* . . . , 194–196.

"The True Story of Ah Q"
McDougall, Bonnie S., and Kam Louie. *The Literature of China* . . . , 96–98.

LU YIN

"Father"
Lieberman, Sally T. *The Mother* . . . , 60–62, 63, 115–116.

"Lishi's Diary"
Lieberman, Sally T. *The Mother* . . . , 113–115.

"Old Friends at the Seaside"
Lieberman, Sally T. *The Mother* . . . , 110–112, 168–170.

CARMEN LUGO FILIPPI

"Milagros, Calle Mercurio"
Homo-Delgado, Asunción. "Voyeurismo, peinetas y otros rizos paródicos: La narrativa de Carmen Lugo Filippi," *Explicación de Textos Literarios*, 24, i–ii (1995–1996), 83–86.
Umpierre, Luzma. "Lesbian Tantalizing in Carmen Lugo Filippi's 'Milagros, Calle Mercurio,' " in Zimmerman, Bonnie, Toni A. H. McNaron, and Margaret Cruikshank, Eds. *The New Lesbian* . . . , 173–176. [see also Umpierre, Luz M. "Lesbian Tantalizing in Carmen Lugo Filippi's 'Milagros, Calle Mercurio,' " in Bergmann, Emilie L., and Paul J. Smith, Eds. *¿Entiendes?* . . . , 306–314.]

"Notas para un obituario"
Homo-Delgado, Asunción. "Voyeurismo . . . ," 88–89.

"Pilar, tus rizos"
Homo-Delgado, Asunción. "Voyeurismo . . . ," 86–88.

DARRELL H. Y. LUM

"Da Beer Can Hat"
Okawa, Gail Y. "Resistance and Reclamation: Hawaii 'Pidgin English'
and Autoethnography in the Short Stories of Darrell H. Y. Lum," in
Brown, Julie, Ed. *Ethnicity* . . . , 184–190.
"The Moiliili Bag Man"
Okawa, Gail Y. "Resistance . . . ," 190.
"Primo Doesn't Take Back Bottles Anymore"
Okawa, Gail Y. "Resistance . . . ," 182–184.

ALISON LURIE

"The Double Poet"
Tintner, Adeline R. *Henry James's Legacy* . . . , 430–431.
"The Highboy"
Tintner, Adeline R. *Henry James's Legacy* . . . , 428–429.
"In the Shadow"
Tintner, Adeline R. *Henry James's Legacy* . . . , 429–430.

COLUM MCCANN

"Cathal's Lake"
Mahony, Christina H. *Contemporary Irish* . . . , 262–263.
"Fishing the Sloe-Black River"
Mahony, Christina H. *Contemporary Irish* . . . , 261–262.
"Stolen Child"
Mahony, Christina H. *Contemporary Irish* . . . , 262.

ROSE MACAULAY

"Miss Anstruther's Letters"
Lassner, Phyllis. *British Women Writers* . . . , 145–146.

BERNARD MACLAVERTY

"My Dear Palestrina"
Mahony, Christina H. *Contemporary Irish* . . . , 237–238.

NELLIE MCCLUNG

"Carried Forward"
Dean, Misao. *Practising Femininity* . . . , 80.

"Men and Money"
    Dean, Misao. *Practising* . . . , 86.
"Neutral Fuse"
    Dean, Misao. *Practising* . . . , 86, 87.

CARSON MCCULLERS

"The Ballad of the Sad Café"
    + Gilbert, Sandra M., and Susan Gubar. "Critical Extracts," in
    Bloom, Harold, Ed. *Lesbian and Bisexual* . . . , 104–106.
    Hannon, Charles. " 'The Ballad of the Sad Café' and Other Stories of
    Women's Wartime Labor," in Foster, Thomas, Carol Siegel, and
    Ellen E. Berry, Eds. *Bodies of Writing* . . . , 97–119.
    + Vickery, John B. "Critical Extracts," in Bloom, Harold, Ed. *Lesbian*
    and Bisexual . . . , 98–99.
    Westling, Louise. "Carson McCullers's Amazon Nightmare," *Mod*
    Fiction Stud, 28 (1982), 472–473; rpt. in Bloom, Harold, Ed.
    Lesbian and Bisexual . . . , 101–102.

DENNIS MCFARLAND

"Nothing to Ask For"
    Warner, Sharon O. "The Way We Write Now: The Reality of AIDS in
    Contemporary Short Fiction," in Lounsberry, Barbara, et al., Eds.
    The Tales We Tell . . . , 187.

JOAQUIM MARÍA MACHADO DE ASSIS

"A Cartomante"
    Douglass, Ellen H. "Machado de Assis's 'A Cartomante': Modern
    Parody and the Making of a 'Brazilian' Text,"*Mod Lang Notes*, 113
    (1998), 1036–1055.

ARTHUR MACHEN

"A Fragment of Life"
    Russell, R. B. "Alternative Lives in Arthur Machen's 'A Fragment of
    Life' and Sylvia Townsend Warner's *Lolly Willowes*," *Stud Weird*
    Fiction, 12 (1993), 17–19.
"The Great God Pan"
    Doussaud, Valérie. "Transformation, déformation et mutation dans
    Tales of Horror and the Supernatural de Machen," in Marigny,
    Jean, Intro., *Images fantastiques du corps*, 176–177, 178.
    Navarette, Susan J. *The Shape* . . . , 188–193, 196, 199–201.
"The Inmost Light"
    Doussaud, Valérie. "Transformation . . . ," 177–178.

"The Novel of the Black Seal"
  Doussaud, Valérie. "Transformation . . . ," 174–175.
"The Novel of the White Powder"
  Doussaud, Valérie. "Transformation . . . ," 175–176.
  Navarette, Susan J. *The Shape* . . . , 179–181.
"Out of the Earth"
  Doussaud, Valérie. "Transformation . . . ," 179.
"The Shining Pyramid"
  Doussaud, Valérie. "Transformation . . . ," 179.

REGINALD MCKNIGHT

"The Kind of Light That Shines in Texas"
  Ford, Joh, and Marjorie Ford. *Instructor's Manual* . . . , 126–127.

NORMAN MACLEAN

"A River Runs Through It"
  Weinberger, Theodore. "Religion and Fly Fishing: Taking Norman
  MacLean Seriously," *Renascence*, 49 (1997), 281–189.

JAMES ALAN MCPHERSON

"A Loaf of Bread"
  Ford, Joh, and Marjorie Ford. *Instructor's Manual* . . . , 105–106.

NADINE MAGLOIRE

"Le Mal de vivre"
  Chancy, Myriam J. A. *Framing Silence* . . . , 109–120, 132.

NAJIB MAHFUZ [NAGUIB MAHFOUZ]

"The Norwegian Rat"
  Ford, Joh, and Marjorie Ford. *Instructor's Manual* . . . , 58–59.
"The Time and the Place"
  Baldwin, Dean. *Instructor's Resource* . . . , 200–202.

MARÍA TERESA MAIORANA

"13–8–1896"
  Burbridge, Martha Vanbiesem de. "Un cuento de María Teresa
  Maiorana frente a uno de Edith Wharton," in Frugoni de Fritzsche,
  Teresita, Ed. *Primeras Jornadas* . . . , 347–348, 351–353.

T. N. MAKUYA

"Vho-Dambala"
Mafela, M. J. "Flashback and the Development of Action in T. N. Makuya's Short Story: 'Vho-Dambala,' " *So African J*, 17, iv (1997), 126–129.

BERNARD MALAMUD

"Angel Levine"
Ford, Joh, and Marjorie Ford. *Instructor's Manual* . . . , 63–64.
Sío-Castiñeira, Begoña. *The Short Stories of* . . . , 32–48.
"Black Is My Favorite Color"
Sío-Castiñeira, Begoña. *The Short* . . . , 51–68.
"The First Seven Years"
Brown, Peter C. "Negative Capability and the Mystery of Hope in Malamud's 'The First Seven Years,' " *Religion & Lit*, 29 (1997), 66–89.
Sío-Castiñeira, Begoña. *The Short* . . . , 9–20.
"God's Wrath"
Sío-Castiñeira, Begoña. *The Short* . . . , 114–131.
"Idiots First"
Bryant, Earle V. "Malamud's 'Idiots First,' " *Explicator*, 55, i (1996), 43–45.
"The Jewbird"
Charters, Ann, and William E. Sheidley. *Resources* . . . , 5th ed., 165.
Sío-Castiñeira, Begoña. *The Short* . . . , 81–89.
"Life Is Better Than Death"
Sío-Castiñeira, Begoña. *The Short* . . . , 70–81.
"The Loan"
Sío-Castiñeira, Begoña. *The Short* . . . , 20–32.
"My Son the Murderer"
Sío-Castiñeira, Begoña. *The Short* . . . , 91–104.
"Rembrandt's Hat"
Sío-Castiñeira, Begoña. *The Short* . . . , 104–113.
"Talking Horse"
Sío-Castiñeira, Begoña. *The Short* . . . , 131–135, 139, 140.

DAVID MALOUF

"The Only Speaker of His Tongue"
Bindella, Maria T. "Crossing Boundaries in David Malouf's *Antipodes*," *Quaderni di Lingue e Letterature*, 19 (1994), 120–121.
"Out of the Stream"
Bindella, Maria T. "Crossing . . . ," 115–119.

"Southern Skies"
    Bindella, Maria T. "Crossing . . . ," 112–115.
"A Traveller's Tale"
    Bindella, Maria T. "Crossing . . . ," 121–123.

THOMAS MANN

"Beim Propheten"
    Marx, Friedhelm. "Künstler, Propheten, Heilige: Thomas Mann und
        die Kunstreligion der Jahrhundertwende," *Thomas Mann Jahrbuch*,
        11 (1998), 51–58.
"Die Betrogene"
    Görner, Rüdiger. "Zauber des Letzten: Thomas Mann im
        spätbürgerlichen Zeitalter," *Thomas Mann Jahrbuch*, 10 (1997),
        13–23.
"Death in Venice"
    Alexander, Doris. *Creating Literature Out* . . . , 11–21.
    Bergenholtz, Rita A. "Mann's 'Death in Venice,' " *Explicator*, 55, iii
        (1997), 145–146.
    Berman, Russell A. "History and Community in 'Death in Venice,' "
        in Ritter, Naomi, Ed. *Thomas Mann* . . . , 263–280.
    Foster, John B. "Why Is Tadzio Polish? *Kultur* and Cultural
        Multiplicity in 'Death in Venice,' " in Ritter, Naomi, Ed. *Thomas
        Mann* . . . , 192–210.
    Furst, Lilian R. "The Potential Deceptiveness of Reading in 'Death in
        Venice,' " in Ritter, Naomi, Ed. *Thomas Mann* . . . , 158–170.
    Lehan, Richard. *The City in Literature* . . . , 149–150.
    Schwarz, Daniel R. *Reconfiguring Modernism* . . . , 10–11, 73–76,
        145, 149.
    Symington, Rodney. "The Eruption of the Other: Psychoanalytic
        Approaches to 'Death in Venice,' " in Ritter, Naomi, Ed. *Thomas
        Mann* . . . , 127–141.
    Tobin, Robert. "The Life and Work of Thomas Mann: A Gay
        Perspective," in Ritter, Naomi, Ed. *Thomas Mann* . . . , 225–244.
"The Fight Between Jappe and Do Escobar"
    Parkes-Perret, Ford B. "Wie Jappe und Do Escobar sich prügelten:
        'Ein Nichts von einer Geschichte'?" *Germ R*, 70 (1995), 138–143.
"Little Herr Friedemann"
    Silberman, Joan. "The Use of Defense Mechanisms in a Short Story
        by Thomas Mann," in Pereira, Frederico, Ed. *Eleventh
        International* . . . , 133–137.
"Mario and the Magician"
    Bewley, Katrine. "Thomas Mann's 'Mario und der Zauberer' and
        Bulgakov's *The Master and Margarita* as Political Commentaries
        on the Events of the 1930s, Noting their Significance on a Personal,
        Ethical Level," *Australian Slavonic*, 9, ii (1995), 119–128.

"Tristan"
Blasberg, Cornelia. "Jugendstil-Literatur: Schwierigkeiten mit einem Bindestrich," *Deutsche Vierteljahrsschrift*, 72 (1998), 702–709.

"Wälsungenblut"
Levesque, Paul. "The Double-Edged Sword: Anti-Semitism and Anti-Wagnerianism in Thomas Mann's 'Wälsungenblut,' " *Germ Stud R*, 20 (1997), 9–21.

"Das Wunderkind"
Marx, Friedhelm. "Künstler, Propheten . . . ," 58–60.

KATHERINE MANSFIELD

"At Lehmann's"
Dunbar, Pamela. *Radical Mansfield* . . . , 29–32.

"At the Bay"
Dunbar, Pamela. *Radical Mansfield* . . . , 156–167.
Weiss, Timothy. "Oriental Elements in Mansfield's *The Garden Party and Other Stories*," in Dubois, Dominique, Laurent Lepaludier, and Jacques Sohier, Eds. *Les Nouvelles* . . . , 33, 35.

"Bains Turcs"
Dunbar, Pamela. *Radical Mansfield* . . . , 37–41.

"Bank Holiday"
Weiss, Timothy. "Oriental Elements . . . ," 30–32.

"A Birthday"
Dunbar, Pamela. *Radical Mansfield* . . . , 27–29.

"Bliss"
Bertrán, Dorian L. "Percances de ocupación en Katherine Mansfield y Violeta López Suria," *Revista de Estudios Hispánicos*, 22 (1995), 368–373, 376–378.
Charters, Ann, and William E. Sheidley. *Resources* . . . , 5th ed., 167.
Dunbar, Pamela. *Radical Mansfield* . . . , 104–113.
Tang-Campon, Maria. " 'Something That's There . . . To Be . . . Not There': Food as Matter and Metaphor in Katherine Mansfield's *Selected Stories*," *Q/W/E/R/T/Y*, 7 (1997), 117–118.
Trodd, Anthea. *Women's Writing in English* . . . , 67–68.

"The Canary"
Dunbar, Pamela. *Radical Mansfield* . . . , 71–72.

"Carnation"
Winston, Janet. "Reading Influences: Homoeroticism and Mentoring in Katherine Mansfield's 'Carnation' and Virginia Woolf's 'Moments of Being: "Slater's Pins Have No Points," ' " in Barrett, Eileen, and Patricia Cramer, Eds. *Virginia Woolf* . . . , 61–68.

"The Child-Who-Was-Tired"
Dunbar, Pamela. *Radical Mansfield* . . . , 34–37.

"The Daughters of the Late Colonel"
Baldwin, Dean. *Instructor's Resource* . . . , 98–101.

Dunbar, Pamela. *Radical Mansfield* . . . , 151–156.
Tang-Campon, Maria. " 'Something That's . . . ,' " 118–119.
Weiss, Timothy. "Oriental Elements . . . ," 38–41.

"Les Deux Étrangères"
Dunbar, Pamela. *Radical Mansfield* . . . , 88–90.

"A Dill Pickle"
Ford, Joh, and Marjorie Ford. *Instructor's Manual* . . . , 41–42.

"The Doll's House"
Dunbar, Pamela. *Radical Mansfield* . . . , 173–175.
O'Sullivan, Vincent. "The New Zealand Stories," *Commonwealth*, 4 (1997), 10.
Stead, C. K. "Katherine Mansfield as Colonial Realist," *Commonwealth*, 4 (1997), 16–17.
Trodd, Anthea. *Women's Writing in English* . . . , 174.

"The Dove's Nest"
Dunbar, Pamela. *Radical Mansfield* . . . , 118–123.

"Die Einsame"
Dunbar, Pamela. *Radical Mansfield* . . . , 59–61.

"The Fly"
Coroneos, Con. "Flies and Violets in Katherine Mansfield," in Raitt, Suzanne, and Trudi Tate, Eds. *Women's Fiction* . . . , 212–216.
Dunbar, Pamela. *Radical Mansfield* . . . , 68–71.

"Frau Brechenmacher Attends a Wedding"
Dunbar, Pamela. *Radical Mansfield* . . . , 32–34.

"Frau Fischer"
Dunbar, Pamela. *Radical Mansfield* . . . , 14–17.

"The Garden Party"
Charters, Ann, and William E. Sheidley. *Resources* . . . , 5th ed., 169–170.
Darrohn, Christine. " 'Blown to Bits!': Katherine Mansfield's 'The Garden Party' and the Great War," *Mod Fiction Stud*, 44 (1998), 513–539.
Dunbar, Pamela. *Radical Mansfield* . . . , 167–171.
Ford, Joh, and Marjorie Ford. *Instructor's Manual* . . . , 42–43.
Harmat, Andrée-Marie. "Bliss Versus Corruption in Katherine Mansfield's Short Stories," *Commonwealth*, 4 (1997), 64–65.
O'Sullivan, Vincent. "The New Zealand . . . ," 9–10.

"Germans at Meat"
Dunbar, Pamela. *Radical Mansfield* . . . , 21–22.

"The Green Tea"
Dunbar, Pamela. *Radical Mansfield* . . . , 3–4.

"His Sister's Keeper"
Dunbar, Pamela. *Radical Mansfield* . . . , 99–100.

"How the Pearl Button Was Kidnapped"
Dunbar, Pamela. *Radical Mansfield* . . . , 41–43.

"An Indiscreet Journey"
Coroneos, Con. "Flies and Violets . . . ," 202–209, 211–212.

"Je ne parle pas français"
Dunbar, Pamela. *Radical Mansfield . . .* , 73–83.
Lamy-Vialle, Élisabeth. "Le Corps absent: Travestissement et fragmentation dans les nouvelles de Katherine Mansfield," *Q/W/E/R/T/Y,* 7 (1997), 93–95.
Sharma, Lakshmi R. "Metaphor and Narrative: A Strange Relationship," *Lit Criterion*, 26, iv (1991), 19–24.

"Juliet"
Dunbar, Pamela. *Radical Mansfield . . .* , 4–5.

"Life of Ma Parker"
Marshall, Tim. "Death and the Abyss: The Representation of Pauperland in Katherine Mansfield's 'Life of Ma Parker,' " *Q/W/E/R/T/Y,* 7 (1997), 99–104.

"The Little Governess"
Dunbar, Pamela. *Radical Mansfield . . .* , 62–64.

"The Little Girl"
Dunbar, Pamela. *Radical Mansfield . . .* , 132–135.

"The Luft Bad"
Dunbar, Pamela. *Radical Mansfield . . .* , 17–20.

"The Man Without a Temperament"
Dunbar, Pamela. *Radical Mansfield . . .* , 125–128.
Tang-Campon, Maria. " 'Something That's . . . ,' " 114–116.

"A Married Man's Story"
Dunbar, Pamela. *Radical Mansfield . . .* , 83–87.

"Mary"
Dunbar, Pamela. *Radical Mansfield . . .* , 1–2.

"Millie"
Dunbar, Pamela. *Radical Mansfield . . .* , 54–57.

"Miss Brill"
Baldwin, Dean. *Instructor's Resource . . .* , 101–103.
Dunbar, Pamela. *Radical Mansfield . . .* , 64–67.

"Mr. And Mrs. Dove"
Dunbar, Pamela. *Radical Mansfield . . .* , 115–117.

"Ole Underwood"
Dunbar, Pamela. *Radical Mansfield . . .* , 49–54.

"Poison"
Dunbar, Pamela. *Radical Mansfield . . .* , 123–125.

"Prelude" [originally "The Aloe"]
Dunbar, Pamela. *Radical Mansfield . . .* , 138–148.
Harmat, Andrée-Marie. "Bliss Versus . . . ," 64, 65.
Tang-Campon, Maria. " 'Something That's . . . ,' " 112–114.
Trodd, Anthea. *Women's Writing in English . . .* , 65–67.

"Psychology"
Dunbar, Pamela. *Radical Mansfield* . . . , 100–104.
Harmat, Andrée-Marie. "Polyphonie de la nouvelle mansfieldienne:
L'Exemple de 'Psychology,' " *Études Anglaises*, 50 (1997),
411–421.
Tang-Campon, Maria. " 'Something That's . . . ,' " 116–117.
"The Singing Lesson"
Coroneos, Con. "Flies and Violets . . . ," 211.
"Six Years After"
Reid, Ian. "Reframing 'The Child in the House': Short Stories and
Neighboring Forms," in Kaylor, Noel H., Ed. *Creative and
Critical* . . . , 326.
"Something Childish But Very Natural"
Dunbar, Pamela. *Radical Mansfield* . . . , 94–99.
"Stay-Laces"
O'Sullivan, Vincent. "The New Zealand . . . ," 6.
"The Stranger"
Dunbar, Pamela. *Radical Mansfield* . . . , 113–115.
"The Tiredness of Rosabel"
Dunbar, Pamela. *Radical Mansfield* . . . , 5–8.
"The Voyage"
Dunbar, Pamela. *Radical Mansfield* . . . , 171–173.
"Widowed"
Dunbar, Pamela. *Radical Mansfield* . . . , 128–130.
"The Woman at the Store"
Dunbar, Pamela. *Radical Mansfield* . . . , 44–49.

EDUARDA MANSILLA DE GARCÍA

"El ramito de romero"
Frederick, Bonnie. *Wily Modesty* . . . , 95–98.

MAO DUN

"At One O'Clock"
Findeisen, Raoul D. "*Kairos* or the Due Time: On Date and Dates in
Modern Chinese Literature," in Findeisen, Raoul D., and Robert H.
Gassmann, Eds. *Autumn Floods* . . . , 235.
"Creation"
Chung, Hilary. "Questing the Goddess: Mao Dun and the New
Woman," in Findeisen, Raoul D., and Robert H. Gassmann, Eds.
Autumn Floods . . . , 182–183.
McDougall, Bonnie S. "Dominance and Disappearance: A Post-

Feminist Review of Fiction by Mao Dun and Ling Shuhua," in
Findeisen, Raoul D., and Robert H. Gassmann, Eds. *Autumn
Floods* . . . , 287–288.

"Disillusion"
Chung, Hilary. "Questing the Goddess . . . ," 174–175.
Lieberman, Sally T. *The Mother* . . . , 127–133.

"A Female"
McDougall, Bonnie S. "Dominance . . . ," 289–290.

"Haze"
McDougall, Bonnie S. "Dominance . . . ," 291.

"Poetry and Prose"
McDougall, Bonnie S. "Dominance . . . ," 290–291.

"Pursuit"
Chung, Hilary. "Questing the Goddess . . . ," 176–178, 180.

"Suicide"
McDougall, Bonnie S. "Dominance . . . ," 288–289.

"Vacillation"
Chung, Hilary. "Questing the Goddess . . . ," 174, 175, 176, 180–181.

DAMBUDZO MARECHERA

"The Black Insider"
Levin, Melissa, and Laurice Taitz. "Fictional Autobiographies/
Autobiographical Fictions: (Re)evaluating the Work of Dambudzo
Marechera," *J Commonwealth Lit*, 32, i (1997), 109–110.

"Black Sunlight"
Buuck, David. "African Doppelganger: Hybridity and Identity in the
Work of Dambudzo Marechera," *Research African Lit*, 28, ii
(1997), 123, 125–126.

"Devil's End"
Levin, Melissa, and Laurice Taitz. "Fictional Autobiographies . . . ,"
110.

"The House of Hunger"
Buuck, David. "African Doppelganger . . . ," 123, 124–125, 127.

"What Available Reality"
Levin, Melissa, and Laurice Taitz. "Fictional Autobiographies . . . ,"
105–106.

PAZ MARQUEZ-BENITEZ

"Dead Stars"
Zapanta-Manlapaz, Edna. "A Feminist Reading of Paz Marquez-
Benitez's 'Dead Stars,' " *Philippine Stud*, 41 (1993), 523–528.

PAULE MARSHALL

"Brooklyn"
DeLamotte, Eugenia C. *Places of Silence* . . . , 5–8.

UNA MARSON

"Sojourn"
Jarrett-Macauley, Delia. *The Life of* . . . , 41–42.

JOSÉ MARTÍ

"La muñeca negra"
Serna Arnaiz, Mercedes. "Estética e ideología en *La edad de oro* de
José Martí: 'La muñeca negra,' " *Notas y Estudios Filológicos*, 9
(1994), 203–213.

CARMEN MARTÍN GAITE

"What Lies Buried"
Davies, Catherine. *Spanish Women's Writing* . . . , 236.

HARRIET MARTINEAU

"Sowers not Reapers"
Logan, Deborah A. *Fallenness in Victorian* . . . , 130–137.

BOBBIE ANN MASON

"Airwaves"
Ford, Joh, and Marjorie Ford. *Instructor's Manual* . . . , 100–101.
"Big Bertha Stories"
Wilhelm, Albert. *Bobbie Ann Mason* . . . , 83–86.
———. "Bobbie Ann Mason: Searching for Home," in Folks, Jeffrey
J., and James A. Perkins, Eds. *Southern Writers* . . . ,153–156.
"Bumblebees"
Wilhelm, Albert. *Bobbie Ann Mason* . . . , 54–58.
"Coyotes"
Wilhelm, Albert. *Bobbie Ann Mason* . . . , 79–83.
"Detroit Skyline"
Wilhelm, Albert. *Bobbie Ann Mason* . . . , 28–33.
"Drawing Names"
Wilhelm, Albert. *Bobbie Ann Mason* . . . , 25–28.
"Hunktown"
Wilhelm, Albert. *Bobbie Ann Mason* . . . , 51–54.

Giannone, Richard. "Bobbie Ann Mason . . . ," 555–558; rpt.
Wilhelm, Albert. *Bobbie Ann Mason* . . . , 140–143.
Wilhelm, Albert. *Bobbie Ann Mason* . . . , 61–65.
"Sorghum"
Wilhelm, Albert. *Bobbie Ann Mason* . . . , 13–17.
"State Champions"
Wilhelm, Albert. *Bobbie Ann Mason* . . . , 33–35.
"Still Life with Watermelon"
Wilhelm, Albert. *Bobbie Ann Mason* . . . , 76–79.
"Third Monday"
Giannone, Richard. ". . . Recovery of Mystery," 561–564; rpt.
Wilhelm, Albert. *Bobbie Ann Mason* . . . , 146–150.
Pollack, Harriet. "From 'Shiloh' . . . ," 98.

MTUTUZELI MATSHORA

"Three Days in the Land of a Dying Illusion"
Davis, Geoffrey V. " 'The People Are Claiming Their History':
Reconstructions of History in Recent Black South African Writing,"
in Delrez, Marc, and Bénédicte Ledent, Eds. *The Contact* . . . ,
100–106.

VALERIE MATSUMOTO

"Two Deserts"
Streamas, John. "The Invention of Normality in Japanese American
Internment Narratives," in Brown, Julie, Ed. *Ethnicity* . . . ,
137–138.

ANDREA MATURANA

"Verde en el borde"
Lagos, María I. "Cuerpo y subjetividad en narraciones de Andrea
Maturana, Ana María del Río y Diamela Eltit," *Revista Chilena*, 50
(1997), 99–101.

ANA MARÍA MATUTE

"Algunos muchachos"
Nichols, Geraldine C. "Creced y multiplicad: niños y números en
'Algunos muchachos' de Ana María Matute," *Compás de Letras*, 4
(1994), 219–221.
"Celebration in the Northwest"
Porter, Phoebe A. "Translator's Introduction," *Celebration in the
Northwest* [by Ana María Matute], x–xii.

"Cuaderno para cuentas"
    Nichols, Geraldine C. "Creced y multiplicad . . . ," 223–225.
"Muy contento"
    Nichols, Geraldine C. "Creced y multiplicad . . . ," 221–223.
"Pecado de omisión"
    Pennington, Eric. "Matute's 'Pecado de omisión': A Prophet
    Spurned," *Letras Femeninas*, 20, i-ii (1994), 141–148.

W. SOMERSET MAUGHAM

"The Letter"
    Baldwin, Dean. *Instructor's Resource* . . . , 108–110.
    Choon, Ban K. "Fetishism and Maugham's 'The Letter,' " in Young,
    Robert J. C., Ban K. Choon, and Robbie B. H. Goh, Eds. *The Silent*
    Word . . . , 97–102.
"String of Beads"
    Tintner, Adeline R. *Henry James's Legacy* . . . , 105–106.

GUY DE MAUPASSANT

"Allouma"
    Joseph, Frédérique. "L'Histoire d'Allouma: Une nouvelle de Guy de
    Maupassant," *Littératures*, 38 (1998), 75–78.
"Bellflower"
    Baldwin, Dean. *Instructor's Resource* . . . , 55–57.
"Le Champ d'oliviers"
    Cogman, P. W. M. "Gaps and Gap-Filling in Maupassant's 'Le Champ
    d'oliviers,' " *French Stud Bull*, 60 (1996), 9–13.
"Confessing"
    Ford, Joh, and Marjorie Ford. *Instructor's Manual* . . . , 19–20.
"Deux amis"
    Betts, Christopher J. "Surface Structure and Symmetry in Maupassant:
    An Alternative View of 'Deux Amis,' " *Romanic R*, 88, ii (1997),
    251–266.
    Lindner, Hermann. "Sympathielenkung im Französischen
    naturalismus: Maupassants Novellistik," *Zeitschrift für französische*
    Sprache und Literatur, 101, iii (1991), 249–260.
"Le Horla"
    Calder, Martin. "Something in the Water: Self as Other in Guy de
    Maupassant's 'Le Horla': A Barthesian Reading," *French Stud*, 52
    (1998), 42–57.
    Turcanu, Radu. " 'Le Horla' et 'l'effet de réel,' " *Nineteenth-Century*
    French Stud, 26 (1998), 387–397.
"Le Masque"
    Cordova, Sarah D. "Writing Dance: Textualizing Narrative Poetics in

Maupassant's 'Menuet' and 'Le Masque,' " *Romance Lang Annual*, 9 (1997), 40–45.

"Menuet"
Cordova, Sarah D. "Writing Dance . . . ," 40–45.

"La Mère aux monstres"
Moore, Gene M. "Conrad's 'The Idiots' and Maupassant's 'La Mère aux monstres,' " in Moore, Gene M., Owen Knowles, and J. H. Stape, Eds. *Conrad: Intertexts* . . . , 51–52, 52–53, 54–55.

"The Necklace"
Charters, Ann, and William E. Sheidley. *Resources* . . . , 5th ed., 173–174.
Ford, Joh, and Marjorie Ford. *Instructor's Manual* . . . , 18–19.

"La Nuit"
Harter, Deborah A. "Silenced by the City: Maupassant's *Flâneur* and Uneasy Dreams," in Prier, A., and Gerald Gillespie, Eds. *Narrative Ironies*, 181–190.

"The Signal"
Ireland, John. "A Speculum in the Text: Freud's 'Katharina' and Maupassant's 'Le Signe,' " *Mod Lang Notes*, 113 (1998), 1089–1090, 1092–1094, 1095–1099.

"Sur l'eau"
Goodkin, Richard E. "Terre ferme, terreur des femmes: Le cou[p] de grâce chez Maupassant et Mallarmé," in Booker, John T., and Allan H. Pasco, Eds. *The Play of Terror* . . . , 99–105.

"Tombouctou"
Anyinefa, Koffi. " 'Y a bon banania': L'Afrique et le discours nationaliste dans 'Tombouctou' de Maupassant," *French R*, 71 (1997), 225–236.

"Two Little Soldiers"
Baldwin, Dean. *Instructor's Resource* . . . , 57–59.

JAMES MEEK

"Bonny Boat Speed"
Falconer, Rachel. "Bakhtin's Chronotope and the Contemporary Short Story," *So Atlantic Q*, 97 (1998), 726–728.

MARTA MELONI

"La Invasión"
Montiveros de Mollo, Perla. "Imágenes de los orígenes ante símbolos de su nostalgia mítica en un cuento de Marta Meloni," in Frugoni de Fritzsche, Teresita, Ed. *Primeras Jornadas* . . . , 307–314.

HERMAN MELVILLE

"The Apple-Tree Table"
Camfield, Gregg. *Necessary Madness* . . . , 85–90.

"Bartleby, the Scrivener"
Baldwin, Dean. *Instructor's Resource* . . . , 48–50.
Charters, Ann, and William E. Sheidley. *Resources* . . . , 5th ed.,
175–176.
Curnutt, Kirk. *Wise Economies* . . . , 25, 57–70.
Davis, Clark. *After the Whale* . . . , 38–45.
Davis, Todd F. "The Narrator's Dilemma in 'Bartleby the Scrivener':
The Excellently Illustrated Re-statement of a Problem," *Stud Short
Fiction*, 34 (1997), 183–192.
Delbanco, Andrew. "Afterword," in Levine, Robert S., Ed. *The
Cambridge* . . . , 285.
———. *Required Reading* . . . , 18–20.
Doloff, Steven. "The Prudent Samaritan: Melville's 'Bartleby, the
Scrivener' as Parody of Christ's Parable to the Lawyer," *Stud Short
Fiction*, 34 (1997), 357–361.
Ford, Joh, and Marjorie Ford. *Instructor's Manual* . . . , 12–14.
Furlani, Andre. "Bartleby the Socratic," *Stud Short Fiction*, 34
(1997), 335–355.
Griffith, Clark. *Achilles and the Tortoise* . . . , 219–222, 226, 240,
243–244, 259.
Hans, James S. "Emptiness and Plenitude in 'Bartleby the Scrivener'
and *The Crying of Lot 49*," *Essays Lit*, 22 (1995), 287–292.
Lehan, Richard. *The City in Literature* . . . , 178–179, 180–181.
Morgan, Jack. "Toward an Organic Theory of the Gothic
Conceptualizing Horror," *J Pop Culture*, 32, iii (1998), 67–68, 76,
78–79.
Peach, Linden. *Angela Carter*, 37–38.
Schueller, Malini J. *U. S. Orientalisms* . . . , 127–128.
Siegel, Adrienne. *The Image of the American* . . . , 152–153.
Smock, Ann. "Quiet," *Qui Parle*, 2, ii (1998), 68–100.
Weinstein, Cindy. "Melville, Labor, and the Discourses of
Reception," in Levine, Robert S., Ed. *The Cambridge* . . . ,
214–216.
"Benito Cereno"
Adamson, Joseph. *Melville, Shame* . . . , 40, 58–59, 153, 161,
164–165, 231–233, 287.
Bus, Heiner. "The Power of Stereotypes: Spain in Herman Melville's
'Benito Cereno' (1855) and Nash Candelaria's *Memories of the
Alhambra* (1977)," in Hebel, Udo J., and Karl Ortseifen, Eds.
Transatlantic Encounters . . . , 194–199.
Byrant, John. "The Persistence of Melville: Representative Writer for
a Multicultural Age," in Bryant, John, and Robert Milder, Eds.
Melville's Evermoving . . . , 13–15.
Davis, Clark. *After the Whale* . . . , 84–89.
Delbanco, Andrew. "Afterword," 284.
———. *Required Reading* . . . , 27–28, 30.
Franklin, H. Bruce. "Slavery and Empire: Melville's 'Benito
Cereno,' " in Bryant, John, and Robert Milder, Eds. *Melville's
Evermoving* . . . , 147–158.

Kamuf, Peggy. *The Division of Literature* . . . , 183–201.
Martin, Terry J. *Rhetorical Deception* . . . , 55–72.
Morgan, Jack. "Toward an . . . ," 76–79.
Rampersad, Arnold. "Shadow and Veil: Melville and Modern Black Consciousness," in Bryant, John, and Robert Milder, Eds. *Melville's Evermoving* . . . , 163, 168.
Robbins, Sarah. "Gendering the History of the Antislavery Narrative: Juxtaposing *Uncle Tom's Cabin* and 'Benito Cereno,' *Beloved* and *Middle Passage*," *Am Q*, 49 (1997), 548, 553–559.
Sanborn, Geoffrey. *The Sign of the Cannibal* . . . , 172–177, 183–200.

"Billy Budd"
Adamson, Joseph. *Melville, Shame* . . . , 108–112, 141, 147–150, 159–161, 180–181, 181–183, 189–190, 197–198, 203–204, 205–206, 209–210, 218–220, 224, 230, 233, 240–241, 252–253, 254–255, 270–271, 289–293, 295–296.
Arouimi, Michel. "Les mythes premiers dans la mort de Billy Budd," *Études Anglaises*, 50 (1997), 296–307.
Barnes, Elizabeth. *States of Sympathy* . . . , 120–126.
Bryant, John. "The Persistence of Melville: Representative Writer for a Multicultural Age," in Bryant, John, and Robert Milder, Eds. *Melville's Evermoving* . . . , 6–7.
Buell, Lawrence. "Melville and the Question of American Decolonization," in Bryant, John, and Robert Milder, Eds. *Melville's Evermoving* . . . , 77–79, 93–94.
Davis, Clark. *After the Whale* . . . , 187–200.
Delbanco, Andrew. *Required Reading* . . . , 28–31.
Franklin, H. Bruce. " 'Billy Budd' and Capital Punishment: A Tale of Three Centuries," *Am Lit*, 69 (1997), 337–354.
Garner, Stanton. "Herman Melville and the Customs Service," in Bryant, John, and Robert Milder, Eds. *Melville's Evermoving* . . . , 290–291.
Giles, Paul. " 'Bewildering Intertanglement': Melville's Engagement with British Culture," in Levine, Robert S., Ed. *The Cambridge* . . . , 242–246.
Goodman, Nan. *Shifting the Blame* . . . , 50–51.
Griffith, Clark. *Achilles and the Tortoise* . . . , 238–245.
Loges, Max L. "Melville's 'Billy Budd,' " *Explicator*, 55, iii (1997), 137–138.
Martin, Robert K. "Melville and Sexuality," in Levine, Robert S., Ed. *The Cambridge* . . . , 197–199.
Shattuck, Roger. "Guilt, Justice, and Empathy in Melville and Camus," *Partisan R*, 63, iii (1996), 430–432, 447.
Troy, Mark. " ' it's me, not the sentence they'll suspend'—Billy in the Darbies," *Orbis Litterarum*, 52 (1997), 240–258.
Weinstein, Cindy. "Melville, Labor . . . ," 216–221.
Woods, Gregory. *A History of Gay* . . . , 164–166.
Zimmerman, Brett. *Herman Melville: Stargazer*, 58–69.

"Cock-A-Doodle-Doo!"
Camfield, Gregg. *Necessary Madness* . . . , 82–84.
Davis, Clark. *After the Whale* . . . , 66–68.

"Daniel Orme"
Davis, Clark. *After the Whale* . . . , 202.
"The Encantadas"
Davis, Clark. *After the Whale* . . . , 74–81.
Fetterley, Judith. "Theorizing Regionalism: Celia Thaxter's *Among the Isles of Shoals*," in Inness, Sherrie A., and Diana Royer, Eds. *Breaking Boundaries* . . . , 42–43.
Lueck, Beth L. *American Writers* . . . , 192–193.
"The Fiddler"
Davis, Clark. *After the Whale* . . . , 69–72.
"The Happy Failure"
Davis, Clark. *After the Whale* . . . , 82–83.
"I and My Chimney"
Allison, John. "Conservative Architecture: Hawthorne in Melville's 'I and My Chimney,' " *So Central R*, 13, i (1996), 18, 19–20, 21, 22–23.
Camfield, Gregg. *Necessary Madness* . . . , 78–81.
Davis, Clark. *After the Whale* . . . , 73.
Pearce, Sandra M. "Secret Closets and Ashes: Melville's 'I and My Chimney,' " in Kaylor, Noel H., Ed. *Creative and Critical* . . . , 81–95.
"The Paradise of Bachelors and the Tartarus of Maids"
Covici, Pascal. *Humor and Revelation* . . . , 36–43.
Dimock, Wai Chee. "Reading the Incomplete," in Bryant, John, and Robert Milder, Eds. *Melville's Evermoving* . . . , 101–102, 105.
Lehan, Richard. *The City in Literature* . . . , 179–180.
Petrulionis, Sandra H. "Re-Reading 'Bachelors and Maids': Melville as Feminist?" *Melville Soc Extracts*, 110 (September, 1997), 1, 5–10.
Schwartz, Hillel. *The Culture* . . . , 353.
Siegel, Adrienne. *The Image of the American* . . . , 94–95.
Weinstein, Cindy. "Melville, Labor . . . ," 214.
"The Piazza"
Marshall, Ian. *Story Line* . . . , 167–169, 170–172.
"Poor Man's Pudding and Rich Man's Crumbs"
Davis, Clark. *After the Whale* . . . , 68–69.
"Timoleon"
Adamson, Joseph. *Melville, Shame* . . . , 65, 66, 69, 70–73.
"The Two Temples"
Franchot, Jenny. "Melville's Traveling God," in Levine, Robert S., Ed. *The Cambridge* . . . , 178–180.
Lehan, Richard. *The City in Literature* . . . , 180.

MARÍA CRISTINA MENA

"The Birth of the God of War"
López, Tiffany A. " 'A Tolerance for Contradictions': The Short

Stories of María Cristina Mena," in Kilcup, Karen L., Ed.
Nineteenth-Century American . . . , 70–71.
"The Education of Popo"
Garza-Falcón, Leticia M. *Gente Decente* . . . , 136–148.
"Marriage by Miracle"
López, Tiffany A. " 'A Tolerance . . . ,' " 74–76.
"The Vine-Leaf"
López, Tiffany A. " 'A Tolerance . . . ,' " 72–74.

TUNUNA MERCADO

"Oír"
Buchanan, Rhonda D. "Eros and Writing in Tununa Mercado's *Canon de alcoba*," *Chasqui*, 25, i (1996), 57.
"Ver"
Buchanan, Rhonda D. "Eros . . . ," 56–57.

GEORGE MEREDITH

"The Case of General Opler and Lady Camper"
Deis, Elizabeth J. "Introduction," *George Meredith's 1895 Collection* . . . [by George Meredith], xxiv-xxvi.
"The House on the Beach"
Deis, Elizabeth J. "Introduction," xx-xxiv.
"The Tale of Chloe: An Episode in the History of Beau Beamish"
Deis, Elizabeth J. "Introduction," xvii-xx.

PROSPER MÉRIMÉE

"Carmen"
García, Carlos J. " 'Carmen': documentalismo y lectura alegórica," *Letras Peninsulares*, 8 (1995–1996), 440–450.
Johnson, Warren. " 'Carmen' and Exotic Nationalism: *España à la française*," *Romance Notes*, 38 (1997), 45–49.
Mickelsen, David. "Travel, Transgression, and Possession in Mérimée's 'Carmen,' " *Romanic R*, 87, iii (1996), 329–344.
"Lokis"
Michelucci, Pascal. "Prétérition et ambiguïté énonciative: Les Dobles sens de 'Lokis' de Prosper Mérimée," *Nineteenth-Century French Stud*, 26 (1997–1998), 91–103.
"La Partie de trictrac"
Cogman, Peter W. M. "Cheating at Narrating: Back to Mérimée's 'La Partie de trictrac,' " *Nineteenth-Century French Stud*, 26 (1997–1998), 80–90.
"La Vénus d'Ille"
Finné, Jacques. "Deux corps de Pierre: 'La Vénus d'Ille' de Prosper

Mérimée et 'La Malvenue' de Claude Seignolle," in Marigny, Jean, Intro., *Images fantastiques du corps*, 81–88.
Spica, Jacques. "Mais est-elle Il ou Elle, la Vénus d'Ille," *Recherches et Travaux*, 52 (1997), 147–168.

JUDITH MERRIL

"That Only a Woman"
Donawerth, Jane. *Frankenstein's Daughters . . .* , 132–133.

W. S. MERWIN

"Shepherds"
Hix, H. L. *Understanding W. S. Merwin*, 145–147, 148–151.

CONRAD FERDINAND MEYER

"Angela Borgia"
Sprengel, Peter. "Der andere Tizian Kunst und Wirklichkeit, Lyrik und Novellistik bei C. F. Meyer (Zu 'Angela Borgia' und 'Die Versuchung des Pescara')," *Colloquia Germanica*, 29 (1996), 146–149.
"Die Versuchung des Pescara"
Sprengel, Peter. "Der andere . . . ," 147–153.

HENRI MICHAUX

"Intervention"
Bertrand, Denis. "Figurativité: L'avant-scene des sens," *Versus*, 73–74 (January-August, 1996), 45–59.

RICHARD MIDDLETON

"The Bird in the Garden"
Ferguson, Suzanne. "Local Color and the Function of Setting in the English Short Story," in Kaylor, Noel H., Ed. *Creative and Critical . . .* , 28–30.

ARTHUR MILLER

"Ditchy"
Crandell, George W. " 'Ditchy' Discovered: Arthur Miller's First Published Short Story," *Stud Short Fiction*, 34 (1997), 519–521.
"Fitter's Night"
Bradbury, Malcolm. "Arthur Miller's Fiction," in Bigsby, Christopher, Ed. *The Cambridge . . .* , 226–227.

"I Don't Need You Any More"
Bradbury, Malcolm. "Arthur Miller's . . . ," 225.

"The Misfits"
Bradbury, Malcolm. "Arthur Miller's . . . ," 224–225.
Palmer, R. Barton. "Arthur Miller and the Cinema," in Bigsby,
Christopher, Ed. *The Cambridge* . . . , 201.

"Monte Sant' Angelo"
Bradbury, Malcolm. "Arthur Miller's . . . ," 223–224.

"The Prophecy"
Bradbury, Malcolm. "Arthur Miller's . . . ," 225–226.

"A Search for a Future"
Bradbury, Malcolm. "Arthur Miller's . . . ," 227.

LIANA MILLU

"L'ardua sentenza"
Sodi, Risa. "Many Bridges to Cross: Sex and Sexuality in Liana
Millu's Holocaust Fiction," *Nemla Italian Stud*, 21 (1997),
166–168.

"Lili Marlene"
Sodi, Risa. "Many Bridges . . . ," 164–166.

MISHA [TOTAL NAME]

"Tiny Dust"
Helford, Elyre R. "Going 'Native': Le Guin, Misha, and the Politics
of Speculative Literature," *Foundation*, 71 (1997), 82.

MISHIMA YUKIO

"Swaddling Clothes"
Baldwin, Dean. *Instructor's Resource* . . . , 168–169.
Charters, Ann, and William E. Sheidley. *Resources* . . . , 5th ed.,
177–178.
Ford, Joh, and Marjorie Ford. *Instructor's Manual* . . . , 77–78.

ROHINTON MISTRY

"Condolence Visit"
Kain, Geoffrey. "The Enigma of Departure: The Dynamics of Cultural
Ambiguity in Rohinton Mistry's *Swimming Lessons and Other
Stories from Firozsha Baag*," in Kain, Geoffrey, Ed. *Ideas of
Home* . . . , 66–67.

"Lend Me Your Light"
Kain, Geoffrey. "The Enigma . . . ," 67–69.

"Squatter"
    Kain, Geoffrey. "The Enigma . . . ," 69–70.
"Swimming Lessons"
    Kain, Geoffrey. "The Enigma . . . ," 70–72.

ANA MARÍA MOIX

"Dangerous Virtues"
    Jones, Margaret E. W. "Afterword," *Dangerous Virtues* [by Ana
    María Moix], 146–148.
"The Dead"
    Jones, Margaret E. W. "Afterword," 150–151.
"The Naive Man"
    Jones, Margaret E. W. "Afterword," 149.
"Once Upon a Time"
    Jones, Margaret E. W. "Afterword," 148–149.
"The Problem"
    Jones, Margaret E. W. "Afterword," 150.
"Las virtudes peligrosas"
    Cornejo-Parriego, Rosalía. "Desde el innominado deseo: Transgresión
    y marginalidad de la mirada en 'Las virtudes peligrosas' de Ana
    María Moix," *Anales Literatura*, 23, i-ii (1998), 607–621.
    Costa, Maria D. " 'Las virtudes peligrosas': The Story of Men
    Reading Women Reading Women," *Letras Peninsulares*, 8 (1995),
    89–97.

SUSANNA MOODIE

"The Broken Mirror, a True Tale"
    Dean, Misao. *Practising Femininity* . . . , 29.

C[ATHERINE] L. MOORE

"Shambleau"
    Bredehoft, Thomas A. "Origin Stories: Feminist Science Fiction and
    C. L. Moore's 'Shambleau,' " *Sci-Fiction Stud*, 24 (1997),
    369–386.

GEORGE MOORE

"Alms Giving"
    Davison, Neil R. "Representations of 'Irishness' in *The Untilled Field*:
    Deconstructing Ideological Ethnicity," *Textual Practice*, 12 (1998),
    312–313.

"The Clerk's Quest"
    Davison, Neil R. "Representations . . . ," 312.
"The Exile"
    Davison, Neil R. "Representations . . . ," 303.
    Ferguson, Suzanne. "Local Color and the Function of Setting in the
        English Short Story," in Kaylor, Noel H., Ed. *Creative and
        Critical* . . . , 18–20.
"Homesickness"
    Davison, Neil R. "Representations . . . ," 301.
"A Letter to Rome"
    Davison, Neil R. "Representations . . . ," 307–309.
"A Play-House in the Waste"
    Davison, Neil R. "Representations . . . ," 309–310.
"The Wild Goose"
    Davison, Neil R. "Representations . . . ," 314–316.
"The Window"
    Davison, Neil R. "Representations . . . ," 306–307.

LORRIE MOORE

"How to Become a Writer"
    Charters, Ann, and William E. Sheidley. *Resources* . . . , 5th ed., 179.
"You're Ugly, Too"
    Baldwin, Dean. *Instructor's Resource* . . . , 211–213.

PAUL MORAND

"Mme Fredda"
    Loselle, Andrea. *History's Double: Cultural* . . . , 109–110.
"Monsieur Zéro"
    Loselle, Andrea. *History's Double: Cultural* . . . , 124–125.

ETHAN MORDDEN

"The Dinner Party"
    Woodhouse, Reed. *Unlimited Embrace* . . . , 191–196.
"I Am the Sleuth"
    Woodhouse, Reed. *Unlimited Embrace* . . . , 187–189.
"Sliding into Home"
    Woodhouse, Reed. *Unlimited Embrace* . . . , 189–191.

IRMTRAUD MORGNER

"Notturno"
    Plow, Geoffrey. "What Became of 'Notturno': The Development of

an Early Theme in Irmtraud Morgner's Work," *Germ Life & Letters*, 50 (1997), 241–253.

TOSHIO MORI

"Japanese Hamlet"
  Palumbo-Liu, David. "Universalisms and Minority Culture," *Differences*, 7, i (1995),194–198.
  Wang, Qun. "Asian American Short Stories: Dialogizing the Asian American Experience," in Brown, Julie, Ed. *Ethnicity . . .* , 120–121.
"The Long Journey and the Short Ride"
  Streamas, John. "The Invention of Normality in Japanese American Internment Narratives," in Brown, Julie, Ed. *Ethnicity . . .* , 136–137.

WRIGHT MORRIS

"The Customs of the Country"
  Wydeven, Joseph J. *Wright Morris Revisited*, 169.
"Fellow Creatures"
  Wydeven, Joseph J. *Wright Morris . . .* , 167–169.
"Glimpse into Another Country"
  Wydeven, Joseph J. *Wright Morris . . .* , 170–172.
"The Origin of Sadness"
  Wydeven, Joseph J. *Wright Morris . . .* , 167–168.
"Victrola"
  Wydeven, Joseph J. *Wright Morris . . .* , 169–170.

TONI MORRISON

"Recitatif"
  Abel, Elizabeth. "Black Writing, White Reading: Race and the Politics of Feminist Interpretation," in Abel, Elizabeth, Barbara Christian, and Helene Moglen, Eds. *Female Subjects . . .* , 102–107.
  Goldstein-Shirley, David. "Race and Response: Toni Morrison's 'Recitatif,' " *Short Story*, 5, i, N.S. (1997), 77–86.
"Sula"
  Cadman, Deborah. "When the Back Door Is Closed and the Front Yard is Dangerous: The Space of Girlhood in Toni Morrison's Fiction," in Saxton, Ruth O., Ed. *The Girl . . .* , 66–71.
  Caminero-Santangelo, Marta. *The Madwoman . . .* , 135–136, 145–149, 169–170, 171.
  Cumings, Susan G. " 'Outing' the Hidden Other: Stranger-Women in the Work of Toni Morrison," in Tsuchiya, Kiyoshi, Ed. *Dissent . . .* , 49–52.

Donovan, Kathleen M. *Feminist Readings* . . . , 126–127, 130–131, 132–133, 134, 137.

Duvall, John N. "Toni Morrison and the Anxiety of Faulknerian Influence," in Kolmerten, Carol A., Stephen M. Ross, and Judith B. Wittenberg, Eds. *Unflinching Gaze* . . . , 6.

Feng, Pin-chia. *The Female* Bildungsroman . . . , 7, 40, 41, 77–105.

Gillespie, Diane, and Missy D. Kubitschek. "Who Cares? Women-Centered Psychology in 'Sula,' " in Middleton, David L., Ed. *Toni Morrison's Fiction* . . . , 61–64.

House, Elizabeth B. "Imagery, Figurative Language, and Symbols," in McKay, Nellie Y., and Kathryn Earle, Eds. *Approaches to Teaching* . . . , 99–105.

Johnson, Barbara. *The Feminist Difference* . . . , 74–87, 158–160.

Kennedy, Liam. "Once Upon a Time in America: Race, Ethnicity and Narrative Remembrance," in Youngs, Tim, Ed. *Writing and Race*, 112.

Kubitschek, Missy D. *Toni Morrison* . . . , 47–70.

McCay, Mary A., and Melanie McKay. "The River Narrative in Toni Morrison's 'Sula,' " in Ewell, Barbara C., Ed. *Performance for a Lifetime* . . . , 23–33.

McKee, Patricia. "Spacing and Placing Experience in Toni Morrison's 'Sula,' " in Peterson, Nancy J., Ed. *Toni Morrison* . . . , 37–59.

Matus, Jill. *Toni Morrison*, 55–71.

Powell, Timothy B. "Toni Morrison: The Struggle to Depict the Black Figure on the White Page," in Middleton, David L., Ed. *Toni Morrison's Fiction* . . . , 51–54.

Smith, Jeanne R. *Writing Tricksters* . . . , 115–120.

Stockton, Kathryn Bond. "Heaven's Bottom: Anal Economics and the Critical Debasement of Freud in Toni Morrison's 'Sula,' " in Stanley, Sandra K., Ed. *Other Sisterhoods* . . . , 277–303.

Thomson, Rosemarie G. *Extraordinary Bodies* . . . , 116–118, 120–121.

Weinstein, Philip M. "David and Solomon: Fathering in Faulkner and Morrison," in Kolmerten, Carol A., Stephen M. Ross, and Judith B. Wittenberg, Eds. *Unflinching Gaze* . . . , 56–58, 64.

Whalen-Bridge, John. *Political Fiction* . . . , 131, 133, 134–135, 152–169.

Wilentz, Gay. "An African-Based Reading of 'Sula,' " in McKay, Nellie Y., and Kathryn Earle, Eds. *Approaches to Teaching* . . . , 127–134.

Wilson, Michael. "Affirming Characters, Communities, and Change: Dialogism in Toni Morrison's 'Sula,' " *Midwestern Miscellany*, 24 (1996), 24–36.

EZEKIEL MPHAHLELE

"Blind Alley"
Gaylard, Rob. " 'A Man is a Man Because of Other Men': The

'Lesane' Stories of Es'kia Mphahlele," *Engl Africa*, 22, i (1995), 75–76.

"Down the Quiet Street"
Gaylard, Rob. " 'A Man is a Man . . . ,' " 76–78.

BHARATI MUKHERJEE

"Isolated Incidents"
Kumar, Sudhir. "The Canadian Experience as Textual Politics in Bharati Mukherjee's *Darkness*," *Panjab Univ Research Bull*, 24, i (1993), 80–81.

"The Management of Grief"
Bowen, Deborah. "Spaces of Translation: Bharati Mukherjee's 'The Management of Grief," *ArielE*, 28, iii (1997), 47–60.
Charters, Ann, and William E. Sheidley. *Resources* . . . , 5th ed., 180–181.
Zaman, Niaz. "Old Passions in a New Land: A Critique of Bharati Mukherjee's 'The Management of Grief' and Bapsi Sidhwa's 'Defend Yourself Against Me,' " in Kain, Geoffrey, Ed. *Ideas of Home* . . . , 80–81.

"Tamurlane"
Kumar, Sudhir. "The Canadian Experience . . . ," 81–83.

"The Wife"
Geis, Deborah R. " 'You're Exploiting My Space': Ethnicity, Spectatorship, and the (Post)Colonial Condition in Mukherjee's 'A Wife's Story' and Mamet's *Glengarry Glen Ross*," in Kane, Leslie, Ed. *David Mamet's* . . . , 123–124, 127–129.

"A Wife's Story"
Ford, Joh, and Marjorie Ford. *Instructor's Manual* . . . , 98–99.

"The World According to HSU"
Kumar, Sudhir. "The Canadian Experience . . . ," 79–80.

ROSA MULHOLLAND

"The Hungry Death"
Kelleher, Margaret. *The Feminization* . . . , 115–116.

HEINER MÜLLER

"The Father"
Hell, Julia. *Post-Fascist Fantasies* . . . , 110–113.

"Report about Grandfather"
Hell, Julia. *Post-Fascist Fantasies* . . . , 110.

ALICE MUNRO

"Accident"
Howells, Coral A. *Alice Munro*, 75–78.

"The Albanian Virgin"
Colvile, Georgiana M. M. "Relating (to) the Spec(tac)ular Other:
Alice Munro's 'The Albanian Virgin,' " *Commonwealth*, 21 (1998),
83–91.

"Baptizing"
Howells, Coral A. *Alice Munro*, 42–46.

"Bardon Bus"
Howells, Coral A. *Alice Munro*, 78–81.

"The Beggar Maid"
Howells, Coral A. *Alice Munro*, 60–62.

"Chaddeleys and Flemings"
Howells, Coral A. *Alice Munro*, 71–75.

"Circle of Prayer"
Ford, Joh, and Marjorie Ford. *Instructor's Manual . . .* , 84–85.

"Dance of the Happy Shades"
Howells, Coral A. *Alice Munro*, 28–30.

"Day of the Butterfly"
Kelly, Darlene. "Alice Munro's 'Day of the Butterfly': An American
Source," *ArielE*, 29, ii (1998), 118–126.

"Differently"
Hiscock, Andrew. " 'Longing for a Human Climate': Alice Munro's
Friend of My Youth and the Culture of Love," *J Commonwealth Lit*,
32, ii (1997), 22, 24, 29.
Nunes, Mark. "Postmodern 'Piecing': Alice Munro's Contingent
Ontologies," *Stud Short Fiction*, 34 (1997), 19.

"Epilogue: The Photographer"
Howells, Coral A. *Alice Munro*, 46–50.

"Fits"
Howells, Coral A. *Alice Munro*, 92–95.

"The Flats Road"
Daziron, Heliane. "Alice Munro's 'The Flats Road,' " *Canadian
Women's Stud*, 6, i (1984), 103–104.
Howells, Coral A. *Alice Munro*, 36–39.

"Friend of My Youth"
Forceville, Charles. "Alice Munro's Layered Structures," in Barfoot,
C. C., and Theo D'haen, Eds. *Shades of Empire . . .* , 309–310.
Hiscock, Andrew. " 'Longing . . . ,' " 21–22, 28.
Howells, Coral A. *Alice Munro*, 102–105.
Nunes, Mark. "Postmodern . . . ," 17–18.

"Goodness and Mercy"
Nunes, Mark. "Postmodern . . . ," 16–17, 24.

Study of Linguistic Modality in Alice Munro's Early Fiction," *Stud Canadian Lit*, 21, i (1996), 84, 87–88.

"Something I've Been Meaning to Tell You"
Howells, Coral A. *Alice Munro*, 25–28.
Somacarrera, Pilar. "Exploring . . . ," 83–84, 84–85, 89.

"Simon's Luck"
Howells, Coral A. *Alice Munro*, 62–66.

"Thanks for the Ride"
New, W. H. *Land Sliding* . . . , 123.

"Walker Brothers Cowboy"
Howells, Coral A. *Alice Munro*, 16–19.

"What Do You Want to Know For?"
Howells, Coral A. *Alice Munro*, 146–149.

"White Dump"
Howells, Coral A. *Alice Munro*, 95–98.

"Who Do You Think You Are?"
Howells, Coral A. *Alice Munro*, 63–68..
Lynch, Gerald. "The One and the Many: Canadian Short Story Cycles," in Lounsberry, Barbara, et al., Eds. *The Tales We Tell* . . . , 42–43.

"A Wilderness Station"
Gittings, Christopher E. "Constructing a Scots-Canadian Ground: Family History and Cultural Translation in Alice Munro," *Stud Short Fiction*, 34 (1997), 29–36.
Howells, Coral A. *Alice Munro*, 124–129.

MURAKAMI KARUKI

"The Dancing Dwarf"
Loughman, Celeste. "No Place I Was Meant to Be: Contemporary Japan in the Short Fiction of Haruki Murakami," *World Lit Today*, 71 (1997), 92.

"The Elephant Vanishes"
Loughman, Celeste. "No Place . . . ," 92.

"The Last Lawn of the Afternoon"
Loughman, Celeste. "No Place . . . ," 89.

"The Little Green Monster"
Loughman, Celeste. "No Place . . . ," 91–92.

"The Second Bakery Attack"
Loughman, Celeste. "No Place . . . ," 89.

"Sleep"
Loughman, Celeste. "No Place . . . ," 92–93.

"A Slow Boat to China"
Loughman, Celeste. "No Place . . . ," 90–91.

"The Wind-up Bird and Tuesday's Women"
   Loughman, Celeste. "No Place . . . ," 89–90, 91.
"A Window"
   Ford, Joh, and Marjorie Ford. *Instructor's Manual* . . . , 115–116.
   Loughman, Celeste. "No Place . . . ," 89.

ROBERT MUSIL

"Grigia"
   Zeller, Hans. "Das Arbeitsmanuskript von Musils Novelle 'Grigia' in
   der Bibliotheca Bodmeriana," in Böschenstein, Bernhard, and
   Marie-Louise Roth, Eds. *Homage à Musil*, 58–62.
"Die Portugiesin"
   Thüsen, Joachim von der. " 'Die Portugiesin': Zur Frage der
   literarischen Tradition bei Robert Musil," *Neophilologus*, 81, iii
   (1997), 433–443.
"Die Versuchung der stillen Veronika"
   Totosy de Zepetnek, Steven. "Female Sexuality and Eroticism in
   Musil's 'Die Versuchung der stillen Veronika,' " *Colloquia
   Germanica*, 30 (1997), 131–147.
"Die Verwirrung des Zöglings Törleß"
   Weiss, Walter. "Zur Metaphorik Robert Musils," in Böschenstein,
   Bernhard, and Marie-Louise Roth, Eds. *Homage à Musil*, 177–179.

ÁLVARO MUTIS

"Antes de que cante el gallo"
   Castro García, Óscar. "La muerte, espejo de la vida, en los cuentos de
   Mutis," *Lingüística y Lit*, 15, xxvi (1994), 78–79, 80–81.
"La muerte del Estratega"
   Castro García, Óscar. "La muerte, espejo . . . . ," 69–75.
"Sharaya"
   Castro García, Óscar. "La muerte, espejo . . . . ," 79–80.
"El ultimo rostro"
   Castro García, Óscar. "La muerte, espejo . . . . ," 75–78.

VLADIMIR NABOKOV

"Signs and Symbols"
   Matthews, Jack. "All Is the Cipher and He Is the Theme," *Southern
   R*, 32 (1996), 822–825.

SHIVA NAIPAUL

"The Dolly House"
   Patteson, Richard F. *Caribbean Passages* . . . , 89–90.

"A Man of Mystery"
Patteson, Richard F. *Caribbean Passages* . . . , 88–89.

TAHIRA NAQVI

"Paths Upon Water"
Leach, Laurie. "Conflict over Privacy in Indo-American Short
Fiction," in Brown, Julie, Ed. *Ethnicity* . . . , 198, 205–209.
Wang, Qun. "Asian American Short Stories: Dialogizing the Asian
American Experience," in Brown, Julie, Ed. *Ethnicity* . . . , 120.

R. K. NARAYAN

"An Astrologer's Day"
Ford, Joh, and Marjorie Ford. *Instructor's Manual* . . . , 55–56.
Richardson, Brian. *UnLikely Stories* . . . , 150–151.

GLORIA NAYLOR

"The Two"
Ford, Joh, and Marjorie Ford. *Instructor's Manual* . . . , 117.

NJABULO NDEBELE

"The Prophetess"
Richardson, Brian. *UnLikely Stories* . . . , 146–147.

JOHN NEAL

"Otter-Bag, the Oneida Chief"
Goddu, Teresa A. *Gothic America* . . . , 58–59.

GÉRARD DE NERVAL

"Aurélia"
Barthèlemy, Guy. "Chimères et errance chez Nerval," *Op. Cit.*, 9
(1997), 127–129, 130.
Brix, Michel. " 'Aurélia' et la crise de la représentation en France au
XIXe siècle," *Op. Cit.*, 9 (1997), 139–140.
Iankova, Silvia D. " 'Aurélia' lue par son rêve inaugural," *Revue
d'Histoire Littéraire*, 97, i (1997), 57–70.
Vadé, Yves. "Espace du souvenir et espace du rêve dans 'Sylvie' et
'Aurélia,' *Op. Cit.*, 9 (1997), 159–168.
"Sylvie"
Barthèlemy, Guy. "Chimères et errance . . . ," 127.
Vadé, Yves. "Espace du souvenir . . . ," 159–160, 164, 165–166.

LESLÉA NEWMAN

"A Letter to Harvey Milk"
Aarons, Victoria. "Responding to an Old Story: Susan Fromberg
Schaeffer, Lesléa Newman, and Francine Prose," in Halio, Jay L.,
and Ben Siegel, Eds. *Daughters of Valor* . . . , 113–115, 117–120.

ANAÏS NIN

"The All-Seeing"
Franklin, Benjamin. "Noli Me Tangere: The Structure of Anaïs Nin's
Under a Glass Bell," *Stud Short Fiction*, 34 (1997), 471.

"Birth"
Elkan, Lajos. "Birth and the Linguistics of Gender: Masculine/
Feminine," in Nalbantian, Suzanne, Ed. *Anaïs Nin* . . . , 153–155,
158–162.
Franklin, Benjamin. "Noli Me Tangere . . . ," 468–469, 470, 472.

"The Child Born Out of the Fog"
Franklin, Benjamin. "Noli Me Tangere . . . ," 471.

"The Eye's Journey"
Franklin, Benjamin. "Noli Me Tangere . . . ," 471.

"Hejda"
Franklin, Benjamin. "Noli Me Tangere . . . ," 471–472.

"Hilda and Rango"
Miller, Edmund. "Erato Throws a Curve: Anaïs Nin and the Elusive
Feminine Voice in Erotica," in Nalbantian, Suzanne, Ed. *Anaïs
Nin* . . . , 168–169.

"Je Suis le Plus Malade des Surréalistes"
Franklin, Benjamin. "Noli Me Tangere . . . ," 467–468.

"The Labyrinth"
Franklin, Benjamin. "Noli Me Tangere . . . ," 468.

"Mandra"
Miller, Edmund. "Erato Throws . . . ," 174–175.

"The Mohican"
Franklin, Benjamin. "Noli Me Tangere . . . ," 467.

"The Mouse"
Franklin, Benjamin. "Noli Me Tangere . . . ," 466–467.

"Ragtime"
Franklin, Benjamin. "Noli Me Tangere . . . ," 468.

"Runaway"
Miller, Edmund. "Erato Throws . . . ," 177–178.

"Through the Streets of My Own Labyrinth"
Franklin, Benjamin. "Noli Me Tangere . . . ," 470–471.

"Two Sisters"
Miller, Edmund. "Erato Throws . . . ," 168.

"Under a Glass Bell"
Franklin, Benjamin. "Noli Me Tangere . . . ," 466–467.
"The Woman on the Dunes"
Miller, Edmund. "Erato Throws . . . ," 169.

FRANK NORRIS

"A Memorandum of Sudden Death"
Link, Eric C. "Frank Norris's Blackwood Tale," *Frank Norris Stud*, 23 (1997), 4–6.
"A Salvation Boom in Matabeleland"
Johanningsmeier, Charles. " 'Rediscovering' Frank Norris's 'A Salvation Boom in Matabeleland,' " *Frank Norris Stud*, 22 (1996), 2–3.

MARTA NOS

"La silla"
Lorente-Murphy, Silvia. " 'La silla' de Marta Nos y el teatro del absurdo: Puntos de contacto," in Hernández de López, Ana M., Ed. *Narrativa hispanoamericana . . .* , 179–189.

LINO NOVÁS CALVO

"A Bum"
Borland, Isabel A. *Cuban-American . . .* , 25–56.
"Fernández, To the Firing Squad"
Borland, Isabel A. *Cuban-American . . .* , 22–23.
"The Night Juan Victimized Pedro"
Borland, Isabel A. *Cuban-American . . .* , 26–27.
"No One to Kill"
Borland, Isabel A. *Cuban-American . . .* , 21–22.
"A Sip of Coffee"
Borland, Isabel A. *Cuban-American . . .* , 23–25.

D. B. Z. NTULI

"Ucingo"
Marggraff, M. M. "Verb Stems as Stylistica in D. B. Z. Ntuli's 'Ucingo,' " *So African J*, 17, iv (1997), 136–139.

RICHARD BRUCE NUGENT

"Smoke, Lilies, and Jade"
Boone, Joseph A. *Libidinal Currents . . .* , 220–232.

MUHAMMAD HUSAYN NURI'ZAD

"The Man and Karbala"
Talattof, Kamran. "The Changing Mode of Relationship Between
Modern Persian Literature and Islam: Karbala in Fiction," in
Hawley, John C., Ed. *The Postcolonial Crescent* . . . , 259–262.

FLORA NWAPA

"The Chief's Daughter"
Azodo, Ada U. "Nigerian Women in Search of Identity: Converging
Feminism and Pragmatism," in Umeh, Marie, Ed. *Emerging
Perspectives* . . . , 248–249.

"The Child Thief"
Horne, Naana B. "Flora Nwapa's *This is Lagos*: Valorizing the Female
Through Narrative Agency," in Umeh, Marie, Ed. *Emerging
Perspectives* . . . , 459–463, 473.

"The Delinquent Adults"
Horne, Naana B. "Flora Nwapa's . . . ," 464–472.

"Jide's Story"
Horne, Naana B. "Flora Nwapa's . . . ," 446, 449–454, 472.

"The Loss of Eze"
Horne, Naana B. "Flora Nwapa's . . . ," 454–458.

"Man Palaver"
Azodo, Ada U. "Nigerian Women . . . ," 247, 248.

"My Soldier Brother"
Horne, Naana B. "Flora Nwapa's . . . ," 446, 447–448.

"The Road to Benin"
Horne, Naana B. "Flora Nwapa's . . . ," 463–464.

"Wives at War"
Azodo, Ada U. "Nigerian Women . . . ," 255–256.

JOYCE CAROL OATES

"Accursed Inhabitants of the House of Bly"
Johnson, Greg. *Invisible Writer* . . . , 385.

"Angst"
Johnson, Greg. *Invisible Writer* . . . , 230.

"The Dead"
Johnson, Greg. *Invisible Writer* . . . , 193, 259.

"The Doll"
Robbins, Alexander. "The Fairy-Tale, Façade: Cinderella's Anti-
Grotesque Dream," *J Pop Culture*, 32, iii (1998), 104–105.

"In the Old World"
Johnson, Greg. *Invisible Writer* . . . , 72, 73–74.

ACHY OBEJAS

EDNA O'BRIEN

"The Love Object"
Mahony, Christina H. *Contemporary Irish* . . . , 213–214.
"Sister Imelda"
Mahony, Christina H. *Contemporary Irish* . . . , 213.

TIM O'BRIEN

"The Ghost Soldiers"
Chen, Tina. " 'Unraveling the Deeper Meaning': Exile and the Embodied Poetics of Displacement in Tim O'Brien's *The Things They Carried*," *Contemp Lit*, 39 (1998), 93–94.
"How to Tell a True War Story"
Chen, Tina. " 'Unraveling . . . ,' " 95.
"The Lives of the Dead"
Chen, Tina. " 'Unraveling . . . ,' " 88.
"The Man I Killed"
Ford, Joh, and Marjorie Ford. *Instructor's Manual* . . . , 110–111.
"Night Life"
Chen, Tina. " 'Unraveling . . . ,' " 87.
"On the Rainy River"
Chen, Tina. " 'Unraveling . . . ,' " 86.
Herzog, Tobey C. *Tim O'Brien*, 116–117.
"Speaking of Courage"
Chen, Tina. " 'Unraveling . . . ,' " 92–93.
"Sweetheart of the Song Tra Bong"
Chen, Tina. " 'Unraveling . . . ,' " 89–92.
"The Things They Carried"
Charters, Ann, and William E. Sheidley. *Resources* . . . , 5th ed., 188.
Chen, Tina. " 'Unraveling . . . ,' " 84–86.

SILVINA OCAMPO

"El automóvil"
Salzmann, Elisa. "Muchachas sobre ruedas: Una lectura de 'El automóvil' de Silvina Ocampo y otras piezas de colección," in Frugoni de Fritzsche, Teresita, Ed. *Primeras Jornadas* . . . , 449–450.
Zapata, Monica. "La Métamorphose des corps et l'esthéique du grotesque dans les récits de Silvina Ocampo," in Marigny, Jean, Intro., *Images fantastiques du corps*, 191–192.
"Azabache"
Zapata, Monica. "La Métamorphose . . . ," 184–185.
"Cartas confidenciales"
Zapata, Monica. "La Métamorphose . . . ," 186.

"El diario de Porfiria Bernal"
Zapata, Monica. "La Métamorphose . . . ," 187–189.

"Hombres animals enredareras"
Zapata, Monica. "La Métamorphose . . . ," 189–191.

"Malva"
Zapata, Monica. "La Métamorphose . . . ," 185.

"Ulises"
Zapata, Monica. "La Métamorphose . . . ," 186–187.

"Las vestiduras peligrosas"
Ostrov, Andrea. "Vestidura/escritura/sepultura en la narrativa de Silvina Ocampo," *Hispamérica*, 25, lxxiv (1996), 23–25.

FLANNERY O'CONNOR

"The Artificial Nigger"
Noya, José L. "Flannery O'Connor's 'Demons': Intentionality and Literary Meaning in 'The Artificial Nigger,' " *REDEN*, 5, viii (1994), 33–44.

"The Comforts of Home"
Hewitt, Avis. " 'Sniveler[s] After the Ineffable': Salvific Suffering in Flannery O'Connor's Sullen Sons of the South," in Hallisey, Joan F., and Mary-Anne Vetterling, Eds. *Proceedings: Northeast* . . . , 55–60.
Ragen, Brian A. "Daredevil Charity: Love and Family in O'Connor's 'The Comforts of Home,' " in Hallisey, Joan F., and Mary-Anne Vetterling, Eds. *Proceedings: Northeast* . . . , 102–107.

"The Displaced Person"
Bolton, Betsy. "Placing Violence, Embodying Grace: Flannery O'Connor's 'Displaced Person,' " *Stud Short Fiction*, 34 (1997), 87–104.
Casey, Roger N. *Textual Vehicles* . . . , 103–105.
Donahoo, Robert. "O'Connor's Catholics: A Historical-Cultural Context," in Murphy, John J., Linda H. Adams, Richard H. Cracroft, and Susan E. Howe, Eds. *Flannery O'Connor* . . . , 105–109.
Labrie, Ross. *The Catholic Imagination* . . . , 216.

"The Enduring Chill"
Donahoo, Robert. "O'Connor's Catholics . . . ," 109–112.
Hewitt, Avis. " 'Sniveler[s] After . . . ,' " 55–60.
Labrie, Ross. *The Catholic Imagination* . . . , 217–218.

"Everything That Rises Must Converge"
Charters, Ann, and William E. Sheidley. *Resources* . . . , 5th ed., 189–190.
Hewitt, Avis. " 'Sniveler[s] After . . . ,' " 55–60.

"Good Country People"
Baldwin, Dean. *Instructor's Resource* . . . , 148–150.
Charters, Ann, and William E. Sheidley. *Resources* . . . , 5th ed., 191–192.

Labrie, Ross. *The Catholic Imagination* . . . , 217.

Olson, Barbara K. *Authorial Divinity* . . . , 120–121.

Streight, Irwin H. "A Good Hypogram Is Not Hard to Find," in Murphy, John J., Linda H. Adams, Richard H. Cracroft, and Susan E. Howe, Eds. *Flannery O'Connor* . . . , 235–240.

Waldmeir, Joseph J. *"Miss Tina Did It"* . . . , 107–113.

"A Good Man Is Hard to Find"

Batts, Martin. "Flannery O'Connor: Good and Evil in a Relativistic World," in Hallisey, Joan F., and Mary-Anne Vetterling, Eds. *Proceedings: Northeast* . . . , 9–11.

Baxter, Charles. *Burning Down the House* . . . , 123–125.

Casey, Roger N. *Textual Vehicles* . . . , 102–103.

Charters, Ann, and William E. Sheidley. *Resources* . . . , 5th ed., 193–194.

Demory, Pamela H. "Violence and Transcendence in *Pulp Fiction* and Flannery O'Connor," in Wright, Will, and Steven Kaplan, Eds. *The Image of Violence* . . . , 187–191.

Labrie, Ross. *The Catholic Imagination* . . . , 214–215.

Polette, Keith. "Text and Textile: Sacred and Profane Fashion Statements in Flannery O'Connor's 'A Good Man is Hard to Find,' " *J Assoc Interdisciplinary Stud Arts*, 2, ii (1997), 63–80.

Ross, Cheri L. "The Iconography of Popular Culture in O'Connor's 'A Good Man Is Hard to Find,' " *Notes Contemp Lit*, 27, i (1997), 7–9.

Sloan, Gary. "The Head-Doctor in Flannery O'Connor's 'A Good Man Is Hard to Find,' " *Notes Contemp Lit*, 27, iii (1997), 4–5.

Wood, Ralph C. "Flannery O'Connor's Strange Alliance with Southern Fundamentalists," in Murphy, John J., Linda H. Adams, Richard H. Cracroft, and Susan E. Howe, Eds. *Flannery O'Connor* . . . , 92–97.

"Greenleaf"

Casey, Roger N. *Textual Vehicles* . . . , 105–106.

Schiff, Jonathan. " 'That's a Greenleaf Bull': Totemism and Exogamy in Flannery O'Connor's 'Greenleaf,' " *Engl Lang Notes*, 32, iii (1995), 69–76.

"Judgment Day"

Whitt, Margaret. "Letters from Corinth: Echoes from Greece to Georgia in O'Connor's 'Judgment Day,' " in Murphy, John J., Linda H. Adams, Richard H. Cracroft, and Susan E. Howe, Eds. *Flannery O'Connor* . . . , 61–74.

"The Lame Shall Enter First"

Labrie, Ross. *The Catholic Imagination* . . . , 218–219.

"Parker's Back"

Casey, Roger N. *Textual Vehicles* . . . , 101–102.

Fodor, Sarah J. " 'A World Apparently Without Comment' Or Shouting at the Reader: Narrative Guidance in O'Connor's Fiction," in Murphy, John J., Linda H. Adams, Richard H. Cracroft, and Susan E. Howe, Eds. *Flannery O'Connor* . . . , 226–227.

Hewitt, Eben. "Diapsalmata and Numinous Recapitulation: The
Tropology of 'Parker's Back,' " in Hallisey, Joan F., and Mary-
Anne Vetterling, Eds. *Proceedings: Northeast* . . . , 61–64.
Kilcourse, George. " 'Parker's Back': 'Not Totally Congenial' Icons
of Christ," in Murphy, John J., Linda H. Adams, Richard H.
Cracroft, and Susan E. Howe, Eds. *Flannery O'Connor* . . . , 38–45.
Labrie, Ross. *The Catholic Imagination* . . . , 219–220.
Samuelson, Todd. "Creating the Incommensurate God: Art and Belief
in O'Connor's 'Parker's Back' and Bloom's *The Book of J*," in
Murphy, John J., Linda H. Adams, Richard H. Cracroft, and Susan
E. Howe, Eds. *Flannery O'Connor* . . . , 48–55.

"Revelation"
Fodor, Sarah J. " 'A World Apparently . . . ,' " 224–226.
Ford, Joh, and Marjorie Ford. *Instructor's Manual* . . . , 76–77.
Labrie, Ross. *The Catholic Imagination* . . . , 219.
Sessions, W. A. "How to Read Flannery O'Connor: Passing by the
Dragon," in Murphy, John J., Linda H. Adams, Richard H. Cracroft,
and Susan E. Howe, Eds. *Flannery O'Connor* . . . , 205–213.
Streight, Irwin H. "A Good Hypogram . . . ," 233–235.

"The River"
Labrie, Ross. *The Catholic Imagination* . . . , 216–217.
Zornado, Joseph. "A Becoming Habit: Flannery O'Connor's Fiction
of Unknowing," *Religion & Lit*, 29, ii (1997), 34–35, 36–37,
40–45, 55, 56.

"A Temple of the Holy Ghost"
Donahoo, Robert. "O'Connor's Catholics . . . ," 103–105.

"A View of the Woods"
Casey, Roger N. *Textual Vehicles* . . . , 106.

FRANK O'CONNOR [MICHAEL O'DONOVAN]

"An Act of Charity"
Alexander, James D. "Frank O'Connor's *New Yorker* Stories: The
Serious Side," in Evans, Robert C., and Richard Harp, Eds. *Frank
O'Connor* . . . , 111–113, 114.

"The Adventuress"
Weber, Owene. "A Woman's Voice Speaking: Glimpses of Irish
Womanhood in the Short Stories of Frank O'Connor," in Evans,
Robert C., and Richard Harp, Eds. *Frank O'Connor* . . . , 124–125.

"The American Wife"
Weber, Owene. "A Woman's Voice . . . ," 134.

"Achilles' Heel"
Weber, Owene. "A Woman's Voice . . . ," 137.

"The Awakening"
Weber, Owene. "A Woman's Voice . . . ," 126–127.

"The Babes in the Woods"
Alexander, James D. "Frank O'Connor's . . . ," 116.

"The Bridal Night"
Durrer, Kathleen B., Scott Johnson, Katie Magaw, and Claire
Skowronski. "Theories and Practice: 'Guests of the Nation' and
'The Bridal Night' from Diverse Critical Perspectives," in Evans,
Robert C., and Richard Harp, Eds. *Frank O'Connor . . .* , 219–237.
Harp, Richard. "Frank O'Connor's Stories: Epiphanies of the Heart,"
in Evans, Robert C., and Richard Harp, Eds. *Frank O'Connor . . .* ,
70–71.

"The Cheat"
Weber, Owene. "A Woman's Voice . . . ," 133.

"Christmas Morning"
Neary, Michael. "Off Stage Narrators: The Evocative Narrative Voice
in Frank O'Connor's Stories," in Evans, Robert C., and Richard
Harp, Eds. *Frank O'Connor . . .* , 86–87.

"The Climber"
Weber, Owene. "A Woman's Voice . . . ," 123–124.

"The Corkerys"
Evans, Robert C., and Katie Magaw. "Irony and Paradox in Frank
O'Connor's Style," in Evans, Robert C., and Richard Harp, Eds.
Frank O'Connor . . . , 154–155.

"Counsel for Oedipus"
Weber, Owene. "A Woman's Voice . . . ," 132.

"Darcy in the Land of Youth"
Neary, Michael. "Off Stage Narrators . . . ," 91–92.

"Don Juan's Temptation"
Neary, Michael. "Off Stage Narrators . . . ," 88–89.

"The Drunkard"
Denio, Megan L. "The Child In, Around, and Of Father Fogarty," in
Evans, Robert C., and Richard Harp, Eds. *Frank O'Connor . . .* ,
142.

"The Duke's Children"
White, Julianne. "The Making of Sensibility: Loneliness, Shame, and
the Narrative Voice of Frank O'Connor," in Evans, Robert C., and
Richard Harp, Eds. *Frank O'Connor . . .* , 95–97, 99–102.

"Expectation of Life"
Evans, Robert C., and Katie Magaw. "Irony . . . ," 150–151, 152–153.

"Face of Evil"
Alexander, James D. "Frank O'Connor's . . . ," 110–111.
Harp, Richard. "Frank O'Connor's . . . ," 75–77.

"Freedom"
Harp, Richard. "Frank O'Connor's . . . ," 77–78.

"The Flowering Trees"
Weber, Owene. "A Woman's Voice . . . ," 123.

"The Frying Pan"
Denio, Megan L. "The Child In . . . ," 140–141.
Harp, Richard. "Frank O'Connor's . . . ," 72.

'The Man of the House,' " in Evans, Robert C., and Richard Harp, Eds. *Frank O'Connor* . . . , 173–187.

"The Mass Island"
Alexander, James D. "Frank O'Connor's . . . ," 115–116.
Denio, Megan L. "The Child In . . . ," 146–147.

"Michael's Wife"
Weber, Owene. "A Woman's Voice . . . ," 131, 329–330.

"A Mother's Warning"
Denio, Megan L. "The Child In . . . ," 142–143.

"Music When Soft Voices Die"
Weber, Owene. "A Woman's Voice . . . ," 129.

"News for the Church"
Weber, Owene. "A Woman's Voice . . . ," 128.

"The Old Faith"
Denio, Megan L. "The Child In . . . ," 141–142.

"The Picture"
Weber, Owene. "A Woman's Voice . . . ," 135.

"The Pretender"
Alexander, James D. "Frank O'Connor's . . . ," 117–118.

"The Procession of Life"
Neary, Michael. "Off Stage Narrators . . . ," 84–85.
Steinman, Michael. " 'The Procession of Life': The Writer as Son and Father," in Evans, Robert C., and Richard Harp, Eds. *Frank O'Connor* . . . , 159–172, 337–338.

"The Rebel"
Weber, Owene. "A Woman's Voice . . . ," 132–133.

"Requiem"
Denio, Megan L. "The Child In . . . ," 145–146.

"The Ring"
Weber, Owene. "A Woman's Voice . . . ," 130.

"The School for Wives"
Weber, Owene. "A Woman's Voice . . . ," 134.

"A Set of Variations on a Borrowed Theme"
Alexander, James D. "Frank O'Connor's . . . ," 118–120.
Weber, Owene. "A Woman's Voice . . . ," 137.

"The Sisters"
Weber, Owene. "A Woman's Voice . . . ," 135.

"A Story by Maupassant"
Corcoran, Neil. *After Yeats* . . . , 76.

"The Teacher's Mass"
Alexander, James D. "Frank O'Connor's . . . ," 114–115.
Denio, Megan L. "The Child In . . . ," 144–145.

"There Is a Lone House"
Harp, Richard. "Frank O'Connor's . . . ," 78–79.

"The Ugly Duckling"
Evans, Robert C., and Katie Magaw. "Irony . . . ," 151–152.
Harp, Richard. "Frank O'Connor's . . . ," 79.
Weber, Owene. "A Woman's Voice . . . ," 125.

"Unapproved Route"
Evans, Robert C., and Katie Magaw. "Irony . . . ," 150.
Weber, Owene. "A Woman's Voice . . . ," 132.

"Uprooted"
Harp, Richard. "Frank O'Connor's . . . ," 71–72.

"The Weeping Children"
Alexander, James D. "Frank O'Connor's . . . ," 117.
Weber, Owene. "A Woman's Voice . . . ," 128.

"The Wreath"
Denio, Megan L. "The Child In . . . ," 143–144.

PEADAR O'DONNELL

"Remembering Kitty"
Gonzalez, Alexander G. *Peadar O'Donnell* . . . , 71–72.

"War"
Gonzalez, Alexander G. *Peadar O'Donnell* . . . , 72–74.

"Why Blame the Sea Gulls"
Gonzalez, Alexander G. *Peadar O'Donnell* . . . , 72.

SEAN O'FAOLAIN

"A Broken World"
Corcoran, Neil. *After Yeats and Joyce* . . . , 73–74.

"Lovers of the Lake"
Corcoran, Neil. *After Yeats* . . . , 74.

O. HENRY [WILLIAM SYDNEY PORTER]

"The Gift of the Magi"
Baldwin, Dean. *Instructor's Resource* . . . , 82–84.
Charters, Ann, and William E. Sheidley. *Resources* . . . , 5th ed., 211–212.

OKAMOTO KANOKO

"Portrait of an Old Geisha"
Goossen, Theodore W. "Introduction," in Goossen, Theodore, Ed. *The Oxford Book* . . . , xxvi.

BEN OKRI

"What the Tapster Saw"
Quayson, Ato. *Strategic Transformations* . . . , 116–120.
"When the Lights Return"
Quayson, Ato. *Strategic* . . . , 103–116.

MARGARET OLIPHANT

"The Library Window"
Williams, Merryn. "Margaret Oliphant," in Gifford, Douglas, and
Dorothy McMillan, Eds. *A History* . . . , 289.
"Old Lady Mary"
Williams, Merryn. "Margaret Oliphant," 288–289.
"The Open Door"
Williams, Merryn. "Margaret Oliphant," 287–288.
"Queen Eleanor and Fair Rosamond"
Williams, Merryn. "Margaret Oliphant," 286.

MARIA ANTÓNIA OLIVER

"Muller qui cerca espill"
Pérez, Janet. "Metamorphosis as a Protest Device in Catalan Feminist
Writing: Rodoreda and Oliver," *Catalan R*, 2, ii (1987), 188–192.
"Vegetal i Muller qui cerca espill"
Pérez, Janet. "Metamorphosis . . . ," 181–188.

TILLIE OLSEN

"Hey Sailor, What Ship?"
Cardoni, Agnes T. *Women's Ethical* . . . , 15–31.
"I Stand Here Ironing"
Cardoni, Agnes T. *Women's Ethical* . . . , 62–72.
Charters, Ann, and William E. Sheidley. *Resources* . . . , 5th ed.,
199–200.
Ford, Joh, and Marjorie Ford. *Instructor's Manual* . . . , 62–63.
Hansen, Elaine T. *Mother Without Child* . . . , 182–183.
"O Yes"
Cardoni, Agnes T. *Women's Ethical* . . . , 31–46.
"Tell Me a Riddle"
Cardoni, Agnes T. *Women's Ethical* . . . , 46–59.

JUAN CARLOS ONETTI

"Los adioses"
Lewis, Bart L. "Realizing the Textual Space: Metonymic Metafiction
in Juan Carlos Onetti," *Hispanic R*, 64 (1996), 497–499.

"La cara de la desgracia"
Olivera-Williams, María R. "Entre él y ella: J. C. Onetti y Armonía Somers desde sus cuentos," *Revista de Crítica*, 23, xlvi (1997), 213–214, 217–220.
"Cuando entonces"
Lewis, Bart L. "Realizing the Textual Space . . . ," 502–505.
"A Dream Come True"
Gurski, Edward T. "Revisiting Onetti's 'Un sueño realizado,' " *Indiana J Hispanic Lit*, 10–11 (1997), 223–235.
Lewis, Bart L. "Realizing the Textual Space . . . ," 495–496.
"El infierno tan temido"
Benítez, Edna, and Alicia de Colombí-Monguió. " 'El infierno tan temido' de Juan Carlos Onetti desde su subtexto: nueva lectura," *Torre*, 8, xxxi (1994), 337–383.

JULIO ORTEGA

"Avenida Oeste"
Salto, Graciela N. "El sabor de lo andino en 'Avenida Oeste' de Julio Ortega," *Hispano*, 124 (1998), 101–106.

BERNARDO ORTIZ DE MONTELLANO

"La calle de los sueños"
Forster, Merlin H. "Los relatos breves de Ortiz de Montellano: Incursión en la prosa vanguardista mexicana," in Herrera, Sara P., Ed. *El cuento mexicano* . . . , 226, 227.
"El caso de mi amigo Alfazeta"
Forster, Merlin H. "Los relatos . . . ," 232–233.
"El cabo Muñoz"
Forster, Merlin H. "Los relatos . . . ," 233–234.
"Cinq heures sans cœur"
Forster, Merlin H. "Los relatos . . . ," 230–231.
"Crimen sin castigo"
Forster, Merlin H. "Los relatos . . . ," 227–228.
"Historia de una imagen"
Forster, Merlin H. "Los relatos . . . ," 226.
"La máquina humana"
Forster, Merlin H. "Los relatos . . . ," 223–224.
"Mr. Dream, detective particular"
Forster, Merlin H. "Los relatos . . . ," 229–230.
"Naturaleza muerta"
Forster, Merlin H. "Los relatos . . . ," 228–229.
"La niña de Guatemala"
Forster, Merlin H. "Los relatos . . . ," 224–226.

PEDRO ORTIZ DOMÍNGUEZ

"Adelante muchachos"
Álvarez Clavel, Osmar. "Las relaciones intertextuales, intratextuales e intergenéricas en *Carta al rey*, de Pedro Ortiz," *Texto Crítico*, 2, ii (1996), 161–162.

"Carta al rey"
Álvarez Clavel, Osmar. "Las relaciones . . . ," 149–151.

"Comer con los indios"
Álvarez Clavel, Osmar. "Las relaciones . . . ," 147–148.

"La ciudad del oro"
Álvarez Clavel, Osmar. "Las relaciones . . . ," 146–147, 153–154.

"La hora tercia"
Álvarez Clavel, Osmar. "Las relaciones . . . ," 159, 160.

"Mi otro corazón"
Álvarez Clavel, Osmar. "Las relaciones . . . ," 155–158.

"Mr. Turnbull èn Gibara"
Álvarez Clavel, Osmar. "Las relaciones . . . ," 160–161.

"Nada más que una sombra"
Álvarez Clavel, Osmar. "Las relaciones . . . ," 151–152.

"Primer encuentro"
Álvarez Clavel, Osmar. "Las relaciones . . . ," 144–146, 148–149.

GEORGE ORWELL

"Animal Farm"
+ Alldritt, Keith. " 'Animal Farm' Is Trivial," in O'Neill, Terry, Ed. *Readings on . . .* , 50–53.
Brown, Spencer. "Strange Doings at 'Animal Farm': A Case Study in Cultural Hocus-Pocus," *Commentary* (February, 1955), 155–161; rpt. in O'Neill, Terry, Ed. *Readings on . . .* , 71–81.
+ Hollis, Christopher. " 'Animal Farm' Is a Successful Animal Fable," in O'Neill, Terry, Ed. *Readings on . . .* , 43–49.
Koon-ki, Tommy Ho. "Dystopia as an Alternative Historical Hypothesis of Eutopia: The Life Histories of Eutopia in 'Animal Farm' and *A Utopian Dream*," in Akiyama, Masayuki, and Yiunam Leung, Eds. *Crosscurrents . . .* , 136–142.
+ Kubal, David L. "Orwell Shows That Too Much Civilizing Can Harm Good Instincts," in O'Neill, Terry, Ed. *Readings on . . .* , 82–85.
+ Meyers, Jeffery. " 'Animal Farm' Is a Strong Political Allegory," in O'Neill, Terry, Ed. *Readings on . . .* , 103–115.
Patai, Daphne. *The Orwell Mystique . . .* , 205–206, 206–214, 215–216, 217; rpt. in O'Neill, Terry, Ed. *Readings on . . .* , 117–126.
+ Reilly, Patrick. "The Fairy Tale Distances Us from the Terror," in O'Neill, Terry, Ed. *Readings on . . .* , 61–68.
Sedley, Stephen. "An Immodest Proposal: Animal Farm," in Norris,

Christopher, Ed. *Inside the Myth* . . . , 155–159, 160–162; rpt. in
O'Neill, Terry, Ed. *Readings on* . . . , 54–60.

VINCENT O'SULLIVAN

"Quite an Ordinary Story"
Bachinger, Katrina. "Setting Allegory Adrift in John Ashbery's
Mountains and Rivers, James Joyce's *Portrait of the Artist as a
Young Man*, and Vincent O'Sullivan's *Let the River Stand*," in
Coelsch-Foisner, Sabine, and Wolfgang Görtschacher, Eds. *Trends
in English* . . . , 285–287.

LOUISE OTTO-PETERS

"Paul Flemming: Eine literarisch-historische Skizze aus dem 17.
Jahrhundert"
Diethe, Carol. *Towards Emancipation* . . . , 148–149.
"Eine weibliche Ahasver"
Diethe, Carol. *Towards Emancipation* . . . , 149.

SEMBÉNE OUSMANE

"The Bilal's Fourth Wife"
Adebayo, Aduke. "The African Mother: Her Changing Perceptions in
West African Fiction," in Adebayo, Aduke, Ed. *Feminism and Black
Women's* . . . , 184–185.
"Lettres de France"
Opara, Chioma. "The Emergence of the Female Self: The Liberating
Pen in Mariama Ba's *Une si longue lettre* and Sembéne Ousmane's
'Lettres de France,' " in Adebayo, Aduke, Ed. *Feminism and Black
Women's* . . . , 161–165.
"La Mère"
Adebayo, Aduke. "The African Mother . . . ," 181–184.

THOMAS OWEN

"Une aile de papillon mort"
Joguin, Odile. "Le fantastique ne fait plus le poids: allègement
fantastique du corps dans quelques texts contemporains," in
Marigny, Jean, Intro., *Images fantastiques du corps*, 195–206.

AMOS OZ

"Nomad and Viper"
Ford, Joh, and Marjorie Ford. *Instructor's Manual* . . . , 97–98.

"Strange Fire"
Holtzman, Avner. "Strange Fire and Secret Thunder: Between Micha
Josef Berdyczewski and Amos Oz," *Prooftexts*, 15 (1995),
157–160.

AYSEL ÖZAKIN

"The Dark-Haired Children of Berlin"
Seyhan, Azade. "Scheherazade's Daughters: The Thousand and One
Tales of Turkish-German Women Writers," in Brinker-Gabler,
Gisela, and Sidonie Smith, Eds. *Writing New Identities* . . . ,
238–239.
"Silent Solidarity"
Seyhan, Azade. "Scheherazade's Daughters . . . ," 239.

EMINE SEVGI ÖZDAMAR

"Großvaterzunge"
Neubert, Isolde. "Searching for Intercultural Communication: Emine
Sevgi Özdamar—A Turkish Woman Writer in Germany," in
Weedon, Chris, Ed. *Post-War Women's* . . . , 158–162.
"Mutterzunge"
Neubert, Isolde. "Searching for . . . ," 156–158.
Seyhan, Azade. "Scheherazade's Daughters: The Thousand and One
Tales of Turkish-German Women Writers," in Brinker-Gabler,
Gisela, and Sidonie Smith, Eds. *Writing New Identities* . . . ,
244–245.

CYNTHIA OZICK

"Envy; or, Yiddish in America"
Klingenstein, Susanne. " 'In Life I Am Not Free': The Writer Cynthia
Ozick and Her Jewish Obligations," in Halio, Jay L., and Ben
Siegel, Eds. *Daughters of Valor* . . . , 66–72.
"Levitation"
Horowitz, Sara R. "The 'Pin with which to Stick Yourself': The
Holocaust in Jewish American Women's Writing," in Halio, Jay L.,
and Ben Siegel, Eds. *Daughters of Valor* . . . , 148–149.
"Rosa"
Alkana, Joseph. " 'Do We Not Know the Meaning of Aesthetic
Gratification?': Cynthia Ozick's 'The Shawl,' the Akedah, and the
Ethics of Holocaust Literary Aesthetics," *Mod Fiction Stud*, 43
(1997), 965–968, 969–971, 973, 974–977, 980–983.
Horowitz, Sara R. "The 'Pin with which to Stick Yourself' . . . ,"
149–150.
Stockton, Kathryn B. "Prophylactics and Brains: *Beloved* in the

Cybernetic Age of Aids," *Stud Novel*, 28 (1996), 439–441; rpt. in Sedgwick, Eve K., Ed. *Novel Gazing* . . . , 47–48.

"The Shawl"

Alkana, Joseph. " 'Do We Not . . . ,' " 965, 969, 970, 973, 974, 979, 980.

Charters, Ann, and William E. Sheidley. *Resources* . . . , 5th ed., 201–202.

Horowitz, Sara R. "The 'Pin with which to Stick Yourself' . . . ," 149.

Stockton, Kathryn B. "Prophylactics and Brains . . . ," 439–441; rpt. in Sedgwick, Eve K., Ed. *Novel Gazing* . . . , 46–48.

"Virility"

Malcolm, Cheryl A. "Compromise and Cultural Identity: British and American Perspectives in Anita Brookner's *Providence* and Cynthia Ozick's 'Virility,' " *Engl Stud*, 78 (1997), 459, 461–463, 465, 466, 467, 468, 469, 470.

CRISTINA PACHECO

"Así pasó"

Egan, Linda. "Cristina Pacheco, nómada entre géneros," in Herrera, Sara P., Ed. *El cuento mexicano* . . . , 470–472.

"Conjugal Bliss"

Valdés, María Elena de. *The Shattered Mirror* . . . , 159–160.

"Lost Labor"

Valdés, María Elena de. *The Shattered* . . . , 158–159.

"Man of the House"

Valdés, María Elena de. *The Shattered* . . . , 159.

"The Shade of a Tree"

Valdés, María Elena de. *The Shattered* . . . , 150–151.

"Slavery"

Valdés, María Elena de. *The Shattered* . . . , 158.

"Wife and Martyr"

Valdés, María Elena de. *The Shattered* . . . , 157–158.

FRANK PACKARD

"The Night Operator"

Goodman, Nan. *Shifting the Blame* . . . , 150–151.

NORVELL PAGE

"But Without Horns"

Attebery, Brian. "Super Men," *Sci-Fiction Stud*, 25 (1998), 72–73.

THOMAS NELSON PAGE

"Marse Chan"
   Gebhard, Caroline. "Reconstructing Southern Manhood: Race,
   Sentimentality, and Camp in the Plantation Myth," in Jones, Anne
   G., and Susan V. Donaldson, Eds. *Haunted Bodies* . . . , 142–143.

GRACE PALEY

"A Conversation with My Father"
   Aarons, Victoria. "Selves and 'Other Shadows': Grace Paley's Ironic
   Fictions," in Reesman, Jeanne C., Ed. *Speaking the Other* . . . ,
   190–192.
   Baxter, Charles. *Burning Down the House* . . . , 186–188.
   Charters, Ann, and William E. Sheidley. *Resources* . . . , 5th ed.,
   203–204.
   Ford, Joh, and Marjorie Ford. *Instructor's Manual* . . . , 68–69.
"The Immigrant Story"
   Aarons, Victoria. "Selves . . . ," 192–193.
   Baxter, Charles. *Burning* . . . , 189–190.
"The Little Girl"
   Baxter, Charles. *Burning* . . . , 190–193.
"The Loudest Voice"
   Baldwin, Dean. *Instructor's Resource* . . . , 157–159.
"Love"
   Aarons, Victoria. "Selves . . . ," 188–189.
"The Story Healer"
   Aarons, Victoria. "Selves . . . ," 187–188.

CLEMENTE PALMA

"Vampiras"
   Mora, Gabriela. "Decadencia y vampirismo en el modernismo
   hispanoamericano: Un cuento de Clemente Palma," *Revista de
   Crítica*, 23, xlvi (1997), 191–198.

MRINAL PANDE

"Girls"
   Collu, Gabrielle. "Unleashing Kali: Anger as Resistance in South
   Asian Women's Writing," in Bogaards, Winnifred M., Ed.
   Literature of Region . . . , 404–405.
   Mohanram, Radhika. "The Problems of Reading: Mother-Daughter
   Relationships and Indian Postcoloniality," in Brown-Guillory,
   Elizabeth, Ed. *Women of Color* . . . , 23–24, 25–29.

ALEXANDROS PAPADIAMANDIS

"The Homesick Wife"
Leontsini, Mary. "Gender and Nation: Or, the Gender of Nation: 'The Homesick Wife' of Alexandros Papadiamandis," in Kalogeras, Yiorgos, and Domna Pastourmatzi, Eds. *Nationalism and Sexuality* . . . , 139–144.

EMILIA PARDO BAZÁN

"Afra"
Buedel, Barbara F. "Gender and Literary Interpretation: An Analysis of Emilia Pardo Bazan's 'Afra,' " in Forbes, F. William, Teresa Méndez-Faith, Mary-Anne Vetterling, and Barbara H. Wing, Eds. *Reflections* . . . , 181–191.

"Las cerezas"
Larsen, Kevin S. "Las cerezas de Vives y Pardo Bazán," *Cincinnati Romance R*, 4 (1985), 76–78, 80.

"¿Cobardía?"
Tolliver, Joyce. *Cigar Smoke* . . . , 92–108.

"El comadrón"
McKenna, Susan. "Recalcitrant Endings in the Short Stories of Pardo Bazán," *Letras Peninsulares*, 11 (1998), 648–651.

"El encaje roto"
Tolliver, Joyce. *Cigar Smoke* . . . , 65–79, 88–89.

"En tranvía"
Ugarte, Michael. "The Generational Fallacy and Spanish Women Writing in Madrid at the Turn of the Century," *Siglo*, 12, i-ii (1994), 266–268.

"La flor seca"
McKenna, Susan. "Recalcitrant Endings . . . ," 651–653.

"El indulto"
McKenna, Susan. "Recalcitrant Endings . . . ," 640–642.

"La novia fiel"
McKenna, Susan. "Recalcitrant Endings . . . ," 645–648.

"Mi suicidio"
Tolliver, Joyce. *Cigar Smoke* . . . , 109–130.

"Náufragas"
Tolliver, Joyce. *Cigar Smoke* . . . , 153–170.

"No lo invento"
Tolliver, Joyce. *Cigar Smoke* . . . , 131–151.

"La punta del cigarro"
Tolliver, Joyce. *Cigar Smoke* . . . , 65–68, 79–89.

"Sara y Agar"
Miller, Stephen. "De la cuentística de Alas y Pardo Bazán en los años noventa, con referencia a Galdós," *Romance Q*, 45 (1998), 36–42.

"Voz de la sangre"
McKenna, Susan. "Recalcitrant Endings . . . ," 642–645.

AMÉRICO PAREDES

"The Hammon and the Beans"
Garza-Falcón, Leticia M. *Gente Decente* . . . , 191–194.
Saldívar, José D. *Border Matters* . . . , 50–52.

DOROTHY PARKER

"The Banquet of Crow"
+ Kinney, Arthur F. *Dorothy Parker, Revised*, 136–137.
Melzer, Sondra. *The Rhetoric of Rage* . . . , 137–152.
"Big Blonde"
+ Kinney, Arthur F. *Dorothy Parker, Revised*, 123–125.
Melzer, Sondra. *The Rhetoric of Rage* . . . , 65–82.
"The Bolt Behind the Blue"
Kinney, Arthur F. *Dorothy Parker, Revised*, 135–136.
"Clothe the Naked"
+ Kinney, Arthur F. *Dorothy Parker, Revised*, 130–131.
"From the Diary of a New York Lady"
Kinney, Arthur F. *Dorothy Parker, Revised*, 126.
"Glory in the Daytime"
Melzer, Sondra. *The Rhetoric of Rage* . . . , 108–122.
"Horsie"
Melzer, Sondra. *The Rhetoric of Rage* . . . , 82–95.
"I Live on Your Visits"
Kinney, Arthur F. *Dorothy Parker, Revised*, 134–135.
"Lady with a Lamp"
Kinney, Arthur F. *Dorothy Parker, Revised*, 129–130.
"Little Curtis"
Kinney, Arthur F. *Dorothy Parker, Revised*, 123.
"The Lovely Leave"
Kinney, Arthur F. *Dorothy Parker, Revised*, 134.
Melzer, Sondra. *The Rhetoric of Rage* . . . , 122–137.
"Mr. Durant"
Melzer, Sondra. *The Rhetoric of Rage* . . . , 25–37.
"The Old Gentleman"
Kinney, Arthur F. *Dorothy Parker, Revised*, 123.
"Soldiers of the Republic"
+ Kinney, Arthur F. *Dorothy Parker, Revised*, 131–132.
"Such a Pretty Little Picture"
+ Kinney, Arthur F. *Dorothy Parker, Revised*, 116.
Melzer, Sondra. *The Rhetoric of Rage* . . . , 13–25.

"A Telephone Call"
+ Kinney, Arthur F. *Dorothy Parker, Revised*, 122–123.
Melzer, Sondra. *The Rhetoric of Rage* . . . , 50–65.
"Too Bad"
+ Kinney, Arthur F. *Dorothy Parker, Revised*, 127–128.
"The Waltz"
+ Kinney, Arthur F. *Dorothy Parker, Revised*, 125–126.
Melzer, Sondra. *The Rhetoric of Rage* . . . , 96–108.
"The Wonderful Old Gentleman"
Melzer, Sondra. *The Rhetoric of Rage* . . . , 37–50.

SARA WILLIS PARTON [PSEUDONYM FANNY FERN]

"Fanny Ford"
Camfield, Gregg. *Necessary Madness* . . . , 48–50.

BORIS PASTERNAK

"Aerial Ways"
Rudova, Larissa. *Understanding* . . . , 58–63.
"The Apelles Mark"
Rudova, Larissa. *Understanding* . . . , 48–50.
"Letters from Tula"
Rudova, Larissa. *Understanding* . . . , 50–53.
"Liuvers' Childhood"
Rudova, Larissa. *Understanding* . . . , 53–58.
"The Tale"
Rudova, Larissa. *Understanding* . . . , 63–68.

WALTER PATER

"The Child in the House"
Reid, Ian. "Generic Variations on a Colonial Topos," in Lounsberry,
Barbara, et al., Eds. *The Tales We Tell* . . . , 87.
———. "Reframing 'The Child in the House': Short Stories and
Neighboring Forms," in Kaylor, Noel H., Ed. *Creative and
Critical* . . . , 323–324.

JAMES KIRKE PAULDING

"Childe Roeliff's Pilgrimage"
Lueck, Beth L. *American Writers* . . . , 74–85.

OCTAVIO PAZ

"The Blue Bouquet"
Baldwin, Dean. *Instructor's Resource* . . . , 174–175.

HILDEBRANDO PÉREZ HUARANCCA

"La oración en la tarde"
Nagy, Silvia M. " 'Los ilegítimos' de Pérez Huarancca y la
legitimidad del neo-indigenismo," *Thesaurus*, 47, iii (1993),
597–598.
"Pascual Gutiérrez ha muerto"
Nagy, Silvia M. " 'Los ilegítimos' . . . ," 596–597.
"Somos de Chukara"
Nagy, Silvia M. " 'Los ilegítimos' . . . ," 600–601.

CRISTINA PERI ROSSI

"The City"
Lawless, Cecilia B. "Insights on Key Sites in the Work of Peri Rossi,"
in Wright, Will, and Steven Kaplan, Eds. *The Image of Nature* . . . ,
102.
"The Game"
Lawless, Cecilia B. "Insights on Key . . . ," 100–102.
"Happy Birthday"
Schmidt-Cruz, Cynthia. "The Children's Revolt Against Structures of
Repression in Cristina Peri Rossi's *La rebellion de los niños* [The
Rebellion of the Children]," *Coll Lit*, 25, iii (1998), 151–153.
"El museo de los esfuerzos inútiles"
Noguerol, Francisca. "La proyección del absurdo en *El museo de los
esfuerzos inútiles* de Cristina Peri Rossi," *Antípodas*, 6–7
(1994–1995), 128.
"La peluquería"
Noguerol, Francisca. "La proyección del absurdo . . . ," 137.
"El sentido del deber"
Noguerol, Francisca. "La proyección del absurdo . . . ," 128–129.
"Ulva lactuca"
Schmidt-Cruz, Cynthia. "The Children's . . . ," 148–151.
"El viaje inconcluso"
Noguerol, Francisca. "La proyección del absurdo . . . ," 129.

LYUDMILA PETRUSHEVSKAYA

"Across the Fields"
Belova, T. N. "Postmodernist Tendencies in the Creative Work of

L'udmila Petruevskaja," in Efimov, Nina A., Christine D. Tomei,
and Richard L. Chapple, Eds. *Critical Essays* . . . , 103.

"The Case of the Virgin"
Belova, T. N. "Postmodernist Tendencies . . . ," 100.

"The Daughter of Ksenija"
Belova, T. N. "Postmodernist Tendencies . . . ," 106–107.

"Intimate Circle"
Peterson, Nadya L. *Subversive* . . . , 161–162.

"The Lady with Dogs"
Belova, T. N. "Postmodernist Tendencies . . . ," 104–105.

"The Observation Point"
Belova, T. N. "Postmodernist Tendencies . . . ," 100–101, 104, 107.

"Our Crowd"
Carden, Patricia. "The Art of War in Petrushevskaya's 'Our Crowd,' "
Stud Short Fiction, 34 (1997), 39–54.

"The Time is Night"
Belova, T. N. "Postmodernist Tendencies . . . ," 107–108, 113.

"Uncle Grisha"
Peterson, Nadya L. *Subversive* . . . , 160–161.

ANN PETRY

"In Darkness and Confusion"
Spilka, Mark. *Eight Lessons* . . . , 266.

"Like a Winding Sheet"
Brody, Jennifer D. "Effaced into Flesh: Black Women's Subjectivity,"
in Kibbey, Ann, Thomas Foster, Carol Siegel, and Ellen Berry, Eds.
On Your Left . . . , 185–196.
Spilka, Mark. *Eight Lessons* . . . , 271–280.

"The Witness"
Spilka, Mark. *Eight Lessons* . . . , 264–265.

ELIZABETH STUART PHELPS

"The Angel Over the Right Shoulder"
Fetterley, Judith. "Theorizing Regionalism: Celia Thaxter's *Among
the Isles of Shoals*," in Inness, Sherrie A., and Diana Royer, Eds.
Breaking Boundaries . . . , 39–40.

"The Tenth of January"
Goodman, Nan. *Shifting the Blame* . . . , 112–113.
Siegel, Adrienne. *The Image of the American* . . . , 90–91.
Thomson, Rosemarie G. "Crippled Girls and Lame Old Women:
Sentimental Spectacles of Sympathy in Nineteenth-Century
American Women's Writing," in Kilcup, Karen L., Ed. *Nineteenth-
Century American* . . . , 139–142.

"The Fall of the House of Usher"
Brennan, Matthew C. *The Gothic Psyche* . . . , 135–145.
Foster, Dennis A. *Sublime Enjoyment* . . . , 53–56.
Frey, Matthew. "Poe's 'The Fall of the House of Usher,' " *Explicator*,
54, iv (1996), 215–216.
Leverenz, David. "Poe and Gentry Virginia: Provincial Gentleman,
Textual Aristocrat, Man of the Crowd," in Jones, Anne G., and
Susan V. Donaldson, Eds. *Haunted Bodies* . . . , 91.
Peeples, Scott. *Edgar Allan Poe Revisited*, 84–88.

"The Gold-Bug"
Cassuto, Leonard. *The Inhuman Race* . . . , 160, 161.
Foster, Dennis A. *Sublime Enjoyment* . . . , 56–59.
Navarette, Susan J. *The Shape* . . . , 103–105.
Peeples, Scott. *Edgar Allan Poe Revisited*, 131–132.
Rosenheim, Shawn J. *The Cryptographic* . . . , 42–43, 60–62.

"Hop-Frog"
Ford, Joh, and Marjorie Ford. *Instructor's Manual* . . . , 11–12.
Leverenz, David. "Poe and Gentry . . . ," 100–101.
Peeples, Scott. *Edgar Allan Poe Revisited*, 151–153.

"The Imp of the Perverse"
Elmer, Jonathan. *Reading at the Social Limit* . . . , 130–136.
Peeples, Scott. *Edgar Allan Poe Revisited*, 147–148.
Pillai, Johann. "Death and its Moments . . . ," 858–859.

"King Pest"
Warner, Nicholas O. *Spirits of America* . . . , 75–76.

"Landor's Cottage"
Lueck, Beth L. *American Writers* . . . , 160–162.
Peeples, Scott. *Edgar Allan Poe Revisited*, 166–167.

"Ligeia"
Covici, Pascal. *Humor and Revelation* . . . , 182–183.
Derrick, Scott S. *Monumental Anxieties* . . . , 75–78.
DeShell, Jeffrey. *The Peculiarity* . . . , 131–134.
Frushell, Richard C. "Poe's Name 'Ligeia' and Milton," *ANQ*, 11, i
(1998), 19–20.
Holland-Toll, Linda J. " 'Ligeia': The Facts in the Case," *Stud Weird
Fiction*, 21 (1997), 10–21.
Hume, Beverly A. "The Madness of Art and Science in Poe's
'Ligeia,' " *Essays Arts & Sciences*, 24 (October, 1995), 21–32.
Leverenz, David. "Poe and Gentry . . . ," 92–94.
Peeples, Scott. *Edgar Allan Poe Revisited*, 51–54.
Schueller, Malini J. *U. S. Orientalisms* . . . , 113–123.
Warner, Nicholas O. *Spirits of America* . . . , 89–90.

"Lionizing"
Peeples, Scott. *Edgar Allan Poe Revisited*, 33–34.

"The Literary Life of Thingum Bob, Esq."
Peeples, Scott. *Edgar Allan Poe Revisited*, 112.

"Loss of Breath"
 Armstrong, Tim. *Modernism, Technology* . . . , 91–92.
 Peeples, Scott. *Edgar Allan Poe Revisited*, 42–44.
"The Man of the Crowd"
 Elmer, Jonathan. *Reading at the Social Limit* . . . , 170–173.
 Lehan, Richard. *The City in Literature* . . . , 81–82.
 Leverenz, David. "Poe and Gentry . . . ," 94–100.
 Merivale, Patricia. "Gumshoe Gothics: 'The Man of the Crowd' and
  His Followers," in Prier, A., and Gerald Gillespie, Eds. *Narrative
  Ironies*, 167–172.
 Peeples, Scott. *Edgar Allan Poe Revisited*, 123–124.
"The Man That Was Used Up"
 Armstrong, Tim. *Modernism, Technology* . . . , 92–93.
 Elmer, Jonathan. *Reading at the Social Limit* . . . , 47–56.
 Peeples, Scott. *Edgar Allan Poe Revisited*, 93, 111–112.
 Rosenheim, Shawn J. *The Cryptographic* . . . , 101–103, 105–106.
"MS. Found in a Bottle"
 Goodman, Nan. *Shifting the Blame* . . . , 46–48.
 Peeples, Scott. *Edgar Allan Poe Revisited*, 46–48.
"The Masque of the Red Death"
 DeShell, Jeffrey. *The Peculiarity* . . . , 136–137.
 Ford, Joh, and Marjorie Ford. *Instructor's Manual* . . . , 10.
 Peeples, Scott. *Edgar Allan Poe Revisited*, 103–105.
 Raynaud, Jean. "Du Religieux chez Edgar Poe," in Court, Antoine,
  Ed. *Le Populaire* . . . , 36–43.
 Wägenbaur, Thomas. "Europäische Literatur gegen Rassismus (Kafka
  und Poe)," in Wertheimer, Jürgen, Ed. *Suchbild Europa* . . . ,
  193–194.
"Mellonta Tauta"
 Lehan, Richard. *The City in Literature* . . . , 171, 172.
 Peeples, Scott. *Edgar Allan Poe Revisited*, 155–157.
 Rosenheim, Shawn J. *The Cryptographic* . . . , 106–107.
"Mesmeric Revelations"
 Disch, Thomas M. *The Dream Our Stuff* . . . , 40–46, 54.
 Elmer, Jonathan. *Reading at the Social Limit* . . . , 115–119.
 Peeples, Scott. *Edgar Allan Poe Revisited*, 118–119.
"Metzengerstein"
 DeNuccio, Jerome. "History, Narrative, and Authority: Poe's
  'Metzengerstein,' " *Coll Lit*, 24, ii (1997), 71–81.
 Peeples, Scott. *Edgar Allan Poe Revisited*, 49–50.
"Morella"
 DeShell, Jeffrey. *The Peculiarity* . . . , 134–136.
 Elmer, Jonathan. *Reading at the Social Limit* . . . , 103.
"The Murders in the Rue Morgue"
 Baldwin, Dean. *Instructor's Resource* . . . , 35–37.
 Cassuto, Leonard. *The Inhuman Race* . . . , 160–161.
 Derrick, Scott S. *Monumental Anxieties* . . . , 69.

Edmundson, Mark. *Nightmare on Main* . . . , 147.
Ford, Joh, and Marjorie Ford. *Instructor's Manual* . . . , 10–11.
Foster, Dennis A. *Sublime Enjoyment* . . . , 48–50.
Peeples, Scott. *Edgar Allan Poe Revisited*, 94–96.
Pillai, Johann. "Death and its Moments . . . ," 837–857, 860–864.
"Thou Art the Man"
Peeples, Scott. *Edgar Allan Poe Revisited*, 130.
"The Thousand-and-Second Tale of Scheherazade"
Peeples, Scott. *Edgar Allan Poe Revisited*, 153–154.
"The Unparalleled Adventures of One Hans Pfaall"
Peeples, Scott. *Edgar Allan Poe Revisited*, 35–37.
"Von Kempelen and His Discovery"
Peeples, Scott. *Edgar Allan Poe Revisited*, 154–155.
"William Wilson"
Elmer, Jonathan. *Reading at the Social Limit* . . . , 71–92.
Peeples, Scott. *Edgar Allan Poe Revisited*, 78–84.
Warner, Nicholas O. *Spirits of America* . . . , 85–86.
"X-ing a Paragrab"
Peeples, Scott. *Edgar Allan Poe Revisited*, 153.

JOHN POLIDORI

"The Vampyre"
Tancheva, Kornelia. "Vampires Are Them, Vampires are Us," in
Castillo, Susan, Ed. *Engendering Identities*, 84, 85, 88–89.

ELENA PONIATOWSKA

"La casita de sololoi"
Bruce-Novoa, Juan. "Los cuentos de Elena Poniatowska," in Herrera,
Sara P., Ed. *El cuento mexicano* . . . , 371.
Vargas, Margarita. "Power and Resistance in *De noche vienes* by
Elena Poniatowska," *Hispanic J*, 16, ii (1995), 290–292.
"De Gaulle de Minería"
Bruce-Novoa, Juan. "Los cuentos . . . ," 374.
"De noche vienes"
Ayes, Zulema. "El distanciamiento o la extraposición en el discurso
ficcional: Dos cuentos: 'Letra para salsa y tres soneos por encargo'
de Ana Lydia Vega, 'De noche vienes' de Elena Poniatowska,"
Revista/Review Interamericana, 27, i–iv (1997), 93–108.
Bruce-Novoa, Juan. "Los cuentos . . . ," 375–376.
"La felicidad"
Bruce-Novoa, Juan. "Los cuentos . . . ," 368–370.
"Love story"
Cornejo-Parriego, Rosalía. "*Racialización* colonial y diferencia

femenina en 'Love story' de Poniatowska y 'Cuando las mujeres
quieren a los hombres' de Ferré," *Afro-Hispanic R*, 16, ii (1997),
11–17.
Vargas, Margarita. "Power and Resistance . . . ," 286–290.
"Métase mi Prieta entre el durmiente y el silbatazo"
Bruce-Novoa, Juan. "Los cuentos . . . ," 373–374.
Vargas, Margarita. "Power and Resistance . . . ," 292–294.
"Park Cinema"
Ford, Joh, and Marjorie Ford. *Instructor's Manual . . .* , 86–87.
"El rayo verde"
Bruce-Novoa, Juan. "Los cuentos . . . ," 376–377.

ENA LUCÍA PORTELA

"La urna y el nombre (cuento jovial)"
Cámara, Madeline. "Antropofagia de los sexos como 'metáfora de
incorporación' en 'La urna y el nombre (cuento jovial)' de Ena
Lucía Portela," *Torre de Papel*, 7, iii (1997), 170–180.

KATHERINE ANNE PORTER

"The Cracked Looking Glass"
DeMouy, Jane K. . . . *Porter's Women* . . . , 61–72; rpt. Unrue, Darlene
H., Ed. *Critical Essays on . . .* , 138–148.
+ Warren, Robert P. "Katherine Anne Porter (Irony with a Center),"
in Unrue, Darlene H., Ed. *Critical Essays on . . .* , 61.
"The Fig Tree"
Davis, William V. " 'The Native Land of My Heart': Katherine Anne
Porter's Miranda Stories," in Bogaards, Winnifred M., Ed.
Literature of Region . . . , 426.
"Flowering Judas"
Baldwin, Dean. *Instructor's Resource . . .* , 113–115.
Harwell, Thomas M. *Porter & Eliot . . .* , 11–51.
Lindsey-Hicks, Glenda. "The World of Word, Line, and Labyrinth in
Katherine Anne Porter's 'Flowering Judas,' " in Kaylor, Noel H.,
Ed. *Creative and Critical . . .* , 275–288.
+ Warren, Robert P. "Katherine Anne Porter . . . ," 55–57.
"The Grave"
+ Brooks, Cleanth. "On 'The Grave,' " in Unrue, Darlene H., Ed.
Critical Essays on . . . , 173–176.
Cheatham, George. "Death and Repetition in Porter's Miranda
Stories," *Am Lit*, 61 (1989), 612–617; rpt. Unrue, Darlene H., Ed.
Critical Essays on . . . , 160–163.
Davis, William V. " 'The Native Land . . . ,' " 428–433.
Stout, Janis P. "Katherine Anne Porter's 'The Old Order': Writing in
the Borderlands," *Stud Short Fiction*, 34 (1997), 503–504.

"Hacienda"
+ Perry, Robert L. "Porter's 'Hacienda' and the Theme of Change,"
in Unrue, Darlene H., Ed. *Critical Essays on . . .* , 149–157.
"He"
+ Jorgensen, Bruce W. " 'The Other Side of Silence': Katherine Anne
Porter's 'He' as Tragedy," in Unrue, Darlene H., Ed. *Critical Essays
on . . .* , 110–118.
Skaggs, Merrill M. "Willa Cather's Influence on Katherine Anne
Porter's 'He,' " *Southern Q*, 34, ii (1996), 23, 24, 25–26.
"Holiday"
+ Hardy, John E. "Katherine Anne Porter's 'Holiday,' " in Unrue,
Darlene H., Ed. *Critical Essays on . . .* , 201–206.
"The Jilting of Granny Weatherall"
Charters, Ann, and William E. Sheidley. *Resources . . .* , 5th ed.,
209–210.
Ford, Joh, and Marjorie Ford. *Instructor's Manual . . .* , 43–44.
+ Wiesenfarth, Joseph. "Internal Opposition in Porter's 'Granny
Weatherall,' " in Unrue, Darlene H., Ed. *Critical Essays on . . .* ,
104–108.
"The Journey"
Davis, William V. " 'The Native Land . . . ,' " 425.
Stout, Janis P. "Katherine Anne Porter's . . . ," 500–501.
"The Leaning Tower"
Hendrick, Willene, and George Hendrick. *Katherine Anne Porter*,
90–96; rpt. Unrue, Darlene H., Ed. *Critical Essays on . . .* ,
216–221.
"María Concepción"
Alvarez, Ruth M. " 'Royalty in Exile': Pre-Hispanic Art and Ritual in
'María Concepción,' " in Unrue, Darlene H., Ed. *Critical Essays
on . . .* , 91–98.
Moddelmog, Debra. "Concepts of Justice in the Works of Katherine
Anne Porter," *Mosaic*, 26, iv (1993), 44–45, 46; rpt. Unrue, Darlene
H., Ed. *Critical Essays on . . .* , 70–71, 72.
"Noon Wine"
Moddelmog, Debra. "Concepts of Justice . . . ,"45–46; rpt. Unrue,
Darlene H., Ed. *Critical Essays on . . .* ,71–72.
+ Stout, Janis P. "Mr. Hatch's Volubility and Miss Porter's Reserve,"
in Unrue, Darlene H., Ed. *Critical Essays on . . .* , 207–215.
+ Warren, Robert P. "Katherine Anne Porter . . . ," 61.
"Old Mortality"
Bryant, J. A. *Twentieth-Century Southern . . .* , 71–72.
Cheatham, George. "Death and Repetition . . . ," 618–623; rpt. Unrue,
Darlene H., Ed. *Critical Essays on . . .* , 164–167.
Davis, William V. " 'The Native Land . . . ,' " 426–428.
Jones, Suzanne W. "Reading the Endings in Katherine Anne Porter's
'Old Mortality,' " *Southern Q*, 31, iii (1993), 29–44; rpt. Unrue,
Darlene H., Ed. *Critical Essays on . . .* , 177–192.
+ Warren, Robert P. "Katherine Anne Porter . . . ," 57–60.

"Pale Horse, Pale Rider"
  Cheatham, George. "Death and Repetition . . . ," 621–624; rpt. Unrue, Darlene H., Ed. *Critical Essays on* . . . , 166–167.
"Theft"
  + Givner, Joan. "A Re-Reading of Katherine Anne Porter's 'Theft,' " in Unrue, Darlene H., Ed. *Critical Essays on* . . . , 99–102.

ALEX POSEY

"Chinnubbie and the Owl"
  Kosmider, Alexia. *Tricky Tribal Discourse* . . . , 71–72.
"Moses and Richard"
  Kosmider, Alexia. *Tricky Tribal Discourse* . . . , 56, 60–62.
"The Possum and the Skunk"
  Kosmider, Alexia. *Tricky Tribal Discourse* . . . , 69–70.
"Rabbit and the Wolf"
  Kosmider, Alexia. *Tricky Tribal Discourse* . . . , 52–53.
"Uncle Dick's Sow"
  Kosmider, Alexia. *Tricky Tribal Discourse* . . . , 56, 57–60.

J. F. POWERS

"Dawn"
  Labrie, Ross. *The Catholic Imagination* . . . , 180.
"The Forks"
  Labrie, Ross. *The Catholic Imagination* . . . , 176–177.
"Lions, Harts, Leaping Does"
  Labrie, Ross. *The Catholic Imagination* . . . , 181–183.
"The Lord's Day"
  Labrie, Ross. *The Catholic Imagination* . . . , 177–178.
"The Presence of Grace"
  Labrie, Ross. *The Catholic Imagination* . . . , 179–180.
"Prince of Darkness"
  Labrie, Ross. *The Catholic Imagination* . . . , 174–176.
"The Valiant Woman"
  Labrie, Ross. *The Catholic Imagination* . . . , 178–179.
"Zeal"
  Labrie, Ross. *The Catholic Imagination* . . . , 180–181.

MUNSHI PREMCHAND [DHANPAT RAI SHRIVASTAV]

"The Chess Players"
  Rubin, David. "The Short Stories of Premchand," in Miller, Barbara S., Ed. *Masterworks of Asian* . . . , 171–172.

MARCEL PROUST

"L'Indifférent"
Pancrazi, Jean-Noël. "Premières amours," *Magazine Litteraire*, 350 (1997), 63.

"La Mélancolique villégiature de Mme de Breyves"
Kingcaid, Renée A. "Thorns Among the Roses: Representation and Narration in Proust's 'La Mélancolique villégiature de Mme de Breyves,' " *Cincinnati Romance R*, 1 (1982), 29–42.

K. F. PURDON

"Match-Making in Ardenoo"
Kelly, Joseph. *Our Joyce: From Outcast . . .* , 37–38.

ALEXANDER PUSHKIN

"The Coffinmaker"
Bethea, David M. *Realizing Metaphors . . .* , 190–194.

"The Queen of Spades"
Feinstein, Elaine. *Pushkin: A Biography*, 223–224.
Foshko, Natalie. "On the Interpretation of 'The Queen of Spades,' " *Elementa*, 3, ii (1996), 181–194.
Richardson, Brian. *UnLikely Stories . . .* , 38–39.

"The Stationmaster" [same as "The Postmaster"]
Evsukhov, Ludmila S. "Donna Dunia: 'The Stationmaster' and 'The Stone Guest' as Variations in Two Keys," *Pushkin J*, 2–3 (1994–1995), 3–18.
Feinstein, Elaine. *Pushkin: A Biography*, 193–194.

THOMAS PYNCHON

"Mortality and Mercy in Vienna"
King, Vincent. "Giving Destruction a Name and a Face: Thomas Pynchon's 'Mortality and Mercy in Vienna,' " *Stud Short Fiction*, 35 (1998), 13–21.

AHMAD NADĪM QĀSIMĪ

"Bain"
Malik, Jamal. "The Literary Critique of Islamic Popular Religion in the Guise of Traditional Mysticism, or the Abused Woman," *Welt Islams*, 35, i (1995), 84–94.

HORACIO QUIROGA

"The Decapitated Chicken"
+ Pearson, Lon. "Horacio Quiroga's Obsessions with Abnormal
Psychology and Medicine as Reflected in 'La Gallina Degollada,' "
in Foster, David W., and Daniel Altamiranda, Eds. *Twentieth-
Century* . . . , 58–72.

"The Flies"
Varela Cabezas, Rodrigo. "Comentario de un cuento fantástico: 'Las
moscas. Réplica de *El hombre muerto*,' de Horacio Quiroga,"
Revista Canadiense, 22 (1998), 514–522.

"The Wilderness"
Baldwin, Dean. *Instructor's Resource* . . . , 105–106.

WILHELM RAABE

"Höxter und Corvey"
Krobb, Florian. "Marginal Daubings: On Wilhelm Raabe's Graphic
Œuvre," in Morrison, Jeff, and Florian Krobb, Eds. *Text Into
Image* . . . , 63–64.

"Wunnigel"
Grätz, Katharina. "Erbe und Sammler in Wilhelm Raabes
'Wunnigel,' " *Zeitschrift für Deutsche Philologie*, 116 (1997),
528–544.

RACHILDE [MARGUERITE VALETTE]

"Le Château hermétique"
Ziegler, Robert. "Interpretation as Mirage in Rachilde's 'Le Château
hermétique,' " *Nineteenth-Century French Stud*, 26 (1997–1998),
182–192.

VIKI RADDEN

"Riding the Wheel of Fortune"
Jablon, Madelyn. "Womanist Storytelling: The Voice of the
Vernacular" in Brown, Julie, Ed. *Ethnicity* . . . , 55–56.

MOHAN RAKESH

"Cartload of Rubble"
Rahim, Habibeh. "The Mirage of Faith and Justice: Some
Sociopolitical and Cultural Themes in Post-Colonial Urdu Short
Stories," in Hawley, John C., Ed. *The Postcolonial Crescent* . . . ,
232–233.

SERGIO RAMÍREZ

"El centerfielder"
Febles, Jorge. "Dying Players: Ramírez's 'El centerfielder' and
Dybek's 'Death of the Rightfielder,' " *Confluencia*, 12, i (1996),
156–157, 160–163.

"Charles Atlas Also Dies"
Ford, Joh, and Marjorie Ford. *Instructor's Manual* . . . , 104–105.

RAJA RAO

"Javni"
Sharma, Lakshmi R. "Metaphor and Narrative: A Strange
Relationship," *Lit Criterion*, 26, iv (1991), 20, 24–26.

MUNIRO RAVANIPUR

"Kanizu"
Talattof, Kamran. "Iranian Women's Literature: From Pre-
Revolutionary Social Discourse to Post-Revolutionary Feminism,"
Int'l J Middle East Stud, 29 (1997), 548–549.

"The Sad Story of Love"
Talattof, Kamran. "Iranian Women's . . . ," 547–548.

MARJORIE KINNAN RAWLINGS

"Benny and the Bird Dogs"
Tarr, Rodger. "Introduction," *Short Stories* . . . [by Marjorie Kinnan
Rawlings], 12–13.

"Black Secret"
Tarr, Rodger. "Introduction," 22.

"Cocks Must Crow"
Tarr, Rodger. "Introduction," 12.

"A Crop of Beans"
Tarr, Rodger. "Introduction," 10.

"The Enemy"
Tarr, Rodger. "Introduction," 18.

"Fish Fry and Fireworks"
Tarr, Rodger. "Introduction," 13.

"Gal Young Un"
Tarr, Rodger. "Introduction," 10–11.

"In the Heart"
Tarr, Rodger. "Introduction," 20.

"Jacob's Ladder"
Tarr, Rodger. "Introduction," 9–10.

"Jessamine Springs"
Tarr, Rodger. "Introduction," 23.
"Lord Bill of the Suwannee River"
Tarr, Rodger. "Introduction," 18–19.
"Miss Moffatt Steps Out"
Tarr, Rodger. "Introduction," 16.
"A Mother in Mannville"
Tarr, Rodger. "Introduction," 14.
"The Pelican's Shadow"
Tarr, Rodger. "Introduction," 14–15.
"A Plumb Clare Conscience"
Tarr, Rodger. "Introduction," 17.
"The Provider"
Tarr, Rodger. "Introduction," 23.
"The Shell"
Tarr, Rodger. "Introduction," 15–16.
"Varmints"
Tarr, Rodger. "Introduction," 13.

ELISABETH REICHART

"Fotze"
Fliedl, Konstanze. "Etymology of Violence: Elisabeth Reichart's Prose," in Williams, Arthur, Stuart Parkes, and Julian Preece, Eds. *Contemporary* . . . , 258–259.
"Die Kammer"
Davies, Mererid P. "Elisabeth Reicharts 'Die Kammer' " *Germ Life & Letters*, 50 (1997), 499–502.
"La Valse"
Fliedl, Konstanze. "Etymology of Violence . . . ," 259.

ALFONSO REYES

"La cena"
Gallo, Marta. "Proyección de 'La cena' de Alfonso Reyes en 'Aura' de Carlos Fuentes," in Herrera, Sara P., Ed. *El cuento mexicano* . . . , 237–256.

JEAN RHYS

"Again the Antilles"
Sternlicht, Sanford. *Jean Rhys*, 28.
Stouck, Jordan. "Locating Other Subjectivities in Jean Rhys's 'Again the Antilles,' " *Jean Rhys R*, 8, i–ii (1997), 1–5.

"The Day They Burned the Books"
Raiskin, Judith. "7 Days/6 Nights at 'Plantation Estates': A Critique of Cultural Colonialism by Caribbean Writers," in Buelens, Gert, and Ernst Rudin, Eds. *Deferring a Dream* . . . , 97–89.

"From a French Prison"
Sternlicht, Sanford. *Jean Rhys*, 26–27.

"Goodbye Marcus, Goodbye Rose"
Sternlicht, Sanford. *Jean Rhys*, 126.

"Illusion"
Bender, Todd K. *Literary Impressionism* . . . , 92.

"In the Luxembourg Garden"
Sternlicht, Sanford. *Jean Rhys*, 25–26.

"The Insect World"
Sternlicht, Sanford. *Jean Rhys*, 128–129.

"La Grosse Fifi"
Sternlicht, Sanford. *Jean Rhys*, 29.

"The Lotus"
Sternlicht, Sanford. *Jean Rhys*, 124.

"Mannequin"
Sternlicht, Sanford. *Jean Rhys*, 24.

"Mixing Cocktails"
Sternlicht, Sanford. *Jean Rhys*, 27–28.

"Night Out 1925"
Sternlicht, Sanford. *Jean Rhys*, 128.

"Outside the Machine"
Sternlicht, Sanford. *Jean Rhys*, 124.

"Rapunzel, Rapunzel"
Sternlicht, Sanford. *Jean Rhys*, 129.

"Sleep It Off, Lady"
Sternlicht, Sanford. *Jean Rhys*, 129–130.

"A Spiritualist"
Savory, Elaine. *Jean Rhys*, 46–47.

"Tea with an Artist"
Sternlicht, Sanford. *Jean Rhys*, 24.

"Temps Perdi"
Lonsdale, Thorunn. " 'One of the Most Beautiful Islands in the World and One of the Unluckiest': Jean Rhys and Dominican National Identity," in Anim-Addo, Joan, Ed. *Framing the Word* . . . , 201–202.
Savory, Elaine. *Jean Rhys*, 170–173.

"Tigers Are Better Looking"
Sternlicht, Sanford. *Jean Rhys*, 123–124.

"Till September Petronella"
Sternlicht, Sanford. *Jean Rhys*, 122–123.

"Vienne"
Sternlicht, Sanford. *Jean Rhys*, 29–31.

JEAN RICHEPIN

"Les Trente Braves"
Zarini, Vincent. "D'une lettre de Symmaque à un conte de Richepin,
ou d'une 'décadence' à une autre," *Travaux de Littérature*, 9 (1996),
202–216.

CARME RIERA

"Jo pos per terstimoni les gavines"
Glenn, Kathleen M. "Reading and Writing the Other Side of the Story
in Two Narratives by Carme Riera," *Catalan R*, 7, i (1993), 56–61.
"Letra de ángel"
Vásquez, Mary S. "Epistolaridad, marginación y deseo en un cuento
de Carme Riera," *Cuadernos de Aldeeu*, 10, ii (1994), 215–220.
"El reportaje"
Aldrich, Mark C. " 'El reportaje' de Carme Riera y 'Las Reglas del
Juego,' " *Hispano*, 120 (1997), 57–65.
"Sí, me llamo Helena"
Vásquez, Mary S. "Epistolarity, Confession and Textual Seduction in
Carme Riera's 'Sí, me llamo Helena,' " in Tibbitts, Mercedes V.,
Ed. *Studies in Honor* . . . , 359–366.
"Te deix, amor, la mar com a penyora"
Epps, Brad. "Virtual Sexuality: Lesbianism, Loss, and Deliverance in
Carme Riera's 'Te deix, amor, la mar com a penyora," in Bergmann,
Emilie L., and Paul J. Smith, Eds. *¿Entiendes?* . . . , 317–345.
Glenn, Kathleen M. "Reading and Writing . . . ," 53–57.

RAINER MARIA RILKE

"Geschichten vom lieben Gott"
Dzikowska, Katarzyna. "Spuren der Transzendenz: Wie religiös sind
Rilkes 'Geschichten vom lieben Gott,' " in Auckenthaler, Karlheinz
F., Ed. *Numinoses und Heiliges* . . . , 104–110.

ANA MARÍA DEL RÍO

"Óxido de Carmen"
Lagos, María Inés. "Cuerpo y subjetividad en narraciones de Andrea
Maturana, Ana María del Río y Diamela Eltit," *Revista Chilena*, 50
(1997), 101–103.

ALBERTO RÍOS

"Not Like Us"
Ford, Joh, and Marjorie Ford. *Instructor's Manual* . . . , 118–119.

TOMÁS RIVERA

"First Communion"
Allen, Paula, and Wendell Aycock. "Subversion of the First Holy
Communion in Contemporary Hispanic Fiction," *Confluencia*, 13, i
(1997), 206–208, 210.

"Under the House"
Sáchez Manzano, María J. "Character and Protagonist in *And the
Earth Did Not Part*," *REDEN*, 7, xi (1996), 44–45.

"When We Arrive"
Fredericksen, Brooke. "Cuando lleguemos/When We Arrive: The
Paradox of Migration in Tomás Rivera's *Y no se lo tragó la tierra*,"
Bilingual R, 19, ii (1994), 145–146, 149.

CHARLES G. D. ROBERTS

"The Little Homeless One"
Dean, Misao. "Political Science: Realism in Roberts's Animal
Stories," *Stud Canadian Lit*, 21, i (1995), 6–7, 8.

"Mothers of the North"
Dean, Misao. "Political . . . ," 7.

"Vagrants of the Barren"
Dean, Misao. "Political . . . ," 12–13.

SHEILA ROBERTS

"The Weekenders"
Sheckels, Theodore F. *The Lion* . . . , 148–155.

MERCÈ RODOREDA

"Carnaval"
McNerney, Kathleen. "Masks and Metamorphoses, Dreams and
Illusions in Mercè Rodoreda's 'Carnaval,' " *Catalan R*, 7, i (1993),
71–77.

"Una fulla de gerani blanc"
Glenn, Kathleen M. "Muted Voices in Mercé Rodoreda's *La meva
Cristina i alters contes*," *Catalan R*, 2, ii (1987), 139–140.

"El mar"
Glenn, Kathleen M. "Muted Voices . . . ," 132–136.

"La meva Cristina"
Glenn, Kathleen M. "Muted Voices . . . ," 140–142.

"El riu i la barca"
Glenn, Kathleen M. "Muted Voices . . . ," 136.

"La sala de les nines"
Glenn, Kathleen M. "Muted Voices . . . ," 137–138.

"La salamandra"
Davies, Catherine. *Spanish Women's* . . . , 218–220.
Glenn, Kathleen M. "Muted Voices . . . ," 139.
Pérez, Janet. "Metamorphosis as a Protest Device in Catalan Feminist Writing: Rodoreda and Oliver," *Catalan R*, 2, ii (1987), 192–196.

"Zerafina"
Glenn, Kathleen M. "Muted Voices . . . ," 137.

MARGARET RODRÍGUEZ

"I Had a Colored Maid"
Mullen, Bill. "Marking Race/Marketing Race: African American Short Fiction and the Politics of Genre, 1933–1946," in Brown, Julie, Ed. *Ethnicity* . . . , 38–39.

FRANCISCO ROJAS GONZÁLEZ

"La cabra en dos patas"
Membrez, Nancy J. "The Roots of *Raices*: The Genesis of *El diosero* into Film," in Cabello-Castellet, George, Jaume Martí-Olivella, and Guy H. Wood, Eds. *Cine-Lit II* . . . , 46.

"Nuestra señora de Nequeteje"
Membrez, Nancy J. "The Roots . . . ," 42–43.

"La parábola del joven tuerto"
Membrez, Nancy J. "The Roots . . . ," 45, 47–48.

"La tona"
Membrez, Nancy J. "The Roots . . . ," 43–44.

"Las vacas de Quiviquinta"
Membrez, Nancy J. "The Roots . . . ," 41–42.

SALLIE RHETT ROMAN

"Mrs. Grundy, An Etching"
Dixon, Nancy. "An Introduction to 'Mrs. Grundy, An Etching' by Sallie Rhett Roman (1844–1921)," *Louisiana Lit*, 13, ii (1996), 79–81.

DEOGRACIAS A. ROSARIO

"Ako'y Mayroong Isang Ibon"
  Liwag, Jesse H. "DAR's 'Ako'y Mayroong Isang Ibon," *Philippine Stud*, 45 (1997), 552–557.

DILYS ROSE

"Red Tides"
  Gifford, Douglas. "Contemporary Fiction II: Seven Writers in Scotland," in Gifford, Douglas, and Dorothy McMillan, Eds. *A History* . . . , 627–628.
"Wings"
  Gifford, Douglas. "Contemporary Fiction . . . ," 628.

NORMA ROSEN

"The Cheek of the Trout"
  Kremer, S. Lillian. "Norma Rosen: An American Literary Response to the Holocaust," in Halio, Jay L., and Ben Siegel, Eds. *Daughters of Valor* . . . , 165–167.
"Fences"
  Kremer, S. Lillian. "Norma Rosen . . . ," 170–172.
"The Inner Light and the Fire"
  Kremer, S. Lillian. "Norma Rosen . . . ," 167–169.
"What Must I Say to You"
  Kremer, S. Lillian. "Norma Rosen . . . ," 169–170.

PHILIP ROTH

"The Conversion of the Jews"
  Baldwin, Dean. *Instructor's Resource* . . . , 152–154.
"Eli the Fanatic"
  Fisch, Harold. *New Stories for Old* . . . , 143–153.
" 'I Always Wanted You to Admire My Fasting'; or Looking at Kafka"
  Charters, Ann, and William E. Sheidley. *Resources* . . . , 5th ed., 213.
"My True Story"
  Greenberg, Robert M. "Transgression in the Fiction of Philip Roth," *Twentieth Century Lit*, 43 (1997), 491–492.

ROU SHI

"A Slave-Mother"
  Lieberman, Sally T. *The Mother* . . . , 206–209.

"The Story of Rengui and His Wife"
   Lieberman, Sally T. *The Mother* . . . , 204–206.

GABRIELLE ROY

"Un Jardin au bout du monde"
   Madigan, M. Kathleen. "Uncommon Ground in Gabrielle Roy's 'Un
   Jardin au bout du monde,' " *Women French Stud*, 5 (1997), 69–76.
"Le Puits de Dunrea"
   Socken, Paul. "The Structure of Dichotomy and the Art of
   Storytelling: Gabrielle Roy's 'Le Puits de Dunrea,' " *Études
   Canadiennes*, 44 (1998), 7–13.
"The Well of Dunrea"
   Charters, Ann, and William E. Sheidley. *Resources* . . . , 5th ed.,
   214–215.

GERMÁN N. ROZENMACHER

"Blues en la noche"
   Lichtblau, Myron I. "La rememoración y la ironía en 'Blues en la
   noche' de Germán Rozenmacher," in Galván, Delia V., Anita K.
   Stoll, and Philippa B. Yin, Eds. *Studies in Honor* . . . , 95–99.

RU ZHIJUAN

"Lilies"
   McDougall, Bonnie S., and Kam Louie. *The Literature of China* . . . ,
   253–254.

BERTA RUCK

"Infant in Arms"
   Potter, Jane. " 'A Great Purifier': The Great War in Women's
   Romances and Memoirs, 1914–1918," in Raitt, Suzanne, and Trudi
   Tate, Eds. *Women's Fiction* . . . , 87–89.
"Wanted—A Master"
   Potter, Jane. " 'A Great Purifier' . . . ," 89–91.

JUAN RULFO

"Anacleto Morones"
   Duffey, J. Patrick. "Vírgenes, madres y prostitutas: la figura femenina
   en *El llano en llamas*," *GénEros*, 4, x (1996), 21–22.
"La Cuesta de las Comadres"
   Capuano, Thomas M. "La caracterización del viejo en 'La Cuesta de

las Comadres' de Juan Rulfo," *Cincinnati Romance R*, 4 (1985), 37–51.

"¡Diles que no me maten!"
Arreola Medina, Angélica, and Javier Alvarado Moguel. " '¡Diles que no me maten!': Ética y estética," in López Mena, Sergio, Ed. *Revisión crítica* . . . , 41–47.
Trejo Villafuerte, Arturo. "Rasgos autobiográficos en '¡Diles que no me maten!' " in López Mena, Sergio, Ed. *Revisión crítica* . . . , 35–40.

"En la madrugada"
Duffey, J. Patrick. "Vírgenes, madres . . . ," 17.

"Es que somos muy pobres"
Duffey, J. Patrick. "Vírgenes, madres . . . ," 16–17.
McGuirk, Bernard. *Latin American* . . . , 251–252.

"El hombre"
Borgeson, Paul W. "The Turbulent Flow: Stream of Consciousness Techniques in the Short Stories of Juan Rulfo," *Revista de Estudios Hispánicos*, 13 (1979), 239–240; rpt. Foster, David W., and Daniel Altamiranda, Eds. *Twentieth-Century Spanish* . . . , 127–128.

"El Llano en llamas"
Ávila Díaz, Patricia. "El mundo mexicano antiguo en 'El Llano en llamas,' " in López Mena, Sergio, Ed. *Revisión crítica* . . . , 53–54.

"La noche que lo dejaron solo"
Borgeson, Paul W. "The Turbulent . . . ," 241, 248–249; rpt. Foster, David W., and Daniel Altamiranda, Eds. *Twentieth-Century Spanish* . . . , 129, 136–137.
Hong, Hyeran. "Acerca de 'La noche que lo dejaron solo,' " in López Mena, Sergio, Ed. *Revisión crítica* . . . , 63–67.

"Luvina"
Borgeson, Paul W. "The Turbulent . . . ," 233, 236, 242; rpt. Foster, David W., and Daniel Altamiranda, Eds. *Twentieth-Century Spanish* . . . , 121, 124, 130.
Duffey, J. Patrick. "Vírgenes, madres . . . ," 18.
Huaman López, Carlos. "Los condenados de 'Luvina,' " in López Mena, Sergio, Ed. *Revisión crítica* . . . , 55–62.

"Macario"
Duffey, J. Patrick. "Vírgenes, madres . . . ," 19.

"No oyes ladrar los perros"
Duffey, J. Patrick. "Vírgenes, madres . . . ," 18–19.

"Un pedazo de noche"
Castillo, Debra A. *Easy Women* . . . , 63–65, 69–77.

"Talpa"
Borgeson, Paul W. "The Turbulent . . . ," 233–234, 236–237; rpt. Foster, David W., and Daniel Altamiranda, Eds. *Twentieth-Century Spanish* . . . , 121–122, 124–125.
Duffey, J. Patrick. "Vírgenes, madres . . . ," 20.

SALMAN RUSHDIE

"The Firebird's Nest"
   Charters, Ann, and William E. Sheidley. *Resources* . . . , 5th ed.,
   216–217.

BERTRAND RUSSELL

"Satan in the Suburbs"
   Monk, Ray. "Devilish Repressions: Bertrand Russell's Use of Fiction
   as Autobiography," in Gould, Warwick, and Thomas E. Staley, Eds.
   Writing the Lives . . . , 257–263.

ERNESTO SÁBATO

"The Tunnel"
   Frame, Scott M. "Vanishing Point: The World View of Juan Pablo
   Castel in 'El túnel,'" *Hispano*, 121 (1997), 11–20.
   Hahn, Hannelore. " 'La metamorfosis (Die Verwandlung)' de Franz
   Kafka y 'El túnel' de Ernesto Sábato," *Círculo*, 24 (1995), 80–85.

GHOLAM-HOSAIN SA'EDI

"Dandil"
   Zarrin, Ali. "The Rhetoric of Self and Other in Selected Iranian Short
   Stories, 1906–1979," *Int'l Fiction R*, 24, i–ii (1997), 39.

IBNE SAID

"The Way It Was"
   Rahim, Habibeh. "The Mirage of Faith and Justice: Some
   Sociopolitical and Cultural Themes in Post-Colonial Urdu Short
   Stories," in Hawley, John C., Ed. *The Postcolonial Crescent* . . . ,
   231–232.

SAKI [HECTOR HUGH MUNRO]

"A Matter of Sentiment"
   Birden, Lorene M. "Saki's 'A Matter of Sentiment,' " *Explicator*, 56,
   iv (1998), 201–204.
"Sredni Vashtar"
   Baldwin, Dean. *Instructor's Resource* . . . , 85–86.

SEVERINO SALAZAR

"Yalula, la mujer de fuego"
Herrera Galván, Alejandra, and Joaquina Rodríguez Plaza. "El juego
es narrar y entramar historias: Dos cuentos contemporáneos de la
literatura mexicana," *Dactylus*, 16 (1997), 32–35, 37–40, 41–43.

PEDRO SALINAS

"Entrada en Sevilla"
Gertz, Audrey R. "Sensuality, Reality, and the Poetic Process in Pedro
Salinas's 'Entrada en Sevilla,' " in Paolini, Claire J., Ed. *La Chispa*
'97 . . . , 163–173.

J. D. SALINGER

"For Esmé"
Korte, Barbara. *Body Language* . . . , 47, 48–49.
"Franny"
Alsen, Eberhard. "The Role of Vedanta Hinduism in Salinger's
Seymour Novel," *Renascence*, 33, ii (1981), 99–116.
"Hapworth 16, 1924"
Alsen, Eberhard. "The Role of Vedanta . . . ," 99–116.
"A Perfect Day for Bananafish"
Alsen, Eberhard. "The Role of Vedanta . . . ," 99–116.
Hochman, Will. "Swimming with Bananafish: The Literary Suicides
of Seymour Glass and J. D. Salinger," in Wright, Will, and Steven
Kaplan, Eds. *The Image of Violence* . . . , 460–461.
"Pretty Mouth"
Korte, Barbara. *Body Language* . . . , 108–109.
"Raise High the Roofbeam, Carpenters"
Alsen, Eberhard. "The Role of Vedanta . . . ," 99–116.
"Seymour—An Introduction"
Alsen, Eberhard. "The Role of Vedanta . . . ," 99–116.
"Uncle Wiggily in Connecticut"
Goodman, Nan. *Shifting the Blame* . . . , 162–163.
"Zooey"
Alsen, Eberhard. "The Role of Vedanta . . . ," 99–116.

DANIÈLE SALLENAVE

"L'Accomplissement"
Thibault, Bruno. "Danièle Sallenave et le thème de la vie séparée dans
les nouvelles d'*Un printemps froid*," *French Forum*, 22 (1997),
86–89.

"Louise"
Thibault, Bruno. "Danièle Sallenave . . . ," 78–83.
"La Séparation"
Thibault, Bruno. "Danièle Sallenave . . . ," 83–86.

JAMES SALTER

"Akhnilo"
Dowie, William. *James Salter*, 101–102.
"American Express"
Dowie, William. *James Salter*, 102–103.
"Am Strand von Tanger"
Dowie, William. *James Salter*, 96–97.
"The Cinema"
Dowie, William. *James Salter*, 97–98.
"Comet"
Dowie, William. *James Salter*, 106–107.
"The Destruction of Goetheanum"
Dowie, William. *James Salter*, 98–100.
"Dirt"
Dowie, William. *James Salter*, 100–101.
"Dusk"
Dowie, William. *James Salter*, 104.
"Foreign Shores"
Dowie, William. *James Salter*, 105–106.
"Lost Sons"
Dowie, William. *James Salter*, 102.
"Twenty Minutes"
Dowie, William. *James Salter*, 106.
"Via Negativa"
Dowie, William. *James Salter*, 99–100.

RAMZI M. SALTI

"Checkpoint"
Wise, Chris. "Re-Orienting the Subject: Arab American Ethnicity in
Ramzi M. Salti's *The Native Informant: Six Tales of Defiance from
the Arab World*," in Brown, Julie, Ed. *Ethnicity* . . . , 217, 220–221.
"The Native Informant"
Wise, Chris. "Re-Orienting . . . ," 223–234.
"The Taxi Driver"
Wise, Chris. "Re-Orienting . . . ," 219–220.
"Vivian and Her Son"
Wise, Chris. "Re-Orienting . . . ," 215–217.

GEORGIANA VALOYCE SANCHEZ

"The Heart of the Flower"
Hansen, Elaine T. *Mother Without Child . . .* , 156–157.

ROLANDO SÁNCHEZ MEJÍAS

"La noche del mundo"
Alvarez, José B. "(Re)escritura de la violencia: El individuo frente la historia en la cuentística novísima cubana," *Chasqui*, 26, ii (1997), 89–90.

ANGEL SANTIESTEBAN PRATTS

"Sueño de un día de verano"
Alvarez, José B. "(Re)escritura de la violencia: El individuo frente la historia en la cuentística novísima cubana," *Chasqui*, 26, ii (1997), 90–91.

BIENVENIDO SANTOS

"The Day the Dancers Came"
Manuel, Dolores de. "Imagined Homecomings: Strategies for Reconnection in the Writing of Asian Exiles," in Kain, Geoffrey, Ed. *Ideas of Home . . .* , 41–42.
"Scent of Apples"
Manuel, Dolores de. "Imagined . . . ," 40–41.
Wang, Qun. "Asian American Short Stories: Dialogizing the Asian American Experience," in Brown, Julie, Ed. *Ethnicity . . .* , 118.

WILLIAM SAROYAN

"The Acrobats"
Balakian, Nona. *The World of William Saroyan*, 148–149.
"And Man"
Balakian, Nona. *The World . . .* , 90–92, 133.
"Another Summer"
Balakian, Nona. *The World . . .* , 146–147.
"At Sundown"
Balakian, Nona. *The World . . .* , 134–135, 139.
"The Broken Wheel"
Balakian, Nona. *The World . . .* , 51–52.
"The Cat"
Balakian, Nona. *The World . . .* , 131.

DOROTHY L. SAYERS

"Die Weissagung"
Weigel, Robert. "Schnitzlers . . . ," 155–162.

HELGA SCHUBERT

"The Forbidden Room"
Mabee, Barbara. "The Wall as a Kafkaesque Symbol: Helga
Schubert's 'Das Verbotene Zimmer,' " *Neophilologus*, 80 (1996),
599–612.

BRUNO SCHULZ

"Sanatorium Under the Sign of the Hourglass"
Doležel, Lubomír. *Heterocosmica* . . . , 179–180.

LYNN SHARON SCHWARTZ

"The Melting Pot"
Mellard, James M. "Resisting the Melting Pot: The Jewish Back-Story
in the Fiction of Lynne Sharon Schwartz," in Halio, Jay L., and Ben
Siegel, Eds. *Daughters of Valor* . . . , 183–190.
"The Opiate of the People"
Aarons, Victoria. "Responding to an Old Story: Susan Fromberg
Schaeffer, Lesléa Newman, and Francine Prose," in Halio, Jay L.,
and Ben Siegel, Eds. *Daughters of Valor* . . . , 116–117.
Mellard, James M. "Resisting . . . ," 179–183.

IRIS SCLAVO ARMAN

"Primer premio"
Cunha-Giabbai, Gloria da. "Variaciones sobre el olvido,"
Monographic R, 11 (1995), 332–334.

DONALD SECREAST

"The Rat Becomes Light"
Luscher, Robert M. "The Deep Grain of the South in Donald
Secreast's Fiction," *Short Story*, 5, ii, N.S. (1997), 93–94.
"When Loads Shift"
Luscher, Robert M. "The Deep Grain . . . ," 91–92.
"White Trash, Red Velvet"
Luscher, Robert M. "The Deep Grain . . . ," 96.

ANNA SEGHERS

"Aufstand der Fischer von St. Barbara"
Sauval, Alain. "Der Aufstand der Fischer von St. Barbara d'Anna
Seghers, 1928" *Cahiers d'Etudes Germ*, 19 (1990), 159–168.

"Das Licht auf dem Galgen"
Mast, Thomas. "Representing the Colonized/Understanding the
Other? A Rereading of Anna Seghers' *Karibische Geschichten*,"
Colloquia Germanica, 30 (1997), 34–35, 37–40.

"Cristanta"
Kaufmann, Eva. "Developments in East German Women's Writing
Since Autumn 1989," in Weedon, Chris, Ed. *Post-War
Women's* . . . , 178.

"The Excursion of the Dead Girls"
Hell, Julia. *Post-Fascist Fantasies* . . . , 79, 81–85, 87, 90, 91, 92–96.

"Die Hochzeit von Haiti"
Mast, Thomas. "Representing the Colonized . . . ," 32–34, 35–36, 40.

"Letters to the Promised Land"
Hell, Julia. *Post-Fascist* . . . , 77–79, 87–88.

"Die Toten auf der Insel Djal"
Hell, Julia. *Post-Fascist* . . . , 97–99.

"Wiedereinfuhrung der Sklaverei in Guadeloupe"
Mast, Thomas. "Representing the Colonized . . . ," 34, 36–37.

MABEL SEGUN

"Ahimie's Wife"
Osha, Sanya. "Feminism or Cynicism in Mabel Segun's *The
Surrender and Other Stories*," in Adebayo, Aduke, Ed. *Feminism
and Black Women's* . . . , 69.

"Bola"
Osha, Sanya. "Feminism . . . ," 63–64.

"By the Silent Stream"
Osha, Sanya. "Feminism . . . ," 67.

"A Child Is a Child"
Osha, Sanya. "Feminism . . . ," 66–67.

"The Confidante"
Osha, Sanya. "Feminism . . . ," 69–70.

"The Feast"
Osha, Sanya. "Feminism . . . ," 64–66.

"Man of the House"
Osha, Sanya. "Feminism . . . ," 66.

"The Mat"
Osha, Sanya. "Feminism . . . ," 68.

"The Surrender"
Osha, Sanya. "Feminism . . . ," 60–63.

"The Voice by the Lagoon"
Osha, Sanya. "Feminism . . . ," 70.

"Who Will Bury Me?"
Osha, Sanya. "Feminism . . . ," 68–69.

CLAUDE SEIGNOLLE

"La Malvenue"
Finné, Jacques. "Deux corps de Pierre: 'La Vénus d'Ille' de Prosper Mérimée et 'La Malvenue' de Claude Seignolle," in Marigny, Jean, Intro., *Images fantastiques du corps*, 81–88.

VICTOR SÉJOUR [JEAN FRANÇOIS LOUIS VICTOR SÉJOUR MARCOU FERRAND]

"Le Mulâtre"
Sollors, Werner. *Neither Black Nor White* . . . , 164–167.

HUBERT SELBY

"The Coat"
Giles, James R. *Understanding Hubert Selby, Jr.*, 135–140.

"Fat Phils Day"
Giles, James R. *Understanding* . . . , 118.

"Fortune Cookie"
Giles, James R. *Understanding* . . . , 124–125.

"Hi Champ"
Giles, James R. *Understanding* . . . , 122–124, 125.

"I'm Being Good"
Giles, James R. *Understanding* . . . , 133–135.

"Liebesnacht"
Giles, James R. *Understanding* . . . , 125–129.

"The Musician"
Giles, James R. *Understanding* . . . , 140–141.

"Of Whales and Dreams"
Giles, James R. *Understanding* . . . , 118–119, 142.

"The Song of Silent Snow"
Giles, James R. *Understanding* . . . , 115, 120–122.

"The Sound"
Giles, James R. *Understanding* . . . , 130–132.

SAMUEL SELVON

"Come Back to Grenada"
  Kuhlmann, Deborah J. "Selvon's 'Come Back to Grenada': Bridges
  and Boundaries," *Griot*, 17, ii (1998), 39–41.

RICHARD SELZER

"Brute"
  King, Nancy M. P., and Ann F. Stanford. "Patient Stories, Doctor
  Stories, and True Stories: A Cautionary Reading," *Lit & Medicine*,
  11 (1992), 192–194.

OLIVE SENIOR

"The Arrival of the Snake Woman"
  Beittel, Mark, and Giovanna Covi. "Talking of Households: Olive
  Senior's Postcolonial Identities," in Zach, Wolfgang, and Ken L.
  Goodwin, Eds. *Nationalism vs. Internationalism* . . . , 392–393.
  Patteson, Richard F. "The Fiction of Olive Senior: Traditional Society
  and the Wider World," *ArielE*, 24, i (1993), 27–31; rpt. in his
  Caribbean Passages . . . , 43–47.
  Richardson, Brian. *UnLikely Stories* . . . , 148.
"Ascot"
  Patteson, Richard F. "The Fiction . . . ," 17, 23; rpt. in his *Caribbean
  Passages* . . . , 20–21, 30.
"Ballad"
  Patteson, Richard F. "The Fiction . . . ," 21–23; rpt. in his *Caribbean
  Passages* . . . , 27–30.
"The Boy Who Loved Ice Cream"
  Patteson, Richard F. *Caribbean Passages* . . . , 23–24.
"Bright Thursdays"
  Beittel, Mark, and Giovanna Covi. "Talking . . . ," 393–394.
  Patteson, Richard F. "The Fiction . . . ," 20–21; rpt. in his *Caribbean
  Passages* . . . , 25.
"Confirmation Day"
  Allen, Paula, and Wendell Aycock. "Subversion of the First Holy
  Communion in Contemporary Hispanic Fiction," *Confluencia*, 13, i
  (1997), 208–211.
"Country of the One-Eye God"
  Patteson, Richard F. *Caribbean Passages* . . . , 19–20.
"Discerner of Hearts"
  Patteson, Richard F. *Caribbean Passages* . . . , 36–38.
"Lily, Lily"
  Patteson, Richard F. "The Fiction . . . ," 26–27; rpt. in his *Caribbean
  Passages* . . . , 40–41, 42–43.

"Real Old Time T'ing"
  Mühleisen, Susanne. "Encoding the Voice: Caribbean Women's
  Writing and Creole," in Anim-Addo, Joan, Ed. *Framing the
  Word* . . . , 179–180.
  Patteson, Richard F. "The Fiction . . . ," 17–18; rpt. in his *Caribbean
  Passages* . . . , 21–22.
"See the Tiki-Tiki Scatter"
  Patteson, Richard F. *Caribbean Passages* . . . , 38–39.
"Summer Lightning"
  Patteson, Richard F. *Caribbean Passages* . . . , 26–27.
"Tears of the Sea"
  Patteson, Richard F. *Caribbean Passages* . . . , 38–39.
"The Tenantry of Birds"
  Beittel, Mark, and Giovanna Covi. "Talking . . . ," 394–396.
  Patteson, Richard F. "The Fiction . . . ," 24–26; rpt. in his *Caribbean
  Passages* . . . , 34–35.
"The Two Grandmothers"
  Patteson, Richard F. *Caribbean Passages* . . . , 38.
"The View from the Terrace"
  Patteson, Richard F. "The Fiction . . . ," 23–24; rpt. in his *Caribbean
  Passages* . . . , 31–32.
"Window"
  Patteson, Richard F. *Caribbean Passages* . . . , 35–36.
"Zig-Zag"
  Patteson, Richard F. *Caribbean Passages* . . . , 33–34.

ENRIQUE SERNA

"El alimento del artista"
  Herrera Galván, Alejandra, and Joaquina Rodríguez Plaza. "El juego
  es narrar y entramar historias: Dos cuentos contemporáneos de la
  literatura mexicana," *Dactylus*, 16 (1997), 35–38, 40–43.

ACHILLE SERRAO

"Cammeo"
  Capek-Habekovic, Romana. "Deconstructed Text: Achille Serrao's
  Retropalco," *Forum Italicum*, 31 (1997), 124–125.
"Il silenzio"
  Capek-Habekovic, Romana. "Deconstructed . . . ," 117–119.

ROBBIE CLIPPER SETHI

"Grace"
  Leach, Laurie. "Conflict over Privacy in Indo-American Short
  Fiction," in Brown, Julie, Ed. *Ethnicity* . . . , 198, 201–204.

SHA TING

"In Qixiangju Teahouse"
McDougall, Bonnie S., and Kam Louie. *The Literature of China* . . . ,
218.

VARLAM SHALAMOV

"Cherry Brandy"
Petrochenkov, Valery. "State-Sponsored Persecution as Violence:
Varlam Shalamov's *Kolyma Tales*," in Wright, Will, and Steven
Kaplan, Eds. *The Image of Violence* . . . , 496.
"Descendant of a Decembrist"
Ziolkowski, Margaret. *Literary Exorcisms* . . . , 163.
"My Trial"
Petrochenkov, Valery. "State-Sponsored . . . ," 496–497.
"The Procurator of Judea"
Petrochenkov, Valery. "State-Sponsored . . . ," 495–496.
Ziolkowski, Margaret. *Literary Exorcisms* . . . , 81–82.

ABU JAFAR SHAMSUDDIN

"The Leader"
Kelleher, Margaret. *The Feminization* . . . , 204–207.

ELLIS SHARP

"The Aleppo Button"
Daly, Macdonald. "Malice Aforethought: The Fictions of Ellis
Sharp," *Critique*, 39 (1998), 145.
"Dobson's Zone"
Daly, Macdonald. "Malice . . . ," 146–147.
"The Hay Wain"
Daly, Macdonald. "Malice . . . ," 147–150.
"Tinctures, Stains, Relics"
Daly, Macdonald. "Malice . . . ," 145–146.

MARY WOLLSTONECRAFT SHELLEY

"A Bride of Modern Italy"
Conger, Syndy M. "Mary Shelley's Women in Prison," in Conger,
Syndy M., Frederick S. Frank, and Gregory O'Dea, Eds.
Iconoclastic Departures . . . , 85–88.
"The Elder Son"
Hofkosh, Sonia. *Sexual Politics* . . . , 100–101.

"The False Rhyme"
   Conger, Syndy M. "Mary Shelley's . . . ," 89–90.
   Hofkosh, Sonia. *Sexual Politics* . . . , 90–93.
"The Heir of Mondolfo"
   Conger, Syndy M. "Mary Shelley's . . . ," 88–89.
"The Invisible Girl"
   Hofkosh, Sonia. *Sexual Politics* . . . , 1–6.
"The Mortal Immortal"
   Hoeveler, Diane L. "Mary Shelley and Gothic Feminism: The Case of
      'The Mortal Immortal,' " in Conger, Syndy M, Frederick S. Frank,
      and Gregory O'Dea, Eds. *Iconoclastic Departures* . . . , 154–160.
   Hofkosh, Sonia. *Sexual Politics* . . . , 93–97.
"A Tale of the Passions"
   Conger, Syndy M. "Mary Shelley's . . . ," 90–92.
"The Transformation"
   Hofkosh, Sonia. *Sexual Politics* . . . , 97–100.

SHEN CONGWEN

"Xiaoxiao"
   McDougall, Bonnie S., and Kam Louie. *The Literature of China* . . . ,
      126–127.

SHEN RONG [ALSO CHEN RONG]

"At Middle Age"
   Thakur, Ravni. *Rewriting Gender* . . . , 135–145, 147–149.
"Regarding the Problem of Newborn Piglets in Winter"
   Ford, Joh, and Marjorie Ford. *Instructor's Manual* . . . , 88–89.

LUCIUS SHEPARD

"Mengele"
   Franklin, H. Bruce. "The Vietnam War as American Science Fiction
      and Fantasy," in Cooke, Brett, George E. Slusser, and Jaume Marti-
      Olivella, Eds. *The Fantastic Other* . . . , 182.
"Salvador"
   Franklin, H. Bruce. "The Vietnam . . . ," 182–183.

SAM SHEPARD

"Hollywood"
   Nischik, Reingard M. "Illusion, Meta-Illusion, Counter-Illusion,
      Illusionism: The Function of Film in American Film Stories," in

Hebel, Udo J., and Karl Ortseifen, Eds. *Transatlantic Encounters* . . . , 301.

MARY MARTHA BUTT SHERWOOD

"Dazee, The Re-captured Negro"
　Ferguson, Moira. "Fictional Constructions of Liberated Africans:
　　Mary Butt Sherwood," in Fulford, Tim, and Peter J. Kitson, Eds.
　　Romanticism . . . , 152–162.

SHI TIESHENG

"Strings of Life"
　McDougall, Bonnie S., and Kam Louie. *The Literature of China* . . . ,
　　403.

CAROL SHIELDS

"Mirrors"
　Charters, Ann, and William E. Sheidley. *Resources* . . . , 5th ed., 218.

SHIGA NAOYA

"Night Fires"
　Goossen, Theodore W. "Introduction," in Goossen, Theodore, Ed. *The
　　Oxford Book* . . . , xxii–xxiii.

RAZIUDDIN SIDDIQI

"Last Stone"
　Rahim, Habibeh. "The Mirage of Faith and Justice: Some
　　Sociopolitical and Cultural Themes in Post-Colonial Urdu Short
　　Stories," in Hawley, John C., Ed. *The Postcolonial Crescent* . . . ,
　　245–246.

BAPSI SIDHWA

"Defend Yourself Against Me"
　Zaman, Niaz. "Old Passions in a New Land: A Critique of Bharati
　　Mukherjee's 'The Management of Grief' and Bapsi Sidhwa's
　　'Defend Yourself Against Me,' " in Kain, Geoffrey, Ed. *Ideas of
　　Home* . . . , 81–84.

LESLIE MARMON SILKO

"Coyote Holds a Full House in His Hand"
Jaskoski, Helen. *Leslie Marmon Silko: A Study* . . . , 67–76.
Rader, Dean. "Dealing With Coyote: Sexuality and Trickery in
'Coyote Holds a Full House in His Hand,' " in Jaskoski, Helen.
Leslie Marmon Silko: A Study . . . , 145–150.

"A Geronimo Story"
Jaskoski, Helen. *Leslie Marmon Silko: A Study* . . . , 57–67.

"Lullaby"
Jaskoski, Helen. *Leslie Marmon Silko: A Study* . . . , 22–32.
Palmer, Linda. "Healing Ceremonies: Native American Stories of
Cultural Survival," in Brown, Julie, Ed. *Ethnicity* . . . , 101–110,
111–112.

"The Man to Send Rain Clouds"
Jaskoski, Helen. *Leslie Marmon Silko: A Study* . . . , 53–57.

"Tony's Story"
Jaskoski, Helen. *Leslie Marmon Silko: A Study* . . . , 40–47.
Ruoff, A. LaVonne B. "Ritual and Renewal: Keres Traditions in the
Short Fiction of Leslie Silko, *MELUS*, 5 (1978), 5–8; rpt. Jaskoski,
Helen. *Leslie Marmon Silko: A Study* . . . , 154–158.

"Uncle Tony's Goat"
Jaskoski, Helen. *Leslie Marmon Silko: A Study* . . . , 47–53.

"Yellow Woman"
Charters, Ann, and William E. Sheidley. *Resources* . . . , 5th ed.,
219–220.
Ford, Joh, and Marjorie Ford. *Instructor's Manual* . . . , 112–113.
García, Alesia. "Politics and Indigenous Theory in Leslie Marmon
Silko's 'Yellow Woman' and Sandra Cisneros' 'Woman Hollering
Creek,' " in Preston, Cathy L., Ed. *Folklore, Literature* . . . , 11–12.
Jaskoski, Helen. *Leslie Marmon Silko: A Study* . . . , 32–40.
Ruoff, A. LaVonne B. "Ritual and Renewal . . . ," 9–15; rpt. Jaskoski,
Helen. *Leslie Marmon Silko: A Study* . . . , 160–166.

WILLIAM GILMORE SIMMS

"Caloya: or, The Loves of the Driver"
Boyd, Molly. "Southwestern Humor in *The Wigwam and the Cabin*,"
in Guilds, John C., and Caroline Collins, Eds. *William Gilmore
Simms* . . . , 169, 170, 171, 173, 175–176.

"Grayling; or 'Murder Will Out' "
Boyd, Molly. "Southwestern . . . ," 169, 170, 171–172.

"The Lazy Crow; A Story of the Cornfields"
Boyd, Molly. "Southwestern . . . ," 169–170, 172–173.

"The Two Camps: A Legend of the Old North State"
Boyd, Molly. "Southwestern . . . ," 169, 170, 171, 172, 174–175.

MAY SINCLAIR

"Khaki"
Raitt, Suzanne. " 'Contagious Ecstasy': May Sinclair's War Journals,"
in Raitt, Suzanne, and Trudi Tate, Eds. *Women's Fiction* . . . , 69–70.
"Red Tape"
Raitt, Suzanne. " 'Contagious Ecstasy' . . . ," 69–71.

ISAAC BASHEVIS SINGER

"The Bread"
Hadda, Janet. *Isaac Bashevis Singer* . . . , 188.
"Gimpel the Fool"
Charters, Ann, and William E. Sheidley. *Resources* . . . , 5th ed.,
221–222.
Hadda, Janet. *Isaac Bashevis Singer* . . . , 21, 123–125.
"The Little Shoemakers"
Baldwin, Dean. *Instructor's Resource* . . . , 146–148.
Hadda, Janet. *Isaac Bashevis Singer* . . . , 120–123.
"Pigeons"
Hadda, Janet. *Isaac Bashevis Singer* . . . , 144–145.
"The Séance"
Ford, Joh, and Marjorie Ford. *Instructor's Manual* . . . , 54–55.
"Short Friday"
Hadda, Janet. *Isaac Bashevis Singer* . . . , 126–127.
"The Son"
Hadda, Janet. *Isaac Bashevis Singer* . . . , 151–152.
"The Wife Killer"
Spilka, Mark. *Eight Lessons* . . . , 334–336.
"The Witch"
Spilka, Mark. *Eight Lessons* . . . , 328–332.
"Yentl the Yeshiva Boy"
Hadda, Janet. *Isaac Bashevis Singer* . . . , 134–135.

ANTONIO SKÁRMETA

"La Cenicienta en San Francisco"
Shaw, Donald L. *The Post-Boom* . . . , 73.
"El ciclista del San Cristóbal"
Shaw, Donald L. *The Post-Boom* . . . , 74.
"El cigarrillo"
Shaw, Donald L. *The Post-Boom* . . . , 75.
"Nupcias"
Flores, David. " 'Nupcias': sentido y forma en su contexto literario,"
Revista Chilena, 50 (1997), 5–19.

"Primera preparatoria"
Shaw, Donald L. *The Post-Boom* . . . , 75.

JOHN SHERBURNE SLEEPER

"The Drunken Captain, or Ned Rollins's Story"
Goodman, Nan. *Shifting the Blame* . . . , 63–64.
"The Unlucky Ship, or Ned Spanker's Story"
Goodman, Nan. *Shifting the Blame* . . . , 61–62.

FLORENCE MARGARET SMITH [STEVIE]

"Beside the Seaside"
Civello, Catherine A. *Patterns of Ambivalence* . . . , 20–21, 57.
"Getting Rid of Sadie"
Civello, Catherine A. *Patterns of Ambivalence* . . . , 21.
"The Story of a Story"
Civello, Catherine A. *Patterns of Ambivalence* . . . , 21–22.

LEE SMITH

"All the Days of Our Lives"
Smith, Rebecca. *Gender Dynamics* . . . , 130–131.
"Artists"
Smith, Rebecca. *Gender Dynamics* . . . , 140–142.
"Between the Line"
Smith, Rebecca. *Gender Dynamics* . . . , 126–128.
"Bob, a Dog"
Smith, Rebecca. *Gender Dynamics* . . . , 145–146.
"Cakewalk"
Smith, Rebecca. *Gender Dynamics* . . . , 142–143.
Wesley, Debbie. "A New Way of Looking at an Old Story: Lee
Smith's Portrait of Female Creativity," *Southern Lit J*, 30, i (1997),
89–91.
"Dear Phil Donahue"
Smith, Rebecca. *Gender Dynamics* . . . , 128–130.
"Desire on Domino Island"
Smith, Rebecca. *Gender Dynamics* . . . , 144–145.
"Dreamers"
Smith, Rebecca. *Gender Dynamics* . . . , 149–150.
"Fatback Season"
Parrish, Nancy C. *Lee Smith* . . . , 183–185.
"Georgia Rose"
Smith, Rebecca. *Gender Dynamics* . . . , 138–139.

ALEXANDER SOLZHENITSYN

ARMONÍA SOMERS

Somers desde sus cuentos," *Revista de Crítica*, 23, xlvi (1997), 215–217, 220–221.

"La inmigrante"
Moore, Charles B. "El papel del lector en 'La inmigrante' de Armonía Somers," *Chasqui*, 26, i (1997), 45–55.

SUSAN SONTAG

"The Way We Live Now"
Charters, Ann, and William E. Sheidley. *Resources* . . . , 5th ed., 222–223.
Warner, Sharon O. "The Way We Write Now: The Reality of AIDS in Contemporary Short Fiction," in Lounsberry, Barbara, et al., Eds. *The Tales We Tell* . . . , 185–187.

GARY SOTO

"El Radio"
Ford, Joh, and Marjorie Ford. *Instructor's Manual* . . . , 119–120.

SEVGI SOYSAL

"The Junk Peddler"
Bertram, Carel. "Restructuring the House, Restructuring the Self: Renegotiating the Meanings of Place in the Turkish Short Story," in Arat, Zehra F., Ed. *Deconstructing Images* . . . , 271–272.

MURIEL SPARK

"The Playhouse Called Remarkable"
Carruthers, Gerard. "The Remarkable Fictions of Muriel Spark," in Gifford, Douglas, and Dorothy McMillan, Eds. *A History* . . . , 514–515.

MICHELE SPINA

"Night"
Serpillo, Giuseppe. "Introduction," *Night and Other* . . . , [by Michele Spina], 2–3, 7.
"Paso Doble"
Serpillo, Giuseppe. "Introduction," 3, 5–6.

NORMAN SPINRAD

"The Big Flash"
Franklin, H. Bruce. "The Vietnam War as American Science Fiction

and Fantasy," in Cooke, Brett, George E. Slusser, and Jaume Marti-Olivella, Eds. *The Fantastic Other* . . . , 172–173.

HARRIET PRESCOTT SPOFFORD

"Desert Sands"
Schueller, Malini J. *U. S. Orientalisms* . . . , 123–126.

BRIAN STABLEFORD

"The Man Who Loved the Vampire Lady"
Stableford, Brian. *"Sang* for Supper: Notes on the Metaphorical Use of Vampires in *The Empire of Fear* and *Young Blood,"* in Gordon, Joan, and Veronica Hollinger, Eds. *Blood Read* . . . , 75–77.

"A True Story of a Vampire"
Holmes, Trevor. "Coming Out of the Coffin: Gay Males and Queer Goths in Contemporary Vampire Fiction," in Gordon, Joan, and Veronica Hollinger, Eds. *Blood Read* . . . , 176–178.

JEAN STAFFORD

"Beatrice Trueblood's Story"
Caminero-Santangelo, Marta. *The Madwoman* . . . , 72–82.

WILBUR DANIEL STEELE

"Footfalls"
Baldwin, Dean. *Instructor's Resource* . . . , 103–105.

WALLACE STEGNER

"Balance His, Swing Yours"
Benson, Jackson J. *Wallace Stegner* . . . , 28–30.

"The Berry Patch"
Benson, Jackson J. *Wallace Stegner* . . . , 58–61.

"Beyond the Glass Mountain"
Benson, Jackson J. *Wallace Stegner* . . . , 35–37.

"The Blue-Winged Teal"
Benson, Jackson J. *Wallace Stegner* . . . , 37–41.
Ferguson, J. M. "Cellars of Consciousness: Stegner's 'The Blue-Winged Teal,' " *Stud Short Fiction*, 14 (1977), 180–182; rpt. Benson, Jackson J. *Wallace Stegner* . . . , 156–159.

"Bugle Song"
Benson, Jackson J. *Wallace Stegner* . . . , 7–9.

"The Volunteer"
Benson, Jackson J. *Wallace Stegner* . . . , 25–26.
"The Women on the Wall"
Benson, Jackson J. *Wallace Stegner* . . . , 68–70.

GERTRUDE STEIN

"Ada"
Blackmer, Corinne E. "Lesbian Modernism in the Shorter Fiction of Virginia Woolf and Gertrude Stein," in Barrett, Eileen, and Patricia Cramer, Eds. *Virginia Woolf* . . . , 91–92.

"As a Wife Has a Cow"
Blackmer, Corinne E. "Lesbian Modernism . . . ," 92.

"Melanctha"
Blackmer, Corinne E. "Lesbian Modernism . . . ," 89–91.
Weiss, M. Lynn. *Gertrude Stein and Richard* . . . , 17–18, 82–84.

"Miss Furr and Miss Skeene"
Charters, Ann, and William E. Sheidley. *Resources* . . . , 5th ed., 224–225.
Curnutt, Kirk. *Wise Economies* . . . , 145–157.

JOHN STEINBECK

"The Chrysanthemums"
Charters, Ann, and William E. Sheidley. *Resources* . . . , 5th ed., 225–227.
Davison, Richard A. "Hemingway, Steinbeck, and the Art of the Short Story," *Steinbeck Q*, 21, iii–iv (1988), 80–83.
Ford, Joh, and Marjorie Ford. *Instructor's Manual* . . . , 53–54.
Piwinski, David J. "Floral Gold in Steinbeck's 'The Chrysanthemums,' " *Notes Contemp Lit*, 27, v (1997), 4–5.

"Flight"
Davison, Richard A. "Hemingway, Steinbeck . . . ," 77–79.

"The Gift"
Johnson, Claudia D. *Understanding* . . . , 2–8.

"The Great Mountains"
Johnson, Claudia D. *Understanding* . . . , 8–10.

"The Leader of the People"
Johnson, Claudia D. *Understanding* . . . , 14–15.

"The Murder"
Spilka, Mark. *Eight Lessons* . . . , 245–250.

"The Promise"
Johnson, Claudia D. *Understanding* . . . , 11–14.

GEORGE STEINER

"A Conversation Piece"
Horowitz, Sara R. *Voicing the Void* . . . , 179–180.

STENDHAL [MARIE HENRI BEYLE]

"Mina de Vanghel"
Augry, Muriel. "Rêveries et séductions dans les nouvelles stendhaliennes," in Guglielminetti, Marziano, Intro. *Studi di storia* . . . , 658–659, 662–663.
"Le Philtre"
Augry, Muriel. "Rêveries et séductions . . . ," 660–661.
"Une Position Sociale"
Augry, Muriel. "Rêveries et séductions . . . ," 665–667.
"Les Priviléges"
Augry, Muriel. "Rêveries et séductions . . . ," 664–665.

ROBERT LOUIS STEVENSON

"The Enchantress"
Linehan, Katherine. "Revaluing Women and Marriage in Robert Louis Stevenson's Short Fiction," *Engl Lit Transition*, 40 (1997), 47–49.
"Providence and the Guitar"
Linehan, Katherine. "Revaluing Women . . . ," 40–42.
"The Story of a Lie"
Linehan, Katherine. "Revaluing Women . . . ," 50, 51–52.
"The Strange Case of Dr. Jekyll and Mr. Hyde"
Armstrong, Tim. *Modernism, Technology* . . . , 109–193.
Clunas, Alex. "Comely External Utterance: Reading Space in 'The Strange Case of Dr. Jekyll and Mr. Hyde,' " *J Narrative Technique*, 24 (1994), 173–189.
Currie, Mark. *Postmodern Narrative Theory*, 117–134.
Hendershot, Cyndy. *The Animal Within* . . . , 105–114.
Manlove, Colin N. " 'Closer Than an Eye': The Interconnections of Stevenson's 'Dr. Jekyll and Mr. Hyde,' " in Sullivan, C. W., Ed. *The Dark Fantastic* . . . , 3–13.
Phelan, James E. "Freudian Commentary on the Parallels of the Male Homosexual Analysand to Robert Louis Stevenson's 'The Strange Case of Dr. Jekyll and Mr. Hyde,' " *J Evolutionary Psych*, 19, iii–iv (1998), 215–222.
Rosner, Mary. " 'A Total Subversion of Character': Dr. Jekyll's Moral Insanity," *Victorian News*, 93 (1998), 27–31.
Youngs, Tim. "White Apes at the *Fin de Siècle*," in Youngs, Tim, Ed. *Writing and Race*, 171–172.
"The Treasures of Franchard"
Linehan, Katherine. "Revaluing Women . . . ," 52–53.

"Will o' the Mill"
Linehan, Katherine. "Revaluing Women . . . ," 42–45.

ADALBERT STIFTER

"Bergkristall"
Beckmann, Martin. "Das ästhetische Erfahrungsverhältnis in Adalbert
Stifters Erzählung 'Bergkristall,' " *Literatur für Leser*, 1 (1994),
37–51.
Gray, Richard T. "The (Mis)Fortune of Commerce: Economic
Transformation in Adalbert Stifter's 'Bergkristall,' " in Bjorklund,
Beth, and Mark E. Cory, Eds. *Politics in German* . . . , 36–59.
"Brigitta"
Block, Richard. "Stone Deaf: The Gentleness of Law in Stifter's
'Brigitta,' " *Monatshefte*, 90 (1998), 17–33.
"Ein Gang durch die Katakomben"
Bernard, Veronika. "Das Bild von einem unterirdischen Wien: Vom
periegetischen Topos zum literarischen Motiv," *Zeitschrift für
Germanistik*, 8, ii (1998), 419–423.
"Granit"
McDonald, Edward R. "The Family's Legacy of Values as the
Redemptive Rock of Ages in Stifter's 'Granit,' " *Mod Lang Stud*,
24, ii (1994), 75–98.
"Nachkommenschaften"
Müller, Dominik. "Self-Portraits of the Poet as a Painter: Narratives
on Artists and the Bounds between the Arts (Hoffmann—Balzac—
Stifter)," in Morrison, Jeff, and Florian Krobb, Eds. *Text Into
Image* . . . , 173–174.

TERJE STIGEN

"Kisten"
Sjåvik, Jan. "A Rhetorical Approach to Three Norwegian Short
Stories," *Selecta*, 14 (1993), 81.

ELIZABETH STODDARD

"Collected by a Valetudinarian"
Weinauer, Ellen. "Alternative Economies: Authorship and Ownership
in Elizabeth Stoddard's 'Collected by a Valetudinarian,' " *Stud Am
Fiction*, 25 (1997), 167–182.

BRAM STOKER [ABRAHAM STOKER]

"Lies and Lilies"
Bierman, Joseph S. "A Crucial Stage in the Writing of *Dracula*," in

Hughes, William, and Andrew Smith, Eds. *Bram Stoker* . . . ,
156–159.
"The Squaw"
Bierman, Joseph S. "A Crucial Stage . . . ," 169–171.
"Under the Sunset"
Bierman, Joseph S. "A Crucial Stage . . . ," 152, 160–161.

LESLIE F. STONE

"The Conquest of Gola"
Weinbaum, Batya. "Sex-Role Reversal in the Thirties: Leslie F.
Stone's 'The Conquest of Gola,' " *Sci-Fiction Stud*, 24 (1997),
471–482.
"Out of the Void"
Donawerth, Jane. *Frankenstein's Daughters* . . . , 157–159.

THEODOR STORM

"Am Kamin"
Cozic, Alain. "Histoires de fantômes contées au coin du feu:
Fonctionnement et fonctions du fantastique chez Theodor Storm: A
propos du recueil 'Am Kamin,' " in David, Claude, Intro. *Les
Songes* . . . , 163–190.
"Aquis submersus"
Strehl, Wiebke. "Kinderlose Ehen: Fluch der Geldgier und
Lieblosigkeit sowie Zeichen der 'ewigen Reinheit,' " *Selecta*, 18
(1997), 66–69.
"Ein Bekenntnis"
Burns, Barbara. "Heyse and Storm on the Slippery Slope: Two
Differing Approaches to Euthenasia," *Germ Life & Letters*, 51
(1998), 34–42.
"Ein Doppelgänger"
Ladenthin, Volker. "Erinnerndes Erzählen: Ein Beitrag zur
Interpretation der Novelle 'Ein Doppelgänger' von Theodor Storm,"
Literatur für Leser, 2 (1994), 77–83.
"Ein grünes Blatt"
Wapnewski, Peter. "Diese grünen Träume oder: Der Schwärmer im
Feldlager zu Theodor Storms Novelle 'Ein Grünes Blatt,' "
Euphorion, 91 (1997), 183–205.
"Immensee"
Andreotti, Adriana, and Hedwig Bärtsch. "Theodor Storm:
'Immensee' (1850)," in Tarot, Rolf, and Gabriela Scherer, Eds.
Erzählkunst der Vormoderne, 199–208.
Coulson, Anthony S. "Veit Harlan's *Immensee*: A Study in the
Perversion of a Literary Classic," in Morrison, Jeff, and Florian
Krobb, Eds. *Text Into Image* . . . , 277–280, 283–284.

Schweitzer, Christoph E. *Men Viewing Women* . . . , 83–87.
Strehl, Wiebke. "Kinderlose Ehen . . . ," 65–69.
"Im Nachbarhaus links"
Strehl, Wiebke. "Kinderlose Ehen . . . ," 68–69.
"Zur Wald- und Wasserfreude"
Schröder, Stefan. "Von Feen und Nixen: Theodor Storms 'Zur
Wald—und Wasserfreude,' " *Zeitschrift für Deutsche Philologie*,
117, iv (1998), 543–563.
Schröder, Stefan. " 'Zur Wald- und Wasserfreude'—Von Feen und
Nixen—," *Zeitschrift für Deutsche Philologie*, 117 (1998), 543,
546–551, 563.

HARRIET BEECHER STOWE

"Uncle Lot"
Baldwin, Dean. *Instructor's Resource* . . . , 43–44.
Pryse, Marjorie. "Origins of American Literary Regionalism: Gender
in Irving, Stowe, and Longstreet," in Inness, Sherrie A., and Diana
Royer, Eds. *Breaking Boundaries* . . . , 25–28.
"The Widow's Bandbox"
Camfield, Gregg. *Necessary Madness* . . . , 74–76.

BOTHO STRAUß

"Die Widmung"
Harbers, Henk. "Psst! Oder Das im Entwischen Erwischte: Über
Paradoxe im Werk von Botho Strauß. Mit einer Interpretation der
'Widmung,' " *Monatshefte*, 85 (1993), 41, 45–53.

WHITLEY STRIEBER

"Pain"
Disch, Thomas M. *The Dreams Our Stuff* . . . , 24–25.

AUGUST STRINDBERG

"Day of Judgment"
Carlson, Harry G. *Out of Inferno* . . . , 83–85.
"Pangs of Conscience"
Carlson, Harry G. *Out of Inferno* . . . , 16–19.

RUTH MCENERY STUART

"A Golden Wedding"
McKinley, Gena. " 'The Delightful Accent of the South Land': Ruth

McEnery Stuart's Dialect Fiction," *Stud Am Fiction*, 26 (1998), 104–105.

"Queen O'Sheba's Triumph"
Sneller, Judy. " 'Old Maids' and Wily 'Widders': The Humor of Ruth McEnery Stuart," in Sloane, David E. E., Ed. *New Directions . . .* , 124–125.

"The Second Mrs. Simms"
Sneller, Judy. " 'Old Maids' . . . ," 121–122.

"Uncle Mingo's Speculations"
McKinley, Gena. " 'The Delightful Accent . . . ,' " 98–102.

"The Widder Johnsing"
Sneller, Judy. " 'Old Maids' . . . ," 123–124.

"The Woman's Exchange of Simpkinsville"
Sneller, Judy. " 'Old Maids' . . . ," 119–121.

WILLIAM STYRON

"The Brothers"
West, James L. W. *William Styron, A Life*, 163.

"A Chance in a Million"
West, James L. W. *William Styron . . .* , 75–76.

"The Ducks"
West, James L. W. *William Styron . . .* , 136.

"The Long Dark Road"
West, James L. W. *William Styron . . .* , 106.

"Shadrach"
West, James L. W. *William Styron . . .* , 420.

"Sun on the River"
West, James L. W. *William Styron . . .* , 106–107.

"This Is My Daughter"
West, James L. W. *William Styron . . .* , 136.

"A Tidewater Morning"
West, James L. W. *William Styron . . .* , 447–450.

D. F. SUTHERLAND

"The True Story of Estelle Ramon of Kentucky"
Stange, Margit. *Personal Property . . .* , 1, 7, 118, 119–122, 125–126.

LINDA SVENDSEN

"White Shoulders"
Fiamengo, Janice. "Linda Svendsen's *Marine Life*: Undoing Narrative Consolation," *Stud Canadian Lit*, 23, ii (1998), 9–17.

"Who He Slept By"
Fiamengo, Janice. "Linda Svendsen's . . . ," 4–8.

ARTHUR SYMONS

"Christian Trevalga"
Waters, Karen V. *The Perfect Gentleman* . . . , 135–136.

WAJIDA TABASSUM

"Hand-Me-Downs"
Collu, Gabrielle. "Unleashing Kali: Anger as Resistance in South Asian Women's Writing," in Bogaards, Winnifred M., Ed. *Literature of Region* . . . , 408–409.

ANTONIO TABUCCHI

"Il gioco del rovescio"
Setzkorn, Sylvia. "Ein Gemälde in der Erzählung: *Las Meninas* von Velázquez in Antonio Tabucchis 'Il gioco del rovescio,' " in Knabe, Peter-Eckhard, and Johannes Thiele, Eds. *Über Texte* . . . , 242–252.

RABINDRANATH TAGORE

"The Hungry Stones"
Smith, Evans L. "Myths of Poesis, Hermeneusis, and Psychogenesis: Hoffmann, Tagore, and Gilman," *Stud Short Fiction*, 34 (1997), 229–230, 232–233.

ELIZABETH TALLENT

"Ciudad Juarez"
Ford, Joh, and Marjorie Ford. *Instructor's Manual* . . . , 125–126.

AMY TAN

"Best Quality"
Ford, Joh, and Marjorie Ford. *Instructor's Manual* . . . , 120–121.
"Two Kinds"
Baldwin, Dean. *Instructor's Resource* . . . , 213–214.
Charters, Ann, and William E. Sheidley. *Resources* . . . , 5th ed., 228–229.

TANIZAKI JUN'ICHIRO

"The Tattooer"
Ito, Ken K. *"Seven Japanese Tales* by Tanizaki Jun'ichiro," in Miller,
Barbara S., Ed. *Masterworks of Asian . . .* , 429–430.

ELIZABETH TAYLOR

"A Dedicated Man"
Tintner, Adeline R. *Henry James's Legacy . . .* , 382–383.
"Poor Girl"
Tintner, Adeline R. *Henry James's Legacy . . .* , 376–378.
"Troubled State of Mind"
Tintner, Adeline R. *Henry James's Legacy . . .* , 363–364.

PETER TAYLOR

"Bad Dreams"
Robinson, David M. *World of Relations . . .* , 159–166.
"The Captain's Son"
Robinson, David M. *World of Relations . . .* , 61–62.
"Cookie"
Robinson, David M. *World of Relations . . .* , 150–153, 159.
"Dean of Men"
Robinson, David M. *World of Relations . . .* , 15–20.
"The Decline and Fall of the Episcopal Church (in the Year of Our Lord
1952)"
Donahue, Peter. "Genteel Companions: The Narrators in Peter
Taylor's *The Oracle at Stoneleigh Court,*" *Southern Q*, 36, i (1997),
40–41.
"The Fancy Woman"
Robinson, David M. *World of Relations . . .* , 94–99.
"A Friend and Protector"
Robinson, David M. *World of Relations . . .* , 148–149, 159.
"The Gift of the Prodigal"
Robinson, David M. *World of Relations . . .* , 14–15.
"In the Miro District"
Bryant, J. A. *Twentieth-Century Southern . . .* , 127–128.
Robinson, David M. *World of Relations . . .* , 4, 20–28, 143.
"A Long Fourth"
Robinson, David M. *World of Relations . . .* , 124, 126–132, 149–150,
153.
"Miss Leonora When Last Seen"
Caesar, Judith. " 'Miss Leonora When Last Seen': Why Americans
Run Away From Home," *Stud Short Fiction*, 34 (1997), 450–457.
Robinson, David M. *World of Relations . . .* , 124–125, 138–146.

ALEV TEKINAY

Tales of Turkish-German Women Writers," in Brinker-Gabler,
Gisela, and Sidonie Smith, Eds. *Writing New Identities* . . . ,
242–244.
"Der Todesengel"
Mattson, Michelle. "The Function . . . ," 74–75.

VLADIMIR TENDRIAKOV

"Donna Anna"
Ziolkowski, Margaret. *Literary Exorcisms* . . . , 123.
"Bread for a Dog"
Ziolkowski, Margaret. *Literary Exorcisms* . . . , 118.

EDWARD WILLIAM THOMSON

"The Privilege of the Limits"
New, W. H. *Land Sliding* . . . , 106–107.

JANE THOMPSON

"The Precious Possession of the Hollow Tree"
Clark, Daniel A., and P. Andrew Miller. "Variations on the Plantation
Romance: Five Stories by Southern Women Writers," *Stud Popular
Culture*, 19, ii (1996), 114–116.

JAMES THURBER

"A Call on Mrs. Forrester"
Tintner, Adeline R. *Henry James's Legacy* . . . , 357–358.
"The Secret Life of Walter Mitty"
Charters, Ann, and William E. Sheidley. *Resources* . . . , 5th ed., 230.

JOHANN LUDWIG TIECK

"Die Elfen"
Crisman, William. *The Crises of* . . . , 113–117.
"Die Gemälde"
Crisman, William. *The Crises of* . . . , 133–141.
"Liebeszauber"
Crisman, William. *The Crises of* . . . , 117–118.
"Der Pokal"
Crisman, William. *The Crises of* . . . , 118–120.
"Der Runenberg"
Sullivan, Heather I. *The Intercontextuality* . . . , 111–134.

LYNNE TILLMAN

"Weird fucks"
   Annesley, James. *Blank Fictions* . . . , 59–62.

JAMES TIPTREE, JR. [ALICE HASTINGS SHELDON]

"And I Awoke and Found Me Here on the Cold Hill's Side"
   Carter, Margaret L. "The Vampire as Alien in Contemporary Fiction,"
      in Gordon, Joan, and Veronica Hollinger, Eds. *Blood Read* . . . , 30.
"The Girl Who Was Plugged In"
   Donawerth, Jane. *Frankenstein's Daughters* . . . , 65–66.
"Houston, Houston, Do You Read?"
   Landon, Brooks. *Science Fiction* . . . , 138–140.
"The Women Men Don't See"
   Disch, Thomas M. *The Dreams Our Stuff* . . . , 191–192.
   Donawerth, Jane. *Frankenstein's Daughters* . . . , 125–127.
   Landon, Brooks. *Science Fiction* . . . , 137–138.

HAROLD TITUS

"A Little Action"
   Goodman, Nan. *Shifting the Blame* . . . , 149–150.

TATIANA TOLSTAYA

"Fire and Dust"
   Polowy, Teresa. "Female Space in Contemporary Russian Women's
      Writing: Tat'jana Tolstaja's 'Ogon' i Pyl,' " in Efimov, Nina A.,
      Christine D. Tomei, and Richard L. Chapple, Eds. *Critical
      Essays* . . . , 68–69, 71–82.
"Okkervile River"
   Peterson, Nadya L. *Subversive* . . . , 169–170, 172.

LEO TOLSTOY

"The Death of Ivan Ilyich"
   Charters, Ann, and William E. Sheidley. *Resources* . . . , 5th ed.,
      231–232.
   Squillace, Robert. *Modernism, Modernity* . . . , 167–170.
"The Kreutzer Sonata"
   Felman, Shoshana. "Forms of Judicial Blindness, or the Evidence of
      What Cannot Be Seen: Traumatic Narratives and Legal Repetitions
      in the O. J. Simpson Case and in Tolstoy's 'The Kreutzer Sonata,' "
      Critical Inquiry, 23 (1997), 739, 751–757, 758–762, 769–772,
      776–777, 783–788.

"Notes of a Madman"
Blank, Ksana. "Lev Tolstoy's Suprematist Icon-Painting," *Elementa*, 2, i (1995), 67–69.
"Three Deaths"
Ford, Joh, and Marjorie Ford. *Instructor's Manual* . . . , 14–15.
"The Three Questions"
Sperrle, Irmhild C. "Leskov, Tolstoy, and the Three Questions," *Tolstoy Stud J*, 10 (1998), 63–79.

CHARLOTTE ELIZABETH TONNA

"The Forsaken Home"
Zlotnick, Susan. *Women, Writing* . . . , 164–165.
"The Little Pin-Headers"
Zlotnick, Susan. *Women, Writing* . . . , 130–132.

JEAN TOOMER

"Fern"
Clary, Françoise. " 'The Waters of My Heart': Mythe et Identité dans *Cane* de Jean Toomer," *Études Anglaises*, 50 (1997), 424, 425–426.
"Karintha"
Clary, Françoise. " 'The Waters . . . ,' " 425.
"Rhobert"
Clary, Françoise. " 'The Waters . . . ,' " 423–424.

MICHEL TOURNIER

"Les amants taciturnes"
Klettke, Cornelia. "Die *mythécriture* als *commémoration*: Von der Wiederholung des Gedächtnisses zur Wiederholung des Todes in *Le médianoche amoureux*. Zum Tournier der 80er Jahre," in Asholt, Wolfgang, Ed. *Intertextualität und Subversivität* . . . , 146–147.
"Les deux banquets ou La commémoration"
Klettke, Cornelia. "Die *mythécriture* . . . ," 139–142.
"La légende de la peinture"
Klettke, Cornelia. "Die *mythécriture* . . . ," 145.
"Lucie ou La femme sans ombre"
Klettke, Cornelia. "Die *mythécriture* . . . ," 144–145.
"Pyrotechnie ou La commémoration"
Klettke, Cornelia. "Die *mythécriture* . . . ," 139–142.

JEAN-PHILIPPE TOUSSAINT

"La Salle de bain"
Gray, Margaret E. "Pascal in the Bathtub: Parodying the *Pensées*," *Symposium*, 5 (1997), 20–29.

ESTELA PORTILLA TRAMBLEY

"The Trees"
Herrera-Sobek, María. "The Politics of Rape: Sexual Transgression in Chicana Fiction," in St. Joan, Jacqueline, and Annette B. McElhiney, Eds. *Beyond Portia* . . . , 223–224.

WILLIAM TREVOR [TREVOR COX]

"Attracta"
Mahony, Christina H. *Contemporary Irish* . . . , 205–206.
"The Ballroom of Romance"
Mahony, Christina H. *Contemporary Irish* . . . , 202–204.
"The Blue Dress"
Bonaccorso, Richard. "William Trevor's Martyrs for Truth," *Stud Short Fiction*, 34 (1997), 115–116.
"Beyond the Pale"
Corcoran, Neil. *After Yeats and Joyce* . . . , 80.
"Death in Jerusalem"
Mahony, Christina H. *Contemporary Irish* . . . , 204–205.
"The Distant Past"
Corcoran, Neil. *After Yeats* . . . , 80.
Mahony, Christina H. *Contemporary Irish* . . . , 204.
"A Dream of Butterflies"
Bonaccorso, Richard. "William Trevor's . . . ," 116–117.
"The News from Ireland"
Kelleher, Margaret. *The Feminization* . . . , 132–134.
"The Third Party"
Bonaccorso, Richard. "William Trevor's . . . ," 114–115.

JEAN-LOUIS TRUDEL

"Remember, the Dead Say"
Weiss, Allan. "Separations and Unities: Approaches to Québec Separatism in English- and French-Canadian Fantastic Literature," *Sci-Fiction Stud*, 25 (1998), 58.

IVAN SERGEEVICH TURGENEV

"Yermolai and the Miller's Wife"
Baldwin, Dean. *Instructor's Resource* . . . , 46–48.

ESTHER TUSQUETS

"The Cousins"
Davies, Catherine. *Spanish Women's* . . . , 257–259.

"Las sutiles leyes de la simetría"
Valdivieso, Jorge H. "Transmutación de los personajes en 'Las sutiles leyes de la simetría,' " in Tibbitts, Mercedes V., Ed. *Studies in Honor* . . . , 367–374.

"The Man Who Painted Butterflies"
Davies, Catherine. *Spanish Women's* . . . , 256–257.

LISA TUTTLE

"Lézard du désir"
Gourion-Duhennois, Sylvia. "Du Fantasme au fantastique: dans quelques nouvelles de Lisa Tuttle," in Marigny, Jean, Intro., *Images fantastiques du corps*, 58, 59–60, 62–63, 64–65, 67.

"Des Maris"
Gourion-Duhennois, Sylvia. "Du Fantasme . . . ," 58–59, 65–66, 67.

"La Plaie"
Gourion-Duhennois, Sylvia. "Du Fantasme . . . ," 58, 60–61, 63, 66–67.

MARK TWAIN [SAMUEL L. CLEMENS]

"An Awful—Terrible Medieval Romance"
Quirk, Tom. *Mark Twain* . . . , 35–36.

"The Belated Russian Passport"
Quirk, Tom. *Mark Twain* . . . , 113.

"Buck Fanshaw's Funeral"
Quirk, Tom. *Mark Twain* . . . , 52–54.

"The Californian's Tale"
Quirk, Tom. *Mark Twain* . . . , 91–92.

"Cannibalism in the Cars"
Quirk, Tom. *Mark Twain* . . . , 37–41.

"The Charmed Life"
Quirk, Tom. *Mark Twain* . . . , 30.

"The Celebrated Jumping Frog of Calaveras County" [same as "The Notorious Jumping Frog . . ."]
Griffith, Clark. *Achilles and the Tortoise* . . . , 57–63.

"The Dandy Frightening the Squatter"
Covici, Pascal. *Humor and Revelation* . . . , 14–15.

"The Death Disk"
Quirk, Tom. *Mark Twain* . . . , 113–114.

"Dick Baker and His Cat"
Quirk, Tom. *Mark Twain* . . . , 50–52.

"A Dog's Tale"
Raveendran, P. P. "Focalizing Narration: Reflections on a Mark Twain Story," *Indian J Am Stud*, 22, i (1992), 81–83.

"The Man Who Put Up at Gadsby's"
    Quirk, Tom. *Mark Twain* . . . , 72–73.
"Medieval Romance"
    Skandera-Trombley, Laura. "Mark Twain's . . . ," 83.
"Mrs. McWilliams and the Lightning"
    Quirk, Tom. *Mark Twain* . . . , 63–64.
"A Mysterious Visit"
    Quirk, Tom. *Mark Twain* . . . , 46–47.
"No. 44: A Mysterious Stranger"
    Griffith, Clark. *Achilles and the Tortoise* . . . , 253–258.
"Political Economy"
    Ford, Joh, and Marjorie Ford. *Instructor's Manual* . . . , 15–16.
"The £1,000,000 Bank Note"
    Quirk, Tom. *Mark Twain* . . . , 92–93.
"1,002d Arabian Night"
    Skandera-Trombley, Laura. "Mark Twain's . . . ," 87–88.
"The Stolen White Elephant"
    Quirk, Tom. *Mark Twain* . . . , 80–81.
"The Story of the Good Little Boy Who Did Not Prosper"
    Quirk, Tom. *Mark Twain* . . . , 30–32.
"The $30,000 Bequest"
    Quirk, Tom. *Mark Twain* . . . , 109–110.
    Skandera-Trombley, Laura. "Mark Twain's . . . ," 92.
"A Trial"
    Quirk, Tom. *Mark Twain* . . . , 48–49.
"A True Story, Repeated Word for Word as I Heard It"
    Quirk, Tom. *Mark Twain* . . . , 57–62.
"Was It Heaven? or Hell?"
    Quirk, Tom. *Mark Twain* . . . , 114–115.

UMEHARI TAKESHI

"How the Gods Came to Kumano"
    McCarthy, Paul. "Umehari Takeshi and 'How the Gods Came to
    Kumano,' " *Lit R*, 39, ii (1996), 220–222.

MIGUEL DE UNAMUNO

"Abel Sánchez"
    Franz, Thomas R. "Abel's 'Second' Manner in 'Abel Sánchez,' " in
    Paolini, Claire J., Ed. *La Chispa '97* . . . , 145–152.
    Tubert, Silvia. "Unbearable Alterity: Using Unanumo to
    Reconceptualize Envy," *Mosaic*, 30, ii (1997), 19–36.

"Saint Manuel the Good, Martyr"
Orringer, Nelson R. "Unamuno and St. José Martí, the Good," *Revista Canadiense*, 21 (1996), 196–200.

JOHN UPDIKE

"A & P"
Charters, Ann, and William E. Sheidley. *Resources* . . . , 5th ed., 234.
Saldívar, Toni. "The Art of John Updike's 'A & P,' " *Stud Short Fiction*, 34 (1997), 215–225.
Schiff, James A. *John Updike Revisited*, 114–117.
"Ace in the Hole"
Greiner, Donald J. "No Place to Run: Rabbit Angstrom as Adamic Hero," in Broer, Lawrence R., Ed. *Rabbit Tales* . . . , 10–12.
"The Blessed Man of Boston, My Grandmother's Thimble, and Fanning Island"
Luscher, Robert M. "John Updike and the Montage Story: 'Farraginous Narrative,' " in Kaylor, Noel H., Ed. *Creative and Critical* . . . , 157–160.
"The Brown Chest"
Ford, Joh, and Marjorie Ford. *Instructor's Manual* . . . , 85–86.
"The Bulgarian Poetess"
Schiff, James A. *John Updike Revisited*, 117–121.
"Packed Dirt, Churchgoing, A Dying Cat, A Traded Car"
Luscher, Robert M. "John Updike . . . ," 160–161.
"Separating"
Schiff, James A. *John Updike Revisited*, 121–126.
"Trust Me"
Luscher, Robert M. "John Updike . . . ," 163–164.

GLEB USPENSKY

"She Straightened"
Mondry, Henrietta. "How 'Straight' Is the Venus de Milo? Regendering Statues and Women's Bodies in Gleb Uspensky's 'Vypriamila,' " *Slavic & East European J*, 41 (1997), 415–430.

HELENA VALENTÍ

"Anna's Solitude"
McNemey, Kathleen. "Tensions and Suspensions: The Fiction of Helena Valentí," *Explicación de Textos Literarios*, 24, i–ii (1995–1996), 115–116.
"The Wandering Woman"
McNemey, Kathleen. "Tensions . . . ," 116–117.

LUISA VALENZUELA

"Aquí pasan cosas raras"
   Shaw, Donald L. *The Post-Boom* . . . , 100, 101.
"Cambio de armas"
   Geisdorfer Feal, Rosemary. "The Politics of 'Wargasm': Sexuality,
   Domination and Female Subversion in Luisa Valenzuela's *Cambio
   de armas*," in Peavler, Terry J., and Peter Standish, Eds. *Structures
   of Power* . . . , 161–168, 169–173.
   Lagos, María Inés. "Sujeto, sexualidad y literatura en 'Cambio de
   armas' y *Novela negra con argentinos* de Luisa Valenzuela," in
   Díaz, Gwendolyn, and María I. Lagos, Eds. *La palabra en vilo* . . . ,
   133–143.
   Morello-Frosch, Marta. "Relecturas del cuerpos en *Cambio de armas*
   de Luisa Valenzuela," in Díaz, Gwendolyn, and María I. Lagos, Eds.
   La palabra en vilo . . . , 119–122.
   Shaw, Donald L. *The Post-Boom* . . . , 108–109.
"Camino al Ministerio"
   Shaw, Donald L. *The Post-Boom* . . . , 100, 101.
"Ceremonias de rechazo"
   Geisdorfer Feal, Rosemary. "The Politics . . . ," 179–180.
   Morello-Frosch, Marta. "Relecturas . . . ," 118–119.
   Shaw, Donald L. *The Post-Boom* . . . , 107.
"Cuarta version"
   Franco, Jean. "Self-Destructing Heroines," *Minnesota R*, 22 (1984),
   113–114; rpt. in Foster, David W., and Daniel Altamiranda, Eds.
   Twentieth-Century Spanish . . . , 277–278.
   Geisdorfer Feal, Rosemary. "The Politics . . . ," 173–177.
   Morello-Frosch, Marta. "Relecturas . . . ," 124–126.
   Shaw, Donald L. *The Post-Boom* . . . , 104–106.
   Trevizan, Liliana. "Luisa Valenzuela: Los riesgos de una versión
   plural y democrática," *Confluencia*, 12, i (1996), 93–105.
"De noche soy tu caballo"
   Morello-Frosch, Marta. "Relecturas . . . ," 123–124.
   Shaw, Donald L. *The Post-Boom* . . . , 106–107.
"El don de las palabras"
   Shaw, Donald L. *The Post-Boom* . . . , 100–101.
"La palabra asesino"
   Geisdorfer Feal, Rosemary. "The Politics . . . ," 177–179.
   Morello-Frosch, Marta. "Relecturas . . . ," 116–118.
   Shaw, D. L. "The Narrative Strategy of 'La palabra asesino,' "
   Antípodas, 6–7 (1994–1995), 173–181.
   Shaw, Donald L. *The Post-Boom* . . . , 107–108.
"Si esto es la vida, yo soy Caperucita Roja"
   Muñoz, Willy O. "Luisa Valenzuela y la subversión normativa en los
   cuentos de hadas: 'Si esto es la vida, yo soy Caperucita Roja,' " in
   Díaz, Gwendolyn, and María I. Lagos, Eds. *La palabra en vilo* . . . ,
   221–246.

"Unlimited Rapes United, Argentina"
Geisdorfer Feal, Rosemary. "The Politics . . . ," 168–169.

RIMA DE VALLBONA

"Alma en pena"
Galván, Delia V. "Medios de distanciamiento de la realidad en
Cosecha de pecadores," in Alcira Arancibia, Juana, and Luis A.
Jiménez, Eds. *Protestas, interrogantes* . . . , 197–198.
Silvestri, Daniel A. "Acercamiento psicocrítico a cuentos de Rima de
Vallbona," in Alcira Arancibia, Juana, and Luis A. Jiménez, Eds.
Protestas, interrogantes . . . , 167.

"Bajo pena de muerte"
Daniel, Lee A. "Angustia y evasión en la narrativa de Rima de
Vallbona," *Revista Filología y Ling*, 1 (1995), 26.

"Balada de un sueño"
Gómez Parham, Mary. "La imagen del hombre en la obra de las
escritoras contemporáneas: El caso de Rima de Vallbona," in Alcira
Arancibia, Juana, and Luis A. Jiménez, Eds. *Protestas,
interrogantes* . . . , 48.
Molina, Nory, and Julia E. Patiño. "La escritura femenina en 'Balada
de un sueño,' " in Alcira Arancibia, Juana, and Luis A. Jiménez,
Eds. *Protestas, interrogantes* . . . , 98–108.

"Beto y Betina"
Daniel, Lee A. "Angustia y evasión . . . ," 25–26.

"Brigada de la paz"
Matarrita, Estébana. "Macroestructuación en el cuentario *Los
infiernos de la mujer y algo más* de Rima de Vallbona," in Alcira
Arancibia, Juana, and Luis A. Jiménez, Eds. *Protestas,
interrogantes* . . . , 268–269, 271.[See also *Revista Filología y Ling*,
1 (1995), 46].

"Caña hueca"
Dowling, Lee. "Perspectivas de la narración y desafíos ideológicos en
algunas de las obras tempranas de Rima de Vallbona," in Alcira
Arancibia, Juana, and Luis A. Jiménez, Eds. *Protestas,
interrogantes* . . . , 26–27.

"El carro de la rutina"
Matarrita, Estébana. "Macroestructuación . . . ," 265–267. [See also
Revista Filología y Ling, 1 (1995), 44–45].

"Cementerio de camions"
Dowling, Lee. "Perspectivas . . . ," 24–25.

"El corrector de la historia"
Matarrita, Estébana. "Macroestructuación . . . ," 263–265. [See also
Revista Filología y Ling, 1 (1995), 43–44].

"Cosecha de pecadores"
Lasarte Dishman, Amalia C. "*Cosecha de pecadores*: Una carcajada

solapada," in Alcira Arancibia, Juana, and Luis A. Jiménez, Eds.
Protestas, interrogantes . . . , 203–205.

"Cruzada Intergaláctica"
Matarrita, Estébana. "Macroestructuación . . . ," 271–272.

"Desde aquí"
Galván, Delia V. "Medios de . . . ," 195–196.
Silvestri, Daniel A. "Acercamiento . . . ," 160.

"Una estrella fugaz"
Matarrita, Estébana. "Macroestructuación . . . ," 269–270.

"El hondón de las sorpresas"
Galván, Delia V. "Medios de . . . ," 191–192.
Izaguirre, Ester de. "Kafka y Vallbona: Exilio del ser o la busca de
respuesta al enigma de la existencia," in Alcira Arancibia, Juana,
and Luis A. Jiménez, Eds. *Protestas, interrogantes* . . . , 173–175.
Lasarte Dishman, Amalia C. "*Cosecha* . . . ," 202–203.
Silvestri, Daniel A. "Acercamiento . . . ," 144–148.

"El impostor"
Cruz, Julia G. "Tema antiguo, trato Nuevo en 'El impostor' de Rima
de Vallbona," *Confluencia*, 10, i (1994), 98–103; rpt. as "Relectura
de 'El impostor' de Rima de Vallbona," *Revista Filología y Ling*, 1
(1995), 51–57.
Daniel, Lee A. "Angustia y evasión . . . ," 26–28.
Daniel, Lee A. "Ekphrasis en 'El impostor' de Rima de Vallbona," in
Alcira Arancibia, Juana, and Luis A. Jiménez, Eds. *Protestas,
interrogantes* . . . , 183–189.

"Infame retorno"
Galván, Delia V. "Medios de . . . ," 196–197.
Gómez Parham, Mary. "La imagen . . . ," 45–46.
Gómez Parham, Mary, and Ingrid Hansz. "La Presencia masculina en
los cuentos de Rima de Vallbona," *Revista Filología y Ling*, 1
(1995), 33–34.

"El infierno"
Matarrita, Estébana. "Macroestructuación . . . ," 269. [See also *Revista
Filología y Ling*, 1 (1995), 47].

"Justicia distributive"
Matarrita, Estébana. "Macroestructuación . . . ," 272–273.

"El legado de la venerable María de Jesús de Agreda"
Galván, Delia V. "Medios de . . . ," 194–195.

"Libelo de repudio"
Matarrita, Estébana. "Macroestructuación . . . ," 270. [See also *Revista
Filología y Ling*, 1 (1995), 47–48].

"Lo inconfesable"
Gómez Parham, Mary. "La imagen . . . ," 43–45.
Gómez Parham, Mary, and Ingrid Hansz. "La Presencia . . . ," 32–33.

"Los males venideros"
Jiménez, Luis A. "Construyendo el sujeto femenino en *Los infiernos*

RAMÓN MARÍA DEL VALLE-INCLÁN

"Beatriz"
Serrano Alonso, Javier. "La estrategia de la escritura en Valle-Inclán:
La historia textual de 'Beatriz,' " *Anthropos*, 158–159 (1994),
69–74.

MARGUERITE VALLETTE [RACHILDE]

"Le Château hermétique"
Ziegler, Robert. "Interpretation as Mirage in Rachilde's 'Le Château
hermétique,' " *Nineteenth-Century French Stud*, 26 (Fall–Winter,
1997–1998), 182–192.

ANA LYDIA VEGA

"Ajustes, S.A."
Galván, Delia V. "Sincretismo cultural en estructura policíaca: Ana
Lydia Vega y su *Pasión de historia*," *Americas R*, 21, iii–iv (1993),
141.

"El baúl de Miss Florence: Fragmentos para un novelón romántico"
Unruh, Vicky. "Like English for Spanish: Mediataciones desde la
frontera anglorriqueña," *Siglo*, 15 (1997), 155–158.

"Caso omiso"
Boling, Becky. " 'What's Wrong with This Picture?': Ana Lydia
Vega's 'Caso omiso,' " *Revista de Estudios Hispánicos*," 23 (1996),
315–324.
Galván, Delia V. "Sincretismo cultural . . . ," 141–142.

"Letra para salsa y tres soneos por encargo"
Ayes, Zulema. "El distanciamiento o la extraposición en el discurso
ficcional: Dos cuentos: 'Letra para salsa y tres soneos por encargo'
de Ana Lydia Vega, 'De noche vienes' de Elena Poniatowska,"
Revista/Review Interamericana, 27, i–iv (1997), 93–108.

"Pasión de historia"
Galván, Delia V. "Sincretismo cultural . . . ," 140–141.

"Sobre tumbas y héroes"
Galván, Delia V. "Sincretismo cultural . . . ," 142–143.

"Three Love Aerobics"
Puleo, Augustus C. "Subverting and Re-defining Sexuality in 'Three
Love Aerobics' by Ana Lydia Vega," *Letras Femeninas*, 21, i–ii
(1995), 57–67.

ED VEGA

"Sometimes, If You Listen Closely, You Can Hear Crying in the Zoo"
Christie, John S. *Latino Fiction* . . . , 126–127.

GIOVANNI VERGA

"The She-Wolf"
Verdicchio, Pasquale. "Verismo, Narrator, and Reality: Giovanni
Verga's 'The She-Wolf,' " *Selecta*, 12 (1991), 74–78.

[COUNT] VILLIERS DE L'ISLE-ADAM [JEAN MARIE MATTHIAS PHILIPPE AUGUSTE]

"L'Inconnue"
Leroy, Claude. "La Passante passe toujours deux fois: 'L'Inconnue'
de Villiers de l'Isle-Adam," *Confronto Letterario*, 13, xxv (1996),
55–66.

VERNOR VINGE

"The Accomplice"
Schweitzer, Darrell. "Genuinely Prophetic Science Fiction?" *New
York R Sci Fiction*, 9, i (1996), 14–15.

HELENA MARÍA VIRAMONTES

"Birthday"
Christie, John S. *Latino Fiction* . . . , 29–30, 96.
"The Broken Web"
Swyt, Wendy. "*Hungry Women*: Borderlands Mythos in Two Stories
by Helena María Viramontes," *MELUS*, 23, ii (190–196, 198, 200.
"The Cariboo Café"
Caminero-Santangelo, Marta. *The Madwoman* . . . , 160–162, 165–69.
Garza-Falcón, Leticia M. *Gente Decente* . . . , 201–210.
Saldívar, José D. *Border Matters* . . . , 97–107.
Swyt, Wendy. "*Hungry Women*: Borderlands . . . ," 190, 196–200.
"Miss Clairol"
Gonzalez, Maria. "Love and Conflict: Mexican American Women
Writers as Daughters," in Brown-Guillory, Elizabeth, Ed. *Women of
Color* . . . , 157–158.
"The Moths"
Charters, Ann, and William E. Sheidley. *Resources* . . . , 5th ed.,
235–236.
"Neighbors"
Christie, John S. *Latino Fiction* . . . , 78.
Garza-Falcón, Leticia M. *Gente Decente* . . . , 210–214.
Saldívar-Hull, Sonia. "Political Identities in Contemporary Chicana
Literature: Helena Viramontes's Visions of the U.S. Third World,"
in D'haen, Theo, and Hans Bertens, Eds. *"Writing" Nation* . . . ,
158–159.

"Paris Rats in L.A."
Saldívar-Hull, Sonia. "Political Identities . . . ," 159–160.
"Tears on My Pillow"
Saldívar-Hull, Sonia. "Political Identities . . . ," 160, 162–164.

GERALD VIZENOR

"Almost Browne"
Ford, Joh, and Marjorie Ford. *Instructor's Manual* . . . , 87–88.

WALTER VOGT

"Der Irre und sein Arzt"
Pender, Malcolm. *Contemporary Images* . . . , 170–171, 173.
"Die roten Tiere von Tsavo"
Pender, Malcolm. *Contemporary Images* . . . , 172–173.

VLADIMIR VOINOVICH

"The Fur Hat"
Lewis, Barry. "Homunculi Sovietici: The Soviet 'Writers' in Voinovich's 'Shapka,' " *Australian Slavonic*, 10, i (1996), 17–28.
"In a Circle of Friends"
Ziolkowski, Margaret. *Literary Exorcisms* . . . , 32, 36.

KURT VONNEGUT

"Adam"
Reed, Peter J. *The Short Fiction* . . . , 50–51.
Thorson, James. "Kurt Vonnegut's Cold War: The Short Stories of the Fifties," in Meyer, Martin, Gabriele Spengemann, and Wolf Kindermann, Eds. *Tangenten* . . . , 109–111.
"All the King's Horses"
Thorson, James. "Kurt Vonnegut's Cold . . . ," 106–108.
"Ambitious Sophomore"
Reed, Peter J. *The Short* . . . , 42–43.
"Any Reasonable Offer"
Reed, Peter J. *The Short* . . . , 36–37.
"Bagombo Snuff Box"
Reed, Peter J. *The Short* . . . , 51–52.
"The Big Space Fuck"
Reed, Peter J. *The Short* . . . , 106–108.
"The Big Trip Up Yonder"
Reed, Peter J. *The Short* . . . , 66–67.

"Unready to Wear"
Reed, Peter J. *The Short* . . . , 64–66.
"Welcome to the Monkey House"
Reed, Peter J. *The Short* . . . , 99–102, 142–143.

DAVID WAGONER

"The Bird Watcher"
McFarland, Ron. *The World of* . . . , 195.
"Holiday"
McFarland, Ron. *The World of* . . . , 39.
"The Spinning Ladies"
McFarland, Ron. *The World of* . . . , 141–148.

ALICE WALKER

"Advancing Luna—and Ida B. Wells"
Smith, Valerie. *Not Just Race* . . . , 21–31.
"The Child Who Favored Daughter"
Larson, Angela. "An Adamantine Emotion," in Wright, Will, and
Steven Kaplan, Eds. *The Image of Violence* . . . , 443–447.
Lester, Neal A. " 'Not my mother, not my sister, but it's me, O Lord,
standing . . .': Alice Walker's 'The Child Who Favored Daughter'
as Neo-Slave Narrative," *Stud Short Fiction*, 34 (1997), 290–305.
"The Flowers"
Loeb, Monica. "Walker's 'The Flowers,' " *Explicator*, 55, i (1996),
60–62.
"Elitheia"
Ewell, Barbara C. "Southern Women Reconstruct the South: Limit as
Aesthetic in the Short Story," in Lounsberry, Barbara, et al., Eds.
The Tales We Tell . . . , 68, 69.
"Everyday Use"
Baxter, Charles. *Burning Down the House* . . . , 115–116.
King, Debra W. *Deep Talk* . . . , 197.
"The Lover"
Butler, Robert. *Contemporary African American* . . . , 66.
"Nineteen Fifty-Five"
Baldwin, Dean. *Instructor's Resource* . . . , 198–200.
"Really, Doesn't Crime Pay?"
Butler, Robert. *Contemporary African American* . . . , 65.
"Roselily"
Butler, Robert. *Contemporary African American* . . . , 65.
Charters, Ann, and William E. Sheidley. *Resources* . . . , 5th ed.,
238–239.
Ford, Joh, and Marjorie Ford. *Instructor's Manual* . . . , 106–107.

"Source"
  Butler, Robert. *Contemporary African American* . . . , 66.
  McDowell, Deborah E. "Reading Family Matters" in Jones, Anne G.,
    and Susan V. Donaldson, Eds. *Haunted Bodies* . . . , 401–410.

HUGH WALPOLE

"Adventure of the Beautiful Things"
  Tintner, Adeline R. *Henry James's Legacy* . . . , 93–95.

MARTIN WALSER

"A Runaway Horse"
  Plouffe, Bruce. *The Post-War Novella* . . . , 191–254.

ANNA LEE WALTERS

"The Sun Is Not Merciful"
  Meredith, Howard. "Metaphor and Meaning in Anna Lee Walters's
    'The Sun Is Not Merciful,' " *Southwestern Am Lit*, 22, ii (1997),
    63–67.
"The Warriors"
  Steinberg, Marc. "Myth, Folk Tale and Ritual in Anna Lee Walters's
    'The Warriors,' " *Stud Short Fiction*, 34 (1997), 55–60.

WANG ANYI

"A Century on a Small Hillock"
  Chen, Helen H. "Gender, Subjectivity, Sexuality: Defining a
    Subversive Discourse in Wang Anyi's Four Tales of Sexual
    Transgression," in Zhang, Yingjin, Ed. *China in a Polycentric
    World* . . . , 102–105.
"Love in a Small Town"
  Chen, Helen H. "Gender, Subjectivity . . . ," 100–102.
"Love in Splendor Valley"
  Chen, Helen H. "Gender, Subjectivity . . . ," 105–108.
"Love in a Wild Mountain"
  Chen, Helen H. "Gender, Subjectivity . . . ," 97–100.

WANG MENG

"Bolshevik Salute"
  McDougall, Bonnie S., and Kam Louie. *The Literature of China* . . . ,
    380.

"Butterfly"
McDougall, Bonnie S., and Kam Louie. *The Literature of China* . . . ,
380–381.

"The Young Newcomer in the Organisation Department"
McDougall, Bonnie S., and Kam Louie. *The Literature of China* . . . ,
257.

WANG SHUO

"The Operators"
McDougall, Bonnie S., and Kam Louie. *The Literature of China* . . . ,
417.

"The Rubber Man"
McDougall, Bonnie S., and Kam Louie. *The Literature of China* . . . ,
417.

WANG ZENGQI

"The Love Story of a Young Monk"
McDougall, Bonnie S., and Kam Louie. *The Literature of China* . . . ,
371–372.

"The Tale of Big Nur"
McDougall, Bonnie S., and Kam Louie. *The Literature of China* . . . ,
372.

ALAN WARNER

"Car Hung, Upside Down"
Falconer, Rachel. "Bakhtin's Chronotope and the Contemporary
Short Story," *So Atlantic Q*, 97 (1998), 723–726.

SYLVIA TOWNSEND WARNER

"Oxenhope"
Baxter, Charles. *Burning Down the House* . . . , 150–158.

MYRIAM WARNER-VIEYRA

"Sidonie"
Proulx, Patrice J. "Inscriptions of Silence and Violence in the
Antillean Text: Reading Warner-Vieyra's *Juletane* and 'Sidonie,' "
French R, 70 (1997), 698–709.

ROBERT PENN WARREN

"The Circus in the Attic"
Blotner, Joseph. *Robert Penn Warren* . . . , 234–235.
Bradley, Patricia L. "The Three Ring Self: Robert Penn Warren's
Circus Personae," *Kentucky Philol R*, 11 (1996), 14–18.
"Prime Leaf"
Blotner, Joseph. *Robert Penn Warren* . . . , 103–104.

EMMA LEE WARRIOR

"Compatriots"
McKinnon, Ann. "Morality Destabilised: Reading Emma Lee
Warrior's 'Compatriots,' " *Stud Am Indian Lit*, 10, iv (1998),
54–66.

FRANK WEDEKIND

"Der greise Freier"
Lewis, Ward B. *The Ironic Dissident* . . . , 141–142.
"Die Fürstin Russalka"
Lewis, Ward B. *The Ironic Dissident* . . . , 138–139.
"Mine-Haha"
Lewis, Ward B. *The Ironic Dissident* . . . , 143–146.
"Rabbi Esra"
Lewis, Ward B. *The Ironic Dissident* . . . , 139–140.

STANLEY WEINBAUM

"Flight on Titan"
Baxter, Stephen. "Under Titan's Green Sky: Titan in Science Fiction
and Science," *Foundation*, 71 (1997), 6–7.

FAY WELDON

"Alopecia"
Dowling, Finuala. *Fay Weldon's Fiction*, 40.
"In the Great War"
Dowling, Finuala. *Fay Weldon's Fiction*, 40–41, 42.
"Polaris"
Dowling, Finuala. *Fay Weldon's Fiction*, 37–40.
"Redundant! or The Wife's Revenge"
Dowling, Finuala. *Fay Weldon's Fiction*, 44–45.

H. G. WELLS

"The Country of the Blind"
Doležel, Lubomír. *Heterocosmica* . . . , 119–120.
"The Door in the Wall"
Navarette, Susan J. *The Shape* . . . , 121–122.
"A Story of the Stone Age"
Disch, Thomas M. *The Dreams Our Stuff* . . . , 64–66.
"The Time Machine"
Navarette, Susan J. *The Shape* . . . , 193, 197, 232–233.

EUDORA WELTY

"At the Landing"
Henderson, Joel. "Tracking the Storms of Life: Eudora Welty as
Meteorologist," *Alpha Chi Recorder*, 40, i (1997), 28–29.
Johnston, Carol A. *Eudora Welty* . . . , 22–26.
Waldron, Ann. *Eudora: A Writer's Life*, 137–139.
Warren, Colleen. "(R)evolutions of Change: Female Alterability in
'The Children' and 'At the Landing,' " *Southern Q*, 36, i (1997),
53–62.
Warren, Robert P. *The Robert Penn Warren Reader*, 203–204; rpt.
Johnston, Carol A. *Eudora Welty* . . . , 164–166.
"The Bride of the Innisfallen"
Marrs, Suzanne. "Place and the Displaced in Eudora Welty's *The
Bride of Innisfallen*," *Mississippi Q*, 50 (1997), 656–660.
Pollack, Harriet. "Photographic Convention and Story Composition:
Eudora Welty's Uses of Detail, Plot, Genre, and Expectation from
'A Worn Path' Through *The Bride of Innisfallen*," *So Central R*, 14,
ii (1997), 29–30.
"The Burning"
Ewell, Barbara C. "Southern Women Reconstruct the South: Limit as
Aesthetic in the Short Story," in Lounsberry, Barbara, et al., Eds.
The Tales We Tell . . . , 67–68, 69, 70.
Johnston, Carol A. *Eudora Welty* . . . , 32–35.
Waldron, Ann. *Eudora: A Writer's Life*, 212–213.
"The Children"
Warren, Colleen. "(R)evolutions . . . ," 52–62.
"Circe"
Marrs, Suzanne. "Place and the Displaced . . . ," 650–653.
"Clytie"
Johnston, Carol A. *Eudora Welty* . . . , xiii, 19, 46, 73–74.
"A Curtain of Green"
Cox, Rosemary. "Green Curtains and Wide Nets: The Sublime in
Eudora Welty's Early Fiction," *J Assoc Interdisciplinary Stud Arts*,
2, ii (1997), 54–58.
Johnston, Carol A. *Eudora Welty* . . . , 71–73.

"Death of a Traveling Salesman"
Johnston, Carol A. *Eudora Welty* . . . , 42–45.
Waldron, Ann. *Eudora: A Writer's Life*, 86–87.
"The Demonstrators"
Johnston, Carol A. *Eudora Welty* . . . , 170–172.
Oates, Joyce C. "The Art of Eudora Welty," *Shenandoah*, 20, iii
(1969), 56–57; rpt. Johnston, Carol A. *Eudora Welty* . . . , 170–172.
Thornton, Naoko F. "Voices and Aphasia in Eudora Welty's 'The
Demonstrators,' " *Stud Engl Lit*, n.v. (1998), 69–82.
Waldron, Ann. *Eudora: A Writer's Life*, 278–279.
"First Love"
Ritter, Alexander. "Natchez in the Fiction of Three Centuries:
Variations of Literary Regionalism in Chateaubriand, Sealsfield and
Welty," *Southern Q*, 35, i (1996), 23–24.
"Flowers for Marjorie"
Mortimer, Gail L. "Memory, Despair, and Welty's MacLain Twins,"
So Central R, 14, ii (1997), 40–41.
"Going to Naples"
Marrs, Suzanne. "Place and the Displaced . . . ," 665–668.
Trouard, Dawn. "Welty's Anti-Ode to Nightingales: Gabriella's
Southern Passage," *Mississippi Q*, 50 (1997), 675–687.
"The Hitch-Hikers"
Mortimer, Gail L. "Memory, Despair . . . ," 41.
"June Recital"
Caminero-Santangelo, Marta. *The Madwoman* . . . , 56–68.
Johnston, Carol A. *Eudora Welty* . . . , 27, 28, 87–92.
Pollack, Harriet. "Story-Making in *The Golden Apples*: Point of View,
Gender and the Importance of Cassie Morrison," *Southern Q*, 34, ii
(1996), 75–80.
Waldron, Ann. *Eudora: A Writer's Life*, 174–175.
Yaeger, Patricia S. " 'Because a Fire Was in My Head': Eudora Welty
and the Dialogic Imagination," *PMLA*, 99 (1984), 965–968; rpt.
Johnston, Carol A. *Eudora Welty* . . . , 215–221.
———. "Beyond the Hummingbird: Southern Women Writers and
the Southern Gargantua," in Jones, Anne G., and Susan V.
Donaldson, Eds. *Haunted Bodies* . . . , 294–299, 301.
"Kella"
Mortimer, Gail L. "Memory, Despair . . . ," 41.
"Kin"
Pitavy-Souques, Danièle. "A Blazing Butterfly: The Modernity of
Eudora Welty," *Mississippi Q*, 39 (1986), 556–559; rpt. Johnston,
Carol A. *Eudora Welty* . . . , 196–198.
"Livvie"
Johnston, Carol A. *Eudora Welty* . . . , 21–22.
"A Memory"
Donaldson, Susan V. "Making a Spectacle: Welty, Faulkner, and
Southern Gothic," *Mississippi Q*, 50 (1997), 582–583.

Johnston, Carol A. *Eudora Welty* . . . , 47–52, 55–61.
Pitavy-Souques, Danièle. "A Blazing . . . ," 543–548; rpt. Johnston, Carol A. *Eudora Welty* . . . , 184–188.
Prenshaw, Peggy W. "The Female South and Eudora Welty's Art," in Gretlund, Jan N., and Karl-Heinz Westarp, Eds. *The Late Novels* . . . , 189–192.
Yaeger, Patricia S. "Beyond . . . ," 289–290, 303, 304–310, 312–313.

"Moon Lake"
Johnston, Carol A. *Eudora Welty* . . . , 92–98.
Mortimer, Gail. "Musical Echoes of World War I in Welty's 'Moon Lake,' " *Eudora Welty Newsletter*, 22, ii (1998), 11–12.
Pitavy-Souques, Danièle. "A Blazing . . . ," 550–552; rpt. Johnston, Carol A. *Eudora Welty* . . . , 190–192.
Waldron, Ann. *Eudora: A Writer's Life*, 179–180.
Wesley, Marilyn C. "The Woman Traveler and the Dynamic Journey: Narrative, Psychological, and Social Process in Eudora Welty's Short Fiction," *Southern Stud*, 4, iii (1993), 255–256.

"Music from Spain"
Bayne, John. "Music from 'Music from Spain': Textual Variants," *Eudora Welty Newsletter*, 22, i (1998), 8–16.
Johnston, Carol A. *Eudora Welty* . . . , 82–87, 91–92, 101–102.
Mortimer, Gail L. "Memory, Despair . . . ," 36, 38–39.
Waldron, Ann. *Eudora: A Writer's Life*, 175–176.

"No Place for You, My Love"
Marrs, Suzanne. "Place and the Displaced . . . ," 660–664.
Wesley, Marilyn C. "The Woman Traveler . . . ," 261–264.

"Old Mr. Marblehall"
Pitavy-Souques, Danièle. "A Blazing . . . ," 554–556; rpt. Johnston, Carol A. *Eudora Welty* . . . , 193–196.
Polk, Noel. "Welty, Hawthorne, and Poe: Men of the Crowd and the Landscape of Alienation," *Mississippi Q*, 50 (1997), 557–563.
Ritter, Alexander. "Natchez in the Fiction . . . ," 22–23.

"A Piece of News"
Johnston, Carol A. *Eudora Welty* . . . , 46–47, 68–71.

"Powerhouse"
Yaeger, Patricia S. "Beyond . . . ," 294–295.

"A Shower of Gold"
Johnston, Carol A. *Eudora Welty* . . . , 74–75.

"Sir Rabbit"
Johnston, Carol A. *Eudora Welty* . . . , 75–77, 79–80.
Yaeger, Patricia. "Beyond . . . ," 207–211.

"A Still Moment"
Baldwin, Dean. *Instructor's Resource* . . . , 136–138.
Johnston, Carol A. *Eudora Welty* . . . , 53.
Pitavy-Souques, Danièle. "A Blazing . . . ," 548–550; rpt. Johnston, Carol A. *Eudora Welty* . . . , 188–190.
Waldron, Ann. *Eudora: A Writer's Life*, 133–134.

"A Visit of Charity"
  Ford, Joh, and Marjorie Ford. *Instructor's Manual* . . . , 56–57.
"The Wanderers"
  Johnston, Carol A. *Eudora Welty* . . . , 29–30, 98–105.
  Wesley, Marilyn C. "The Woman Traveler . . . ," 257–259.
  Yaeger, Patricia S. " 'Because a Fire . . . ,' " 962–964; rpt. Johnston,
    Carol A. *Eudora Welty* . . . , 211–214.
"Where Is the Voice Coming From"
  Harrison, Suzan. " 'It's Still a Free Country': Constructing Race,
    Identity, and History in Eudora Welty's 'Where Is the Voice Coming
    From?' " *Mississippi Q*, 50, iv (1997), 637–646.
"The Whole World Knows"
  Johnston, Carol A. *Eudora Welty* . . . , 80–82.
  Mortimer, Gail L. "Memory, Despair . . . ," 36–38, 39–40.
"Why I Live at the P.O."
  Baldwin, Dean. *Instructor's Resource* . . . , 134–136.
  Charters, Ann, and William E. Sheidley. *Resources* . . . , 5th ed.,
    241–242.
  Johnston, Carol A. *Eudora Welty* . . . , 16–19.
"The Wide Net"
  Cox, Rosemary. "Green Curtains . . . ," 58–60.
  Warren, Robert P. *The Robert Penn Warren Reader*, 202; rpt. Johnston,
    Carol A. *Eudora Welty* . . . , 163–164.
  Wesley, Marilyn C. "The Woman Traveler . . . ," 264–267.
"The Winds"
  Henderson, Joel. "Tracking the Storms . . . ," 26–28.
  Kreyling, Michael. "History and Imagination: Writing 'The Winds,' "
    Mississippi Q, 50 (1997), 593–598.
"A Worn Path"
  Butterworth, Nancy K. "From Civil War to Civil Rights: Race
    Relations in Welty's 'A Worn Path,' " in Trouard, Dawn, Ed.
    Eudora Welty . . . , 165–172; rpt. Johnston, Carol A. *Eudora
    Welty* . . . , 227–234.
  Charters, Ann, and William E. Sheidley. *Resources* . . . , 5th ed., 243.
  Ford, Joh, and Marjorie Ford. *Instructor's Manual* . . . , 57–58.
  Pollack, Harriet. "Photographic Convention . . . ," 19–22.
  Ritter, Alexander. "Natchez in the Fiction . . . ," 23.
  Sykes, Dennis J. "Welty's 'The Worn Path,' " *Explicator*, 56, iii
    (1998), 151–152.
  Waldron, Ann. *Eudora: A Writer's Life*, 111.

NATHANAEL WEST

"The Fake"
  Veitch, Jonathan. *American Superrealism* . . . , 23–26.
"Miss Lonelyhearts"
  Budniakiewicz, Therese. "The Value of the Notion of Contract to

Literary Interpretation: Greimas, Propp, and West's 'Miss
Lonelyhearts,' " in Rauch, Irmengard, and Gerald F. Carr, Eds.
Semiotics Around the World . . . , 381–384.
Ravvin, Norman. *A House of Words* . . . , 108–109, 111–115, 121–123.
Veitch, Jonathan. *American Superrealism* . . . , xix, 57, 62, 69–87,
99–100, 116–117.

REBECCA WEST

"Adela"
Rollyson, Carl. *The Literary Legacy* . . . , 32–34.
"Indissoluble Matrimony"
Rollyson, Carl. *The Literary Legacy* . . . , 10–12.
"Life Sentence"
Rollyson, Carl. *The Literary Legacy* . . . , 83–84.
"Madame Sara's Magic Crystal"
Rollyson, Carl. *The Literary Legacy* . . . , 175–180.
"The Only Poet"
Rollyson, Carl. *The Literary Legacy* . . . , 218–220.
"The Salt of the Earth"
Rollyson, Carl. *The Literary Legacy* . . . , 112–115.
"There is No Conversation"
Rollyson, Carl. *The Literary Legacy* . . . , 85–87.

EDITH WHARTON

"All Souls"
Beer, Janet. *Kate Chopin, Edith Wharton* . . . , 137–142.
Burleson, Donald R. "Sabbats: Hawthorne/Wharton," *Stud Weird
Fiction*, 12 (1993), 13–16.
"The Angel at the Grave"
Beer, Janet. *Kate Chopin, Edith Wharton* . . . , 126–130.
"Bewitched"
Beer, Janet. *Kate Chopin, Edith Wharton* . . . , 134–137.
Sweeney, Gerard M. "Wharton's 'Bewitched,' " *Explicator*, 56, iv
(1998), 198–201.
"Bunner Sisters"
Campbell, Donna M. *Resisting Regionalism* . . . , 154–160, 171–172.
"The Daunt Diana"
Montgomery, Maureen E. *Displaying Women* . . . , 70–71.
"The Dilettante"
Ford, Joh, and Marjorie Ford. *Instructor's Manual* . . . , 31–32.
"Ethan Frome"
Asya, Ferdâ. "Edith Wharton's Dream of Incest: 'Ethan Frome,' "
Stud Short Fiction, 35 (1998), 23–40.

"Eyes"
Tintner, Adeline R. *Henry James's Legacy* . . . , 27–29.

"False Dawn"
Burbridge, Martha Vanbiesem de. "Un cuento de María Teresa Maiorana frente a uno de Edith Wharton," in Frugoni de Fritzsche, Teresita, Ed. *Primeras Jornadas* . . . , 346–347, 349–353.

"Friends"
Beer, Janet. *Kate Chopin, Edith Wharton* . . . , 123–126.

"Her Son"
Hoeller, Hildegard. "Competing Mothers: Edith Wharton's Late Vision of Family Life," in Herrera, Andrea O., Elizabeth M. Nollen, and Sheila R. Foor, Eds. *Family Matters* . . . , 174–180.

"The Lady's Maid's Bell"
Wilson-Jordan, Jacqueline S. "Telling the Story That Can't Be Told: Hartley's Role as Dis-eased Narrator in 'The Lady's Maid's Bell,' " *Edith Wharton R*, 14, i (1997), 12–17.

"The Legend"
Ware, Michele S. "Making Fun of the Critics: Edith Wharton's Anticipation of the Postmodern Academic Romance," in Sloane, David E. E., Ed. *New Directions* . . . , 151–159.

"The Looking Glass"
Sweeney, Susan E. "Mirror, Mirror, on the Wall: Gazing in Edith Wharton's 'Looking Glass,' " in Reesman, Jeanne C., Ed. *Speaking the Other* . . . , 54–75.

"Mrs. Manstey's View"
Campbell, Donna M. *Resisting Regionalism* . . . , 151–154.

"New Year's Day"
Montgomery, Maureen E. *Displaying Women* . . . , 35–37.

"The Old Maid"
Hoeller, Hildegard. "Competing Mothers. . . ," 168–174.

"The Other Two"
Stange, Margit. *Personal Property* . . . , 46–47.

"The Quicksand'
Singley, Carol J. "Edith Wharton, Religion, and Moral 'Quicksand,' " *Lit & Belief*, 15 (1995), 75–93.

"Roman Fever"
Charters, Ann, and William E. Sheidley. *Resources* . . . , 5th ed., 245–246.

"Writing a War Story"
Gallagher, Jean. "The Great War and the Female Gaze: Edith Wharton and the Iconography of War Propaganda," *Lit Int Theory*, 7, i (1996), 32–37.

"The Young Gentlemen"
Beer, Janet. *Kate Chopin, Edith Wharton* . . . , 130–133.

EDMUND WHITE

"Cinnamon Skin"
Woodhouse, Reed. *Unlimited Embrace* . . . , 287–290.

"An Oracle"
Fulk, Robert D. "Greece and Homosexual Identity in Edmund White's
'An Oracle,' " *Coll Lit*, 24, i (1997), 229–238.

ROBIN WHITE

"Padma"
Nair, Nirmala R. "Images of India and an Affirmation of Being in
Robin White's *Foreign Soil*," *Indian J Am Stud*, 24, i (1994), 27–28.

"Showers of Ashes"
Nair, Nirmala R. "Images of India . . . ," 28, 30.

ZOË WICOMB

"Another Story"
Sicherman, Carol. "Zoë Wicomb's *You Can't Get Lost in Cape Town*:
The Narrator's Identity," *Bucknell R*, 37, i (1993), 119–120.

"A Clearing in the Bush"
Sicherman, Carol. "Zoë Wicomb's . . . ," 115–116.

"Home Sweet Home"
Sicherman, Carol. "Zoë Wicomb's . . . ," 116–117.

JOHN EDGAR WIDEMAN

"Across the Wide Missouri"
Byerman, Keith E. *John Edgar Wideman* . . . , 13–19.

"All Stories Are True"
Byerman, Keith E. *John Edgar Wideman* . . . , 56–60.
Charters, Ann, and William E. Sheidley. *Resources* . . . , 5th ed.,
247–248.

"Backseat"
Byerman, Keith E. *John Edgar Wideman* . . . , 64–70.

"The Beginning of Homewood"
Byerman, Keith E. *John Edgar Wideman* . . . , 29–33.
Rushdy, Ashraf H. A. "Fraternal Blues: John Edgar Wideman's
Homewood Trilogy," *Contemp Lit*, 32, iii (1991), 328; rpt.
Byerman, Keith E. *John Edgar Wideman* . . . , 112.

"Damballah"
Byerman, Keith E. *John Edgar Wideman* . . . , 4–7.

"Doc's Story"
Byerman, Keith E. *John Edgar Wideman* . . . , 39–42.
Ford, Joh, and Marjorie Ford. *Instructor's Manual* . . . , 101–102.

OSCAR WILDE

MICHAEL WILDING

"I Like Him to Write"
Maver, Igor. " 'My Beloved . . . ,' " 88.
"Joe's Absence"
Maver, Igor. " 'My Beloved . . . ,' " 84–85.
"Kayf"
Maver, Igor. " 'My Beloved . . . ,' " 87–88.
"Somewhere New"
Maver, Igor. " 'My Beloved . . . ,' " 84.
"Under Saturn"
Maver, Igor. " 'My Beloved . . . ,' " 87.

KATE WILHELM

"The Village"
Franklin, H. Bruce. "The Vietnam War as American Science Fiction
and Fantasy," in Cooke, Brett, George E. Slusser, and Jaume Marti-
Olivella, Eds. *The Fantastic Other . . .* , 175–177.

JOY WILLIAMS

"Escapes"
Casey, Roger N. *Textual Vehicles . . .* , 144–145.
"Health"
Casey, Roger N. *Textual Vehicles . . .* , 145–146.
"The Last Generation"
Casey, Roger N. *Textual Vehicles . . .* , 147.
"The Little Winter"
Casey, Roger N. *Textual Vehicles . . .* , 145.
"Rot"
Casey, Roger N. *Textual Vehicles . . .* , 140–142.
"The Route"
Casey, Roger N. *Textual Vehicles . . .* , 142–144.

TENNESSEE WILLIAMS

"Hard Candy"
Martin, Robert K. "Gustav von Aschenbach Goes to the Movies:
Thomas Mann in the Joy Rio Stories of Tennessee Williams," *Int'l
Fiction R*, 24, i–ii (1997), 62–63.
Woodhouse, Reed. *Unlimited Embrace . . .* , 43–50.
"The Mysteries of Joy Rio"
Martin, Robert K. "Gustav . . . ," 58–62.
"One Arm"
Woodhouse, Reed. *Unlimited Embrace . . .* , 39–41.

WILLIAM CARLOS WILLIAMS

"A Face of Stone"
King, Nancy M. P., and Ann F. Stanford. "Patient Stories, Doctor Stories, and True Stories: A Cautionary Reading," *Lit & Medicine*, 11 (1992), 194–195.

"Mind and Body"
Crawford, T. Hugh. "The Politics of Narrative Form," *Lit & Medicine*, 11 (1992), 150–160.

"The Use of Force"
Charters, Ann, and William E. Sheidley. *Resources . . .* , 5th ed., 249.

EDMUND WILSON

"The Death of a Soldier"
Castronovo, David. *Edmund Wilson Revisited*, 21.

"Ellen Terhune"
Castronovo, David. *Edmund Wilson Revisited*, 97–98.

"Glimpses of Wilbur Flick"
Castronovo, David. *Edmund Wilson Revisited*, 98–99.

"The Man Who Shot Snapping Turtles"
Castronovo, David. *Edmund Wilson Revisited*, 96–97.

"The Men from Rumpelmayer's"
Castronovo, David. *Edmund Wilson Revisited*, 53–54.

"The Milhollands and Their Damned Soul"
Castronovo, David. *Edmund Wilson Revisited*, 104.

"Mr. and Mrs. Blackburn at Home"
Castronovo, David. *Edmund Wilson Revisited*, 104–105.

"The Princess with the Golden Hair"
Castronovo, David. *Edmund Wilson Revisited*, 99–104.

HARRIET E. WILSON

"Our Nig; or, Sketches from the Life of a Free Black"
Bassard, Katherine C. "Harriet E. Wilson's 'Our Nig' and the American Racial Dream-Text," in Abel, Elizabeth, Barbara Christian, and Helene Moglen, Eds. *Female Subjects . . .* , 187–188, 189–199.
Fishburn, Katherine. *The Problem . . .* , 102–115.
Johnson, Ronna C. "Said But Not Spoken: Ellision and the Representation of Rape, Race, and Gender in Harriet E. Wilson's 'Our Nig,' " in Reesman, Jeanne C., Ed. *Speaking the Other . . .* , 96–116.
Twagilimana, Aimable. *Race and Gender . . .* , 125–131.

THYRA SAMTER WINSLOW

"A Cycle of Manhattan"
Koppelman, Susan. "The Naming of Katz: Who Am I? Who Am I
Supposed to Be? Who Can I Be? Passing, Assimilation, and
Embodiment in Short Fiction by Fannie Hurst and Thyra Samter
Winslow with a Few Jokes Thrown in and Various References to
Other Others," in Brown, Julie, Ed. *Ethnicity* . . . , 237–240.

JEANETTE WINTERSON

"The Poetic of Sex"
Swanson, Diana L. "Playing in Jeanette Winterson's 'The Poetics of
Sex': Rescuing Words for Lesbians," *Lit Int Theory*, 7, iv (1997),
325–337.

CHRISTA WOLF

"June Afternoon"
Resch, Margit. *Understanding Christa Wolf* . . . , 50–53.

"Kassandra"
Hell, Julia. *Post-Fascist Fantasies* . . . , 18, 184, 199, 216–245.

"Moscow Novella"
Hell, Julia. *Post-Fascist Fantasies* . . . , 146–153, 157–163.
Lehnert, Herbert. "Novellentradition und neueste deutsche
Geschichte: Christa Wolfs 'Was bleibt' als 'Gegennovelle' zur ihrer
'Moskauer Novelle,' " in Cramer, Sabine, Ed. *Neues zu Altem* . . . ,
185, 187–201.
Resch, Margit. *Understanding* . . . , 30–33.

"Nagelprobe"
Baldwin, Claire. "Speaking of Art: Ekphrastic Reflections in Postwar
German Literature," in Weninger, Robert, and Brigitte Rossbacher,
Eds. *Wendezeiten* . . . , 144–146.
Hell, Julia. *Post-Fascist Fantasies* . . . , 245–247.

"Self-Experiment: Appendix to a Report"
Resch, Margit. *Understanding* . . . , 77–79.

"Sommerstück"
Resch, Margit. *Understanding* . . . , 138–148.

"Störfall"
Rechtien, Renate. "Christa Wolf and Bertolt Brecht: A Case of
Extended Intertexuality," in Williams, Arthur, Stuart Parkes, and
Julian Preece, Eds. *Contemporary* . . . , 47–49.

"A Tomcat's New Views on Life"
Resch, Margit. *Understanding* . . . , 75–77.

"Unter den Linden"
Resch, Margit. *Understanding* . . . , 71–75.

"Was bleibt"
  Lehnert, Herbert. "Novellentradition . . . ," 194–201.
  Resch, Margit. *Understanding* . . . , 163–168.
  Roethke, Gisela. " 'Was bleibt'—'Nun Ja! Das nächste Leben geht
    aber heute an'—Zur politisch-literarischen Gratwanderung von
    Christa Wolf im Jahre 1979," *Germ Life & Letters*, 48 (1995),
    86–89, 91–95.

GENE WOLFE

"The Detective of Dreams"
  Locey, Kathryn. "Three Dreams, Seven Nights, and Gene Wolfe's
    Catholicism," *New York R Sci Fiction*, 8, xi (1996), 1, 8–9.
"Seven American Nights"
  Locey, Kathryn. "Three Dreams . . . ," 9–12.

THOMAS WOLFE

"Chickamauga"
  Madden, David. "Lost Men: From Gettysburg to Chickamauga,"
    Thomas Wolfe R, 21, ii (1997), 13–14.
"The Four Lost Men"
  Madden, David. "Lost Men . . . ," 10–12.
"The Lost Boy"
  Boyer, James D. "Revisions of Thomas Wolfe's 'The Lost Boy,' "
    Stud Short Fiction, 35 (1998), 8–9.
  Souris, Stephen. "Dialogic Agreement: Thomas Wolfe's 'The Lost
    Boy' and the Multiple Narrator Novel," *Thomas Wolfe R*, 22, ii
    (1998), 17–27.

TOBIAS WOLFF

"Lady's Dream"
  Ford, Joh, and Marjorie Ford. *Instructor's Manual* . . . , 109–110.
"Say Yes"
  Charters, Ann, and William E. Sheidley. *Resources* . . . , 5th ed.,
    250–251.

NORMAN WONG

"Ordinary Chinese People"
  Cheung, King-kok. "Of Men and Men: Reconstructing Chinese
    American Masculinity," in Stanley, Sandra K., Ed. *Other
    Sisterhoods* . . . , 183–185, 186.
"Robbed"
  Cheung, King-kok. "Of Men and Men . . . ," 183.

VIRGINIA WOOLF

"The Fisherman and His Wife"
Goldman, Jane. *The Feminist Aesthetics* . . . , 175–176.

"The Introduction"
Maze, John R. *Virginia Woolf: Feminism* . . . , 80–81.

"Kew Gardens"
Baldwin, Dean. *Instructor's Resource* . . . , 96–98.
Charters, Ann, and William E. Sheidley. *Resources* . . . , 5th ed., 251–252.
Trodd, Anthea. *Women's Writing in English* . . . , 69–70.

"The Mark on the Wall"
Rosenbaum, S. P. *Aspects of Bloomsbury* . . . , 7–9.
Trodd, Anthea. *Women's Writing in English* . . . , 68–69.

"Memoirs of a Novelist"
Blackmer, Corinne E. "Lesbian Modernism in the Shorter Fiction of Virginia Woolf and Gertrude Stein," in Barrett, Eileen, and Patricia Cramer, Eds. *Virginia Woolf* . . . , 82–85.

"Moments of Being: 'Slater's Pins Have No Points' "
Winston, Janet. "Reading Influences: Homoeroticism and Mentoring in Katherine Mansfield's 'Carnation' and Virginia Woolf's 'Moments of Being: "Slater's Pins Have No Points,' " " in Barrett, Eileen, and Patricia Cramer, Eds. *Virginia Woolf* . . . , 68–75.

"Mrs. Dalloway in Bond Street"
Maze, John R. *Virginia Woolf: Feminism* . . . , 61–62.

"The Mysterious Case of Miss V."
Blackmer, Corinne E. "Lesbian Modernism . . . ," 80–82.

"A Simply Melody"
Lackey, Michael. "The Gender of Atheism in Virginia Woolf's 'A Simple Melody,' " *Stud Short Fiction*, 35 (1998), 49–63.

"A Society"
Blackmer, Corinne E. "Lesbian Modernism . . . ," 86–89.

"The Symbol"
Ford, Joh, and Marjorie Ford. *Instructor's Manual* . . . , 37–38.

CONSTANCE FENIMORE WOOLSON

"The Lady of Little Fishing"
Levander, Caroline F. *Voices of the Nation* . . . , 141–145.

RICHARD WRIGHT

"Big Boy Leaves Home"
Osinubi Viktor. "African American Writers and the Use of Dialect in Literature: The Foregrounding of Ethnicity," *J Commonwealth & Postcolonial Stud*, 4, i (1996), 73–75.

"Fire and Cloud"
Mullen, Bill. "Marking Race/Marketing Race: African American Short Fiction and the Politics of Genre, 1933–1946," in Brown, Julie, Ed. *Ethnicity* . . . , 30–31.

"The Man Who Lived Underground"
Rand, William E. "The Structure of the Outsider in the Short Fiction of Richard Wright and F. Scott Fitzgerald," *Coll Lang Assoc J*, 40 (1996), 233–234, 235, 236, 237–242, 243–245.
Weiss, M. Lynn. *Gertrude Stein and Richard* . . . , 9–10.

"The Man Who Was Almost a Man" [originally "Almos' a Man"]
Charters, Ann, and William E. Sheidley. *Resources* . . . , 5th ed., 253–254.
Curnutt, Kirk. *Wise Economies* . . . , 144, 187–199.

WU ZUXIANG

"The Night Before Leaving Home"
Lieberman, Sally T. *The Mother* . . . , 141–142.

"Two Sparrow Chicks"
Lieberman, Sally T. *The Mother* . . . , 161–162.

"The World at Peace"
McDougall, Bonnie S., and Kam Louie. *The Literature of China* . . . , 145.

XIAO JUN

"Goats"
McDougall, Bonnie S., and Kam Louie. *The Literature of China* . . . , 143–144.

XIE BINGYING

"Abandoned"
Lieberman, Sally T. *The Mother* . . . , 142, 149–153.

XU DISHAN

"Big Sister Liu"
McDougall, Bonnie S., and Kam Louie. *The Literature of China* . . . , 101–102.

HISAYE YAMAMOTO

"Las Vegas Charley"
Wang, Qun. "Asian American Short Stories: Dialogizing the Asian

American Experience," in Brown, Julie, Ed. *Ethnicity . . .* ,
117–118.

"The Legend of Miss Sasagawara"
   Streamas, John. "The Invention of Normality in Japanese American
   Internment Narratives," in Brown, Julie, Ed. *Ethnicity . . .* ,
   128–133.

"Seventeen Syllables"
   Baldwin, Dean. *Instructor's Resource . . .* , 144–146.
   Jay, Gregory S. *American Literature . . .* , 127–130.
   Wang, Qun. "Asian American . . . ," 121.

"Wilshire Bus"
   Mullins, Maire. "Esther's Smile: Silence and Action in Hisaye
   Yamamoto's 'Wilshire Bus,' " *Stud Short Fiction*, 35 (1998),
   77–84.

YANG GANG

"Fragment from a Lost Diary"
   Lieberman, Sally T. *The Mother . . .* , 142, 153–154.

YE SHENGTAO

"A Ju"
   Lieberman, Sally T. *The Mother . . .* , 41–43.

"A Life"
   McDougall, Bonnie S., and Kam Louie. *The Literature of China . . .* ,
   103.

"Mr. Pan in Difficulty"
   McDougall, Bonnie S., and Kam Louie. *The Literature of China . . .* ,
   103.

"She and He"
   Lieberman, Sally T. *The Mother . . .* , 38–41.

"Spring Outing"
   Lieberman, Sally T. *The Mother . . .* , 36–38.

ABRAHAM B. YEHOSHUA

"Early in the Summer of 1970"
   Fisch, Harold. *New Stories for Old . . .* , 170–176.

VIKTOR YEROFEYEV

"Death and the Maiden"
   Roll, Serafima. "Re-Surfacing: The Shades of Violence in Viktor
   Yerofeyev's Short Stories," *Australian Slavonic*, 9 ii (1995), 29–32.

"Galoshes"
Roll, Serafima. "Re-Surfacing . . . ," 32–35.
"How We Slew a Frenchman"
Roll, Serafima. "Re-Surfacing . . . ," 39–40.
"Life with an Idiot"
Roll, Serafima. "Re-Surfacing . . . ," 41–44.
"The Parrot"
Roll, Serafima. "Re-Surfacing . . . ," 35–39.
"A White Castrated Cat with the Eyes of a Beauty"
Roll, Serafima. "Re-Surfacing . . . ," 40–41.

ANZIA YEZIERSKA

"The Free Vacation House"
Konzett, Delia C. "Administered Identities and Linguistic
Assimilation: The Politics of Immigrant English in Anzia
Yezierska's *Hungry Hearts*," *Am Lit*, 69 (1997), 606–613.

YIN FU

"King Coal"
Lyell, William A. "Down the Road that Mei Took: Women in Yin Fu's
Work," in Findeisen, Raoul D., and Robert H. Gassmann, Eds.
Autumn Floods . . . , 346–349.
"Little Mother"
Lyell, William A. "Down the Road . . . ," 343–346.
"The Three Eight-ers"
Lyell, William A. "Down the Road . . . ," 341–342.

MARGUERITE YOURCENAR

"Antigone or the Choice"
King, Katherine C. "Antigone's Lyric Heart: Marguerite Yourcenar's
Revision of Sophocles' *Antigone*," in Komar, Kathleen L., and Ross
Shideler, Eds. *Lyrical Symbols* . . . , 67–68, 72–73, 75.

YU DAFU

"Blood and Tears"
Lieberman, Sally T. *The Mother* . . . , 92–94.
"In a Cold Wind"
Lieberman, Sally T. *The Mother* . . . , 94–97.
"Sinking"
Lieberman, Sally T. *The Mother* . . . , 97–102.

McDougall, Bonnie S., and Kam Louie. *The Literature of China* . . . ,
107.

TASKEEN ZAIDI

"The Victor"
Rahim, Habibeh. "The Mirage of Faith and Justice: Some
Sociopolitical and Cultural Themes in Post-Colonial Urdu Short
Stories," in Hawley, John C., Ed. *The Postcolonial Crescent* . . . ,
246–247.

EVGENY I. ZAMIATIN
[SAME AS EVGENIZ ZAMJATIN, EVGENIĬ OR EVGENIJ ZAMJATIN]

"Comrade Churygin Has the Floor"
Platt, Kevin M. F. *History in a Grotesque* . . . , 130–144.

RUF' ALEKSANDROVNA ZERNOVA

"Elizabet Arden"
Ziolkowski, Margaret. *Literary Exorcisms* . . . , 128.

ZHANG CHENGZHI

"Rivers of the North"
McDougall, Bonnie S., and Kam Louie. *The Literature of China* . . . ,
396.

ZHANG JIE

"The Child from the Forest"
McDougall, Bonnie S., and Kam Louie. *The Literature of China* . . . ,
386.

ZHANG TIANYI

"Mr. Hua Wei"
McDougall, Bonnie S., and Kam Louie. *The Literature of China* . . . ,
138–139.

ZHANG XIANLIANG

"Flesh and Soul"
McDougall, Bonnie S., and Kam Louie. *The Literature of China* . . . ,
386–87.

ZHAO SHULI

"Registration"
  McDougall, Bonnie S., and Kam Louie. *The Literature of China* . . . ,
  223–224.

"The Rhymes of Li Youcai"
  McDougall, Bonnie S., and Kam Louie. *The Literature of China* . . . ,
  222–223.

ZHU LIN

"Snake's Pillow"
  King, Richard. "Translator's Postscript: Zhu Lin's Literary Mission,"
  Snake's Pillow . . . [by Zhu Lin], 196–197.

ZITKALA-ŠA

"The School Days of an Indian Girl"
  Ruoff, A. LaVonne B. "Early Native American Women Authors: Jane
  Johnston Schoolcraft, Sarah Winnemucca, S. Alice Callahan, E.
  Pauline Johnson, and Zitkala-Ša," in Kilcup, Karen L., Ed.
  Nineteenth-Century American . . . , 103–104.

PAMELA ZOLINE

"The Heat Death of the Universe"
  Landon, Brooks. *Science Fiction* . . . , 27–30.

MIKHAIL ZOSHCHENKO

"Apollo and Tamara"
  Siniavskii, Andrei. "The Myths of Mikhail Zoshchenko," *Russian
  Stud Lit*, 33, i (1996), 51–55.

"The Electrician"
  Zholkovsky, A. K. "Zoshchenko's 'Electrician,' or the Complex
  Theatrical Mechanism," *Russian Stud Lit*, 33, i (1996–1997),
  59–79.

"The Goat"
  Siniavskii, Andrei. "The Myths . . . ," 40–49.

"Soul's Simplicity"
  Zholkovsky, A. K. "Reinterpreting Zoshchenko: The Case of 'Soul's
  Simplicity,' " *Russian Stud Lit*, 33, ii (1997), 41–48.

"A Terrible Night"
  Siniavskii, Andrei. "The Myths . . . ," 55–57.

ARNOLD ZWEIG

"Die Bestie"
    Cohen, Robert. "Lernprozeß mit offenem Ausgang: Arnold Zweigs
        Kriegsnovellen von 1914 und ihre Frassungen," in Alt, Arthur T.,
        Julia Bernhard, Hans-Harald Müller, and Deborah Vietor-
        Engländer, Eds. *Arnold Zweig* . . . , 147–149.
"Der Feind"
    Cohen, Robert. "Lernprozeß . . . ," 145–146.
"Der Kaffee"
    Cohen, Robert. "Lernprozeß . . . ," 144.
"Quartett von Schönberg"
    Cohen, Robert. "Lernprozeß . . . ," 138–140, 142.
"Die Quittung"
    Cohen, Robert. "Lernprozeß . . . ," 143.
"Der Schießplatz"
    Cohen, Robert. "Lernprozeß . . . ," 145.
"Unterwerfung"
    Cohen, Robert. "Lernprozeß . . . ," 138–139.

STEFAN ZWEIG

"Angst"
    Godé, Maurice. "Innovation littéraire et stéréotypes sociaux dans la
        nouvelle de Stefan Zweig 'Angst (1925),' " *Cahiers d'Etudes Germ*,
        19 (1990), 172–179.
"Schachnovelle"
    Christophe, Alain. "Literarischer Phrasemgebrauch in Stefan Zweigs
        Schachnovelle," in Gréciano, Gertrud, and Annely Rothkegel, Eds.
        Phraseme in Kontext . . . , 17–29.

A Checklist of Books Used

Abel, Elizabeth, Barbara Christian, and Helene Moglen, Eds. *Female Subjects in Black and White: Race, Psychoanalysis, Feminism.* Berkeley: Univ. of California Press, 1997.

Acheson, James. *Samuel Beckett's Artistic Theory and Practice: Criticism, Drama and Early Fiction.* London: MacMillan Press, 1997; Am. ed. New York: St. Martin's Press, 1997.

Aching, Gerard. *The Politics of Spanish American Modernismo: By Exquisite Design.* Cambridge: Cambridge Univ. Press, 1997.

Adamson, Joseph. *Melville, Shame, and the Evil Eye: A Psychoanalytic Reading.* Albany: State Univ. of New York Press, 1997.

Adebayo, Aduke, Ed. *Feminism and Black Women's Creative Writing: Theory, Practice, and Criticism.* Ibadan, Nigeria: AMD, 1996.

Aizenberg, Edna. *Borges, el tejedor del Aleph y otros ensayos: Del hebraísmo al poscolonialismo.* Madrid: Iberoamericana, 1997.

Akiyama, Masayuki, and Yiu-nam Leung, Eds. *Crosscurrents in the Literatures of Asia and the West: Essays in Honor of A. Owen Aldridge.* Cranbury, N.J.: Assoc. Univ. Presses [for Univ. of Delaware Press], 1997.

Alcira Arancibia, Juana, and Luis A. Jiménez, Eds. *Protestas, interrogantes y agonías en la obra de Rima de Vallbona,* III. Westminster, Calif.: Instituto Literario y Cultura Hispánico, 1997.

Alexander, Doris. *Creating Literature Out of Life: The Making of Four Masterpieces.* University Park: Pennsylvania State Univ., 1996.

Alkana, Joseph. *The Social Self: Howells, William James, and Nineteenth-Century Psychology.* Lexington: Univ. Press of Kentucky, 1997.

Allen, Carol. *Black Women Intellectuals: Strategies of Nation, Family, and Neighborhood in the Works of Pauline Hopkins, Jessie Fauset, and Marita Bonner.* New York: Garland, 1998.

Alley, Henry. *The Quest for Anonymity: The Novels of George Eliot.* Cranbury, N. J.: Assoc. Univ. Presses [for Univ. of Delaware Press], 1997.

Almon, Bert. *William Humphrey: Destroyer of Myths.* Denton: Univ. of North Texas Press, 1998.

Alonso, Carlos J., Ed. *Julio Cortázar: New Readings.* Cambridge: Cambridge Univ. Press, 1998.

Alt, Arthur T., Julia Bernhard, Hans-Harald Müller, and Deborah Vietor-Engländer, Eds. *Arnold Zweig: Berlin—Haifa—Berlin; Perspektiven des Gesamtwerks; Akten des III. Internationalen Arnold-Zweig-Symposiums, Berlin 1993.* Bern, Switzerland: Peter Lang, 1995.

Andermatt, Michael, Ed. *Grenzgänge: Studien zu L. Achim von Arnim.* Bonn, Germany: Bouvier, 1994.

Anderson, Bo, and Gernot Müller, Eds. *Kleine Beiträge zur Germanistik: Festschrift für John Evert Härd.* Uppsala, Sweden: Uppsala Univ., 1997.

Anim-Addo, Joan, Ed. *Framing the Word: Gender and Genre in Caribbean Women's Writing.* London: Whiting & Birch, 1997; Am. ed. Concord, Mass.: Paul & Company, 1997.

Annesley, James. *Blank Fictions: Consumerism, Culture and the Contemporary American Novel.* New York: St. Martin's Press, 1998.

Arat, Zehra F., Ed. *Deconstructing Images of "The Turkish Woman."* New York: St. Martin's Press, 1998.

Armstrong, Tim. *Modernism, Technology, and the Body: A Cultural Study.* Cambridge: Cambridge Univ. Press, 1998.

Asholt, Wolfgang, Ed. *Intertextualität und Subversivität: Studien zur Romanliteratur der achtziger Jahre in Frankreich.* Heidelberg: Carl Winter Univ.-verl, 1994.

Auckenthaler, Karlheinz F., Ed. *Numinoses und Heiliges in der österreichischen Literatur.* Bern, Switzerland: Peter Lang, 1995.

Bacarisse, Pamela, Ed. *Tradición y actualidad de la literatura iberoamericana.* Pittsburgh, Penn.: Univ. of Pittsburgh Press, 1995.

Baker, Phil. *Beckett and the Mythology of Psychoanalysis.* London: MacMillan Press, 1997; Am. ed. New York: St. Martin's Press, 1997.

Balakian, Nona. *The World of William Saroyan.* Cranbury, N.J.: Assoc. Univ. Presses [for Bucknell Univ. Press], 1998.

Baldwin, Dean. *Instructor's Resource Manual [for] "The Riverside Anthology of Short Fiction: Convention and Innovation."* Boston: Houghton Mifflin, 1998.

Barfoot, C. C., and Theo D'haen, Eds. *Shades of Empire in Colonial and Post-Colonial Literatures.* Amsterdam: Rodopi, 1993.

Barnes, Elizabeth. *States of Sympathy: Seduction and Democracy in the American Novel.* New York: Columbia Univ. Press, 1997.

Barnstone, Aliki, Michael T. Manson, and Carol J. Singley, Eds. *The Calvinist Roots of the Modern Era.* Hanover, N.H.: Univ. Press of New England, 1997.

Barrett, Eileen, and Patricia Cramer, Eds. *Virginia Woolf: Lesbian Readings.* New York: New York Univ. Press, 1997.

Bassanese, Fiora A. *Understanding Luigi Pirandello.* Columbia: Univ. of South Carolina Press, 1997.

Baxter, Charles. *Burning Down the House: Essays on Fiction.* Saint Paul, Minn.: Graywolf Press, 1997.

Becket, Fiona. *D. H. Lawrence: The Thinker as Poet.* London: MacMillan Press, 1997; Am. ed. New York: St. Martin's Press, 1997.

Beekman, E. M. *Troubled Pleasures: Dutch Colonial Literature from the East Indies, 1600–1950.* Oxford: Clarendon Press, 1996.

Beer, Janet. *Kate Chopin, Edith Wharton and Charlotte Perkins Gilman: Studies in Short Fiction.* London: MacMillan Press, 1997; Am. ed. New York: St. Martin's Press, 1997.

Bell, Michael. *Literature, Modernism and Myth: Belief and Responsibility in the Twentieth Century.* Cambridge: Cambridge Univ. Press, 1997.

Bender, Todd K. *Literary Impressionism in Jean Rhys, Ford Madox Ford, Joseph Conrad, and Charlotte Brontë.* New York: Garland, 1997.

Benson, Jackson J. *Wallace Stegner: A Study of the Short Fiction.* New York: Twayne, 1998.

Berg, William J., and Laurey K. Martin. *Gustave Flaubert.* New York: Twayne, 1997.

Bergmann, Emilie L., and Paul J. Smith, Eds. *¿Entiendes? Queer Readings, Hispanic Writings.* Durham: Duke Univ. Press, 1995.

Bethea, David M. *Realizing Metaphors: Alexander Pushkin and the Life of the Poet.* Madison: Univ. of Wisconsin Press, 1998.

Bigsby, Christopher, Ed. *The Cambridge Companion to Arthur Miller.* Cambridge: Cambridge Univ. Press, 1997.

Billy, Ted. *A Wilderness of Words: Closure and Disclosure in Conrad's Short Fiction.* Lubbock: Texas Tech Univ. Press, 1997.

Bivona, Daniel. *British Imperial Literature, 1870–1940: Writing and the Administration of Empire.* Cambridge: Cambridge Univ. Press, 1998.

Bjorklund, Beth, and Mark E. Corey, Eds. *Politics in German Literature.* Columbia, S.C.: Camden House, 1998.

Blanchot, Maurice. *Awaiting Oblivion (L'Attente l'oubli)*, trans. John Gregg. Lincoln: Univ. of Nebraska Press, 1997.

Bloom, Clive, Ed. *Creepers: British Horror and Fantasy in the Twentieth Century.* London: Pluto Press, 1993.

——, Ed. *Gothic Horror: A Reader's Guide from Poe to King and Beyond.* New York: St. Martin's Press, 1998.

Bloom, Harold, Ed. *Hispanic-American Writers.* Philadelphia: Chelsea House, 1998.

——, Ed. *Lesbian and Bisexual Fiction Writers.* Philadelphia: Chelsea House, 1997.

Bloom, James D. *The Literary Bent: In Search of High Art in Contemporary American Writing.* Philadelphia: Univ. of Pennsylvania Press, 1997.

Blotner, Joseph. *Robert Penn Warren: A Biography.* New York: Random House, 1997.

Bodi, Leslie, Günter Helmes, Egon Schwarz, and Friedrich Voit, Eds. *Weltbürger— Textwelten.* Frankfurt: Peter Lang, 1995.

Bogaards, Winnifred M., Ed. *Literature of Region and Nation: Proceedings of the 6th International Literature of Region and Nation Conference,* I-II. Saint John, Canada: Univ. of New Brunswick in Saint John, 1998.

Bondanella, Peter. *Umberto Eco and the Open Text: Semiotics, Fiction, Popular Culture.* Cambridge: Cambridge Univ. Press, 1997.

Booker, John T., and Allan H. Pasco, Eds. *The Play of Terror in Nineteenth-Century France.* Cranbury, N. J.: Assoc. Univ. Presses [for Univ. of Delaware Press], 1997.

Boone, Joseph A. *Libidinal Currents: Sexuality and the Shaping of Modernism.* Chicago: Univ. of Chicago Press, 1998.

Borland, Isabel A. *Cuban-American Literature of Exile: From Person to Persona.* Charlottesville: Univ. Press of Virginia, 1998.

Böschenstein, Bernhard, and Marie-Louise Roth, Eds. *Homage à Musil.* New York: Peter Lang, 1995.

Bosinelli, Rosa M. B., and Harold F. Mosher, Eds. *ReJoycing: New Readings of Dubliners.* Lexington: Univ. Press of Kentucky, 1998.

Bowers, Bege K., and Barbara Brothers, Eds. *Reading and Writing Women's Lives: A Study of the Novel of Manners.* Ann Arbor: UMI Research Press, 1990.

Brannigan, John. *New Historicism and Cultural Materialism.* New York: St. Martin's Press, 1998.

——, Geoff Ward, and Julian Wolfreys, Eds. *Re:Joyce: Text, Culture, Politics.* London: MacMillan Press, 1998; Am. ed. New York: St. Martin's Press, 1998.

Brennan, Matthew C. *The Gothic Psyche: Disintegration and Growth in Nineteenth-Century English Literature.* Columbia, S.C.: Camden House, 1997.

Brinker-Gabler, Gisela, and Sidonie Smith, Eds. *Writing New Identities: Gender, Nation, and Immigration in Contemporary Europe.* Minneapolis: Univ. of Minnesota Press, 1997.

Bristow, Joseph, and Trev L. Broughton, Eds. *The Infernal Desires of Angela Carter: Fiction, Femininity, Feminism.* London: Longman, 1997.

Broer, Lawrence R., Ed. *Rabbit Tales: Poetry and Politics in John Updike's Rabbit Novels.* Tuscaloosa: Univ. of Alabama Press, 1998.

Brokoph-Mauch, Gudrun, Ed. *Thunder Rumbling at My Heels: Tracing Ingeborg Bachmann.* Riverside, Calif.: Ariadne Press, 1998.

Brown, Hilda M. *Heinrich von Kleist: The Ambiguity of Art and the Necessity of Form.* Oxford: Clarendon Press, 1998.

Brown, Janice. *The Seven Deadly Sins in the Work of Dorothy L. Sayers.* Kent: Kent State Univ. Press, 1998.

Brown, Julia P. *Cosmopolitan Criticism: Oscar Wilde's Philosophy of Art.* Charlottesville: Univ. Press of Virginia, 1997.

Brown, Julie, Ed. *Ethnicity and the American Short Story.* New York: Garland, 1997.

Brown-Guillory, Elizabeth, Ed. *Women of Color: Mother-Daughter Relationships in 20th-Century Literature.* Austin: Univ. of Texas Press, 1996.

Brownlow, Jeanne P., and John W. Kronik, Eds. *Intertextual Pursuits: Literary Mediations in Modern Spanish Narrative.* Cranbury, N. J.: Assoc. Univ. Presses [for Bucknell Univ. Press], 1998.

Bryant, J. A. *Twentieth-Century Southern Literature.* Lexington: Univ. Press of Kentucky, 1997.

Bryant, John, and Robert Milder, Eds. *Melville's Evermoving Dawn: Centennial Essays.* Kent: Kent State Univ. Press, 1997.

Brydon, Diana. *Timothy Findley.* New York: Twayne, 1998.

Buelens, Gert, Ed. *Enacting History in Henry James: Narrative, Power, and Ethics.* Cambridge: Cambridge Univ. Press, 1997.

Buelens, Gert, and Ernst Rudin, Eds. *Deferring a Dream: Literary Sub-Versions of the American Columbiad.* Basel, Switzerland: Birkhäuser Verlag, 1994.

Buisine, Alain, and Norbert Dodille, Eds. *L'Exotisme.* Paris: Didier-Erudition, 1998.

Bullivant, Keith, Ed. *Beyond 1989: Re-Reading German Literary History Since 1945.* Providence, R.I.: Berghahn, 1997.

Buning, Marius, Danielle De Ruyter, Matthijs Engelberts, and Sjef Houppermans, Eds. *Beckett Versus Beckett.* Amsterdam: Rodopi, 1998.

Butler, Robert. *Contemporary African American Fiction: The Open Journey.* Cranbury, N.J.: Assoc. Univ. Presses [for Fairleigh Dickinson Univ. Press], 1998.

Byerman, Keith E. *John Edgar Wideman: A Study of the Short Fiction.* New York: Twayne, 1998.

Bygrave, Stephen, Ed. *Romantic Writings.* New York: Routledge, 1996.

Cabello-Castellet, George, Jaume Martí-Olivella, and Guy H. Wood, Eds. *Cine-Lit II: Essays on Hispanic Film and Fiction.* Portland: Portland State Univ. Press, 1995.

Caesar, Ann H. *Characters and Authors in Luigi Pirandello.* Oxford: Clarendon Press, 1998.

Callow, Philip. *Chekhov: The Hidden Ground, A Biography.* Chicago: Ivan R. Dee, 1998.

Camfield, Gregg. *Necessary Madness: The Humor of Domesticity in Nineteenth-Century American Literature.* Oxford: Oxford Univ. Press, 1997.

Caminero-Santangelo, Marta. *The Madwoman Can't Speak: Or Why Insanity Is Not Subversive.* Ithaca: Cornell Univ. Press, 1998.

Campbell, Donna M. *Resisting Regionalism: Gender & Naturalism in American Fiction, 1885–1915.* Athens: Ohio Univ. Press, 1997.

Caponi, Gena D. *Paul Bowles.* New York: Twayne, 1998.

Carabine, Keith, Owen Knowles, and Paul Armstrong, Eds. *Conrad, James and Other Relations.* Boulder, Colo.: Social Science Monographs, 1998.

Cardoni, Agnes T. *Women's Ethical Coming-of-Age: Adolescent Female Characters in the Prose Fiction of Tillie Olsen.* Lanham, Md.: Univ. Press of America, 1998.

Cardy, Michael, George Evans, and Gabriel Jacobs, Eds. *Narrative Voices in Modern French Fiction: Studies in Honour of Valerie Minogue on the Occasion of Her Retirement.* Cardiff: Univ. of Wales Press, 1997.

Carlson, Harry G. *Out of Inferno: Strindberg's Reawakening as an Artist.* Seattle: Univ. of Washington Press, 1996.

Carmean, Karen. *Ernest J. Gaines: A Critical Companion.* Westport, Conn.: Greenwood Press, 1998.

Carter, Steven R. *James Jones: An American Literary Orientalist Master.* Urbana: Univ. of Illinois Press, 1998.

Casey, Janet G. *Dos Passos and the Ideology of the Feminine.* Cambridge: Cambridge Univ. Press, 1998.

Casey, Roger N. *Textual Vehicles: The Automobile in American Literature.* New York: Garland, 1997.

Cassuto, Leonard. *The Inhuman Race: The Racial Grotesque in American Literature and Culture.* New York: Columbia Univ. Press, 1997.

Castillo, Debra A. *Easy Women: Sex and Gender in Modern Mexican Fiction.* Minneapolis: Univ. of Minnesota Press, 1998.

Castillo, Susan, Ed. *Engendering Identities.* Porto, Portugal: Universidade Fernando Pessoa, 1996.

Castronovo, David. *Edmund Wilson Revisited.* New York: Twayne, 1998.

Cather, Willa. *Alexander's Bridge,* ed. Marilee Lindemann. Oxford: Oxford Univ. Press, 1997.

Chancy, Myriam J. A. *Framing Silence: Revolutionary Novels by Haitian Women.* New Brunswick, N.J.: Rutgers Univ. Press, 1997.

Charters, Ann, and William E. Sheidley. *Resources for Teaching "The Story and Its Writer: An Introduction to Short Fiction, Fifth Edition."* Boston: St. Martin's Press, 1998.

Cheung, King-Kok, Ed. *An Interethnic Companion to Asian American Literature.* Cambridge: Cambridge Univ. Press, 1997.

Christie, John S. *Latino Fiction and the Modernist Imagination: Literature of the Borderlands.* New York: Garland, 1998.

Civello, Catherine A. *Patterns of Ambivalence: The Fiction and Poetry of Stevie Smith.* Columbia, S. C.: Camden House, 1997.

Clark, Suzanne. *Sentimental Modernism: Women Writers and the Revolution of the Word.* Bloomington: Indiana Univ. Press, 1991.

Clayton, J. Douglas, Ed. *Chekhov Then and Now: The Reception of Chekhov in World Culture.* New York: Peter Lang, 1997.

Clifford, Stephen P. *Beyond the Heroic "I": Reading Lawrence, Hemingway, and "Masculinity."* Cranbury, N.J.: Assoc. Univ. Presses [for Bucknell Univ. Press], 1998.

Coates, John. *The Day's Work: Kipling and the Idea of Sacrifice.* Cranbury, N. J.: Assoc. Univ. Presses [for Fairleigh Dickinson Univ. Press], 1997.

Coelsch-Foisner, Sabine, and Wolfgang Görtschacher, Eds. *Trends in English and American Studies: Literature and the Imagination.* Lewiston, N.Y.: Edwin Mellen, 1996.

Colacurcio, Michael J. *Doctrine and Difference:Essays in the Literature of New England.* New York: Routledge, 1997.

Coleman, Daniel. *Masculine Migrations: Reading the Postcolonial Male in 'New Canadian' Narratives.* Toronto: Univ. of Toronto Press, 1998.

Collard, Patrick, Ed. *La memoria histórica en las letras hispánicas contemporáneas.* Geneva, Switzerland: Droz, 1997.

Coloquio Internacional: El texto latinoamericano, I-II. Madrid: Editorial Fundamentos, 1994.

Conger, Syndy M., Frederick S. Frank, and Gregory O'Dea, Eds. *Iconoclastic Departures: Mary Shelley After* Frankenstein: *Essays in Honor of the Bicentenary of Mary Shelley's Birth.* Cranbury, N.J.: Assoc. Univ. Presses [for Fairleigh Dickinson Univ. Press], 1997.

Cooke, Brett, George E. Slusser, and Jaume Marti-Olivella, Eds. *The Fantastic Other: An Interface of Perspectives.* Amsterdam: Rodopi, 1998.

Corcoran, Neil. *After Yeats and Joyce: Reading Modern Irish Literature.* Oxford: Oxford Univ. Press, 1997.

Corpa Vargas, Mirta. *Los cuentos de Liliana Heker: Testimonios de vida.* New York: Peter Lang, 1996.

Court, Antoine, Ed. *Le Populaire à l'ombre des clochers.* Saint-Étienne, France: Publications de l'Université de Saint-Étienne, 1997.

Covici, Pascal. *Humor and Revelation in American Literature: The Puritan Connection.* Columbia: Univ. of Missouri Press, 1997.

Craig, David M. *Tilting at Mortality: Narrative Strategies in Joseph Heller's Fiction.* Detroit: Wayne State Univ. Press, 1997.

Cramer, Sabine, Ed. *Neues zu Altem: Novellen der Vergangenheit und der Gegenwart.* Munich: Fink, 1996.

Crane, Ralph J., and Jennifer Livett. *Troubled Pleasures: The Fiction of J. G. Farrell.* Dublin: Four Courts Press, 1997.

Crisman, William. *The Crises of "Language and Dead Signs" in Ludwig Tieck's Prose Fiction.* Columbia, S.C.: Camden House, 1996.

Crockett, Roger A. *Understanding Friedrich Dürrenmatt.* Columbia: Univ. of South Carolina Press, 1998.

Cronin, Gloria L., Ed. *Critical Essays on Zora Neale Hurston.* New York: G. K. Hall, 1998.

Curnutt, Kirk. *Wise Economies: Brevity and Storytelling in American Short Stories.* Moscow: Univ. of Idaho Press, 1997.

Currie, Mark. *Postmodern Narrative Theory.* New York: St. Martin's Press, 1998.

Dadlez, E. M. *What's Hecuba to Him?: Fictional Events and Actual Emotions.* University Park: Pennsylvania State Univ. Press, 1997.

Daleski, H. M. *Thomas Hardy and Paradoxes of Love.* Columbia: Univ. of Missouri Press, 1997.

Danow, David K. *Models of Narrative: Theory and Practice.* New York: St. Martin's Press, 1997.

Danson, Lawrence. *Wilde's Intentions: The Artist in His Criticism.* Oxford: Oxford Univ. Press, 1997.

David, Claude, Intro. *Les Songes de la raison: Mélanges offerts à Dominique Iehl.* Bern, Switzerland: Peter Lang, 1995.

Davies, Catherine. *Spanish Women's Writing, 1849–1996.* London: Athlone Press, 1998.

Davis, Clark. *After the Whale: Melville in the Wake of Moby-Dick.* Tuscaloosa: Univ. of Alabama Press, 1995.

Davis, Terry. *Presenting Chris Crutcher.* New York: Twayne, 1997.

Davison, Ray. *Camus: The Challenge of Dostoevsky.* Exeter: Univ. of Exeter Press, 1997.

Day, Aidan. *Angela Carter: The Rational Glass.* Manchester: Manchester Univ. Press, 1998.

Dean, Misao. *Practising Femininity: Domestic Realism and the Performance of Gender in Early Canadian Fiction.* Toronto: Univ. of Toronto Press, 1998.

Debatin, Bernhard, Timothy R. Jackson, and Daniel Steuer, Eds. *Metaphor and Rational Discourse.* Tübingen, Germany: Niemeyer, 1997.

Delamater, Jerome H., and Ruth Prigozy, Eds. *The Detective in American Fiction, Film, and Television.* Westport, Conn.: Greenwood Press, 1998.

————, Eds. *Theory and Practice of Classic Detective Fiction.* Westport, Conn.: Greenwood Press, 1997.

DeLamotte, Eugenia C. *Places of Silence, Journeys of Freedom: The Fiction of Paule Marshall.* Philadelphia: Univ. of Pennsylvania Press, 1998.

Delbanco, Andrew. *Required Reading: Why Our American Classics Matter Now.* New York: Farrar, Straus and Giroux, 1997.

Delrez, Marc, and Bénédicte Ledent, Eds. *The Contact and the Culmination.* Liège, Belgium: Liège Language and Literature, 1997.

DeMouy, Jane K. *Katherine Anne Porter's Women: The Eye of Her Fiction.* Austin: Univ. of Texas Press, 1983.

Derrick, Scott S. *Monumental Anxieties: Homoerotic Desire and Feminine Influence in 19th-Century U.S. Literature.* New Brunswick, N.J.: Rutgers Univ. Press, 1997.

DeShell, Jeffrey. *The Peculiarity of Literature: An Allegorical Approach to Poe's Fiction.* Cranbury, N. J.: Assoc. Univ. Presses [for Fairleigh Dickinson Univ. Press], 1997.

D'haen, Theo, and Hans Bertens, Eds. *"Writing" Nation and "Writing" Region in America.* Amsterdam: VU Univ. Press, 1996.

Díaz, Gwendolyn, and María I. Lagos, Eds. *La palabra en vilo: Narrativa de Luisa Valenzuela*. Santiago, Chile: Editorial Cuarto Propio, 1996.

Diethe, Carol. *Towards Emancipation: German Women Writers of the Nineteenth Century*. New York: Berghahn Books, 1998.

Disch, Thomas M. *The Dreams Our Stuff Is Made Of: How Science Fiction Conquered the World*. New York: Free Press, 1998.

Doležel, Lubomír. *Heterocosmica: Fiction and Possible Worlds*. Baltimore: Johns Hopkins Univ. Press, 1998.

Donawerth, Jane. *Frankenstein's Daughters: Women Writing Science Fiction*. Syracuse: Syracuse Univ. Press, 1997.

Donovan, Kathleen M. *Feminist Readings of Native American Literature: Coming to Voice*. Tucson: Univ. of Arizona Press, 1998.

Dowie, William. *James Salter*. New York: Twayne, 1998.

Dowling, Finuala. *Fay Weldon's Fiction*. Cranbury, N.J.: Assoc. Univ. Presses [for Fairleigh Dickinson Univ. Press], 1998.

Drews, Jörg, Ed. *Vergangene Gegenwart—Gegenwärtige Vergangenheit: Studien, Polemiken und Laudationes zur deutschprachigen Literatur, 1960–1964*. Bielefeld, Germany: Aisthesis, 1994.

Dubois, Dominique, Laurent Lepaludier, and Jacques Sohier, Eds. *Les Nouvelles de Katherine Mansfield*. Angers, France: Presses Univ. d'Angers, 1998.

Dubois, Lionel, Ed. *Albert Camus entre la misère et le soleil*. Poitiers, France: Pont-Neuf, 1997.

Dunbar, Pamela. *Radical Mansfield: Double Discourse in Katherine Mansfield's Short Stories*. London: MacMillan Press, 1997; Am. ed. New York: St. Martin's Press, 1997.

Duncan, Charles. *The Absent Man: The Narrative Craft of Charles W. Chesnutt*. Athens: Ohio Univ. Press, 1998.

Durzak, Manfred, and Hartmut Steinecke, Eds. *F. C. Delius: Studien über sein literarisches Werk*. Tübingen, Germany: Stauffenburg, 1997.

Edmundson, Mark. *Nightmare on Main Street: Angels, Sadomasochism, and the Culture of Gothic*. Cambridge: Harvard Univ. Press, 1997.

Efimov, Nina A., Christine D. Tomei, and Richard L. Chapple, Eds. *Critical Essays on the Prose and Poetry of Modern Slavic Women*. Lewiston, N.Y.: Edwin Mellen, 1998.

Eggert, Paul, and John Worthen, Eds. *Lawrence and Comedy*. Cambridge: Cambridge Univ. Press, 1996.

Elfenbein, Anna S. *Women on the Color Line: Evolving Stereotypes and the Writings of George Washington Cable, Grace King, and Kate Chopin*. Charlottesville: Univ. Press of Virginia, 1989.

Elkins, Marilyn, Ed. *Critical Essays on Kay Boyle*. New York: G. K. Hall, 1997.

Ellis, David. *D. H. Lawrence: Dying Game, 1922–1930*. Cambridge: Cambridge Univ. Press, 1998.

Elmer, Jonathan. *Reading at the Social Limit: Affect, Mass Culture, and Edgar Allan Poe*. Stanford: Stanford Univ. Press,1995.

Evans, Robert C., and Richard Harp, Eds. *Frank O'Connor: New Perspectives*. West Cornwall, Conn.: Locust Hill Press, 1998.

Ewell, Barbara C., Ed. *Performance for a Lifetime: A Festschrift Honoring Dorothy Harrell Brown: Essays on Women, Religion, and the Renaissance*. New Orleans: Loyola Univ. Press, 1997.

Ezenwa-Ohaeto. *Chinua Achebe: A Biography*. Oxford: James Curry, 1997; Am. ed. Bloomington: Indiana Univ. Press, 1997.

Farrell, James T. *Chicago Stories*, ed. Charles Fanning. Urbana: Univ. of Illinois Press, 1998.

Feinstein, Elaine. *Pushkin: A Biography*. Hopewell, N.J.: Ecco Press, 1998.

Felton, Sharon, and Michelle C. Loris, Eds. *The Critical Response to Gloria Naylor.* Westport, Conn.: Greenwood Press, 1997.

Feng, Pin-chia. *The Female* Bildungsroman *by Toni Morrison and Maxine Hong Kingston: A Postmodern Reading.* New York: Peter Lang, 1998.

Fiddian, Robin, Ed. *García Márquez.* London: Longman, 1995.

Findeisen, Raoul D., and Robert H. Gassmann, Eds. *Autumn Floods: Essays in Honour of Marián Gálik.* Bern, Switzerland: Peter Lang, 1998.

Fisch, Harold. *New Stories for Old: Biblical Patterns in the Novel.* London: MacMillan Press, 1998; Am. ed. New York: St. Martin's Press, 1998.

Fischer, Susanne, Ed. *"Umgängliche Nachbarn erwarten euch": Zu Arno Schmidts "Die Umsiedler."* Bargfeld, Germany: Arno Schmidt Stiftung, 1995.

Fishburn, Katherine. *The Problem of Embodiment in Early African American Narrative.* Westport, Conn.: Greenwood Press, 1997.

Fisher, Barbara M. *Noble Numbers, Subtle Words: The Art of Mathematics in the Science of Storytelling.* Cranbury, N. J.: Assoc. Univ. Presses [for Fairleigh Dickinson Univ. Press], 1997.

Folks, Jeffrey J., and James A. Perkins, Eds. *Southern Writers at Century's End.* Lexington: Univ. Press of Kentucky, 1997.

Forbes, F. William, Teresa Méndez-Faith, Mary-Anne Vetterling, and Barbara H. Wing, Eds. *Reflections on the Conquest of America: Five Hundred Years After.* Durham: Univ. of New Hampshire, 1996.

Ford, Jane M. *Patriarchy and Incest from Shakespeare to Joyce.* Gainesville: Univ. Press of Florida, 1998.

Ford, Joh, and Marjorie Ford. *Instructor's Manual [for] "The Web of Stories."* Upper Saddle River, N.J.: Prentice Hall, 1998.

Foster, David W., and Daniel Altamiranda, Eds. *Theoretical Debates in Spanish American Literature.* New York: Garland, 1997.

———, Eds. *Twentieth-Century Spanish American Literature since 1960.* New York: Garland, 1997.

———, Eds. *Twentieth-Century Spanish American Literature to 1960.* New York: Garland, 1997.

Foster, Dennis A. *Sublime Enjoyment: On the Perverse Motive in American Literature.* Cambridge: Cambridge Univ. Press, 1997.

Foster, Thomas, Carol Siegel, and Ellen E. Berry, Eds. *Bodies of Writing, Bodies in Performance.* New York: New York Univ. Press, 1996.

Foulke, Robert. *The Sea Voyage Narrative.* New York: Twayne, 1997.

Fowler, Doreen. *Faulkner: The Return of the Repressed.* Charlottesville: Univ. Press of Virginia, 1997.

Franci, Giovanna, Ed. *Remapping the Boundaries: A New Perspective in Comparative Studies.* Bologna, Italy: CLUEB, 1997.

Frederick, Bonnie. *Wily Modesty: Argentine Women Writers, 1860–1910.* Tempe: Arizona State Univ. Center for Latin American Studies Press, 1998.

Freedman, Jonathan, Ed. *The Cambridge Companion to Henry James.* Cambridge: Cambridge Univ. Press, 1998.

Frugoni de Fritzsche, Teresita, Ed. *Primeras Jornadas Internacionales de Literatura Argentina/Comparística: Actas.* Buenos Aires: Facultad de Filosofía y Letras, Univ. de Buenos Aires, 1996.

Fulford, Tim, and Peter J. Kitson, Eds. *Romanticism and Colonialism: Writing and Empire, 1780–1830.* Cambridge: Cambridge Univ. Press, 1998.

Furman, Andrew. *Israel Through the Jewish-American Imagination: A Survey of Jewish-American Literature on Israel, 1928–1995.* Albany: State Univ. of New York Press, 1997.

Gaard, Greta, and Patrick D. Murphy, Eds. *Ecofeminist Literary Criticism: Theory, Interpretation, Pedagogy.* Urbana: Univ. of Illinois Press, 1998.

Gaggi, Silvio. *From Text to Hypertext: Decentering the Subject in Fiction, Film, the Visual Arts, and Electronic Media.* Philadelphia: Univ. of Pennsylvania Press, 1997.

Galván, Delia V., Anita K. Stoll, and Philippa B. Yin, Eds. *Studies in Honor of Bleznick.* Newark, Del: Juan de la Cuesta, 1995.

Gamble, Sarah. *Angela Carter: Writing from the Front Line.* Edinburgh: Edinburgh Univ. Press, 1997.

Gambrell, Alice. *Women Intellectuals, Modernism, and Difference: Transatlantic Culture, 1919–1945.* Cambridge: Cambridge Univ. Press, 1997.

Gandal, Keith. *The Virtues of the Vicious: Jacob Riis, Stephen Crane, and the Spectacle of the Slum.* Oxford: Oxford Univ. Press, 1997.

García de Juan, Miguel Ángel. *Los cuentos de Pío Baroja: Creación, recepción y discurso.* Madrid: Editorial Pliegos, 1997.

Gardner, Jared. *Master Plots: Race and the Founding of an American Literature, 1787–1845.* Baltimore: Johns Hopkins Univ. Press, 1998.

Garza-Falcón, Leticia M. *Gente Decente: A Borderlands Response to the Rhetoric of Dominance.* Austin: Univ. of Texas Press, 1998.

Gasperetti, David. *The Rise of the Russian Novel: Carnival, Stylization, and Mockery of the West.* DeKalb: Northern Illinois Univ. Press, 1998.

Gassenmeier, Michael, Petra Bridzun, Jens M. Gurr, and Frank E. Pointner, Eds. *British Romantics as Readers: Intertextualities, Maps of Misreadings, Reinterpretations.* Heidelberg, Germany: Winter, 1998.

Gatta, John. *American Madonna: Images of the Divine Woman in Literary Culture.* Oxford: Oxford Univ. Press, 1997.

Gifford, Douglas, and Dorothy McMillan, Eds. *A History of Scottish Women's Writing.* Edinburgh: Edinburgh Univ. Press, 1997.

Giles, James R. *Understanding Hubert Selby, Jr.* Columbia: Univ. of South Carolina Press, 1998.

Gilman, Sander L., and Jack Zipes, Eds. *Yale Companion to Jewish Writing and Thought in German Culture, 1096–1996.* New Haven: Yale Univ. Press, 1997.

Gilmartin, Sophie. *Ancestry and Narrative in Nineteenth-Century British Literature: Blood Relations from Edgeworth to Hardy.* Cambridge: Cambridge Univ. Press, 1998.

Giordano, Paolo A., and Anthony J. Tamburri, Eds. *Beyond the Margin: Readings in Italian Americana.* Cranbury, N. J.: Assoc. Univ. Presses [for Fairleigh Dickinson Univ. Press], 1998.

Girard, René. *Resurrection from the Underground: Feodor Dostoevsky,* ed. and trans. James G. Williams. New York: Crossroad, 1997.

Gitay, Yehoshua, Ed. *Literary Responses to the Holocaust: 1945–1995.* San Francisco: International Scholars Publications, 1998.

Glassman, Steve, and Kathryn L. Seidel, Eds. *Zora in Florida.* Orlando: Univ. of Central Florida Press, 1991.

Goddu, Teresa A. *Gothic America: Narrative, History, and Nation.* New York: Columbia Univ. Press, 1997.

Goldman, Jane. *The Feminist Aesthetics of Virginia Woolf: Modernism, Post-Impressionism and the Politics of the Visual.* Cambridge: Cambridge Univ. Press, 1998.

Gölz, Sabine I. *The Split Scene of Reading: Nietzsche / Derrida / Kafka / Bachmann.* Atlantic Highlands, N.J.: Humanities Press, 1998.

Gonzalez, Alexander G. *Peadar O'Donnell: A Reader's Guide.* Chester Springs, Penn.: Dufour, 1997.

González, José E. *Borges and the Politics of Form.* New York: Garland, 1998.

Goodman, Nan. *Shifting the Blame: Literature, Law, and the Theory of Accidents in Nineteenth-Century America.* Princeton: Princeton Univ. Press, 1998.

Goodman, Susan. *Ellen Glasgow: A Biography.* Baltimore: Johns Hopkins Univ. Press, 1998.

Goossen, Theodore, Ed. *The Oxford Book of Japanese Short Stories*. Oxford: Oxford Univ. Press, 1997.

Gordon, Joan, and Veronica Hollinger, Eds. *Blood Read: The Vampire as Metaphor in Contemporary Culture*. Philadelphia: Univ. of Pennsylvania Press, 1997.

Gorra, Michael. *After Empire: Scott, Naipaul, Rushdie*. Chicago: Univ. of Chicago Press, 1997.

Gough, Val, and Jill Rudd, Eds. *A Very Different Story: Studies on the Fiction of Charlotte Perkins Gilman*. Liverpool: Liverpool Univ. Press, 1998.

Gould, Warwick, and Thomas E. Staley, Eds. *Writing the Lives of Writers*. London: MacMillan Press, 1998; Am. ed. New York: St. Martin's Press, 1998.

Graziano, Frank. *The Lust of Seeing: Themes of the Gaze and Sexual Rituals in the Fiction of Felisberto Hernández*. Cranbury, N.J.: Assoc. Univ. Presses [for Bucknell Univ. Press], 1997.

Gréciano, Gertrud, and Annely Rothkegel, Eds. *Phraseme in Kontext und Kontrast*. Bochum, Germany: Brockmeyer, 1997.

Gretlund, Jan N., and Karl-Heinz Westarp, Eds. *The Late Novels of Eudora Welty*. Columbia: Univ. of South Carolina Press, 1998.

Griffin, Clive. *Los de abajo*. London: Grant & Cutler, 1993.

Griffith, Clark. *Achilles and the Tortoise: Mark Twain's Fictions*. Tuscaloosa: Univ. of Alabama Press, 1998.

Guglielminetti, Marziano, Intro. *Studi di storia della civiltà letteraria francese*, II. Paris: Champion, 1996.

Guilds, John C., and Caroline Collins, Eds. *William Gilmore Simms and the American Frontier*. Athens: Univ. of Georgia Press, 1997.

Gutiérrez, Mariela A. *Lydia Cabrera: Aproximaciones mítico-simbólicas a su cuentística*. Madrid: Editorial Verbum, 1997.

Haber, Edythe C. *Mikhail Bulgakov: The Early Years*. Cambridge: Harvard Univ. Press, 1998.

Hadda, Janet. *Isaac Bashevis Singer: A Life*. Oxford: Oxford Univ. Press, 1997.

Halio, Jay L., and Ben Siegel, Eds. *Daughters of Valor: Contemporary Jewish American Women Writers*. Cranbury, N. J.: Assoc. Univ. Presses [for Univ. of Delaware Press], 1997.

Hall, Caroline K. B. *Sylvia Plath, Revised*. New York: Twayne, 1998.

Hallisey, Joan F., and Mary-Anne Vetterling, Eds. *Proceedings: Northeast Regional Meeting of the Conference on Christianity and Literature*. Weston, Mass.: Regis College, 1996.

Hansen, Elaine T. *Mother Without Child: Contemporary Fiction and the Crisis of Motherhood*. Berkeley: Univ. of California Press, 1997.

Hanson, Ellis. *Decadence and Catholicism*. Cambridge: Harvard Univ. Press, 1997.

Härle, Gerhard, Maria Kalveram, and Wolfgang Popp, Eds. *Erkenntniswunsch und Diskretion: Erotik in biographischer und autobiographischer Literatur*. Berlin: Rosa Winkel, 1992.

Harrison, Elizabeth J., and Shirley Peterson, Eds. *Unmanning Modernism: Gendered Re-Readings*. Knoxville: Univ. of Tennessee Press, 1997.

Harrison, Russell. *Patricia Highsmith*. New York: Twayne, 1997.

Hart, Clive, C. George Sandulescu, Bonnie K. Scott, and Fritz Senn, Eds. *Images of Joyce*. Gerrards Cross, England: Colin Smythe, 1998.

Harwell, Thomas M. *Porter & Eliot: "Flowering Judas" & "Burbank-Bleistein,"* Two *Essays in Interpretation*. Lewiston, N.Y.: Edwin Mellen, 1996.

Haviland, Beverly. *Henry James's Last Romance: Making Sense of the Past and the American Scene*. Cambridge: Cambridge Univ. Press, 1997.

Hawley, John C., Ed. *The Postcolonial Crescent: Islam's Impact on Contemporary Literature*. New York: Peter Lang, 1998.

Hebel, Udo J., and Karl Ortseifen, Eds. *Transatlantic Encounters: Studies in European-American Relations*. Trier, Germany: Wissenschaftlicher Verlag, 1995.

Heise, Ursula K. *Chronoschisms: Time, Narrative, and Postmodernism*. Cambridge: Cambridge Univ. Press, 1997.

Hell, Julia. *Post-Fascist Fantasies: Psychoanalysis, History, and the Literature of East Germany*. Durham: Duke Univ. Press, 1997.

Helmuth, Chalene. *The Postmodern Fuentes*. Cranbury, N.J.: Assoc. Univ. Presses [for Bucknell Univ. Press], 1997.

Hendershot, Cyndy. *The Animal Within: Masculinity and the Gothic*. Ann Arbor: Univ. of Michigan Press, 1998.

Hendrick, Willene, and George Hendrick. *Katherine Anne Porter*. New York: Twayne, 1995.

Herminghouse, Patricia, and Magda Mueller, Eds. *Gender and Germanness: Cultural Productions of Nations*. Providence, R.I.: Berghahn Books, 1997.

Hernández de López, Ana M., Ed. *Narrativa hispanoamericana contemporánea: Entre la vanguardia y el posboom*. Madrid: Editorial Pliegos, 1996.

Herrera, Andrea O., Elizabeth M. Nollen, and Sheila R. Foor, Eds. *Family Matters in the British and American Novel*. Bowling Green: Bowling Green State Univ. Popular Press, 1997.

Herrera, Sara P., Ed. *El cuento mexicano: Homenaje a Luis Leal*. Mexico City: Universidad Nacional Autónoma de México, 1996.

Herzog, Tobey C. *Tim O'Brien*. New York: Twayne, 1997.

Higbie, Robert. *Dickens and Imagination*. Gainesville: Univ. Press of Florida, 1998.

Hinds, Elizabeth J. W. *Private Property: Charles Brockden Brown's Gendered Economies of Virtue*. Cranbury, N.J.: Assoc. Univ. Presses [for Univ. of Delaware Press], 1997.

Hiney, Tom. *Raymond Chandler: A Biography*. New York: Atlantic Monthly Press, 1997.

Hix, H. L. *Understanding W. S. Merwin*. Columbia: Univ. of South Carolina Press, 1997.

Hofkosh, Sonia. *Sexual Politics and the Romantic Author*. Cambridge: Cambridge Univ. Press, 1998.

Hollis, Daniel W. *The ABC-CLIO World History Companion to Utopian Movements*. Santa Barbara, Calif.: ABC-CLIO, 1998.

Hönnighausen, Lothar. *Faulkner: Masks and Metaphors*. Jackson: Univ. Press of Mississippi, 1997.

Horan, Patrick M. *The Importance of Being Paradoxical: Maternal Presence in the Works of Oscar Wilde*. Cranbury, N. J.: Assoc. Univ. Presses [for Fairleigh Dickinson Univ. Press], 1997.

Horner, Avril, and Sue Zlosnik. *Daphne du Maurier: Writing, Identity and the Gothic Imagination*. London: MacMillan Press, 1998; Am. ed. New York: St. Martin's Press, 1998.

Horowitz, Sara R. *Voicing the Void: Muteness and Memory in Holocaust Fiction*. Albany: State Univ. of New York Press, 1997.

Horvath, Brooke, Irving Malin, and Paul Ruffin, Eds. *A Goyen Companion: Appreciations of a Writer's Writer*. Austin: Univ. of Texas Press, 1997.

Howells, Coral A. *Alice Munro*. Manchester: Manchester Univ. Press, 1998.

Howells, William Dean. *Selected Short Stories of William Dean Howells*, ed. Ruth Bardon. Athens: Ohio Univ. Press, 1997.

Hsia, Adrian, Ed. *Kafka and China*. Bern, Switzerland: Peter Lang, 1996.

Hughes, Kathryn. *George Eliot: The Last Victorian*. New York: Farrar Straus Giroux, 1998.

Hughes, William, and Andrew Smith, Eds. *Bram Stoker: History, Psychoanalysis and the Gothic*. London: MacMillan Press, 1998; Am. ed. New York: St. Martin's Press, 1998.

Hurston, Zora Neale. *The Complete Stories*, intro. Henry L. Gates and Sieglinde Lemke. New York: HarperCollins, 1995.

Hutchings, Stephen C. *Russian Modernism: The Transfiguration of the Everyday*. Cambridge: Cambridge Univ. Press, 1997.

Hyvernaud, Georges. *The Cattle Car*, trans. Dominic Di Bernardi and Austryn Wainhouse. Evanston, Ill.: The Marlboro Press/Northwestern, 1997.

Inness, Sherrie A., and Diana Royer, Eds. *Breaking Boundaries: New Perspectives on Women's Regional Writing*. Iowa City: Univ. of Iowa Press, 1997.

James, William C. *Locations of the Sacred: Essays on Religion, Literature, and Canadian Culture*. Waterloo, Ontario: Wilfrid Laurier Univ. Press, 1998.

Jarrett-Macauley, Delia. *The Life of Una Marson, 1905–65*. Manchester: Manchester Univ. Press, 1998; Am. ed. New York: St. Martin's Press, 1998.

Jaskoski, Helen. *Leslie Marmon Silko: A Study of the Short Fiction*. New York: Twayne, 1998.

Jay, Gregory S. *American Literature and the Culture Wars*. Ithaca: Cornell Univ. Press, 1997.

Johnson, Barbara. *The Feminist Difference: Literature, Psychoanalysis, Race, and Gender*. Cambridge: Harvard Univ. Press, 1998.

Johnson, Claudia D. *Understanding "Of Mice and Men," "The Red Pony," and "The Pearl": A Student Casebook to Issues, Sources, and Historical Documents*. Westport, Conn.: Greenwood Press, 1997.

Johnson, Greg. *Invisible Writer: A Biography of Joyce Carol Oates*. New York: Dutton, 1998.

Johnson, Steven. *Interface Culture: How New Technology Transforms the Way We Create and Communicate*. New York: HarperCollins, 1997.

Johnston, Carol A. *Eudora Welty: A Study of the Short Fiction*. New York: Twayne, 1997.

Jones, Anne G., and Susan V. Donaldson, Eds. *Haunted Bodies: Gender and Southern Texts*. Charlottesville: Univ. Press of Virginia, 1997.

Jones, Gayl. *Liberating Voices: Oral Tradition in African American Literature*. Cambridge: Harvard Univ. Press, 1991.

Jones, Michael P. *Conrad's Heroism: A Paradise Lost*. Ann Arbor, Mich.: UMI Research Press, 1985.

Judd, Catherine. *Bedside Seductions: Nursing and the Victorian Imagination, 1830–1880*. New York: St. Martin's Press, 1998.

Kain, Geoffrey, Ed. *Ideas of Home: Literature of Asian Migration*. East Lansing: Michigan State Univ. Press, 1997.

Kalogeras, Yiorgos, and Domna Pastourmatzi, Eds. *Nationalism and Sexuality: Crises of Identity*. Thessaloníki, Greece: Hellenic Association of American Studies, Aristotle University, 1996.

Kamuf, Peggy. *The Division of Literature: Or the University in Deconstruction*. Chicago: Univ. of Chicago Press, 1997.

Kane, Leslie, Ed. *David Mamet's* Glengarry Glen Ross: *Text and Performance*. New York: Garland, 1996.

Kartiganer, Donald M., and Ann J. Abadie, Eds. *Faulkner in Cultural Context: Faulkner and Yoknapatawpha, 1995*. Jackson: Univ. Press of Mississippi, 1997.

———, Eds. *Faulkner and Gender: Faulkner and Yoknapatawpha, 1994*. Jackson: Univ. Press of Mississippi, 1996.

Kaylor, Noel H., Ed. *Creative and Critical Approaches to the Short Story*. Lewiston, N.Y.: Edwin Mellen, 1997.

Keefe, Terry. *Simone de Beauvoir*. New York: St. Martin's Press, 1998.

Kelleher, Margaret. *The Feminization of Famine: Expressions of the Inexpressible?* Durham: Duke Univ. Press, 1997.

Kelly, Joseph. *Our Joyce: From Outcast to Icon*. Austin: Univ. of Texas Press, 1998.

Kelly, Kathleen C. *A. S. Byatt*. New York: Twayne, 1996.

Kennedy, J. Gerald, and Jackson R. Bryer, Eds. *French Connections: Hemingway and Fitzgerald Abroad*. New York: St. Martin's Press, 1998.

Kestner, Joseph A. *Sherlock's Men: Masculinity, Conan Doyle, and Cultural History.* Aldershot, England: Ashgate, 1997.

Kibbey, Ann, Thomas Foster, Carol Siegel, and Ellen Berry, Eds. *On Your Left: The New Historical Materialism in the 1990s.* New York: New York Univ. Press, 1996.

Kilcup, Karen L., Ed. *Nineteenth-Century American Women Writers: A Critical Reader.* Oxford: Blackwell, 1998.

King, Debra W. *Deep Talk: Reading African American Literary Names.* Charlottesville: Univ. Press of Virginia, 1998.

Kinney, Arthur F. *Dorothy Parker, Revised.* New York: Twayne, 1998.

Klinkowitz, Jerome. *Vonnegut in Fact: The Public Spokesmanship of Personal Fiction.* Columbia: Univ. of South Carolina Press, 1998.

Knabe, Peter-Eckhard, and Johannes Thiele, Eds. *Uber Texte: Festschrift für Karl-Ludwig Selig.* Tübingen, Germany: Stauffenburg, 1997.

Knight, Denise D. *Charlotte Perkins Gilman: A Study of the Short Fiction.* New York: Twayne, 1997.

Kolmerten, Carol A., Stephen M. Ross, and Judith B. Wittenberg, Eds. *Unflinching Gaze: Morrison and Faulkner Re-Envisioned.* Jackson: Univ. Press of Mississippi, 1997.

Koloski, Bernard. *Kate Chopin: A Study of the Short Fiction.* New York: Twayne, 1996.

Komar, Kathleen L., and Ross Shideler, Eds. *Lyrical Symbols and Narrative Transformations: Essays in Honor of Ralph Freedman.* Columbia, S. C.: Camden House, 1998.

Kontje, Todd. *Women, the Novel, and the German Nation, 1771–1871: Domestic Fiction in the Fatherland.* Cambridge: Cambridge Univ. Press, 1998.

Korte, Barbara. *Body Language in Literature.* Toronto: Univ. of Toronto Press, 1997.

Kosmider, Alexia. *Tricky Tribal Discourse: The Poetry, Short Stories, and Fus Fixico Letters of Creek Writer Alex Posey.* Moscow: Univ. of Idaho Press, 1998.

Kossew, Sue, Ed. *Critical Essays on J. M. Coetzee.* New York: G. K. Hall, 1998.

Kramer, Michael, Ed. *New Essays on Seize the Day.* Cambridge: Cambridge Univ. Press, 1998.

Kubitschek, Missy D. *Toni Morrison: A Critical Companion.* Westport, Conn.: Greenwood Press, 1998.

Kumbier, William, and Ann Colley, Eds. *Afterimages: A Festschrift in Honor of Irving Massey.* Buffalo, N.Y.: Shuffaloff, 1996.

Kurczaba, Alex S., Ed. *Conrad and Poland.* Boulder, Colo.: East European Monographs, 1996.

Kuribayashi, Tomoko, and Julie Tharp, Eds. *Creating Safe Space: Violence and Women's Writing.* Albany: State Univ. of New York Press, 1998.

Labrie, Ross. *The Catholic Imagination in American Literature.* Columbia: Univ. of Missouri Press, 1997.

Lachmann, Renate. *Memory and Literature: Intertextuality in Russian Modernism,* trans. Roy Sellars and Anthony Wall. Minneapolis: Univ. of Minnesota Press, 1997.

Lahusen, Thomas. *How Life Writes the Book: Real Socialism and Socialist Realism in Stalin's Russia.* Ithaca: Cornell Univ. Press, 1997.

Lamb-Faffelberger, Margarete, Ed. *Out from the Shadows: Essays on Contemporary Austrian Women Writers and Filmmakers.* Riverside, Calif.: Ariadne Press, 1997.

Landon, Brooks. *Science Fiction After 1900: From the Steam Man to the Stars.* New York: Twayne, 1997.

Lassner, Phyllis. *British Women Writers of World War II: Battlegrounds of Their Own.* London: MacMillan Press, 1998; Am. ed. New York: St. Martin's Press, 1998.

Leff, Leonard J. *Hemingway and His Conspirators: Hollywood, Scribners, and the Making of American Celebrity Culture.* New York: Rowman & Littlefield, 1997.

Lehan, Richard. *The City in Literature: An Intellectual and Cultural History.* Berkeley: Univ. of California Press, 1998.

Lerner, Laurence. *Angels and Absences: Child Deaths in the Nineteenth Century.* Nashville: Vanderbilt Univ. Press, 1997.

Levander, Caroline F. *Voices of the Nation: Women and Public Speech in Nineteenth-Century American Literature and Culture.* Cambridge: Cambridge Univ. Press, 1998.

Levine, Robert S., Ed. *The Cambridge Companion to Herman Melville.* Cambridge: Cambridge Univ. Press, 1998.

Lewis, Sinclair. *If I Were Boss: The Early Business Stories of Sinclair Lewis*, ed. Anthony Di Renzo. Carbondale: Southern Illinois Univ. Press, 1997.

Lewis, Ward B. *The Ironic Dissident: Frank Wedekind in the View of His Critics.* Columbia, S. C.: Camden House, 1997.

Lieberman, Sally T. *The Mother and Narrative Politics in Modern China.* Charlottesville: Univ. Press of Virginia, 1998.

Lindstrom, Naomi. *The Social Conscience of Latin American Writing.* Austin: Univ. of Texas Press, 1998.

Little, Jonathan. *Charles Johnson's Spiritual Imagination.* Columbia: Univ. of Missouri Press, 1997.

Lloyd, Tom. *Crises of Realism: Representing Experience in the British Novel, 1816–1910.* Cranbury, N.J.: Assoc. Univ. Presses [for Bucknell Univ. Press], 1997.

Lockerbie, D. Bruce. *Dismissing God: Modern Writers' Struggle Against Religion.* Grand Rapids, Mich.: Baker Books, 1998.

Logan, Deborah A. *Fallenness in Victorian Women's Writing: Marry, Stitch, Die, or Do Worse.* Columbia: Univ. of Missouri Press, 1998.

López Mena, Sergio, Ed. *Revisión crítica de la obra de Juan Rulfo.* Mexico: Editorial Praxis, 1998.

Lord, Ursula. *Solitude Versus Solidarity in the Novels of Joseph Conrad: Political and Epistemological Implications of Narrative Innovation.* Montreal: McGill-Queen's Univ. Press, 1998.

Loselle, Andrea. *History's Double: Cultural Tourism in Twentieth-Century French Writing.* New York: St. Martin's Press, 1997.

Lounsberry, Barbara, et al., Eds. *The Tales We Tell: Perspectives on the Short Story.* Westport, Conn.: Greenwood Press, 1998.

Lowe, John. *Jump at the Sun: Zora Neale Hurston's Classic Comedy.* Urbana: Univ. of Illinois Press, 1994.

Luckhurst, Roger. *"The Angle Between Two Walls": The Fiction of J. G. Ballard.* New York: St. Martin's Press, 1997.

Lueck, Beth L. *American Writers and the Picturesque Tour: The Search for National Identity, 1790–1860.* New York: Garland, 1997.

Luis, William. *Dance Between Two Cultures: Latino Caribbean Literature Written in the United States.* Nashville: Vanderbilt Univ. Press, 1997.

Lungstrum, Janet, and Elizabeth Sauer, Eds. *Agonistics: Arenas of Creative Contest.* Albany: State Univ. of New York Press, 1997.

Lurie, Susan. *Unsettled Subjects: Restoring Feminist Politics to Poststructuralist Critique.* Durham: Duke Univ. Press, 1997.

McCarthy, Desmond F. *Reconstructing the Family in Contemporary American Fiction.* New York: Peter Lang, 1997.

McCarthy, Patrick A., and Paul Tiessen, Eds. *Joyce/Lowry: Critical Perspectives.* Lexington: Univ. Press of Kentucky, 1997.

McCormack, Jerusha, Ed. *Wilde the Irishman.* New Haven: Yale Univ. Press, 1998.

McDougall, Bonnie S., and Kam Louie. *The Literature of China in the Twentieth Century.* New York: Columbia Univ. Press, 1997.

McFarland, Ron. *The World of David Wagoner.* Moscow: Univ. of Idaho Press, 1997.

McGlathery, James M. *E. T. A. Hoffmann.* New York: Twayne, 1997.

McGuirk, Bernard. *Latin American Literature: Symptoms, Risks and Strategies of Post-Structuralist Criticism.* London: Routledge, 1997.

McKay, Nellie Y., and Kathryn Earle, Eds. *Approaches to Teaching the Novels of Toni Morrison*. New York: Modern Language Association, 1997.

McKnight, Natalie J. *Suffering Mothers in Mid-Victorian Novels*. New York: St. Martin's Press, 1997.

McLaren, Joseph. *Langston Hughes: Folk Dramatist in the Protest Tradition, 1921–1943*. Westport, Conn.: Greenwood Press, 1997.

McLaughlin, Martin. *Italo Calvino*. Edinburgh: Edinburgh Univ. Press, 1998.

Mahony, Christina H. *Contemporary Irish Literature: Transforming Tradition*. New York: St. Martin's Press, 1998.

Maier, John. *Desert Songs: Western Images of Morocco and Moroccan Images of the West*. Albany: State Univ. of New York, 1996.

Marigny, Jean, Intro. *Images fantastiques du corps: Actes du colloque, 13–14–15 mars 1997*. Grenoble: Université Stendhal, 1998.

Marin, Louis. *Cross-Readings*, trans. Jane M. Todd. Atlantic Highlands, N.J.: Humanities Press, 1998.

Marrero Henríquez, José M. *Documentación y lirismo en la narrativa de Ignacio Aldecoa*. Las Palmas: Universidad de las Palmas de Gran Canaria, 1997.

Marshall, Ian. *Story Line: Exploring the Literature of the Appalachian Trail*. Charlottesville: Univ. Press of Virginia, 1998.

Martin, Robert K., and George Piggford, Eds. *Queer Forster*. Chicago: Univ. of Chicago Press, 1997.

Martin, Robert K., and Eric Savoy, Eds. *American Gothic: New Interventions in a National Narrative*. Iowa City: Univ. of Iowa Press, 1998.

Martin, Terry J. *Rhetorical Deception in the Short Fiction of Hawthorne, Poe, and Melville*. Lewiston, N.Y.: Edwin Mellen, 1998.

Matus, Jill. *Toni Morrison*. Manchester: Manchester Univ. Press, 1998; Am. ed. New York: St. Martin's Press, 1998.

Matute, Ana María. *Celebration in the Northwest*, trans. Phoebe A. Porter. Lincoln: Univ. of Nebraska Press, 1997.

Maze, John R. *Virginia Woolf: Feminism, Creativity, and the Unconscious*. Westport, Conn.: Greenwood Press, 1997.

Meij, Dick van der, Ed. *India and Beyond: Aspects of Literature, Meaning, Ritual and Thought*. London: Kegan Paul International, 1997.

Meletinsky, Eleazar M. *The Poetics of Myth*, trans. Guy Lanoue and Alexandre Sadetsky. New York: Garland, 1998.

Melzer, Sondra. *The Rhetoric of Rage: Women in Dorothy Parker*. New York: Peter Lang, 1997.

Meredith, George. *George Meredith's 1895 Collection of Three Stories: Explorations of Gender and Power*, ed. Elizabeth J. Deis. Lewiston, N.Y.: Edwin Mellen, 1997.

Meyer, Martin, Gabriele Spengemann, and Wolf Kindermann, Eds. *Tangenten: Literatur & Geschichte*. Münster, Germany: Lit, 1996.

Middleton, David L., Ed. *Toni Morrison's Fiction: Contemporary Criticism*. New York: Garland, 1997.

Miller, Barbara S., Ed. *Masterworks of Asian Literature in Comparative Perspective: A Guide for Teaching*. Armonk, N.Y.: Sharpe, 1994.

Miller, J. Hillis. *Reading Narrative*. Norman: Univ. of Oklahoma Press, 1998.

Moix, Ana María. *Dangerous Virtues*, trans. Margaret E. W. Jones. Lincoln: Univ. of Nebraska Press, 1997.

Monteiro, George. *The Presence of Pessoa: English, American, and Southern African Literary Responses*. Lexington: Univ. Press of Kentucky, 1998.

Montgomery, Maureen E. *Displaying Women: Spectacles of Leisure in Edith Wharton's New York*. New York: Routledge, 1998.

Moore, Gene M., Owen Knowles, and J. H. Stape, Eds. *Conrad: Intertexts & Appropriations: Essays in Memory of Yves Hervouet*. Amsterdam: Rodopi, 1997.

Morrison, Jeff, and Florian Krobb, Eds. *Text Into Image: Image Into Text, Proceedings*

*of the Interdisciplinary Bicentenary Conference Held at St. Patrick's College May-
nooth (The National University of Ireland) in September 1995.* Amsterdam: Rodopi,
1997.

Moseley, Merritt. *Understanding Julian Barnes.* Columbia: Univ. of South Carolina
Press, 1997.

Müller-Waldeck, Gunnar, and Roland Ulrich, Eds. *Hans Fallada: Beiträge zu Leben
und Werk.* Rostock, Germany: Hinstorff, 1995.

Murphy, John J., Linda H. Adams, Richard H. Cracroft, and Susan E. Howe, Eds.
Flannery O'Connor and the Christian Mystery. Provo, Utah: Center for the Study
of Christian Values in Literature, Brigham Young Univ., 1997.

Najder, Zdzisław. *Conrad in Perspective: Essays on Art and Fidelity.* Cambridge:
Cambridge Univ. Press, 1997.

Nalbantian, Suzanne, Ed. *Anaïs Nin: Literary Perspectives.* New York: St. Martin's
Press, 1997.

Nanney, Lisa. *John Dos Passos.* New York: Twayne, 1998.

Natanson, Maurice. *The Erotic Bird: Phenomenology in Literature.* Princeton:
Princeton Univ. Press, 1998.

Navarette, Susan J. *The Shape of Fear: Horror and the Fin de Siècle Culture of Decadence.* Lexington: Univ. Press of Kentucky, 1998.

Nelles, William. *Frameworks: Narrative Levels and Embedded Narrative.* New York:
Peter Lang, 1997.

New, W. H. *Land Sliding: Imagining Space, Presence, and Power in Canadian Writing.* Toronto: Univ. of Toronto Press, 1997.

Nickerson, Catherine R. *The Web of Iniquity: Early Detective Fiction by American
Women.* Durham: Duke Univ. Press, 1998.

Nielsen, Aldon L. *C. L. R. James: A Critical Introduction.* Jackson: Univ. Press of
Mississippi, 1997.

Niemi, Robert. *Russell Banks.* New York: Twayne, 1997.

Norris, Christopher, Ed. *Inside the Myth: Orwell: Views from the Left.* London: Lawrence & Wishart, 1984.

Nuernberg, Susan M., Ed. *The Critical Response to Jack London.* Westport, Conn.:
Greenwood Press, 1995.

Nutter, Ronald G. *A Dream of Peace: Art and Death in the Fiction of John Gardner.*
New York: Peter Lang, 1997.

O'Dwyer, Michael. *Julien Green: A Critical Study.* Portland, Ore.: Four Courts Press,
1997.

O'Farrell, Mary A. *Telling Complexions: The Nineteenth-Century English Novel and
the Blush.* Durham: Duke Univ. Press, 1997.

O'Hara, J. D. *Samuel Beckett's Hidden Drives: Structural Uses of Depth Psychology.*
Gainesville: Univ. Press of Florida, 1997.

Olson, Barbara K. *Authorial Divinity in the Twentieth Century: Omniscient Narration
in Woolf, Hemingway, and Others.* Cranbury, N.J.: Assoc. Univ. Presses [for Bucknell Univ. Press], 1997.

O'Neill, Terry, Ed. *Readings on* Animal Farm. San Diego: Greenhaven Press, 1998.

Østergaard, Svend. *The Mathematics of Meaning,* trans. Kenneth Tindall. Oxford:
Alden Press [for Aarhus Univ. Press], 1997.

Paolini, Claire J., Ed. *La Chispa '97: Selected Proceedings.* New Orleans: Tulane
Univ.Press, 1997.

Parlej, Piotr. *The Romantic Theory of the Novel: Genre and Reflection in Cervantes,
Melville, Flaubert, Joyce, and Kafka.* Baton Rouge: Louisiana State Univ. Press,
1997.

Parrish, Nancy C. *Lee Smith, Annie Dillard, and the Hollins Group: A Genesis of
Writers.* Baton Rouge: Louisiana State Univ. Press, 1998.

Patai, Daphne. *The Orwell Mystique: A Study of Male Ideology.* Amherst: Univ. of
Massachusetts Press, 1984.

Patteson, Richard F. *Caribbean Passages: A Critical Perspective on New Fiction from the West Indies.* Boulder, Colo.: Lynne Rienner, 1998.

Pattillo-Hess, John, and Wilhelm Petrasch, Eds. *Ingeborg Bachmann: Die Schwarz-kunst der Worte.* Vienna, Austria: Verein Volksbildungshaus Weiner Urania, 1993.

Peach, Linden. *Angela Carter.* New York: St. Martin's Press, 1998.

Peavler, Terry J., and Peter Standish, Eds. *Structures of Power: Essays on Twentieth-Century Spanish-American Fiction.* Albany: State Univ. of New York Press, 1996.

Peck, John. *War, the Army and Victorian Literature.* London: MacMillan Press, 1998; Am. ed. New York: St. Martin's Press, 1998.

Peeples, Scott. *Edgar Allan Poe Revisited.* New York: Twayne, 1998.

Pender, Malcolm. *Contemporary Images of Death and Sickness: A Theme in German-Swiss Literature.* Sheffield: Sheffield Academic Press, 1998.

Pereira, Frederico, Ed. *Eleventh International Conference on Literature and Psychology.* Lisbon: Instituto Superior de Psicologia Aplicada, 1995.

Peters, Pearlie M.F. *The Assertive Women in Zora Neale Hurston's Fiction, Folklore, and Drama.* New York: Garland, 1998.

Peterson, Nadya L. *Subversive Imaginations: Fantastic Prose and the End of Soviet Literature, 1970s-1990s.* Boulder, Colo: Westview Press, 1997.

Peterson, Nancy J., Ed. *Toni Morrison: Critical and Theoretical Approaches.* Baltimore: Johns Hopkins Univ. Press, 1997.

Peyser, Thomas. *Utopia & Cosmopolis: Globalization in the Era of American Literary Realism.* Durham: Duke Univ. Press, 1998.

Pilipp, Frank, Ed. *The Legacy of Kafka in Contemporary Austrian Literature.* Riverside, Calif.: Ariadne, 1997.

Pilling, John. *Beckett Before Godot.* Cambridge: Cambridge Univ. Press, 1997.

Platt, Kevin M. F. *History in a Grotesque Key: Russian Literature and the Idea of Revolution.* Stanford: Stanford Univ. Press, 1997.

Plouffe, Bruce. *The Post-War Novella in German-Language Literature: An Analysis.* New York: AMS Press, 1998.

Preston, Cathy L., Ed. *Folklore, Literature, and Cultural Theory: Collected Essays.* New York: Garland, 1995.

Prier, A., and Gerald Gillespie, Eds. *Narrative Ironies.* Amsterdam: Rodopi, 1997.

Putney, Charles R., Joseph A. C. King, and Sally Sugarman, Eds. *Sherlock Holmes: Victorian Sleuth to Modern Hero.* Lanham, Md.: Scarecrow Press, 1996.

Quayson, Ato. *Strategic Transformations in Nigerian Writing: Orality and History in the Work of Rev. Samuel Johnson, Amos Tutuola, Wole Soyinka and Ben Okri.* Oxford: James Currey, 1997; Am. ed. Bloomington: Indiana Univ. Press, 1997.

Quirk, Tom. *Mark Twain: A Study of the Short Fiction.* New York: Twayne, 1997.

Raby, Peter, Ed. *The Cambridge Companion to Oscar Wilde.* Cambridge: Cambridge Univ. Press, 1997.

Rado, Lisa, Ed. *Modernism, Gender, and Culture: A Cultural Studies Approach.* New York: Garland, 1997.

Raitt, Suzanne, and Trudi Tate, Eds. *Women's Fiction and the Great War.* Oxford: Clarendon Press, 1997.

Rauch, Irmengard, and Gerald F. Carr, Eds. *Semiotics Around the World: Synthesis in Diversity, Proceedings of the Fifth Congress of the International Association for Semiotic Studies, Berkeley 1994,* I-II. Berlin: Mouton de Gruyter, 1997.

Ravitz, Abe C. *Imitations of Life: Fannie Hurst's Gaslight Sonatas.* Carbondale: Southern Illinois Univ. Press, 1997.

Ravvin, Norman. *A House of Words: Jewish Writing, Identity, and Memory.* Montreal: McGill-Queen's Univ. Press, 1997.

Rawlings, Marjorie Kinnan. *Short Stories by Marjorie Kinnan Rawlings,* ed. Rodger L. Tarr. Gainesville: Univ. Press of Florida, 1994.

Recherches croisées Aragon/Elsa Triolet, IV. Besançon, France: Univ. de Franche-Comté, 1992.

Reed, Peter J. *The Short Fiction of Kurt Vonnegut.* Westport, Conn.: Greenwood Press, 1997.

Reesman, Jeanne C., Ed. *Speaking the Other Self: American Women Writers.* Athens: Univ. of Georgia Press, 1997.

Reeve, N. H., Ed. *Henry James: The Shorter Fiction, Reassessments.* London: Mac-Millan Press, 1997; Am. ed. New York: St. Martin's Press, 1997.

Reichardt, Mary R. *Mary Wilkins Freeman: A Study of the Short Fiction.* New York: Twayne, 1997.

Resch, Margit. *Understanding Christa Wolf: Returning Home to a Foreign Land.* Columbia: Univ. of South Carolina Press, 1997.

Reynolds, David S., and Debra J. Rosenthal, Eds. *The Serpent in the Cup: Temperance in American Literature.* Amherst: Univ. of Massachusetts Press, 1997.

Rice, Thomas J. *Joyce, Chaos, and Complexity.* Urbana: Univ. of Illinois Press, 1997.

Richardson, Brian. *UnLikely Stories: Causality and the Nature of Modern Narrative.* Cranbury, N.J.: Assoc. Univ. Presses [for Univ. of Delaware Press], 1997.

Riordan, Colin, Ed. *Jurek Becker.* Cardiff: Univ. of Wales Press, 1998.

Ritter, Naomi, Ed. *Thomas Mann: "Death in Venice."* Boston: Bedford Books, 1998.

Rizzuto, Anthony. *Camus: Love and Sexuality.* Gainesville: Univ. Press of Florida, 1998.

Roberson, Susan L., Ed. *Women, America, and Movement: Narratives of Relocation.* Columbia: Univ. of Missouri Press, 1998.

Roberts, Andrew M., Ed. *Joseph Conrad.* London: Longman, 1998.

Roberts, Graham. *The Last Soviet Avant-Garde: OBERIU—Fact, Fiction, Metafiction.* Cambridge: Cambridge Univ. Press, 1997.

Roberts, Nancy. *Schools of Sympathy: Gender and Identification Through the Novel.* Montreal: McGill-Queen's Univ. Press, 1997.

Robertson, Linda K. *The Power of Knowledge: George Eliot and Education.* New York: Peter Lang, 1997.

Robertson, Michael. *Stephen Crane, Journalism, and the Making of Modern American Literature.* New York: Columbia Univ. Press, 1997.

Robinson, David M. *World of Relations: The Achievement of Peter Taylor.* Lexington: Univ. Press of Kentucky, 1998.

Rodgers, Lawrence R. *Canaan Bound: The African-American Great Migration Novel.* Urbana: Univ. of Illinois Press, 1997.

Rollyson, Carl. *The Literary Legacy of Rebecca West.* San Francisco: International Scholars Publications, 1998.

Rosello, Mireille. *Declining the Stereotype: Ethnicity and Representation in French Cultures.* Hanover, N.H.: Univ. Press of New England, 1998.

Rosenbaum, S. P. *Aspects of Bloomsbury: Studies in Modern English Literary and Intellectual History.* London: MacMillan Press, 1998; Am. ed. New York: St. Martin's Press, 1998.

Rosenheim, Shawn J. *The Cryptographic Imagination: Secret Writing from Edgar Poe to the Internet.* Baltimore: Johns Hopkins Univ. Press, 1997.

Roth, Michael S., Ed. *Rediscovering History: Culture, Politics, and the Psyche.* Stanford: Stanford Univ. Press, 1994.

Rowe, John C. *At Emerson's Tomb: The Politics of Classic American Literature.* New York: Columbia Univ. Press, 1997.

———. *The Other Henry James.* Durham: Duke Univ. Press, 1998.

Rudova, Larissa. *Understanding Boris Pasternak.* Columbia: Univ. of South Carolina Press, 1997.

Rutherford, Jonathan. *Forever England: Reflections on Race, Masculinity and Empire.* London: Lawrence & Wishart, 1997.

St. Joan, Jacqueline, and Annette B. McElhiney, Eds. *Beyond Portia: Women, Law, and Literature in the United States.* Boston: Northeastern Univ. Press, 1997.

Saldívar, José D. *Border Matters: Remapping American Cultural Studies*. Berkeley: Univ. of California Press, 1997.

Salmon, Richard. *Henry James and the Culture of Publicity*. Cambridge: Cambridge Univ. Press, 1997.

Sanborn, Geoffrey. *The Sign of the Cannibal: Melville and the Making of a Postcolonial Reader*. Durham: Duke Univ. Press, 1998.

Sander, Gabriele, Ed. *Internationales Alfred-Döblin-Kolloquium, Leiden 1995*. Bern, Switzerland: Peter Lang, 1997.

Sarbu, Aladár. *The Reality of Appearances: Vision and Representation in Emerson, Hawthorne, and Melville*. Budapest, Hungary: Akadémiai Kiadó, 1996.

Savory, Elaine. *Jean Rhys*. Cambridge: Cambridge Univ. Press, 1998.

Saxton, Ruth O., Ed. *The Girl: Constructions of the Girl in Contemporary Fiction by Women*. New York: St. Martin's Press, 1998.

Schaefer, Michael W. *Just What War Is: The Civil War Writings of De Forest and Bierce*. Knoxville: Univ. of Tennessee Press, 1997.

Schaller, Barry R. *A Vision of American Law: Judging Law, Literature, and the Stories We Tell*. Westport, Conn.: Praeger, 1997.

Scheick, William J., Ed. *Alice Maude Ewell's* Atlantic Monthly *Fiction, 1892–1905*. Delmar, N. Y.: Scholar's Facsimiles & Reprints, 1997.

Schiff, James A. *John Updike Revisited*. New York: Twayne, 1998.

Schmitt, Cannon. *Alien Nation: Nineteenth-Century Gothic Fictions and English Nationality*. Philadelphia: Univ. of Pennsylvania Press, 1997.

Scholz, Bernhard F., Ed. *Mimesis: Studien zur literarischen Repräsentation/ Studies on Literary Representation*. Tübingen, Germany: Francke, 1998.

Schrader, Hans J., Elliott M. Simon, and Charlotte Wardi, Eds. *The Jewish Self-Portrait in European and American Literature*. Tübingen, Germany: Niemeyer, 1996.

Schueller, Malini J. *U. S. Orientalisms: Race, Nation, and Gender in Literature, 1790–1890*. Ann Arbor: Univ. of Michigan Press, 1998.

Schuldiner, Michael, Ed. *Studies in Puritan American Spirituality: Literary Calvinism and Nineteenth-Century American Women Authors*. Lewiston, N.Y.: Edwin Mellen, 1997.

Schwarz, Daniel R., Ed. *Joseph Conrad: "The Secret Sharer,"* New York: St. Martin's Press, 1997.

———. *Reconfiguring Modernism: Explorations in the Relationship Between Modern Art and Modern Literature*. New York: St. Martin's Press, 1997.

Schwartz, Hillel. *The Culture of the Copy: Striking Likenesses, Unreasonable Facsimiles*. New York: Zone Books, 1996.

Schweitzer, Christoph E. *Men Viewing Women as Art Objects: Studies in German Literature*. Columbia, S. C.: Camden House, 1998.

Sedgwick, Eve K., Ed. *Novel Gazing: Queer Readings in Fiction*. Durham: Duke Univ. Press, 1997.

Segrest, Mab. *My Mama's Dead Squirrel*. Ithaca: Firebrand Books, 1985.

Serpillo, Giuseppe, and Donatella Badin, Eds. *The Classical World and the Mediterranean*. Cagliari, Italy: Tema, 1996.

Shaw, Donald L. *The Post-Boom in Spanish-American Fiction*. Albany: State Univ. of New York Press, 1998.

Sheckels, Theodore F. *The Lion on the Freeway: A Thematic Introduction to Contemporary South African Literature in English*. New York: Peter Lang, 1997.

Shepherd, Valerie. *Literature about Language*. London: Routledge, 1994.

Sherbinin, Julie W. de. *Chekhov and Russian Religious Culture: The Poetics of the Marian Paradigm*. Evanston: Northwestern Univ. Press, 1997.

Siegel, Adrienne. *The Image of the American City in Popular Literature*. Port Washington, N.Y.: Kennikat Press, 1981.

Simmons, Philip E. *Deep Surfaces: Mass Culture and History in Postmodern American Fiction*. Athens: Univ. of Georgia Press, 1997.

Simón Martínez, Pedro. *Sobre García Márquez*. Montevideo: Biblioteca de Marcha, 1971.

Sinaiko, Herman L. *Reclaiming the Canon: Essays on Philosophy, Poetry, and History*. New Haven: Yale Univ. Press, 1998.

Singal, Daniel J. *William Faulkner: The Making of a Modernist*. Chapel Hill: Univ. of North Carolina Press, 1997.

Sío-Castiñeira, Begoña. *The Short Stories of Bernard Malamud: In Search of Jewish Post-Immigrant Identity*. New York: Peter Lang, 1998.

Skerl, Jennie, Ed. *A Tawdry Place of Salvation: The Art of Jane Bowles*. Carbondale: Southern Illinois Univ. Press, 1997.

Sloane, David E. E., Ed. *New Directions in American Humor*. Tuscaloosa: Univ. of Alabama Press, 1998.

Smadja, Robert. *Corps et Roman: Balzac, Thomas Mann, Dylan Thomas, Marguerite Yourcenar*. Paris: Honoré Champion, 1998.

Smith, Jeanne R. *Writing Tricksters: Mythic Gambols in American Ethnic Literature*. Berkeley: Univ. of California Press, 1997.

Smith, Paul, Ed. *New Essays on Hemingway's Short Fiction*. Cambridge: Cambridge Univ. Press, 1998.

Smith, Rebecca. *Gender Dynamics in the Fiction of Lee Smith: Examining Language and Narrative Strategies*. San Francisco: International Scholars Publications, 1997.

Smith, Valerie. *Not Just Race, Not Just Gender: Black Feminist Readings*. New York: Routledge, 1998.

Sollors, Werner. *Neither Black Nor White Yet Both: Thematic Explorations of Interracial Literature*. Oxford: Oxford Univ. Press, 1997.

Speirs, Ronald, and Beatrice Sandberg. *Franz Kafka*. New York: St. Martin's Press, 1997.

Spilka, Mark. *Eight Lessons in Love: A Domestic Violence Reader*. Columbia: Univ. of Missouri Press, 1997.

Spina, Michele. *Night and Other Short Stories*. Gerrards Cross, England: Colin Smythe, 1998.

Squillace, Robert. *Modernism, Modernity, and Arnold Bennett*. Cranbury, N. J.: Assoc. Univ. Presses [for Bucknell Univ. Press], 1997.

Stange, Margit. *Personal Property: Wives, White Slaves, and the Market in Women*. Baltimore: Johns Hopkins Univ. Press, 1998.

Stanley, Sandra K., Ed. *Other Sisterhoods: Literary Theory and U. S. Women of Color*. Urbana: Univ. of Illinois Press, 1998.

Stephan, Alexander, Ed. *Themes and Structures: Studies in German Literature from Goethe to the Present*. Columbia, S.C.: Camden House, 1997.

Stern, Madeleine B. *Louisa May Alcott: From Blood and Thunder to Hearth and Home*. Boston: Northeastern Univ. Press, 1998.

Sternlicht, Sanford. *Jean Rhys*. New York: Twayne, 1997.

Stevens, Hugh. *Henry James and Sexuality*. Cambridge: Cambridge Univ. Press, 1998.

Stitt, Megan P. *Metaphors of Change in the Language of Nineteenth-Century Fiction: Scott, Gaskell, and Kingsley*. Oxford: Clarendon Press, 1998.

Stout, Janis P. *Through the Window, Out the Door: Women's Narratives of Departure, from Austin and Cather to Tyler, Morrison, and Didion*. Tuscaloosa: Univ. of Alabama Press, 1998.

Strelka, Joseph P., Ed. *Des Mitleids tiefe Liebesfähigkeit: Zum Werk der Marie von Ebner-Eschenbach*. Bern, Switzerland: Peter Lang, 1997.

———, Ed. *Die Seele ist ein weites Land: Kritische Beiträge zum Werk Arthur Schnitzlers*. Bern, Switzerland: Peter Lang, 1996.

Struthers, J. R. (Tim), Ed. *On Coasts of Eternity: Jack Hodgins' Fictional Universe*. Lantzville, British Columbia: Oolichan Books, 1996.

Sullivan, C. W., Ed. *The Dark Fantastic: Selected Essays from the Ninth International Conference on the Fantastic in the Arts*. Westport, Conn.: Greenwood Press, 1997.

Sullivan, Heather I. *The Intercontextuality of Self and Nature in Ludwig Tieck's Early Works*. New York: Peter Lang, 1997.

Sundquist, Eric J. *To Wake the Nations: Race in the Making of American Literature*. Cambridge: Harvard Univ. Press, 1993.

Swisher, Clarice, Ed. *Readings on Joseph Conrad*. San Diego: Greenhaven Press, 1998.

Tamburri, Anthony J. *A Semiotic of Ethnicity: In (Re)cognition of the Italian/American Writer*. Albany: State Univ. of New York Press, 1998.

Tarot, Rolf, and Gabriela Scherer, Eds. *Erzählkunst der Vormoderne*. Bern, Switzerland: Peter Lang, 1996.

Tate, Trudi. *Modernism, History and the First World War*. Manchester: Manchester Univ. Press, 1998.

Teague, David W. *The Southwest in American Literature and Art: The Rise of a Desert Aesthetic*. Tucson: Univ. of Arizona Press, 1997.

Thakur, Ravni. *Rewriting Gender: Reading Contemporary Chinese Women*. London: Zed Books, 1997.

Thomas, Brook. *American Literary Realism and the Failed Promise of Contract*. Berkeley: Univ. of California Press, 1997.

Thomas, D. M. *Alexander Solzhenitsyn: A Century in His Life*. New York: St. Martin's Press, 1998.

Thomas, Neil, and Françoise Le Saux, Eds. *Myth and Its Legacy in European Literature*. Durham, England: Univ. of Durham Press, 1996.

Thompson, Andrew. *George Eliot and Italy: Literary, Cultural and Political Influences from Dante to the Risorgimento*. London: MacMillan Press, 1998; Am. ed. New York: St. Martin's Press, 1998.

Thoms, Peter. *Detection and Its Designs: Narrative & Power in 19th Century Detective Fiction*. Athens: Ohio Univ. Press, 1998.

Thomson, Rosemarie G. *Extraordinary Bodies: Figuring Physical Disability in American Culture and Literature*. New York: Columbia Univ. Press, 1997.

Tibbitts, Mercedes V., Ed. *Studies in Honor of Gilberto Paolini*. Newark, Del.: Cuesta, 1996.

Tintner, Adeline R. *Henry James's Legacy: The Afterlife of His Figure and Fiction*. Baton Rouge: Louisiana State Univ. Press, 1998.

Tolliver, Joyce. *Cigar Smoke and Violet Water: Gendered Discourse in the Stories of Emilia Pardo Bazán*. Cranbury, N.J.: Assoc. Univ. Presses [for Bucknell Univ. Press], 1998.

Travis, Molly A. *Reading Cultures: The Construction of Readers in the Twentieth Century*. Carbondale: Southern Illinois Univ. Press, 1998.

Trodd, Anthea. *Women's Writing in English: Britain 1900–1945*. London: Longman, 1998.

Trouard, Dawn, Ed. *Eudora Welty: Eye of the Storyteller*. Kent: Kent State Univ. Press, 1989.

Tsuchiya, Kiyoshi, Ed. *Dissent and Marginality: Essays on the Borders of Literature and Religion*. London: MacMillan Press, 1997; Am. ed. New York: St. Martin's Press, 1997.

Tusken, Lewis W. *Understanding Herman Hesse*. Columbia: Univ. of South Carolina Press, 1998.

Twagilimana, Aimable. *Race and Gender in the Making of an African American Literary Tradition*. New York: Garland, 1997.

Umeh, Marie, Ed. *Emerging Perspectives on Flora Nwapa*. Trenton, N.J.: Africa World Press, 1998.

Unrue, Darlene H., Ed. *Critical Essays on Katherine Anne Porter*. New York: G. K. Hall, 1997.

Urioste Azcorra, Carmen de. *Narrativa Andaluz (1900–1936): Erotismo, feminismo y regionalismo*. Sevilla: Univ. de Sevilla, 1997.

Valcárcel, Eva, Ed. *Hispanoamérica en sus textos*. La Coruña, Spain: Univ. de Coruña, 1993.

Valdés, María Elena de. *The Shattered Mirror: Representations of Women in Mexican Literature*. Austin: Univ. of Texas Press, 1998.

Valdés, María Elena de, Mario J. Valdés, and Richard A. Young, Eds. *Latin America as Its Literature*. Whitestone, N.Y.: Council on National Literature, 1995.

Valente, Joseph, Ed. *Quare Joyce*. Ann Arbor: Univ. of Michigan Press, 1998.

Van Delden, Maarten. *Carlos Fuentes, Mexico, and Modernity*. Nashville: Vanderbilt Univ. Press, 1998.

Varty, Anne. *A Preface to Oscar Wilde*. London: Longman, 1998.

Veitch, Jonathan. *American Superrealism: Nathanael West and the Politics of Representation in the 1930s*. Madison: Univ. of Wisconsin Press, 1997.

Waldmeir, Joseph J. *"Miss Tina Did It" and Other Fresh Looks at Modern Fiction*. West Cornwall, Conn.: Locust Hill Press, 1997.

Waldron, Ann. *Eudora: A Writer's Life*. New York: Doubleday, 1998.

Wall, Cheryl A., Ed. *Zora Neale Hurston, "Sweat."* New Brunswick, N.J.: Rutgers Univ. Press, 1997.

Wang, Jennie. *Novelistic Love in the Platonic Tradition: Fielding, Faulkner and the Postmodernists*. Lanham, Md.: Rowland & Littlefield, 1997.

Ward, Mark G., Ed. *Perspectives on German Realist Writing: Eight Essays*. Lewiston, N.Y.: Edwin Mellen, 1995.

Warhol, Robyn R., and Diane P. Herndl, Eds. *Feminisms: An Anthology of Literary Theory and Criticism*. New Brunswick, N.J.: Rutgers Univ. Press, 1997.

Warner, Nicholas O. *Spirits of America: Intoxication in Nineteenth-Century American Literature*. Norman: Univ. of Oklahoma Press, 1997.

Warren, Robert P. *The Robert Penn Warren Reader*. New York: Random House, 1987.

Waters, Catherine. *Dickens and the Politics of the Family*. Cambridge: Cambridge Univ. Press, 1997.

Waters, Karen V. *The Perfect Gentleman: Masculine Control in Victorian Men's Fiction, 1870–1901*. New York: Peter Lang, 1997.

Watt, Ian. *Conrad in the Nineteenth Century*. Berkeley: Univ. of California Press, 1979.

Watts, Philip. *Allegories of the Purge: How Literature Responded to the Postwar Trials of Writers and Intellectuals in France*. Stanford: Stanford Univ. Press, 1998.

Wawrzycka Jolanta W., and Marlena G. Corcoran, Eds. *Gender in Joyce*. Gainesville: Univ. Press of Florida, 1997.

Weaver, Jack W. *Joyce's Music and Noise: Theme and Variation in His Writings*. Gainesville: Univ. Press of Florida, 1998.

Weedon, Chris, Ed. *Post-War Women's Writing in German: Feminist Critical Approaches*. Providence, R.I.: Berghahn, 1997.

Weiss, M. Lynn. *Gertrude Stein and Richard Wright: The Poetics and Politics of Modernism*. Jackson: Univ. of Mississippi, 1997.

Weisser, Susan O. *A "Craving Vacancy": Women and Sexual Love in the British Novel, 1740–1880*. New York: New York Univ. Press, 1997.

Weninger, Robert, and Brigitte Rossbacher, Eds. *Wendezeiten Zeitenwenden: Positionsbestimmungen zur deutschsprachigen Literatur, 1945–1995*. Tübingen, Germany: Stauffenburg, 1997.

Wertheimer, Jürgen, Ed. *Suchbild Europa—künstlerische Konzepte der Moderne*. Amsterdam: Rodopi, 1995.

West, James L. W. *William Styron, A Life*. New York: Random House, 1998.

Westervelt, Linda A. *Beyond Innocence, or the Altersroman in Modern Fiction*. Columbia: Univ. of Missouri Press, 1997.

Whalen-Bridge, John. *Political Fiction and the American Self*. Urbana: Univ. of Illinois Press, 1998.

Wiedemann, Barbara. *Josephine Herbst's Short Fiction: A Window to Her Life and Times.* Cranbury, N.J.: Assoc. Univ. Presses [for Susquehanna Univ. Press], 1998.

Wiesenthal, Chris. *Figuring Madness in Nineteenth-Century Fiction.* London: Mac-Millan Press, 1997; Am. ed. New York: St. Martin's Press, 1997.

Wiley, Catherine, and Fiona R. Barnes, Eds. *Homemaking: Women Writers and the Politics and Poetics of Home.* New York: Garland, 1996.

Wilhelm, Albert. *Bobbie Ann Mason: A Study of the Short Fiction.* New York: Twayne, 1998.

Williams, Arthur, Stuart Parkes, and Julian Preece, Eds. *Contemporary German Writers, Their Aesthetics and Their Language.* Bern, Switzerland: Peter Lang, 1996.

Williams, John. *Fictions as False Document: The Reception of E. L. Doctorow in the Postmodern Age.* Columbia, S.C.: Camden House, 1996.

Williams, Trevor L. *Reading Joyce Politically.* Gainesville: Univ. Press of Florida, 1997.

Wolfreys, Julian. *The Rhetoric of Affirmative Resistance: Dissonant Identities from Carroll to Derrida.* New York: St. Martin's Press, 1997.

Wonham, Henry B. *Charles W. Chesnutt: A Study of the Short Fiction.* New York: Twayne, 1998.

Woodhouse, Reed. *Unlimited Embrace: A Canon of Gay Fiction, 1945–1995.* Amherst: Univ. of Massachusetts Press, 1998.

Woods, Gregory. *A History of Gay Literature: The Male Tradition.* New Haven: Yale Univ. Press, 1998.

Wright, Will, and Steven Kaplan, Eds. *The Image of Nature: In Literature, the Media, and Society: Selected Papers, 1993 Conference, Society for the Interdisciplinary Study of Social Imagery, March 11–13, 1993, Colorado Springs, Colorado.* Pueblo: Univ. of Southern Colorado Press, 1993.

————. *The Image of Violence in Literature, the Media, and Society: Selected Papers [from the] 1995 Conference [of the]Society for Interdisciplinary Study of Social Imagery.* Pueblo: Univ. of Southern Colorado Press, 1995.

Wussow, Helen. *The Nightmare of History: The Fictions of Virginia Woolf and D. H. Lawrence.* Cranbury, N.J.: Assoc. Univ. Presses [for Lehigh Univ. Press], 1998.

Wydeven, Joseph J. *Wright Morris Revisited.* New York: Twayne, 1998.

Yee, Cordell D. K. *The Word According to James Joyce: Reconstructing Representation.* Cranbury, N.J.: Assoc. Univ. Presses [for Bucknell Univ. Press], 1997.

Yoon, Hye-Joon. *Physiognomy of Capital in Charles Dickens: An Essay in Dialectical Criticism.* San Francisco: International Scholars Publications, 1998.

Young, Robert J. C., Ban K. Choon, and Robbie B. H. Goh, Eds. *The Silent Word: Textual Meaning and the Unwritten.* Singapore: Singapore Univ. Press, 1998.

Youngs, Tim, Ed. *Writing and Race.* New York: Longman, 1997.

Zach, Wolfgang, and Ken L. Goodwin, Eds. *Nationalism vs. Internationalism: (Inter)-National Dimensions of Literatures in English.* Tübingen: Stauffenburg-Verl., 1996.

Zamora, Lois P. *The Usable Past: The Imagination of History in Recent Fiction of the Americas.* Cambridge: Cambridge Univ. Press, 1997.

Zhang, Aiping. *Enchanted Places: The Use of Setting in F. Scott Fitzgerald's Fiction.* Westport, Conn.: Greenwood Press, 1997.

Zhang, Xudong. *Chinese Modernism in the Era of Reforms: Cultural Fever, Avant-Garde Fiction, and the New Chinese Cinema.* Durham: Duke Univ. Press, 1997.

Zhang, Yingjin, Ed. *China in a Polycentric World: Essays in Chinese Comparative Literature.* Stanford: Stanford Univ. Press, 1998.

Zhu Lin. *Snake's Pillow and Other Stories,* trans. Richard King. Honolulu: Univ. of Hawaii Press, 1998.

Zimmerman, Bonnie, Toni A. H. McNaron, and Margaret Cruikshank, Eds. *The New Lesbian Studies: Into the Twenty-First Century.* New York: Feminist Press at the City Univ. of New York, 1996.

Zimmerman, Brett. *Herman Melville: Stargazer*. Montreal: McGill-Queen's Univ. Press, 1998.

Ziolkowski, Margaret. *Literary Exorcisms of Stalinism: Russian Writers and the Soviet Past*. Columbia, S.C.: Camden House, 1998.

Zlotnick, Susan. *Women, Writing, and the Industrial Revolution*. Baltimore: Johns Hopkins Univ. Press, 1998.

A Checklist of Journals Used

Das Achtzehnte Jahrhundert

African Am R   African American Review

Afro-Hispanic R   Afro-Hispanic Review

Alba de América

Alpha Chi Recorder

Am Imago   American Imago: Studies in Psychoanalysis and Culture

Am J Psychoanalysis   American Journal of Psychoanalysis

Am Lit   American Literature: A Journal of Literary History, Criticism, and Bibliography

Am Lit Hist   American Literary History

Am Lit Realism   ALR: American Literary Realism [formerly ALR: American Literary Realism, 1870–1910.]

Am Q   American Quarterly

Americas R   The Americas Review: A Review of Hispanic Literature and Art of the USA

Anales Literatura   Anales de la Literatura Española Contemporánea

Anglophonia   Anglophonia: French Journal of English Studies

Annales Centre Recherches   Annales du Centre de Recherches dur l'Amérique Anglophone

L'Année Balzacienne

ANQ   ANQ: A Quarterly Journal of Short Articles, Notes, and Reviews

Anthropos   Anthropos: Revista de Documentación Científica de la Cultura

Antípodas   Antípodas: Journal of Hispanic Studies of the University of Auckland and La Trobe University

377

Antipodes	*Antipodes: A North American Journal of Australian Literature*
Arete	*Arete: The Journal of Sport Literature*
ArielE	*Ariel: A Review of International English Literature*
	Atlantic Monthly
ATQ	*American Transcendental Quarterly*
Australian J French Stud	*Australian Journal of French Studies*
Australian Slavonic	*Australian Slavonic & East European Studies*
Auto/Bio Stud	*Auto/Biography Studies*
Bilingual R	*The Bilingual Review/La Revista Bilingue*
	Boletín de la Biblioteca de Menéndez Pelayo
Brecht Yearbook	*The Brecht Yearbook/Das Brecht-Jahrbuch*
British & Am Stud	*B.A.S. British and American Studies* (Timidsoara, Romania)
Brno Stud Engl	*Brno Studies in English*
Bucknell R	*Bucknell Review: A Scholarly Journal of Letters, Arts and Sciences*
Bull Hispanic Stud	*Bulletin of Hispanic Studies*
Bull de la Soc Théophile Gautier	*Bulletin de la Société Théophile Gautier*
Cahiers d'Etudes Germ	*Cahiers d'Etudes Germaniques*
Cahiers de la Nouvelle	*Cahiers de la Nouvelle: Journal of the Short Story in English*
Cahiers Victoriens et Edouardiens	*Cahiers Victoriens et Edouardiens: Revue du Centre d'Études et de Recherches Victoriennes et Edouardiennes de l'Université Paul Valéry, Montpellier*
Cambridge Q	*The Cambridge Quarterly*
Canadian Lit	*Canadian Literature*
Canadian R Am Stud	*Canadian Review of American Studies*
Canadian Women's Stud	*Canadian Women's Studies—Les Cahiers de la Femme*

Catalan R	Catalan Review
CEA Critic	College English Association Critic
CEAMAG	CEAMAGazine: A Journal of the College English Association, Middle Atlantic Group
Centennial R	Centennial Review
Champs du Signe	Champs du Signe: Sémantique, Poétique, Rhétorique [formerly Champs du Signe: Cahiers de Stylistique]
Chasqui	Chasqui: Revista de Literatura Latinoamericana
Cincinnati Romance R	Cincinnati Romance Review
Círculo	Círculo: Revista de Cultura
Clio	Clio:A Journal of Literature, History and the Philosophy of History
Clues	Clues: A Journal of Detection
Colby Q	Colby Quarterly
Coll Engl	College English
Coll Lang Assoc J	College Language Association Journal
Coll Lit	College Literature
Colloquia Germanica	Colloquia Germanica: Internationale Zeitschrift für Germanische Sprach-und Literaturwissenschaft
	Colloquium Helveticum
	Commentary
	Commonwealth [Rodez, France]
Commonwealth Essays & Stud	Commonwealth Essays and Studies
Comparatist	The Comparatist: Journal of the Southern Comparative Literature Association
Compás de Letras	Compás de Letras: Monografías de Literatura Española
Comp Lit Stud	Comparative Literature Studies
Confluencia	Confluencia: Revista Hispánica de Cultura y Literatura
Confronto Letterario	Il Confronto Letterario: Quaderni del Dipartimento di Lingue e Litterature Straniere moderne

	dell'Università di Paviae del Diparitmento di Linguistica e Letterature Comparate dell'Università di Bergamo
Connotations	Connotations: A Journal for Critical Debate
Conradian	The Conradian: Journal of the Joseph Conrad Society (U. K.)
Conradiana	Conradiana: A Journal of Joseph Conrad Studies
Contemp Lit	Contemporary Literature
	Critical Inquiry
Critical S	Critical Survey
Criticism	Criticism: A Quarterly for Literature and the Arts
Critique	Critique: Studies in Contemporary Fiction
	Cuadernos de Aldeeu
Cuadernos de Investigación	Cuadernos de Investigación Filológica
	Cycnos
	Dactylus
D. H. Lawrence R	The D. H. Lawrence Review
Dalhousie French Stud	Dalhousie French Studies
Deutsche Vierteljahrsschrift	Deutsche Vierteljahrsschrift fürLiteraturwissenschaft
Differences	Differences: A Journal of Feminist Cultural Studies
	Diogenes
Edith Wharton R	Edith Wharton Review
Elementa	Elementa: Schriften zur Philosophie und ihrer Problemgeschichte
	ELH
	Encuentro de la Cultura Cubana
Engl Africa	English in Africa
Engl Lit Transition	English Literature in Transition
Engl Lang Notes	English Language Notes

Engl Stud	*English Studies: A Journal of English Language and Literature*
L'Epoque Conradienne	*L'Epoque Conradienne: Bulletin annuel de la Societé Conradienne*
Escritura	*Escritura: Revista de Teoría y Crítica Literaria*
Essays Arts & Sciences	*Essays in Arts and Sciences*
Essays Crit	*Essays in Criticism: A Quarterly Journal of Literary Criticism*
Essays Lit	*Essays in Literature* [Macomb, Ill.]
Études Anglaises	*Études Anglaises: Grande-Bretagne, États-Unis*
Études Canadiennes	*Études Canadiennes/Canadian Studies: Revue Interdisciplinaire des Études Canadiennes en France* (Bordeaux, France)
	Etudes Francophones
	Eudora Welty Newsletter
Euphorion	*Euphorion: Zeitschrift für Literaturgeschichte*
	Explicator
	Explicación de Textos Literarios
	Extrapolation
Faulkner J	*The Faulkner Journal*
	Forum Italicum
Forum Mod Lang Stud	*Forum for Modern Language Studies*
Foundation	*Foundation: The International Review of Science Fiction* [formerly *The Review of Science Fiction*]
Francofonia	*Francofonia: Studi e Ricerche Sulle Letterature di Lingua Francese*
Frank Norris Stud	*Frank Norris Studies*
	Französisch Heute
	French Forum
French R	*The French Review: Journal of the American Association of Teachers of French*
French Stud	*French Studies: A Quarterly Review*

French Stud Bull	*French Studies Bulletin: A Quarterly Supplement* (Leeds, England)
French Stud Southern Africa	*French Studies in Southern Africa*
Furman Stud	*Furman Studies*
	GénEros
George Eliot-George Henry Lewes Stud	*George Eliot-George Henry Lewes Studies* [formerly *The George Eliot-George Henry Lewes Newsletter*]
Germ Life & Letters	*German Life and Letters*
Germ Notes & R	*Germanic Notes and Review* [formerly *Germanic Notes*]
Germ R	*The Germanic Review*
Germ Q	*German Quarterly*
Germ Stud R	*German Studies Review*
Griot	*Griot: Official Journal of the Southern Conference on Afro-American Studies*
	Heine Jahrbuch
Hemingway R	*Hemingway Review*
Henry James R	*Henry James Review*
Hispania	*Hispania: A Journal Devoted to the Interests of the Teaching of Spanish and Portuguese*
Hispanic J	*Hispanic Journal*
Hispanic R	*Hispanic Review*
Hispamérica	*Hispamérica: Revista de Literatura*
Hispano	*Hispanófila*
Hist Psychiatry	*History of Psychiatry*
Humor	*Humor* (Berlin, Germany)
Indian J Am Stud	*Indian Journal of American Studies*
Indiana J Hispanic Lit	*Indiana Journal of Hispanic Literatures*
Int'l Fiction R	*International Fiction Review*
Int'l J Middle East Stud	*International Journal of Middle East Studies*

Inti	*Inti: Revista de Literatura Hispánica*
Irish Univ R	*Irish University Review: A Journal of Irish Studies*
Italian Books	*Italian Books and Periodicals*
	Italica
Jack London J	*Jack London Journal*
Jean Rhys R	*Jean Rhys Review*
J Am Stud Turkey	*Journal of American Studies of Turkey*
J Assoc Interdisciplinary Stud Arts	*JAISA: The Journal of the Association for the Interdisciplinary Study of the Arts*
J Black Stud	*Journal of Black Studies*
J Commonwealth Lit	*The Journal of Commonwealth Literature*
J Commonwealth & Postcolonial Stud	*Journal of Commonwealth and Postcolonial Studies*
J Engl Lang & Lit	*Journal of English Language and Literature*
J Evolutionary Psych	*Journal of Evolutionary Psychology*
J Hispanic Philol	*Journal of Hispanic Philology*
J Kafka Soc Am	*Journal of the Kafka Society of America*
J Narrative Technique	*Journal of Narrative Technique*
J Pop Culture	*Journal of Popular Culture*
J So African Stud	*Journal of South African Studies*
Kentucky Philol R	*Kentucky Philological Review*
Kipling J	*The Kipling Journal*
	Kleist-Jahrbuch
Korean Stud	*Korean Studies*
Lang & Lit	*Language and Literature: Journal of the Poetics and Linguistics Association*
	Letras Femeninas
	Letras Peninsulares
Lingüística y Lit	*Lingüística y Literatura* (Medellín, Colombia)

Lit & Belief	*Literature and Belief*
Lit Int Theory	*LIT: Literature Interpretation Theory*
Lit & Medicine	*Literature and Medicine*
	Literatur für Leser
Lit & Psych	*Literature and Psychology*
Lit Criterion	*Literary Criterion*
Lit R	*The Literary Review: An International Journal of Contemporary Writing*
Littératures	*Littératures* (Toulouse, France)
Louisiana Lit	*Louisiana Literature*
Lovecraft Stud	*Lovecraft Studies*
	Lubelskie Materiały Neofilologiczne
Luso-Brazilian R	*Luso-Brazilian Review*
	Magazine Litteraire
Malcolm Lowry R	*Malcolm Lowry Review*
Marvels & Tales	*Marvels & Tales: Journal of Fairy-Tale Studies*
MELUS	*MELUS: The Journal of the Society for the Study of the Multiple-Ethnic Literature of the United States*
Melville Soc Extracts	*Melville Society Extracts* [supersedes *Extracts: An Occasional Newsletter*]
	Mester
	Midwestern Miscellany
MIFLC R	*MIFLC Review: Journal of the Mountain Interstate Foreign Language Conference*
Minnesota R	*Minnesota Review*
Mississippi Q	*Mississippi Quarterly: The Journal of Southern Culture*
Mod Fiction Stud	*Modern Fiction Studies*
Mod Lang Notes	*MLN: Modern Language Notes*
Mod Lang R	*Modern Language Review*

Mod Lang Stud	Modern Language Studies
Monatshefte	Monatshefte: Für Deutschen Unterricht, Deutsche Sprache und Literatur
Monographic R	Monographic Review/Revista Monográfia
Mosaic	Mosaic: A Journal for the Interdisciplinary Study of Literature [formerly Mosaic: A Journal for the Comparative Study of Literature and Ideas for the Interdisciplinary Study of Literature]
Nathaniel Hawthorne R	The Nathaniel Hawthorne Review
Nemla Italian Stud	Nemla Italian Studies
	Neophilologus
New England Q	The New England Quarterly: A Historical Review of New England Life and Letters
	New Republic
New York R Sci Fiction	New York Review of Science Fiction
	New Yorker
Nineteenth-Century French Stud	Nineteenth-Century French Studies
Nineteenth-Century Lit	Nineteenth-Century Literature [formerly Nineteenth-Century Fiction]
	Notas y Estudios Filológicos
Notes & Queries	Notes and Queries
Notes Contemp Lit	Notes on Contemporary Literature
Notes Mod Irish Lit	Notes on Modern Irish Literature
Novel	Novel: A Forum on Fiction
Ojáncano	Ojáncano: Revista de Literatura Española
Op. Cit.	Op. Cit.: Revue de Littératures Française et Comparée
Orbis Litterarum	Orbis Litterarum: International Review of Literary Studies
Österreich Geschichte	Österreich in Geschichte und Literatur (mit Geographie)

Oxford Germ Stud	*Oxford German Studies*
Panjab Univ Research Bull	*Panjab University Research Bulletin (Arts)*
Para-doxa	*Para-doxa: Studies in World Literary Genres*
Partisan R	*Partisan Review*
Philippine Stud	*Philippine Studies* (Manila)
PMLA	*PMLA: Publications of the Modern Language Association of America*
Prooftexts	*Prooftexts: A Journal of Jewish Literary History*
Prospects	*Prospects: An Annual Journal of American Cultural Studies*
	Psychological Perspectives
Pubs Arkansas Philol Assoc	*Publications of the Arkansas Philological Association*
Pubs Engl Goethe Soc	*Publications of the English Goethe Society*
Pushkin J	*The Pushkin Journal: The Journal of the North American Pushkin Society*
	Pynchon Notes
	Quaderni di Lingue e Letterature
Qui Parle	*Qui Parle: Literature, Philosophy, Visual Arts, History* (Berkeley, Calif.) [formerly *Qui Parle: A Journal of Literary and Critical Studies*]
Q/W/E/R/T/Y	*Q/W/E/R/T/Y: Arts, Littératures & Civilisations du Monde Anglophone*
	Recherches et Travaux
REDEN	*REDEN: Revista Española de Estudios Norteamericanos*
Religion & Lit	*Religion and Literature*
Renascence	*Renascence: Essays on Value in Literature*
	Representations
Research African Lit	*Research in African Literatures*
Resources Am Lit Stud	*Resources for American Literature Study*
R Contemp Fiction	*Review of Contemporary Fiction*

Revista Canadiense	*Revista Canadiense de Estudios Hispánicos*
Revista Chilena	*Revista Chilena de Literatura*
Revista de Crítica	*Revista de Crítica Literaria Latinoamericana*
	Revista de Estudios Colombianos
Revista de Estudios Hispánicos	*Revista de Estudios Hispánicos* [Río Piedras, Puerto Rico]
	Revista de la Universidad Nacional Autónoma de México
Revista Filología y Ling	*Revista Filología y Lingüística de la Universidad de Costa Rica. Extraordinario*
	Revista Hispánica Moderna
	Revista Iberoamericana
	Revista/Review Interamericana
Revista Lit Hispanoamericana	*Revista Literatura Hispanoamericana*
Revue de l'ACLA	*Revue de l'ACLA/Journal of the CAAL*
Revue d'Histoire Littéraire	*Revue d'Histoire Littéraire de la France*
La Revue des Lettres Modernes	*La Revue des Lettres Modernes: Histoire des Idées et des Littératures*
	Revue de Littérature Comparée
Roman 20–50	*Roman 20–50: Revue d'Etude du Roman du XX Siècle*
Romance Lang Annual	*RLA: Romance Language Annual*
	Romance Notes
Romance Q	*Romance Quarterly*
Romance R	*Romance Review*
Romanic R	*Romanic Review*
Romantist	*The Romantist*
Russian Lit	*Russian Literature*
Russian Stud Lit	*Russian Studies in Literature*
Sci-Fiction Stud	*Science-Fiction Studies*

Screen	*Screen: The Journal of the Society for Education in Film and Television* [London]
Selecta	*Selecta: Journal of the Pacific Northwest Council on Foreign Languages*
	Shenandoah
	Short Story
Siglo	*Siglo XX/20th Century*
Slavic & East European J	*Slavic and East European Journal*
So African J	*South African Journal of African Languages/Suid-Afrikaanse Tydskrif vir Afrikatale*
So Atlantic Q	*South Atlantic Quarterly*
So Atlantic R	*South Atlantic Review*
So Central R	*South Central Review*
Southerly	*Southerly: the Magazine of the Australian English Association*
Southern Lit J	*Southern Literary Journal*
Southern Q	*The Southern Quarterly: A Journal of the Arts in the South*
Southern R	*Southern Review*
Southern Stud	*Southern Studies: An Interdisciplinary Journal of the South*
Southwestern Am Lit	*Southwestern American Literature*
Steinbeck Q	*Steinbeck Quarterly*
Strumenti Critici	*Strumenti Critici: Rivista Quadrimestrale di Cultura e Critica Letteraria*
Stud Am Fiction	*Studies in American Fiction*
Stud Am Indian Lit	*Studies in American Indian Literatures: The Journal of the Association for the Study of American Indian Literatures*
Stud Canadian Lit	*Studies in Canadian Literature*
Stud English Lit	*Studies in English Literature* (Tokyo, Japan)
Stud Engl Lit 1500–1900	*Studies in English Literature 1500–1900*

Stud Hum	*Studies in the Humanities*
Stud Lit Imagination	*Studies in the Literary Imagination*
Stud Novel	*Studies in the Novel*
Stud Popular Culture	*Studies in Popular Culture*
Stud Short Fiction	*Studies in Short Fiction*
Stud Twentieth-Century Lit	*Studies in Twentieth-Century Literature*
Stud Weird Fiction	*Studies in Weird Fiction*
	Style
SubStance	*SubStance: A Review of Theory and Literary Criticism*
Symposium	*Symposium: A Quarterly Journal of Modern Literatures*
Tamkang R	*Tamkang Review*
	Tangence
	Texto Crítico
Textos	*Textos: Works and Criticism*
	Textual Practice
Thesaurus	*Thesaurus: Boletín del Instituto Caro y Cuervo*
	Thomas Mann Jahrbuch
Thomas Wolfe R	*The Thomas Wolfe Review*
Tolstoy Stud J	*Tolstoy Studies Journal*
	Torre de Papel
Torre	*La Torre: Revista de la Universidad de Puerto Rico*
	Travaux de Littérature
Tulsa Stud Women's Lit	*Tulsa Studies in Women's Literature*
Twentieth Century Lit	*Twentieth Century Literature: A Scholarly and Critical Journal*
Ufahamu	*Ufahamu: Journal of the African Activist Association*
Utah Foreign Lang R	*Utah Foreign Language Review*

Utopian Stud	*Utopian Studies*
Variaciones Borges	*Variaciones Borges: Journal of the Jorge Luis Borges Center for Studies and Documentation*
Venezuelan Lit & Arts J	*Venezuelan Literature and Arts Journal/Revista de Literatura y Artes Venezolanas*
Versus	*Versus: Quaderni di Studi Semiotici*
Victorian News	*The Victorian Newsletter*
War, Lit, & Arts	*War, Literature, and the Arts: An International Journal of the Humanities*
Weber Stud	*Weber Studies: An Interdisciplinary Humanities Journal*
Welt Islams	*Die Welt des Islams: International Journal for the Study of Modern Islam*
	West Coast Line
Western Hum R	*Western Humanities Review*
Westerly	*Westerly: A Quarterly Review*
Women	*Women: A Cultural Review*
Women French Stud	*Women in French Studies*
Women Germ Yearbook	*Women in German Yearbook: Feminist Studies in German Literature and Culture*
Women's Stud	*Women's Studies: An Interdisciplinary Journal*
Women's Writing	*Women's Writing: The Elizabethan to Victorian Period*
World Lit Today	*World Literature Today: A Literary Quarterly of the University of Oklahoma*
	Zeitschrift für Deutsche Philologie
	Zeitschrift für französische Sprache und Literatur
	Zeitschrift für Germanistik

Index of Short Story Writers